Life in Abundance

Studies of John's Gospel in Tribute to Raymond E. Brown, S.S.

Edited by
John R. Donahue, S.J.

I came that they may have life and have it more abundantly.

(John 10:10)

LITURGICAL PRESS
Collegeville, Minnesota

www.litpress.org

Cover design by David Manahan, O.S.B. Detail of painting "Saint John the Evangelist on Patmos," 1474, Hans Memling, Memling Museum, Bruges.

1	2	3	4	5	6	7	8

Library of Congress Catalog-in Publication Data

Life in abundance : studies of John's Gospel in tribute to Raymond E. Brown, S.S. / edited by John R. Donahue.
    p. cm.
    Summary: "Primarily a collection of essays (originally papers) and responses given at 'An International Conference on the Gospel of John: Life in Abundance,' held at St. Mary's Seminary and University in Maryland, October 16–18, 2003; the book includes presentations of Johannine theology, issues of interpretation, considerations of the work of Raymond Brown, and two homilies"—Provided by publisher.
    Includes bibliographical references and indexes.
    ISBN 13: 978-0-8146-3011-2 (pbk. : alk. paper)
    ISBN 10: 0-8146-3011-1
    1. Bible. N.T. John—Criticism, interpretation, etc.—Congresses. 2. Brown, Raymond Edward—Congresses. I. Brown, Raymond Edward. II. Donahue, John R.

BS2615.52.L54 2005
226.5'06—dc22

2004023819

Contents

Preface

The essays in this volume were originally papers delivered at "An International Conference on the Gospel of John: Life in Abundance," held at St. Mary's Seminary and University, Baltimore, Maryland, from October 16-18, 2003 to honor the memory of Raymond E. Brown, s.s. Shortly before his death on August 8, 1998, Raymond Brown had delivered an address at St. Mary's, his alma mater, where he had taught from 1959–1971, and where he wrote his major commentary on the Gospel of John. In response to a question posed by his friend, the longtime rector of the seminary, Robert F. Leavitt, s.s., Father Brown had expressed a desire to bequeath a part of his personal library to St. Mary's after his death. Subsequently this wish helped to spark Father Leavitt's interest in developing a special research collection devoted to Johannine studies that would bear Father Brown's name and would be the centerpiece of an extensive expansion of the library facility at St. Mary's. Thus was born the Raymond E. Brown Center and the Johannine Collection as an addition to the Knott Library of the Seminary.

After Brown's unexpected death, planning for the new facility to house the Johannine collection and related materials began in earnest. In addition to expanded library stacks and classrooms, the facility also houses newly combined archives of early American church history including the archives of the Archdiocese of Baltimore, the U.S. Province of the Society of St. Sulpice, and St. Mary's Seminary and University. The new facility was dedicated in April 2002 and includes over three thousand books from Father Brown's personal library, including some important materials in Judaica.

During the construction of the library, Father Leavitt envisioned the creation of a named chair in honor of Father Brown and shared his vision with Father Ronald Witherup, s.s., Provincial of the Sulpicians, who was instrumental in organizing and bringing Father Brown's Johannine Collection to St. Mary's. After discussions with Father Leavitt, in Spring 2001 I accepted the inaugural appointment at St. Mary's as "The Raymond Brown Distinguished Professor of New Testament Studies." Thanks also to the initiative of Father Leavitt, plans emerged to host an international conference in tribute to Raymond Brown and his special contribution to Johannine studies. As holder of the chair, I had the welcome task of coordinating the conference, with the hope that the conference would spark more interest in the Raymond E. Brown Center as a locus of Johannine research for future scholars for years to come.

Over three hundred people attended the conference, including scholars from Canada, Europe, and New Zealand as well as clergy and lay people with different interests, most of whom had been influenced by Raymond Brown's writings or lectures. The scholars whose papers are included here responded to invitations with complete graciousness, and the excellence of their work reflects not only their own scholarship but also their respect for Father Brown. Participants declared the conference a great success. The lion's share of credit for that success is due to the superb staff at St. Mary's, especially Mrs. Elizabeth Visconage, Vice President for Administration and Advancement, Mr. Richard Childs, Vice-President for Finance, Mrs. Patricia Grega, Director of Information Services and University Registrar, Mrs. Kathy Mignini, Director of Institutional Services, Ms. Marcia Xintas, also from the Advancement office, and the library staff, along with the extraordinary efforts of the whole staff and student body of St. Mary's. Special thanks are owed to Kristin Simms, a 2005 graduate of the Jesuit School of Theology at Berkeley, for great help in preparing the indexes.

We are also very grateful to Cardinal Gottfried Danneels, Archbishop of Malines-Brussels, who had agreed to give the keynote address but had to cancel since he necessarily attended the twenty-fifth anniversary of the pontificate of Pope John Paul II, held in Rome at the same time. Special thanks are then due to Archbishop Terrence T. Prendergast, s.j., of Halifax, Nova Scotia, a New Testament scholar and formerly Rector of Regis College (Toronto). His keynote address, "The Church's Great Challenge: Proclaiming God's Word in the New Millennium," builds on the theme proposed by Cardinal Danneels.

The major purpose of the conference was not to enter into direct dialogue with Raymond E. Brown's extensive writings, but to continue further study of the Gospel of John, which had been his life's work. Following the keynote address, the essays in the volume treat major aspects of Johannine studies, with two essays on "The Challenges of Johannine Studies," followed by examinations of the "The Historical Context of the Gospel of John," and two expositions of Johannine Theology. The final two essays raise issues of interpretation by dealing directly with important aspects of Brown's work. A major contribution of the present volume is the only complete bibliography of Brown's publications, which Michael L. Barre, s.s., produced with incredible diligence, based on an earlier compilation by Ronald D. Witherup, s.s. Such a bibliography always remains a work in progress since Brown's works are still being translated into different languages, most recently his *Introduction to the New Testament* into French, Italian, and Spanish.

The volume also contains a sermon preached at the Interreligious Prayer Service by Dr. Phyllis Trible, Professor Emerita of Old Testament at Union Theological Seminary, New York, and a longtime colleague and close friend of Raymond Brown. Also included is the homily given by myself at the closing liturgy presided over by Father Lawrence B. Terrien, s.s., Superior General of the Sulpicians. Special thanks are due to Rev. Emora T. Brannan, Ph.D., Senior Pastor of Grace United Methodist Church, Baltimore, MD for coordinating the moving Interreligious Service, and to Father Anthony R. Perez, s.s., Professor of Liturgy at St. Mary's, for directing the final liturgy.

Both the Conference and the initial years of the Brown Professorship were funded by the Henry Luce Foundation, through the help of Dr. Michael Gilligan, President of the Foundation. Their vision and generosity help to keep alive the memory and enduring influence of the one of the greatest scholars and teachers of the last century, Raymond E. Brown, s.s.

John R. Donahue, s.j.
Raymond E. Brown Distinguished Professor
of New Testament Studies (2001–2004)

List of Contributors

Most Rev. Terrence T. Prendergast, s.j.
Archbishop of Halifax, Nova Scotia

Rev. Francis J. Moloney, s.d.b.
Dean, School of Theology and Religious Studies
Katharine Drexel Professor of Religion
The Catholic University of America
Washington, D.C.

Prof. R. Alan Culpepper
Dean, McAfee School of Theology
Mercer University
Macon, Georgia

Prof. D. Moody Smith
George Washington Ivey Professor of New Testament
The Divinity School of Duke University
Durham, North Carolina

Professor Rabbi Burton L. Visotzky
Appleman Professor of Midrash and Interreligious Studies
Jewish Theological Seminary
New York, New York

Prof. Adele Reinhartz
Dean of Graduate Studies and Research
Wilfrid Lautier University
Waterloo, Ontario

Prof. Joseph A. Fitzmyer, s.j.
Professor Emeritus and Professorial Lecturer
The Catholic University of America
Washington, D.C.

Prof. Daniel Harrington, S.J.
Professor of New Testament
Weston Jesuit School of Theology
Cambridge, Massachusetts

Prof. Robert Kysar
Bandy Professor Emeritus of New Testament and Homiletics
Candler School of Theology, Emory University
Atlanta, Georgia

Professor Hans-Josef Klauck, O.F.M.
Divinity School, University of Chicago
Chicago, Illinois

Prof. Craig R. Koester
Professor of New Testament
Luther Seminary
St. Paul, Minnesota

Prof. Gail R. O'Day
A. H. Shatford Professor of Preaching and New Testament
Candler School of Theology, Emory University
Atlanta, Georgia

Prof. Sandra M. Schneiders, I.H.M.
Professsor of New Testament and Spirituality
Jesuit School of Theology and Graduate Theological Union
Berkeley, California

Prof. Donald Senior, C.P.
President and Professor of New Testament
Catholic Theological Union
Chicago, Illinois

Rev. Robert F. Leavitt, S.S.
Rector/President St. Mary's Seminary and University
Baltimore, Maryland

Prof. Francis Schüssler Fiorenza
Charles Chauncey Stillmann Professor of Roman Catholic Theological Studies
Harvard Divinity School
Cambridge, Massachusetts

Very Rev. Ronald D. Witherup, S.S.
Provincial of U.S. Province of Sulpicians
Sulpician Provincial House
Baltimore, Maryland

Prof. Michael L. Barré, s.s.
Professor of Old Testament
St. Mary's Seminary and University
Baltimore, Maryland

Prof. Phyllis Trible
Professor Emerita of Old Testament, Union Theological Seminary, New York
University Professor, Divinity School of Wake Forest University,
    Winston-Salem, North Carolina

Prof. John R. Donahue, s.j.
Raymond E. Brown Distinguished Professor
    of New Testament Studies (2001–2004)
St. Mary's Seminary and University
Baltimore, Maryland

Abbreviations for Periodicals, Reference Works, and Serials*

(For abbreviations in the Bibliography of the Publications of Raymond E. Brown, S.S. See p. 259.)

AAS	*Acta Apostolicae Sedis*
AB	Anchor Bible
ABRL	Anchor Bible Reference Library
AGSU	Arbeiten zur Geschichte des Spätjudentums und Urchristentums
AJSRev	*Association for Jewish Studies Review*
ALUOUS	*Annual of the Leeds University Oriental Society*
AnBib	Analecta Biblica
ANES	*Ancient Near Eastern Studies*
ANRW	*Aufstieg und Niedergang der röminschen Welt: Geschichte und Kultur Roms in Spiegel der neueren Forschung.* Edited by H. Temporini and W. Haase. Berlin. 1973
AVTRW	Aufsätze und Vorträge zur Theologie und Religionswissenschaft
BA	*Biblical Archeologist*
BETL	Bibliotheca ephemeridum theologicarum lovaniensium
Bib	*Biblica*
BibInt	*Biblical Interpretation*
BJRL	*Bulletin of the John Rylands Library*
BRev	*Bible Review*
BTB	*Biblical Theology Bulletin*
BTS	Biblische-theologische Studien
BWANT	Beiträge zur Wissenschaft von Alten und Neuen Testament
BZNW	Beihefte zur Zeitschrift für die neutestamentliche Wissenschaft
CahRB	Cahiers de la Revue biblique
CBQ	*Catholic Biblical Quarterly*
CBQMS	Catholic Biblical Quarterly Monograph Series
CCSA	Corpus Christianorum. Series Apocryphorum 1–2

* Abbreviations for journals, series, and major reference works follow those listed in Patrick H. Alexander et al., eds., *The SBL Handbook of Style: For Ancient Near Eastern, Biblical, and Early Christian Studies* (Peabody, MA: Hendrickson, 1999) 89–121. These abbreviations are used in *The Catholic Biblical Quarterly* and *The Journal of Biblical Literature*.

ConBNT	Coniectanea biblica: New Testament Series
EB	Echter Bibel
EgT	*Eglise et théologie*
EKKNT	Evangelisch-katholischer Kommentar zum Neuen Testament
ETL	*Ephemerides theologicae lovanienses*
EvTh	*Evangelische Theologie*
ExpT	*Expository Times*
FG	Fourth Gospel
HTKTN	Herders theologicscher Kommentar zum Neuen Testament
HTR	*Harvard Theological Review*
HTS	Harvard Theological Studies
JAAR	*Journal of the American Academy of Religion*
JBL	*Journal of Biblical Literature*
JSJSup	Supplements for the Journal for the Study of Judaism
JSNT	*Journal for the Study of the New Testament*
JSNTSup	Journal for the Study of the New Testament: Supplement Series
LS	*Louvain Studies*
LXX	Septuagint
MTZ	*Münchener theologische Zeitschrift*
Neot	*Neotestamentica*
NJBC	New Jerome Biblical Commentary
NovT	*Novum Testamentum*
NovTSup	Novum Testamentum, Supplements
NPNF	Nicene and Post Nicene Fathers
NRSV	New Revised Standard Version
NT	New Testament
NTL	New Testament Library
NTS	*New Testament Studies*
OT	Old Testament
ÖTK	*Ökumenischer Taschenbuch-Kommentar*
RBL	*Review of Biblical Literature*
RechBib	*Recherches bibliques*
RevExp	*Review and Expositor*
RevQ	*Revue de Qumran*
RTL	*Revue théologique de Louvain*
SBLDS	Society of Biblical Literature Dissertation Series
SBLsym	Society of Biblical Literature Symposium Series
SBLTT	Society of Biblical Literature Texts and Translations
SJT	*Scottish Journal of Theology*
SP	Sacra Pagina
STR-B	Strack, H. L., and P. Billerbeck, *Kommentar zum Neuen Testament aus Talmud und Midrasch.* 6 vols. Munich, 1922–1961
SubBi	*Subsidia Biblica*

TS	*Theological Studies*
TSAJ	Texte und Studien zum antiken Judentum
UB	Universal-Bibliothek
USQR	*Union Seminary Quarterly Review*
WBC	Word Biblical Commentary
WdF	Wege der Forschung
WMANT	Wissenschäftliche Monographien zum Alten und Neuen Testament
WUNT	Wissenschäftichle Untersuchungen zum Neuen Testament
ZNW	*Zeitschrift für Neutestamentliche Wissenschaft*
ZTK	*Zeitschrift für Theologie und Kirche*

Raymond E. Brown, s.s.
(1928–1998)

The Church's Great Challenge
Proclaiming God's Word in the New Millennium

Most Reverend Terrence T. Prendergast, S.J.

Archbishop of Halifax, Nova Scotia

It is a double honor and privilege for me to be here with you at this International Conference on the Gospel of John at St. Mary's Seminary and University in Baltimore. First and foremost it affords me an opportunity to pay tribute to one of the great Scripture scholars of the church, my brother priest and colleague the late Sulpician Fr. Raymond E. Brown. Second, Cardinal Godfried Danneels was slated to give the keynote address at this conference, but today's celebrations of the silver jubilee of the pontificate of Pope John Paul II in Rome required the Cardinal's presence at the Vatican. Therefore I stand in the footsteps of a great contemporary Church leader—a man of biblical vision and hope—qualities so badly needed for our times.

I come before you as a student and teacher of Scripture and as a priest and shepherd of the church in Atlantic Canada. I have chosen to address the topic that was assigned to Cardinal Danneels with a little variation on the original title: "The Church's Great Challenge: Proclaiming God's Word in the New Millennium." I will approach this topic by first recalling the biblical landscape within which Raymond Brown began his work. Next I will consider some of the challenges and opportunities that have arisen following the great wave of scriptural renewal. Finally, I will look at the church that Raymond Brown left behind, and how this church can continue to respond to the challenges of proclaiming God's Word in fresh ways in this new millennium. In doing so I would like to share with you some personal reflections of Raymond Brown's influence on my life, and on the life of the church.

Raymond Brown's Biblical Landscape

It is important for us to consider for a moment the landscape of Catholic biblical studies in the last century.[1] Physical, historical, and linguistic methods known to us only in approximately the last one hundred twenty-five years have produced a scientifically critical study of the Bible, a study that has revolutionized views held in the past about the authorship, origin, and dating of the biblical books, about how they were composed, and about what their authors meant. In the first forty years of the last century (1900 to 1940 approximately) the Roman Catholic Church very clearly and officially took a stance against such biblical criticism. Modernist heretics at the beginning of the century employed biblical criticism, and the official Vatican condemnations of Modernism made little distinction between the possible intrinsic validity of biblical criticism and the theological misuse of it by the Modernists.[2]

Between 1905 and 1915 the Pontifical Biblical Commission in Rome—of which Raymond Brown would later become a member not once but twice, named by two different popes—issued a series of conservative decisions on the composition and authorship of the Bible. Although phrased with nuance, these decisions ran against the trends of contemporary Old and New Testament investigations.[3] Yet Catholic scholars were obliged to assent to these decisions and to teach them.

You will certainly recall that, after forty years of rigorous opposition, the Catholic Church in the 1940's under the pontificate of Pope Pius XII made an undeniable about-face in attitude toward biblical criticism. The encyclical *Divino Afflante Spiritu* (1943) instructed Catholic scholars to use the methods of scientific approach to the Bible that had hitherto been closed to them.[4] It was now safe for Catholic scholars to take up the methods that were previously forbidden. Translations from the original Hebrew and Greek were now encouraged. A particular aspect of the encyclical definitively steered Catholics away from fundamentalism: namely, the recognition that the Bible includes many different literary forms or genres, not just history.

Within a space of ten to twenty years teachers trained in biblical criticism began to move in large numbers into Catholic classrooms in seminaries and colleges, so that the late 1950's and early 1960's really marked the watershed. By that time the pursuit of the scientific method had led Catholic exegetes to abandon almost all the positions on biblical authorship and composition taken by the Vatican at the beginning of the century.

Divino Afflante Spiritu sparked an enormous growth in Catholic biblical scholarship. New teachers were trained, and the results of the changed approach to the Scriptures were gradually communicated to the people—the very steps the Pope had urged.[5]

Another crucial moment occurred at the beginning of the Second Vatican Council in 1962. Pius XII had died, and it soon became evident that not everyone in Rome approved of the biblical changes he had introduced. The preliminary document on the sources of revelation, sent out by the Holy Office before the Council as a basis for discussion, appealed to positions taken in the early 1900's and would have turned the clock back. This document was rejected by nearly two-thirds of the Council participants and sent back by Pope John XXIII for a thorough rewriting.[6]

As part of the rewriting, the important document "Instruction on the Historical Truth of the Gospels" *(Sancta Mater Ecclesia)*—an Instruction of the Roman Pontifical Biblical Commission (1964), became the basis of the final Vatican II document pertinent to Scripture, *Dei Verbum* (Dogmatic Constitution on Divine Revelation), promulgated on November 18, 1965.[7] The Commission held that the gospels, while retaining the sense of the sayings of Jesus, were not necessarily expressing them literally.

Biblical criticism began to have an enormous effect on theology precisely because the Second Vatican Council raised biblical exegesis from the status of second-class citizenship to which it had been reduced among Catholics by an overreaction to the Protestant claim for its autonomy.

In *Dei Verbum* § 11 we read: "The books of Scripture must be acknowledged as teaching firmly, faithfully, and without error that truth which God wanted put into the sacred writings for the sake of our salvation"[8] That was quite a far cry from assuming that every statement in Scripture had to be literally accurate. And, as a further sign of the church's commitment to biblical criticism, in 1972 Pope Paul VI restructured the Pontifical Biblical Commission so that scholars, instead of being merely consultors, now constituted the commission itself. Those scholars whom he named were, in several instances, men who had suffered in the long battle to get biblical criticism accepted. All those appointed were scholars dedicated to the scientific approach to the Bible that was perfectly consonant with the best in Catholicism—men who moved far beyond the fearful spirit that governed the dark days at the beginning of the last century.

You will also recall that this turnabout was not without opposition and anguish. But in general the change sparked a renewed interest in the Bible, perhaps the greatest flowering of biblical study and writing the Roman Catholic Church had ever seen. Wisely, the church did not reverse the direction taken by Pius XII, despite the objections of those who were opposed to it. Rather, his ideas on the Bible became part of the final schema on Revelation of Vatican II, *Dei Verbum*.

The Vatican Council encouraged ecumenical relations, and Catholic and Protestant biblical specialists started to work together on translations of the sacred texts as well as on sensitive issues that divided the churches (like the biblical presentation of Peter and of Mary). Academics from the different confessions began to teach on the others' university and seminary faculties, for Catholic biblical scholarship and middle-of-the-road Protestant scholarship could agree on the meaning of much of the Scriptures. Within a remarkably short time Catholic scholarly production had reached equality in the eyes of all.

The new era ushered in by *Divino Afflante Spiritu* became the wind beneath the wings of Fr. Raymond Brown. For nearly 40 years Father Brown caught the entire church up into the excitement and new possibilities of scriptural scholarship.[9] He spread for us the feast of God's word and showed us a new landscape. More than simply inviting us to set out into the deep with him upon the new, uncharted waters of biblical scholarship, Raymond Brown excited us, inspired us, moved us, and taught us to envision Christ and the church in a new, fresh, youthful way.

Challenges Arising From the Great Biblical Renewal

In the last third of the last century, since the end of the Second Vatican Council, church needs shaped developments in the Catholic approach to the Bible. A new set of liturgical books provided three years of Sunday Mass readings, involving not only the Old Testament but also almost the complete texts of Mark, Matthew, and Luke. The church as a whole was being exposed to scriptural criticism through the liturgy. For liturgical purposes, translations from the original languages—done according to modern standards of scholarship—were made into the vernacular languages of the world. More than in any other area, it was through liturgy that Catholics experienced the initial impact of the biblical renewal.

As we look back over the sweeping changes in the life of the church following Vatican II we can never underestimate the important relation that exists between liturgy and the interpretation of the Bible. This relation is directly linked to the Church Fathers who were first and foremost individuals of prayer, even when they were writing their learned treatises and pursing their theological investigations. They were never far from the church's worship. In the liturgy they came to know Christ not so much as a historical figure from the past but as a living person present in the Eucharist. When they opened their Bibles they discovered this same Christ not only in the writings of the evangelists and St. Paul but also in the Old Testament. In the liturgy the words of Scripture were alive and filled with the mystery of Christ.

It may surely be said that the Bible provided a lexicon of words for Christian speech and the liturgy a grammar of how they are to be used. This must always be a guiding principle for us in our own efforts to make God's Word come alive for the church today. In spite of its many accomplishments, a strictly historical approach to the Bible can only give us a medley of documents from different times and places in the ancient world. It cannot give us the book of the church, the Scriptures as heard by Christians for centuries, the psalms imprinted on the church's soul, the words and images that bear witness to the Trinity.

If we ignore the first readers and scholars of the Bible we are left with a collection of fragments, interesting in their own right but lacking the unity that only the living Christ can give. And the crowning moment of this unity is given to the Scriptures in our celebration of liturgy and prayer.

There was a tremendous amount of excitement and interest in what was taking place in biblical studies. A cursory examination of the themes of study days for dioceses, Catholic gatherings, and conventions of various groups in those post-Conciliar years would indicate that Scripture was one of the most common topics. Laymen and women were involved in no small numbers in Bible groups, biblical formation programs, and biblical pilgrimages to the Holy Lands. Even among those preparing for ordained ministry in the church a new approach and fervor had entered the scene.

I think that this initial fervor and wave have subsided, and there is a "slow-down" that is hovering over the ecclesial scene, especially in the area of biblical formation and scriptural studies. I also think that some of this slowdown is due to the atomization and dissection of the Scriptures, and a lack of integration of biblical studies with faith and lived spirituality. I have from time to time heard it said among candidates preparing for ordained ministry: "Scripture courses are like doing autopsies in a morgue . . . no one is teaching us how to put the body back together again after the dissection." The real question we must ask ourselves is: Are today's Catholic Scripture scholars adequately prepared to draw from their exegetical knowledge and their own life of faith and prayer to help fellow Catholics discover the meaning of the biblical word for today?

Where are we today with the biblical renewal that enveloped all of us over the past twenty to thirty years? I see five challenges and new opportunities arising from biblical studies and biblical formation in the church:

- First, I would like to look at some of the limitations of the historical-critical method, and consider other methods that are necessary for the continued biblical renewal of the People of God and the church today.
- Second, I will address the issue of biblical fundamentalism that was often addressed by Raymond Brown during his lifetime.
- Third, I will speak about the proliferation of biblical programs and scriptural information on radio, television, and in the electronic media.
- Fourth, I wish to make some comments on the polarization in the church today, especially when it affects biblical studies and scholarship.
- Finally, I would like to address two new "biblical initiatives" that have brought the Scriptures alive to young people.

1. The Challenges of the Historical-Critical Method

Various factors have contributed to the ascendancy of historical-critical exegesis in the contemporary Catholic approach to the Bible. First, fearing that its misuse could undermine dogma, church authorities denied or severely restricted the use of this method up to and including the papacy of Pope John XXIII. It is not surprising that since then a generation of Catholic biblical scholars has devoted itself to catching up. Nor is it surprising that there have been excesses and criticisms along the way.

Ten years ago the Pontifical Biblical Commission published the English version of "The Interpretation of the Bible in the Church" (Rome, 1993).[10] It is clearly one of the most important documents on the topic since Vatican II. While continuing to affirm strongly the importance of the historical-critical method, the Biblical Commission insisted that it is not enough for Christians to understand what the words of Scripture signified at the time they were written. Exegetes must also seek to understand and communicate the meaning of the biblical word for today: "Exegesis is truly faithful to the proper intent of biblical texts when it goes not only to the heart of their formulation to find the reality of faith there, but also seeks to link this reality to the experience of faith in our present world."[11]

"The Interpretation of the Bible in the Church" emphasized the historical-critical method and accorded it primacy of place among the different methods and approaches discussed. The Commission called this method "indispensable" and insisted that the proper understanding of the Bible "not only admits the use of this method but actually requires it."[12] But the Biblical Commission document also speaks of the importance of "actualization," a term that is new to church documents on Scripture.[13] This term, transposed from the original French text, derives from *actualiser,* meaning, "to make present for today."

This emphasis on "actualization" opens new vistas for the manner in which Catholics read, study, and teach the Bible. While useful and necessary, the historical-critical method is not enough: we Catholic exegetes must never forget that what we are interpreting is the *Word of God.* Our common task is not finished when we have simply determined sources, defined forms, or explained literary procedures. We arrive at the true goal of our work only when we have explained the meaning of the biblical text as God's word for today.[14]

To realize the potential of actualizing the word, however, will require a change of attitude and reconsideration of the biblical training Catholic exegetes and seminarians and candidates for ministry receive. Actualization builds on the properly ascertained literal sense, extending it homogeneously to show how what was meant can have meaning today. Any actualized meaning that is not in homogeneous connection with what was meant becomes the projection of an extraneous sense on the text. It thus becomes heterogeneous eisegesis, the opposite of exegesis. If the actualization is not rooted in the historical-critical method, it will only become allegorical and irrelevant.

Actualization is necessary because biblical texts were composed in response to past circumstances and in a language conditioned by the time of their composition. Interpreting Scripture for today must not be a matter of projecting opinions or ideologies on the text, "but of sincerely seeking to discover what the text has to say at the present time."[15]

Actualization, unlike strict historical-critical exegesis, demands personal faith as a prerequisite and concerns itself with the religious meaning of the Bible. According to the Pontifical Biblical Commission, "the Church depends on exegetes, animated by the same Spirit as inspired Scripture . . . ."[16]

Nowhere in the life of the church is it more important that exegesis be linked with actualization than in the training of future priests, permanent deacons, and lay pastoral ministers of the church. However, as in other academic settings, the predominant approach to teaching Scripture in seminaries and other related centers of formation has *often* been to teach historical-critical exegesis without attention to actualization, which is expected to be learned, if at all, in homiletics courses. This inevitably leads to shallowness in homiletic expositions of Scripture.

If the Pontifical Biblical Commission is right about the priority of actualization, and if the eagerness of lay Catholics to learn more from the Bible is to be fostered, there need to be changes in how Catholic Scripture scholars, seminarians, and candidates for lay ministry are trained. For the present, without neglecting the historical meaning of the Bible, the priority needs to be on learning to discern and communicate the meaning of the word of God for today.

2. The Challenges of Fundamentalism

Father Raymond Brown stood firm in his opposition to biblical fundamentalism. Admitting that one of the purposes of religion is to give people security, he called into question the extent to which Jesus really functioned in normal religious terms.[17] "Often he did not make people more secure," Brown would state. "He challenged them and, indeed, shook some of their securities, so that his greatest opposition really came from religious people."[18]

Fundamentalism, Father Brown believed, is an attempt to bend Jesus to religious security. "Fundamentalism is saying, 'You really don't have to think—this ancient document or statement is your answer, all set for you.' In the case of Bible fundamentalism, the Word of God is so stressed that one forgets that human beings wrote the Bible and human beings received it," Brown would say.[19] For Brown the answer to fundamentalism is not skepticism. It is an appreciation of the divine and the human in revelation, with an invitation to take the human seriously.

The message of the Incarnation is that there is no way to avoid the interplay of the divine and the human in approaching God. Biblical literalism, since it makes everything divine, supplies a false certitude that often unconsciously confuses the human limitation with the divine message. A literalist interpretation destroys the very nature of the Bible as a human expression of divine revelation. We must understand that only human beings speak words. Therefore the valid description of the Bible as "God's Word" refers to both the divine element ("God's") and the human element ("Word").

We must never treat fundamentalists as if they were fools. At times biblical literalism is an attitude of self-definition even on the part of extremely intelligent people. They want to preserve their faith in God, and this seems to them the only way. They will understand attacks on them as an attack on their faith. Some fundamentalists are very well informed about biblical technicalities, such as languages. Occasionally evangelists know a lot more about the Bible than the average Catholic priest or mainline Protestant minister.

In the years leading up to the Great Jubilee Year 2000 there was much millennial talk and print about the end times, the end of the world, yet the chief message of Christianity does not consist in knowing exact details about the end of the world. That is not what Jesus came to proclaim. As a matter of fact, there are very few specifics about the future in Jesus' preaching other than that God is going to fulfill the divine purpose and intends to accomplish it through Jesus. When people asked Raymond Brown about the Second Coming he almost always told them that he suspected it would be as big a surprise as the first coming.[20] Brown would speak along the following lines: "It is in God's hands; he will bring about his Kingdom and I think that is what is important."

3. The Challenges of Radio, Television, and Electronic Media

Brown's attentiveness to the movements within the churches of today extended to the "electronic church" as well. Careful to disclaim any special expertise on the subject of TV evangelists, Brown admitted to reacting with some concern to media Bible preaching. The pop-psychology of TV evangelists— what Brown wryly called "the feel-all-right"—was often not heavily biblical or doctrinal, in his opinion, but simply substituted a philosophy of human betterment for biblical content. According to Brown the lack of force in such preaching worked against the biblical message of the prophets and Jesus, which, instead of being a "security blanket" was often a very confronting word.[21]

Radio, television, and now the Internet often complicate a balanced approach to such issues. On the one hand, particularly in the southern and southwestern United States, fundamentalist and literalist preachers occupy a good deal of media time defining the word-for-word historicity of the Bible and issuing predictions based on the misunderstanding that the books of Daniel and Revelation are conceived as precise prophecies of the future. They reject much modern Catholic and centrist Protestant exegesis.

On the other hand, hypotheses based on very little evidence—such as some of those promoted by the "Jesus Seminar"—propose extravagant reinterpretations of Christian origins.[22] These are presented in the media as the latest biblical scholarship. It is difficult to find on the radio or TV a presentation of the centrist approach to Scripture—that which is actually the most commonly taught and held. Fortunately, a good number of books, Catholic and Protestant, embody a centrist scholarly approach.

Father Brown also believed that the tendency for the "electronic church" to become a substitute for full church membership could best be counteracted when individual parishes offered quality Bible presentations. He felt the mainline churches had a long way to go in sponsoring this kind of Bible study, but insisted that solid teaching in churches was the best antidote to the extraordinary appeal of TV and radio evangelism.

Media interest in religious thinking holds potential for some very worthwhile programming. We must strive to assure that an educated Bible voice finds a role in the media. Such a voice, Brown believed, would be able to counteract the impression that "Bible Christians" means only those who take a highly literalistic approach to Scripture. The positive way to do this is to get something worthwhile on TV and not spend our time tearing down the present programming that is shallow or empty of meaning.

We are invited to present the Bible in an intelligent, non-literalist way. There is no use bemoaning the number of fundamentalist media preachers if we have no one in the media presenting the Bible in a sensible, non-literal manner based on modern biblical approaches, and not simply using the text as a jumping-off point for a pietistic homily. When fundamentalists are the only ones to offer them knowledge about the Bible, people will go to the fundamentalists. A solid, scholarly approach to the Bible can be spiritually nourishing and mentally satisfying. We must encourage that in the media.

4. The Challenges of Ecclesial Polarization

The continued support of the magisterium for authentic biblical scholarship is all the more necessary now that dangers both to theology and magisterium have arisen from the ultraconservative right. With increasing frequency ultraconservative or fundamentalist Catholics are usurping the authority of the magisterium by trying to condemn as heretical all theological speculation that shows any sign of nuance with regard to past doctrine. They do not respect the positions of the popes or the bishops who have permitted modern biblical and theological advances; rather, these Catholic fundamentalists denounce as heretical the freer Catholic positions that have emerged from Vatican II.

These voices from the extreme right are alienated and unhappy voices in the Roman Catholic Church today. That is a tragedy that Raymond Brown wished "with all his heart" could have been avoided. But it will be a greater tragedy if, through a manipulation of catechetics that tries to turn the clock back on genuine Catholic theological progress, they succeed in creating a future generation of youth that will be even less at home in the Catholic movements of this new century than their parents were.

An effective way for teachers of Catholic doctrine to combat this divisive tendency is to follow the lead the bishops have given. Teachers should present in catechetics the fundamentals that the Pope and bishops have underscored in their documents, and yet at the same time pedagogically prepare the students for a future encounter with theological discussions about aspects of doctrine that the magisterium has left open.

This will be a challenge, but a challenge that stems from a period of great Christian vitality. After several rather barren centuries in the history of Catholic theological thought we have come alive again theologically and scripturally. Let those who are afraid of the changes of our times condemn them; *our* task is to capitalize on the opportunity of our time to preach with joy the Good News of our faith in what God has done, not only what God has done in the past, but what God is doing today as well, and will continue to do.

5. New Opportunities to Discover the Bible

There are many signs and pockets of hope in the church today that have kept alive the biblical renewal that followed the Second Vatican Council. Here I would like to refer to two programs or projects that have embodied the best of the biblical renewal of the Roman Catholic Church.

First of all I mention the powerful and very successful "Lectio Divina" evenings in Milan's cathedral, led by my Jesuit brother Cardinal Carlo Maria Martini, now emeritus archbishop of the largest diocese in the world. Beginning from the time of his installation as bishop in 1980, and continuing almost up to his retirement over the past year, Martini gathered tens of thousands of young people together each month and taught them the Scriptures. He followed the ancient method of "Lectio Divina" as he led his audience through the Scriptures. The crowds grew so large that the evening sessions had to be telecast from the huge cathedral to various other locations in the city. Martini instilled in the young people of his local church a deep love for the Sacred Scriptures. He truly lived up to the role of a bishop as a teacher of the word of God. He created a momentum and expectation in the young people of his archdiocese that they needed God's word in their life.[23]

Another very hopeful sign in the church has developed in the context of the World Youth Day created by Pope John Paul II himself. Begun eighteen years ago, these events, which alternate between a national event in each country and large mega-gatherings every two to three years have papally-chosen Scripture themes running throughout the event. The theme of Canada's recent World Youth Day—July 2002—was "You are the salt of the earth. You are the light of the world" (Matt 5:13, 14).

During the major international World Youth Days hundreds of bishops and cardinals also attend as catechists. Each day during the World Youth Day week, thousands of young people gather around their pastor-bishops to hear teachings, "catecheses," reflections based on the word of God. This novel invention has taken on a life of its own and become an intrinsic part of the biennial international celebrations of faith and youth culture. Having been a bishop catechist myself at two World Youth Days, I can assure you that it was an extraordinary privilege to proclaim and preach the word of God in such an international setting and to appreciate how much young people need God's word to sustain them and reverence it when they hear it.

At the beginning of this new millennium Pope John Paul II addressed to the church an apostolic exhortation, *Novo Millennio Ineunte,* a very important "signature" document that sets the church on a new biblical trajectory. Quoting from Luke 5:4, the Holy Father invited the entire church to follow the example of the apostle Peter: to "put out into the deep" for a catch. *"Duc in altum"* (Luke 5:4): Peter and his first companions trusted Christ's words, and cast the nets. "When they had done this, they caught a great number of fish" (Luke 5:6).[24]

Duc in altum! These words ring out for us today, and they invite us to remember the past century of tremendous advances in Scripture scholarship with gratitude, to relive the fervor and enthusiasm that enveloped all of us in the years following Vatican II, to rekindle the biblical flame within each of us, and to look forward to the future with confidence.

Raymond Brown's Legacy

Father Raymond Brown, the Auburn Distinguished Professor Emeritus of Biblical Studies at Union Theological Seminary, New York, was twice appointed a member of the Pontifical Biblical Commission, by Pope Paul VI in 1972 and by Pope John Paul II in 1996. He was not only a theologian of international acclaim but also a man with genuine interest in the people and communities that make up the church today. To paraphrase the popular E. F. Hutton ad, when Father Raymond E. Brown, s.s., spoke, all kinds of people listened—from the Catholic hierarchy to Methodist bishops, from theology students to the lay people who bought his books.

Brown once commented that his contributions to *Catholic Update* and *St. Anthony Messenger* reached hundreds of thousands, more than his many books and scholarly works. His editors often remarked that many authors resist any suggestions, but Brown was always open to ideas and editing. He was a gracious man and a brilliant scholar who knew that the fruits of his labor were for everyone. While he reached countless scholars, religious educators, and clergy with his academic books, in his zeal he wanted to reach more: the people in the pew who hungered for a greater understanding of the Bible. In Brown, exegesis was truly at the service of the church.

One of my Scripture colleagues and good friends, Fr. Thomas Rosica, c.s.b., who headed up the recent World Youth Day 2002 in Canada and now is guiding "Salt & Light Television," Canada's first national Catholic television network with a biblical flavor, shared with me his experience of Raymond Brown while he studied at the Biblicum in the early nineties. Father Rosica was one of Brown's students in the course on the "The Death of the Messiah." He said: "Brown's course was a real *tour de force* of my entire scriptural career, not because he dazzled the huge crowd gathered weekly in the Aula

Magna of the Gregorian University, not because he taught with only a small, blue Nestle Aland New Testament and using no notes, but rather because Brown showed me how to spread the biblical feast and how to be a servant, scholar, and pastor of the Church."

As priests, ministers, teachers, and servants of God's Word we are among the stewards and servants of the "table of the Word," that first half of every eucharistic celebration when the Scriptures are broken open and shared, proclaimed and expounded. Here we spread the table before a diverse congregation, letting each person know that the Bible is a unity, a whole work of God, containing a message for everyone and for each one, no matter where they are along their pilgrim path. This is scholarship in service of the church. This is what Fr. Raymond Brown taught each of us here today.

At the end of his life Raymond Brown was quick to point out that many of the biblical studies of our time are of frightening complexity as scholars debate the meaning and origin of every pertinent verse or half-verse of the New Testament. He held that those who do not accept Christian claims about Jesus could not afford to be simplistically skeptical or to dismiss those claims out of hand as if they were based on a "fundamentalist" or uncritically literalistic reading of the evidence. If non-Christians have never spent even a few hours studying Jesus' identity they are depriving themselves of a basic insight into why the lives of so many people have been influenced by the belief that he is the Messiah of God. Father Brown made sure that his scriptural research not only imparted great knowledge but also had a pastoral goal.

While ranking churchmen trusted his teaching, extremist harassment at the grassroots level plagued Brown at times. A packet of materials available from an ultraconservative source was available to individuals upon request in advance of his appearance in a particular area. "Maybe my form of the cross [is to be] a particularly 'open target' for what I regard as Catholic extremists," he once said reflectively. "Often they dislike me more than they've disliked anybody else in the biblical field."[26]

Father Brown's works have helped countless tens of thousands of people throughout the world to preach and teach, and his presentation of the conflicts in the early churches freed many people to see how we can grow through the struggles of our present day. Above and beyond all of those remarkable qualities, Raymond Brown was a man of faith and an eminent scholar who helped shape many people's understanding of the person of Jesus Christ. He remained until the end fascinated by the Bible. He never once gave the impression that he mastered the text. Rather, he taught us how to allow the sacred text to master us.

If there were some who entertained doubts about what to say to a person who had written over forty books on the Bible and collected some thirty honorary degrees from distinguished universities such as Uppsala, Edinburgh, and Louvain, their minds were put at ease. The people who talked with Brown after the lectures found him to be friendly and approachable rather than remote and technical. He enthusiastically asked questions about everything, from parish organization to the type of audiovisual equipment used to tape his talks.

It was fitting that Brown's last book, *A Retreat with John the Evangelist: That You May Have Life* was published just before he died. Brown penned the work as part of the *A Retreat With . . .* series.[27] The book is a seven-day retreat guided by John the Evangelist, author of the Fourth Gospel, as spiritual director. Through his artful appearance in the role of "translator" for John, Brown wove the evangelist's words into a week of prayer and deepening acquaintance, ending with a list of resources to help the reader continue this relationship. Brown brought immediacy to the "gospel message," allowing modern readers to understand and resolve difficulties in the text and its interpretation throughout the centuries. Transcending the political struggles and divisiveness of some modern Christians, this retreat refreshes for the reader what it means to be, first and foremost, a disciple of Jesus.

I would like to conclude my presentation today with a striking passage from Brown's final work:

> We have been cautious during our life to shield ourselves with bank accounts, credit cards and investments, and to protect our future with health plans, life insurance, social security and retirement plans. Yet there comes a moment when neither cash nor "plastic" works. No human support goes with one to the grave; and human companionship stops at the tomb. One enters alone.[28]

On Saturday, August 8, 1998, Fr. Raymond Brown died in California of sudden and unexpected heart failure. He was seventy years old. His entire life exemplified the ability to see how Scripture is vivified in prayer and liturgy. His little books—*A Coming Christ in Advent* (Bibliography A, 34), *An Adult Christ at Christmas* (A, 23) *A Crucified Christ during Holy Week* (A, 31)—are brilliant examples of his desire to make God's word alive for the church especially at the great feasts. For it is in the silent adoration of prayer and in the congregation's act of worship in liturgy that the Bible comes alive.

This is the mystery biblical scholarship serves. Liturgy reveals the fruits of scholarship. Hence we must ask ourselves if our teaching and preaching leads others into celebration, prayer, and adoration of the Lord of history? Or has reliance on scientific methods and writings only compounded the confusion already found in our church and world?

I will now let Raymond Brown pray for us in his own words from his final retreat publication:

> Almighty God, help us to be disciples of your Son. If we are struggling with faith and doubting whether we should believe, overcome our obstacles. If we believe, strengthen our faith when it is tested by the difficulties of life. And as we face the specter of death, grant us the grace to see that already we possess your life that death cannot touch.[29]

May the memory of Father Brown be a blessing for us as we take up the church's great challenge of proclaiming God's word in the new millennium. Through his writings, may he continue to inspire generations of Scripture scholars and students, as we confidently trust that now he possesses life in abundance with the Father and feasts his eyes on the Lord of History, the Word Made Flesh, the One in whose life he was so deeply immersed while on earth, loving him, serving him, and making him known to so many people.

Notes

1. For helpful surveys see Gerald P. Fogarty, *American Catholic Biblical Scholarship: A History from the Early Republic to Vatican II.* (San Francisco: Harper & Row, 1989), and Raymond E. Brown, Joseph A. Fitzmyer, and Roland E. Murphy, eds. , *The New Jerome Biblical Commentary* (Englewood Cliffs, NJ: Prentice Hall, 1990) nos. 69, 70, "Modern Old Testament Criticism" (Alexa Suelzer and John S. Kselman) and "Modern New Testament Cricticism" (John S. Kselman and Ronald D. Witherup); no. 72, "Church Pronouncements" (Raymond E. Brown) and no. 71 "Hermeneutics," (Raymond E. Brown and Sandra M. Schneiders)

2. On Modernism see especially Gabriel Daly, *Transcendence and Immanence: A Study in Catholic Modernism and Integralism.* (Oxford: Clarendon Press; New York: Oxford University Press, 1980) and Alexander Vidler, *The Modernist Movement in the Roman Church, Its Origins and Outcome* (Cambridge: Cambridge University Press, 1934.)

3. The best collection of official Catholic documents on Scripture is Dean P. Bechard, ed. and trans., *The Scripture Documents: An Anthology of Official Catholic Teachings* (Collegeville: Liturgical Press, 2002). The early decrees of the Biblical Commission ranging from 1905 to 1933 are found on pp. 187–211.

4. Issued on September 30, 1943. See *The Scripture Documents,* 115–39; for the official text see *Acta Apostolicae Sedis* 35 (1943) 297–325.

5. When I entered the Jesuit novitiate in 1961 older members of my community told me they were jealous of the scriptural formation we were getting from the likes of Fathers David Michael Stanley, s.j. and R. A. F. MacKenzie, s.j., contemporaries of Father Brown.

6. For development of the Decree on Revelation *(Dei Verbum)* and commentary see Herbert Vorgrimler, ed., *Commentary on the Documents of Vatican II* (New York: Herder and Herder, 1969) 3:155–272; John R. Donahue, "Between Jerusalem and Athens: The Changing Shape of Catholic Biblical Scholarship," in Eleonore Stump and Thomas P. Finn, eds., *Hermes and Athena: Biblical Exegesis and Philosophical Theology* (Notre Dame: University of Notre Dame Press, 1993) 285–313.

7. Pontifical Biblical Commission, "Instruction on the Historical Truth of the Gospels" *(Sancta Mater Ecclesia)* in *The Scripture Documents,* 227–34, official text *AAS* 56 (1964) 712–18; for an excellent commentary on its significance see, Joseph A. Fitzmyer, "The Biblical Commission's Instruction on the Historical Truth of the Gospels," *TS* 25 (1964) 386–408; for the Dogmatic Constitution on Divine Revelation *(Dei Verbum)* see *The Scripture Documents,* 19–31, official text *AAS* 58 (1966) 817–36.

8. In *The Scripture Documents,* 24.

9. See "Biography and Bibliography of the Publications of Raymond E. Brown, s.s.," below, Appendix I.

10. In *The Scripture Documents,* 244–315; for excellent commentary see Joseph A. Fitzmyer, *The Biblical Commission's Document, "The Interpretation of the Bible in the Church." Text and Commentary* (Rome: Biblical Institute Press, 1995).

11. In *The Scripture Documents,* 278.

12. Ibid. 249.

13. Ibid. 303–307.

14. Ibid. 296

15. Ibid. 304

16. Ibid. 294

17. Editor's Note: Raymond Brown gave innumerable lectures and was widely quoted. Many of the following quotations are from the "oral tradition" and certainly represent the *ipsissima vox* if not the *ipsissima verba*. Where his publications touch on the issue mentioned, these will be noted. Full bibliographical data on these books and their translations into multiple languages can be found in Appendix I, "The Publications of Raymond E. Brown, s.s." Works are listed by categories, e.g., A (books), B (articles), and number in the category (A, 40).

18. In his magisterial *The Death of the Messiah,* Brown notes that Jesus' actions and teaching would be offensive to religious people today and that "most of those finding him guilty would identify themselves as Christians and think that they were rejecting an imposter, someone who claimed to be Jesus but did not fit into their conception of who Jesus was, and how he ought to act" (*Death,* 393, Bibliography A, 40).

19. For Brown's comments on fundamentalism see *Responses to 101 Questions on the Bible,* 43–48; 137–42 (Bibliography A, 36)

20. Ibid. 41–42 for Brown's comments on the book of Revelation (Bibliography A, 36).

21. Recollections of a lecture given by Fr. Raymond Brown at St. Michael's College, Toronto.

22. For a critical review of the work of the Jesus Seminar see Luke Timothy Johnson, *The Real Jesus: The Misguided Quest for the Historical Jesus and the Truth of the Traditional Gospels* (San Francisco: HarperSanFrancisco, 1995).

23. See, for example, Carlo Maria Martini, *The Joy of the Gospel. Meditations for Young People,* trans. James McGrath (Collegeville: Liturgical Press, 1994).

24. Apostolic Letter of Pope John Paul II, *Novo Millennio Ineunte* (At the Beginning of the New Millennium), issued on January 6, 2001; quotations are from § 1.

25. For his writings in *Catholic Update* see Bibliography B, 137, 151, 178, 189, 191, 193; for those in *St. Anthony Messenger* see B, 137, 151, 180, 189, 193, 194, 196, 198. Many of these short articles also appeared in his books, especially the commentaries on the liturgical seasons.

26. For a fine presentation of the opposition to and unjust criticisms of Brown's work see Joseph A. Fitzmyer, "Raymond E. Brown, s.s. In Memoriam," *USQR* 52 (1998) 1–18, especially 12–18, "The Unjust Criticism and Persecution of Raymond Brown."

27. *A Retreat With John the Evangelist: That You May Have Life* (Cincinnati: St. Anthony Messenger, 1998).

28. Ibid. 54.

29. Ibid. 98.

Part I
Johannine Studies: Challenges and Prospects

Chapter One

The Gospel of John
The Legacy of Raymond E. Brown and Beyond

Francis J. Moloney, S.D.B.
The Catholic University of America, Washington, D.C.

One of the earliest published articles from the pen of Raymond E. Brown dealt with the Gospel of John. It reflected on the impact that the discovery of the scrolls at Qumran had made upon Johannine studies, and suggested that this may have been the result of a close relationship between John the Baptist and the origins of the Fourth Gospel.[1] Already in this study Brown's basic hermeneutical stance can be sensed: he carefully sifts historical and literary evidence to provide a firm basis for a sane use of the historical-critical method. Since that time, despite major ventures into other crucial New Testament questions, especially in the area of gospel studies,[2] he has rightly been regarded as the premier Johannine scholar in the English-speaking world.

This reputation was established by the publication of his magisterial commentary on the Gospel of John for the Anchor Bible series,[3] an epoch-making publication that changed the very nature of the series.[4] His interest in matters Johannine did not cease there. His years at Union Seminary in New York, working closely with J. Louis Martyn, led to an important development in his and all subsequent approaches to the Johannine literature. These years were marked by a careful assessment of the possible experiences of a Christian community that can be traced behind various literary and theological turning points found in the gospel and pursued into the Johannine epistles.[5] The world at large was introduced to his assessment of that situation in Brown's brief but brilliant book on the life, loves, and hates within the so-called "Community of the Beloved Disciple."[6] His theoretical reconstruction of the experience of the community of the Beloved Disciple undergirds his further major contribution to Johannine studies, the Anchor Bible volume on the Johannine epistles.[7]

Less well known, but equally important, have been his briefer reflections on matters Johannine in some of his shorter writings,[8] and the remarkable presentation of the *persona* of the Beloved Disciple as told by the "voice" of the Evangelist in his *A Retreat with John the Evangelist. That You May Have Life*, published in 1998, the year of Brown's sudden and unexpected death.[9] As is now well known, Brown had turned his mind to a second edition of his Anchor Bible commentary. He had already signed a contract with Doubleday and had done some major work on the introduction. At the time of his death the commentary itself remained largely untouched. We are blessed to have the recently published final thoughts of Raymond Brown on the Fourth Gospel in his posthumous *Introduction to the Gospel of John*.[10] It takes us up to, and perhaps somewhat speculatively even a little "beyond" 1998.

This rapid survey indicates that—despite his intense interest in New Testament scholarship as a whole—from 1955 till 1998 the Gospel of John teased Brown's mind relentlessly.[11] Fortunately, and not only in biblical studies, *first loves* die hard! How can one look to the *contemporary* study of the Gospel of John and succinctly evaluate "the legacy of Raymond E. Brown" in order to gauge better where one might go "beyond" that legacy? The sheer quantity and quality of four decades of intense historical-critical scholarship stand as Brown's major legacy to future generations of Johannine scholarship. To this date no single scholar—certainly in the English-speaking world—can claim to have contributed such quantity and quality to Johannine studies.[12] Given the immensity of the task, and the limitations of this reflection, the goals he stated in 1966 as he began his commentary may serve as a basis for a selective assessment of Brown's legacy. In 1966 he expressed a desire to write a commentary that incorporated "a moderately critical theory of the composition of the Gospel" reflecting his conviction that the Fourth Gospel "is rooted in historical tradition about Jesus of Nazareth." He finally insisted: "sincere confessional commitment to a theological position is perfectly consonant with a stubborn refusal to make a biblical text say more than its author meant it to say."[13]

I. The Legacy

Brown must be located within his own period in the development of critical New Testament scholarship, and especially Johannine scholarship. He has recently been called a "second-generation" American Catholic scholar. Luke Timothy Johnson describes the generations: "The first generation was made up of those who grew to maturity in the 'old world' of Catholic sensibility, whose theological education was traditional, and whose commitment to the Church was expressed through vows or ordination." The second generation, to which Brown belongs, "consists of those who entered more wholeheartedly into the ethos of critical scholarship. . . . These scholars were by no means faithless or negligent. Many still took up theological issues. The main distinguishing feature of this generation is its uncritical acceptance of the dominant historical-critical paradigm, and a style of scholarship that was increasingly directed to . . . other scholars."[14] Against Johnson's assessment of Brown's methodological stance as *uncritical*, I would suggest it was from the *strength* provided by his carefully articulated use of the historical-critical paradigm *within* the Catholic communion that he became a trailblazer within all circles of American and international Johannine scholarship.[15] In my own initial forays into the Fourth Gospel, while I was studying in Europe in the early 1970s, I was stunned to experience the massive influence of two young scholars who were Roman Catholic in their faith tradition and remarkably "catholic" in their scholarship: Rudolph Schnackenburg and Raymond Brown.[16] They formed my generation of Johannine scholars. I trust that the work of both recently deceased giants will continue to play an important role in the formation of the next generation! Given the present distancing of many younger scholars, and indeed Biblical Studies schools and departments, from historical study, there is a danger that this may not be the case. It is to the importance of that legacy that I would now like to turn.

The Legacy of Historical Criticism

In recent years much has been made of the "bankruptcy" of the historical-critical method,[17] but those who do not recognize the past will not create a viable future. If we are not prepared to recognize that we stand on the shoulders of those who went before us, we will not look too far into the future! Brown was a consummate practitioner of the historical-critical method in his approach to the Johannine text. With care and respect he sought the historical origins and developing traditions, reaching back to Jesus where possible, peeling back the various layers, suggesting various *Sitze im Leben* for them, finally putting them together to comment upon the text as a whole. Throughout his commentary, examples of this methodology abound. I mention three here, simply to remind you of the care and calibre of his contribution.

- Along with many scholars of his generation, Brown was convinced that the Prologue (John 1:1-18) was originally a Christian hymn, taken over by the redactor and used as a prologue to the Johannine narrative. The background to the use of λόγος was primarily Jewish Wisdom speculation, and the two passages dealing with John the Baptist (vv. 6-8, 15) were added by the redactor to the original hymn in order to clarify the nature of the relationship between the Baptist and Jesus.[18]
- Influenced by the argument of Günther Bornkamm that the use of σάρξ in 6:63 contradicted its use in 6:52, 53, 54, 55, 56,[19] Brown argued that vv. 51c-58 were added by the redactor. The eucharistic background to 6:1-15 colored the reading of vv. 25-51b, but the discourse was sapiential, summoning the believer to faith in the Son, the one who came from the Father. The work of the redactor, adding vv. 51c-58, highlighted the eucharistic possibilities of the whole of John 6.[20]

- A number of different traditions lay behind John 13:1–17:26. The earliest discourse can be traced in 13:31–14:31 (with its original closure in 14:31, running into 18:1). A later development of 13:31-14:31 can be found in 16:4b-33. The account of the meal and the footwashing (13:1-30), itself the product of a complex literary history blending narrative with moral exhortation, the discourse of 15:1–16:4a, and the prayer of 17:1-26 each had its independent literary prehistory. The account of Jesus' final encounter with his disciples before the Passion is the work of the Evangelist, with some help from the redactor.[21]

Every element of this historical-critical analysis of the Johannine text is nowadays subjected to criticism, and alternative approaches are being developed.[22] But Brown and his contemporaries exercised great discipline in pointing to the *foreignness* of a text that was written in a strange language, that followed strange literary conventions, and that took decades to assume its present shape. However much contemporary Johannine scholarship might agree or disagree with the details of Brown's analysis and might propose methods at variance with the historical-critical paradigm, it must accept and grapple with the foreignness of the biblical text.

Our current move toward "wholistic" readings of ancient texts, whatever form these readings may take, can sometimes claim that the narrative world of the text is sufficient unto itself. For example, in a fine study of "the Jews" in the Fourth Gospel, Gérard Caron rightly traces their *function within the narrative*, and concludes that there are various "forms of Judaism" involved in the Johannine story. The negative use of "the Jews" as characters within the narrative represents one of those forms. He eschews any need to trace the possibility that such a "form of Judaism" ever actually existed, or whether it may have provided a historical context within which the gospel story may have developed. The world that produced the text has lost its relevance, and this is dangerous on both theological and critical grounds.[23] Theologically, it ignores the foundational experience of Jesus and the early Christian community. Critically, it leaves many tensions and questions that arise from a close reading of the text unexplained. There are also some "wholistic" readings that deliberately disregard historical questions and consequently produce a new fundamentalism. The meaning of the text may be *entirely* subjected to the dogmas of an institution[24] or—even worse—to the subjectivity of the contemporary reader. As the literary critic Peter Rabinowitz has rightly remarked: "For once you take seriously the notion that readers 'construct' (even partially) the texts that they read, then the canon (any canon) is not (or not only) the product of the inherent qualities in the text; it is also (at least partly) the product of particular choices by the arbiters of taste who create it—choices always grounded in ideological and cultural values, always enmeshed in class, race and gender."[25]

The legacy of Brown's commitment to the historical-critical method must continue to be taken seriously as we attempt to look "beyond" him. Within that legacy there were, as we have seen, three self-confessed agendas that determined his analysis of the Gospel of John: a theory of the gospel's composition, the traditions—both literary and historical—that formed it, and his confessional commitment.[26]

1. The Composition of the Gospel

In the 1966 commentary, before he turned his attention to the history of the Johannine community,[27] Brown had suggested a five-stage theory for the development of the gospel.[28] By associating a theory of composition, distilled from the strengths and weaknesses of scholars before him, with more recent speculations upon the history of the community, in 1998 he proposed a three-stage development that produced the gospel as we now have it.[29] His more recent proposal may be summarized as follows:

Stage One: Like all the gospels, the Gospel of John had its origins in the ministry and teaching of Jesus, witnessed to by a disciple.

Stage Two: In a fashion similar to the development of the Synoptic Tradition, for several decades Jesus was proclaimed in the post-resurrectional context of a Christian community. It is at this stage that the Beloved Disciple played a crucial role.[30] Not one of the Twelve, but a disciple of Jesus, this figure was the link between the first and the second stage. The bulk of this lengthy period (several decades) would have been marked by the oral transmission of the tradition of the Beloved Disciple, but there may have been something written toward the end of this stage.

Stage Three: There are two moments in this final stage. The first is the creative writing of a remarkable storyteller, whom Brown calls *"the evangelist."* This person is *not* the Beloved Disciple, but faithfully, and indeed brilliantly (see chs. 9, 11, 18–19), receives the tradition of the Beloved Disciple and communicates it through a coherent, theologically motivated story containing signs, discourses, and narratives. He is the author of the bulk of the gospel. To cite Brown: "If in Stage Two the Beloved Disciple was a major instrument of the Paraclete-Spirit in bearing witness, by producing the gospel in Stage Three the evangelist was the instrument of the Paraclete-Spirit."[31] Brown suggests that the evangelist may have worked and reworked the story, but we cannot be sure of this. Finally, *"the redactor"* produced the gospel as we now have it. This figure is responsible for such features as the Prologue (1:1-18), the Epilogue (21:1-25), and shifting certain blocks of material within the evangelist's story from one place to another. Contrary to Bultmann and his many followers, for Brown the redactor was not responsible for making the Gospel of John more acceptable to the so-called "greater church" by introducing material on traditional eschatology and sacraments. The redactor is in deep sympathy with the evangelist who, in his own turn, brilliantly rendered the traditions passed on by the Beloved Disciple into the narrative forms that produced the gospel.[32]

2. The Johannine Tradition

Aware of the increasing interest in the possible *literary* dependence of the Johannine tradition upon the Synoptic Tradition, Brown's most recent work is less forthright, but nevertheless firmly concludes that a theory of *literary independence* best explains the uniqueness of the Johannine narrative.[33] Brown claims that to accept that the evangelist and/or the redactor drew directly from Mark, Matthew, and Luke, as Franz Neirynck has argued,[34] would mean that the evangelist (and the redactor?), writing in the '80s-'90s of the first century, would have known and accepted all three Synoptic Gospels as authoritative Christian documents. If this were the case, it would make him/them the earliest Christian author(s) to know and use them in this fashion. This is hardly likely to have been the case. The better option remains that of Percival Gardner-Smith and Charles Harold Dodd.[35] All four gospels draw on independent traditions, but Brown's most recent work shifts ground here. In a fashion similar to that outlined more recently in the work of Udo Schnelle, Brown suggests that John did not think he was inventing the literary form of "gospel." There was probably some cross-influence, most likely during Brown's "Second Stage" (but one cannot be sure of this), especially from the emerging Lukan tradition.[36] Of course, as Brown carefully points out and subjects to careful analysis, a common use of shared ancient traditions raises the historical question. Is it possible that there may be in the Gospel of John more genuine historical data about Jesus and his world than is often allowed? Here one must return to the commentary of 1966–70. In his analysis of every episode Brown faced the possibility that behind the Johannization of an early Christian tradition lay an event from the life of Jesus.[37]

But what of the world within which the Johannine story developed? As in 1966–70, Brown still turns to Judaism as the gospel's most formative element. But in 1966 he wrote confidently of "Palestinian Judaism." He now broadens his base and suggests that a number of different Jewish worlds played into the stream that formed the Gospel of John: the Old Testament, Jewish practices, and Jewish thought in the world of the time. This world and its thought can be notoriously difficult to identify, but are probably best reflected by the Dead Sea Scrolls. Brown now speaks of a *more broadly based* "traditional Judaism," defined as a Judaism that took its main inspiration from what we call the Old Testament, without adoption of extra-biblical Hellenistic philosophy and theology.[38] Brown questions the exaggerated anti-Baptist polemic often found in this gospel, and rejects an anti-docetic tendency.[39] He argues that the gospel is written to encourage crypto-Christians to take the step into full commitment to the Johannine Jesus but condemns those whose faith is insufficient. Crucial to this treatment, however, is a completely updated and documented study of the use of "the Jews" in the Fourth Gospel. Following the development of difficulties between the historical Jesus and some Jews of his time, through the various stages of the development of the gospel and the history of the community across the latter half of the first Christian century, Brown identifies them as hostile Jews whose *role in the story* is to demonstrate implacable rejection of Jesus and its consequences, both for Jesus and for themselves. However, this identification by "role" is followed by no less than eight "riders" that clarify and circumscribe this position from a number of angles, historically, theologically, literally, and politically.[40] Brown's history of the Johannine community allows him to suggest a geographical move from Palestine to Ephesus, where the gospel finally saw the light. He allows that northern Transjordan may have been part of that journey and has thus left its mark in the Johannine story.[41]

In the end, however, Brown's final words on the task of interpreting the Gospel of John indicate that a second edition of his famous commentary might have taken him into hitherto uncharted waters. Marking a serious shift of position from his earlier approach to the Gospel of John, strongly influenced by positions he took on historical-critical issues, Brown finally comments:

> Even though I think there was both an evangelist and a redactor, the duty of the commentator is not to decide what was composed by whom, or in what order it originally stood, nor whether these composers drew on a written source or an oral tradition. One should deal with the Gospel of John as it now stands, for that is the only form that we are certain has ever existed.[42]

The influence of contemporary Johannine scholarship is apparent in this position. We can only speculate on how seriously this affirmation would have influenced a complete commentary on the Gospel of John from Brown. However, it is a further challenge that this great scholar leaves with those who claim to be reaching "beyond" him.

3. Confessional commitment

I only have to point to the remarkable gathering of Johannine scholars from across the world, and across our many Christian and Jewish traditions, that generated this paper, as proof that Raymond Brown's work on John, as with all his work, affirmed his Catholic confessional commitment in a way that both welcomed and nourished believers from many other traditions. I simply wish to address, briefly, a uniquely American phenomenon: the search for a *Catholic biblical scholarship*. My roots are in Australia, where I did my research and teaching within the ecumenical Melbourne College of Divinity, and then in the equally ecumenical Australian Catholic University, where I was the Foundation Professor of Theology. All of my other research and

teaching have been carried out in Italy, France, Germany, the United Kingdom, Ireland, Hong Kong, the Philippines, and Israel. I have never experienced difficulty from either my many colleagues from other faith traditions or
my religious or ecclesiastical superiors about *how* I work as a biblical scholar,
i.e., my "methodology." Yet, on arrival in the United States, I discovered that a
hand-wringing debate has been generated over this issue. It appears to have
begun in earnest as the result of a heated encounter between Luke Timothy
Johnson and John Meier at the annual meeting of the Catholic Biblical Association in Seattle in 1997. Since that time others have entered the debate. It has
reached its high point in the volume of Luke Timothy Johnson and William S.
Kurz.[43]

I have never felt the need for some form of theoretical underpinning for a
method that would single out Catholic biblical scholarship. It had not crossed
my mind until I met the current discussions in some Catholic circles in the
United States today. Postmodernism has taught us that we need to be more
honest about where we stand before, during, and after the process of interpretation, whatever "method" we are using. I have no quibble with the appeal
from Johnson and Kurz that we recapture the massive and life-giving contributions made by the patristic and medieval interpreters, and that we interpret
the text within the context of the *regula fidei* of our tradition.[44] All of us, be we
Roman Catholic, Anglican, Protestant, or Jewish, know where we stand. And
so do our colleagues. My Lutheran colleagues would wonder what was wrong
with me if I were to claim that Catholics were to live under the catch-cry of
sola Scriptura. My Anglican brethren would be equally perplexed if I were to
discount the importance of Petrine traditions in the New Testament and not
see them as an integral part of emerging Christianity.

We do not have to agree, but we are mutually enriched as we work diligently with an ancient text, giving it all the respect it deserves. This text is,
after all, our canon of Sacred Scripture. It unites us under God, one with Jesus
Christ, enlightened and guided by the same Spirit. Raymond Brown is a shining example of how a professional biblical scholar from any tradition should
set about this task from within the context of a particular ecclesiastical tradition. His influence as a human being as well as a scholar reaches well beyond
what he has published. I remain firmly convinced that there is no place for a
methodological approach to the Bible that is uniquely Roman Catholic. As the
Pontifical Biblical Commission has recently affirmed: "Catholic exegesis does
not claim any particular scientific method as its own."[45] But there is an urgent
need for Catholics to apply themselves to the interpretation of the Bible with a
commitment to the text, the tradition, and the *regula fidei*, following the example of Raymond Brown. "[S]incere confessional commitment to a theological position is perfectly consonant with a stubborn refusal to make a
biblical text say more than its author meant it to say."[46]

II. And Beyond

But Johannine scholarship moves on. Brown's decision to completely rewrite his commentary, a decision frustrated by God's design, is clear indication of that truth. Yet, as I worked through the text that Brown had left unfinished, I noticed a number of tensions and *non-sequiturs*. Brown was working with his 1966 text, but he was straining to go "beyond" that point, and tensions emerged. There are several places where completely new material was inserted into an older text.[47] *Necessarily*, this process of reworking an older text in a somewhat piecemeal fashion, adding new material on the way, creates literary and even theological tensions. I will give two examples. Brown declares that he is not prepared to make use of Revelation as support for a Johannine idea or literary pattern, but at times he continues to do so.[48] Second, there are some occasions when he speaks of the Johannine christology "replacing" the Jewish institutions. Yet there are one or two places where he (more correctly) speaks of Jesus' perfecting or fulfilling the possibilities of the Jewish institutions.[49] If Brown's own work—obviously the work of *a single author* working on the same material across a span of thirty years—can reflect these (and other) tensions and internal contradictions, is it necessary to develop a hypothesis involving a series of different "authors" (Beloved Disciple, evangelist, redactor) to demonstrate the composition history of the Gospel of John? The presence of tensions and internal contradictions in the Gospel of John cannot be denied, but this ancient text probably grew in a far more haphazard fashion than the two editions of Brown's introduction to the Gospel of John, which itself contains tensions and internal contradictions.

In terms of the composition history of this new *Introduction*, there is but one author. The physical *writer* of the original work (1966), is the same writer (and in some ways the same person acting as a redactor) who produced a different, and at times contradictory, text (1998). I am aware that with Brown's work we are dealing with two written texts. This separates it from the development of the Gospel of John, which (one must speculate) had a long pre-literary history. It must always be remembered that respect for received traditions may have caused a certain awkwardness in an evangelist's use of them.[50] But what was the relationship between the evangelist and the Beloved Disciple, whose traditions the former forged into a coherent narrative? The enigma of the historical figure and the literary and even theological function of the Beloved Disciple remain. Could the Beloved Disciple and the evangelist be one and the same figure? Is this perhaps what is meant by 21:24: "This is the disciple who is bearing witness to these things, and who has written these things, and we know that his testimony is true" (21:24)? Should we, perhaps, take these words, obviously from the redactor ("we know that his testimony is true"), more seriously? But why, in this section of my paper that deals with where we must go to reach "beyond" Brown's legacy, do I raise this issue? This is a helpful example of the limitations of a historical-critical method that speculates on data *outside the text*. What must be admitted is that all such reconstructions lie outside our scientific control, and suggests that we need to focus more intensely upon what can be found *within the text*.

Second, a further challenge comes from Brown's recent insistence on the need to comment upon the Gospel of John as we now have it. Charles Harold Dodd once asked that scholars respect the final shape of the gospel because someone was responsible for it, even if it were only "a scribe doing his best." Brown comes close to this in his affirmation that "[o]ne should deal with the Gospel of John as it now stands, for that is the only form that we are certain has ever existed."[51] Would Brown have provided a commentary on 1:1-18 *without* discussing the influence of the *later* (and perhaps apologetic) addition of vv. 6-8 and 15 into a hymn that (for Brown) was itself a late addition from the hand of the redactor?[52] Would he have explained 6:25-59 *without* recourse to the suggestion that vv. 51c-58 were a late insertion (obvious from the contradicting meaning of "flesh" [σάρξ] in vv. 51c-58 and v. 63)?[53] Would he have attempted a synchronic reading of 13:1–17:26?[54] Reaching "beyond" Brown forces us to ask: what would have determined the understanding of the meaning of Jesus' final encounter with his disciples: the tradition history or "the Gospel as it now stands, for that is the only form that we are certain has ever existed"? The more I ponder them, the more I suspect that the latest Raymond Brown was moving in a direction that commissions those of us who have received so much from him to reach "beyond" what he has achieved.

In 1998 Brown continued to insist that the Gospel of John is the product of "traditional Judaism." He rejects any direct influence from Gnosticism, Mandean thought, the *Hermetica*, or extra-biblical Hellenistic influence. Brown's carefully articulated argument reflects a middle-of-the-road position taken by most scholars of his generation who reacted rightly against Bultmann's Gnostic-existentialist reading of John, in its own turn a reflection of the agenda of the earlier History of Religions School.[55] Contemporary studies are suggesting that a more nuanced approach should be considered. As Hans-Josef Klauck describes it:

> One would impose an unnecessary restriction on one's ability to get a proper perspective on this material, if one were *a priori* to subordinate everything *to the question of a possible dependence*—whether particular reasons led one to seek to demonstrate that certain phenomena were originally non-Christian, or an apologetic prejudice led one to dispute the existence of any foreign influence whatsoever. . . . The critical eye will see clearly that the specific characteristic of Christianity in many cases is to be found less in the details and the individual aspects than in the total pattern and in the unifying centre-point, which gives structure to the Christian universe of meaning. Besides this, the acceptance and assimilation of foreign influences can also be assessed positively, as a sign of the integrative power of the Christian faith, which is capable of fusing the different elements together.[56]

As indicated above, Brown shifted away from his original identification of "Palestinian Judaism" to the more *broadly based* "traditional Judaism" as his basic point of reference for the background to the Gospel of John. This shift of position opens the door—ever so slightly—on another possibility that was not articulated in Brown's posthumous text as we have it. His work on the history of the Johannine community enabled him to develop the theory that the Gospel of John was not influenced by Gnostic thought but that, as the community fell into disunity, one direction some of its members took was into Gnosticism. Thus Gnosticism played no role in the formation of the gospel, but it was an important *recipient* of the gospel. In his analysis of the possible influence of philonic-type Jewish-Hellenistic thinking, Brown concludes that Philo and the evangelist shared a common way of working out biblical motifs in a partially Jewish, partially Greek world where Hellenistic thought had taken root.

This theme is developed further by means of Brown's careful listing of the many parallels between the Wisdom tradition and the Johannine thought world, imagery, and terminology.[57] The Wisdom tradition, as is well known, reflects the presence of Jewish-Hellenistic thinking and writing in the pre-Christian era. But as he closes his reflections upon Wisdom, Brown returns to his earlier reflections on the various possible influences on the gospel. He adds, in a note: "What John shows in common with these latter bodies of literature (Gnostic, Mandean or Hermetic) often represents a common but independently received heritage from the Jewish Wisdom Literature."[58] In a fashion parallel with his earlier suggestions concerning the Gnostic *reception* of the Johannine tradition, Brown turns to a theory of "reception" to explain the oft-drawn links between the Gospel of John and other contemporaneous non-Jewish and non-biblical literatures and "cultures." The Gospel of John and these other literatures and streams of thought are to be regarded as *recipients* of common traditions, especially the Wisdom traditions.

Stepping "beyond" Brown, I suggest that the person(s) responsible for the final form of the Gospel of John was/were well aware that this story of Jesus was very different from the Jewish traditions that formed it. The existence of a philonic-like Jewish approach to the life and practices of Israel in the first Christian century is obvious, and Philo himself is evidence of it. But he would not have been alone. It happens that we have his written work and we tend to think that he must have been something of a unique and lone voice. Such was surely not the case. Similarly, by Brown's own admission (and it is commonplace among all scholars of early Christianity),[59] a profound hellenization of Judaism had been going on for some centuries before the Christian movement. As Klauck has rightly remarked of this process: "Like platonic philosophy, sapiential literature and apocalyptic do not simply provide material on which gnosis then worked: they belong to the basic intellectual presuppositions without which gnosis could not have been elaborated."[60]

So much has been said and written about a pre-Christian gnosticism. Did it or did it not exist? I would like to suggest that this is to ask the wrong question in a discussion of the factors that may have influenced the formation of the Gospel of John as we now have it. Clearly the great Gnostic systems that we know from the second century owe a great deal to the Christian tradition, and especially to the Gospel of John.[61] However, did these powerful intellectual movements, which almost took the young Christian Church by storm and aroused angry and voluminous writing from people like Irenaeus, Hippolytus, and Epiphanius, come from nowhere?[62] Did they suddenly appear on the scene in the second century as fully developed systems? As Giovanni Filoramo states the case: "Related, if not prior, to Christianity, it had arisen independently, based on oriental texts and ideas, a genuine religion, in which the *logos* (word/reason) was the son of the *mythos* (myth) *and Christianity one of several elements that came together to make a difficult puzzle.*"[63]

Might it not be better, in the light of Filoramo's comment and the evidence of the second century, to speak of a *pre-gnostic Gnosticism*, or, as Klauck describes it, "a non-Christian gnosis"?[64] Accepting Brown's position that the gospel saw the light of day in its present form at Ephesus,[65] the world *into which* the Gospel of John told its story of Jesus was marked by a maelstrom of religious thought and practices, however eclectic they may have been. It would have been impossible, to my mind, for the author(s) of the Gospel of John *not* to shape the Johannine story of Jesus so that it might address the confused and confusing religious world of one of the great cosmopolitan cities of Asia Minor.[66] The Gospel of John, therefore, told the old story of Jesus in a radically different fashion without betraying the roots of the original Christian tradition: the life, teaching, death, and resurrection of Jesus of Nazareth. One of the reasons for these remarkable differences, might I suggest, was an awareness of the new world into which Jesus' story had to be announced.

Only in recent times have literary critics and people interested in the science of hermeneutics begun to speak about the worlds behind, within, and in front of the text.[67] However, in all ages anyone who tells a story (the world in the text) is influenced by both the material he or she receives (the world behind the text) and the people for whom the story is being told (the world in front of the text). Surely this was the case for the author(s) of the Gospel of John. If so, then the pre-gnostic Gnostic and Hellenistic world of the first century (the world in front of the text), side by side with the formative elements from the story of Jesus and the traditional Judaism within which it was originally told (the world behind the text), also played *a formative role* in the development of the Gospel of John (the world in the text). This preparedness to shape a new story of Jesus to address a new world is one of the many reasons, in my opinion, for the perennial fascination of the Gospel of John. Into these worlds also step the remarkable *personae* of Brown's Beloved Disciple and evangelist if, indeed, they are to be separated. They have inscribed themselves into these inspired and inspiring pages.[68] The Gospel of John builds bridges from one sociocultural and religious world (traditional Judaism) into another (the Gnostic-Hellenistic world of Asia Minor), and in doing so serves as a paradigm for all who seek to tell and retell the story of Jesus.[69]

III. Conclusion

Assessing the challenge of the legacy of one of the greatest Johannine scholars of the twentieth century is a tall order. It cannot be done in a lecture, nor perhaps within the career of any particular scholar. In conclusion I suggest that many of the tasks Brown set himself still remain, and I am sure that he would be the first to admit that such was the case. This means that many of the classical questions in Johannine studies continue to be vigorously debated, and it is our responsibility to go "beyond" what Brown has achieved.[70] Major issues, some of which have been seriously faced by Brown as recently as 1998 but remain unresolved, are:

- The *religionsgeschichtliche Hintergrund* to the Fourth Gospel.
- The history of the Johannine community.[71]
- The dependence of the Fourth Gospel on the Synoptic Tradition.[72]
- The possibility of a genuine redaction-critical study of the Fourth Gospel.[73]
- The relationship between Jesus of Nazareth and the Johannine christology.[74]
- The literary and theological creativity of the Evangelist.[75]

Newer issues are emerging:

- What once might have been limited to the more formal and scientifically reconstructed *religionsgeschichtliche Hintergrund* has now been broadened. Scholars search more widely for possible "intertext" and reconstruct the "repertoire" shared by the implied author and reader of the gospel.[76]
- What function do characters play within the narrative? (the question of "characterization").[77]
- There is an increasing awareness of the pervasive use of symbolism in the Gospel of John.[78]
- We now acknowledge the possibility of an ideological stance "over against the text" as a reading strategy that renders the culturally prejudiced Johannine text more conducive to contemporary reading.[79]
- There is clearly a need, especially among younger generations of English-speaking scholars, to follow the lead of Raymond Brown and his contemporaries by interacting with scholars outside the comfort zones of their own cultural and linguistic world.[80]

This is but a sketch, and the list could no doubt be lengthened. Recent Johannine scholarship, reaching "beyond" Raymond Brown, frankly admits "who I am" and "where I stand." This is an important and honest advance on traditional historical-critical scholarship. However, and again the legacy of Brown looms large, we must continue to pay attention to the question of "where I look." Contemporary hermeneutics, under the influence of reader-focused literary theory, from reader-response to radical postmodern readings, stresses the issues of "who I am" and "where I stand," once elements the historical-critical method claimed to have expunged from biblical criticism. But not even the most rigorous historical critic has ever read the Bible objectively.[81] It is important that all working with text admit that text without context is pretext. All interpreters inscribe something of themselves upon their interpretation.[82] This means that more and more elements need to be drawn into the now-famous Gadamerian *Horizontsverschmelzung*.[83]

Nevertheless, I remain convinced that a reading of the biblical text *within the Christian tradition* must give primacy to the text.[84] The primary focus of the interpreter's attention must be *the text itself*. It is from there that one must move to rediscover the "repertoire," the socio-religious and theological setting and possible other texts that may or may not have generated the text. In the end our interpretations will stand or fall in view of our successful (or unsuccessful) illumination of the primary text, in our case the Gospel of John, read within the secondary text of the Christian tradition.

Contemporary scholarship, and not only biblical scholarship, is uncovering increasing complexities in the worlds behind, within, and in front of the text. It is thus becoming more difficult to give primacy to this fragile collection of τὰ βίβλια, the product of much ambiguous human experience, and perhaps an even more ambiguous reading of it.[85] Yet, *mutatis mutandis*, a contemporary assessment of the task of the literary critic could be applied to the work of the biblical scholar:

> A great literary critic is like a great musician, who uses his knowledge of music to create beautiful interpretations. These interpretations, although they are called interpretations *of*, are in fact interpretations *with* the music—they achieve what the art was made for in the first place.[86]

Johannine scholarship, and hopefully the Christian Church, will be richer if we respectfully and critically embrace the heritage of Raymond Brown but take seriously our further responsibility to reach "beyond" his magnificent contribution. Our goal as professional Johannine scholars is to "achieve what the art was made for in the first place."

Notes

1. The result of a seminar paper presented at Johns Hopkins University in 1955, the most up-to-date version of this essay can now be found in Raymond E. Brown, "The Qumran Scrolls and the Johannine Gospel and Epistles," in idem, *New Testament Essays* (London: Geoffrey Chapman, 1967), 102–31. The original appeared in *CBQ* 17 (1955) 403–19. It had been preceded by a study that arose from his doctoral research, pursued at St Mary's Seminary and University: Raymond E. Brown, "The History and Development of the Theory of a *Sensus Plenior*," *CBQ* 15 (1953) 141–62. Brown's association with William Foxwell Albright at Johns Hopkins made him an early player in the assessment of the Qumran material. He was part of a team (Joseph A. Fitzmyer, Willard Oxtoby, and later Javier Teixidor) that produced a rare aid for the initial study of the scrolls: *A Preliminary Concordance to the Hebrew and Aramaic Fragments from Qumran Caves II–X*. On the history of this working tool for the original scholars, and its later use and abuse, see James C. Vanderkam and Peter Flint, *The Meaning of the Dead Sea Scrolls. Their Significance for Understanding the Bible, Judaism, Jesus and, Christianity* (New York: HarperCollins, 2002) 385, 390–92. Brown's final contribution to Qumran studies was published posthumously: Raymond E. Brown, "John, Gospels and Letters of," in Lawrence H. Schiffman and James C. Vanderkam, eds., *Encyclopedia of the Dead Sea Scrolls*. 2 vols. (New York: Oxford University Press, 2000) 414–17.

2. Incomparable in their depth and breadth have been his two large-scale studies dealing with some of the thorniest questions in New Testament scholarship: *The Birth of the Messiah. A Commentary on the Infancy Narratives in Matthew and Luke*. ABRL (new updated version New York: Doubleday, 1993), and *The Death of the Messiah. From Gethsemane to the Grave. A Commentary on the Passion Narratives in the Four Gospels*. 2 vols. ABRL (New York: Doubleday, 1994).

3. Raymond E. Brown, *The Gospel according to John*. 2 vols. AB 29–29a (Garden City, NY: Doubleday, 1966–70).

4. As the original frontispiece (written by William Foxwell Albright and David Noel Freedman) announced: "The Anchor Bible is aimed at the general reader with no special training in biblical studies." The earliest volumes in the series (pre-Brown) reflected this approach. Freedman continues to insert this note, but Brown's two volumes on the Gospel of John set a new standard that all subsequent contributors (in both Testaments) have attempted to follow. Since Brown's *John*, most volumes are well beyond "the general reader."

5. Martyn, after several explorations into the history of the Johannine community, published, in 1968, a groundbreaking study, *History and Theology in the Fourth Gospel*. The original publication was with Harper & Row (New York). A second edition appeared with Abingdon (Nashville) in 1979, and a third (unchanged, but with an important introduction by D. Moody Smith) with Westminster John Knox (Louisville) in 2003. Martyn's work, so influential on Brown's later Johannine scholarship, has been a watershed in contemporary Johannine studies. For a description and assessment of this development see my added excursus, "Theories of Johannine Community History," in Raymond E. Brown, *Introduction to the Gospel of John,* edited and updated by Francis J. Moloney. ABRL (New York: Doubleday, 2003) 69–75.

6. Raymond E. Brown, *The Community of the Beloved Disciple: The Life, Loves and Hates of an Individual Church in New Testament Times* (New York: Paulist, 1979).

7. Raymond E. Brown, *The Epistles of John*. AB 30 (Garden City, NY: Doubleday, 1982). For the application of his understanding of the history of the Johannine community to the Epistles see pp. 47–115.

8. See especially Raymond E. Brown, *The Churches the Apostles Left Behind* (New York: Paulist, 1984) 84–123; idem, *Introduction to the New Testament*. ABRL (New York: Doubleday, 1997) 333–82. For further reflections on these briefer writings see the essay of Ronald D. Witherup, "The Incarnate Word Revealed: The Pastoral Writing of Raymond Brown," pp. 238–52 below.

9. Cincinnati: St. Anthony Messenger Press, 1998.

10. See above, n. 5. On this volume see Francis J. Moloney, "Raymond Brown's New *Introduction to the Gospel of John*: A Presentation—and Some Questions," *CBQ* 65 (2003) 1–21.

11. The sheer quantity and quality of Brown's publication record is overwhelming. The major works mentioned above are supported by scholarly and popular articles published in journals all over the world from 1955 to 1998. Perhaps the greatest legacy Brown leaves to a newer generation of New Testament scholars is *a relentless dedication to hard work*. I personally regard this as one of his greatest gifts to me.

12. I speak with some authority here. I have published a monograph on the Johannine use of ὁ υἱὸς τοῦ ἀνθρώπου in John, three volumes attending to a narrative reading of John, a single volume commentary on the gospel, and many articles on a number of issues. Side by side with Brown's contribution, I suspect they can be regarded as important, but they reflect my situation as an interpreter, a step "beyond" the legacy of Raymond Brown.

13. All citations from Brown, *John*, 1:vi.

14. Luke Timothy Johnson and William S. Kurz, *The Future of Catholic Biblical Scholarship. A Constructive Conversation* (Grand Rapids: Eerdmans, 2002) 11–12. For explicit reference to Brown see p. 12, n. 11. For an assessment of the strengths and failures of this "generation," to which I shall return, see pp. 11–32. This section of the book was written by Johnson.

15. I have stressed "strength" because, as we have seen, some current appraisal of the work of Brown's generation regards it as introducing an "either" Scripture "or" Tradition distinction into Roman Catholic thought. See Johnson and Kurz, *The Future*, 11–32. For Brown this was not the case. I think it can be justifiably claimed that, while some earlier (or contemporary) Americans made significant contributions to Johannine scholarship (e.g., Benjamin W. Bacon, P. W. Meyer, J. L. Price, Sherman E. Johnson, Bruce Vawter, Gerard Sloyan, Edwin D. Freed, Edward Malatesta, J. Louis Martyn, D. Moody Smith, Robert Kysar), no one excelled Brown's international contribution.

16. See Rudolf Schnackenburg, *The Gospel according to St John*. 3 vols. HTKNT 4/1-3 (London: Burns & Oates; New York: Crossroad, 1968–82). The original German volumes were roughly contemporary with Brown's commentary (1965–75). I must confess two sentiments. I regard Schnackenburg's commentary more highly than Brown's. My main reason for this preference lies in Brown's amazing ability to present succinctly a large number of possible solutions to any exegetical question and see the positive elements in each of them. One often rises from a reading of Brown's commentary wondering exactly what Brown thought. This is *never* the case with Schnackenburg's mature and deeply theological commentary. He always lets his reader know exactly what he thinks. My other sentiment is my disappointment that so few American scholars refer to Schnackenburg. Brown is *de rigeur*, but never Schnackenburg.

17. The work of Johnson and Kurz (see n. 14) is but one among dozens. See, for example, Walter Wink, *The Bible in Human Transformation: Toward a Paradigm for Biblical Study* (Philadelphia: Fortress, 1973). Wink is credited with first recognizing the "bankruptcy" of the historical-critical method. See further A. L. Nations, "Historical Criticism and the Current Methodological Crisis," *SJT* 36 (1983) 59–71; Elisabeth Schüssler Fiorenza, "The Ethics of De-Centering Biblical Scholarship," *JBL* 107 (1988) 3–17.

18. Brown, *John*, 1:21–23. This approach has its origins in the work of W. (Guillaume) Baldensperger, *Der Prolog des vierten Evangeliums. Sein polemisch-apologetischer Zweck* (Tübingen: J. C. B. Mohr [Paul Siebeck], 1898), and was made popular by Rudolf Bultmann, *The Gospel of John. A Commentary* (Oxford: Blackwell, 1971 [original ed. 1943]) 17–18.

19. Günther Bornkamm, "Die eucharistische Rede im Johannes-Evangelium," *ZNW* 47 (1956) 161–69.

20. Brown, *John*, 1:284–91.

21. Brown, *John*, 2:581–604.

22. See, for example, Francis J. Moloney, *The Gospel of John*. SP 4 (Collegeville: Liturgical Press, 1998) 33–41 (on 1:1-18), 193–232 (on 6:1-71), 370–477 (on 13:1–17:26). See especially pp. 477–79 on the literary unity of this section of the narrative. Also see Fernando F. Segovia, "John 1:1-18 as Entrée into Johannine Reality, Representation and Ramifications," in John

Painter, R. Alan Culpepper, and Fernando F. Segovia, eds., *Word, Theology, and Community in John* (St. Louis: Chalice, 2002) 33–64; Johnson and Kurz, *The Future,* 159–78 (these pages are from Kurz); Francis J. Moloney, "The Function of Prolepsis in the Interpretation of John 6," in R. Alan Culpepper, ed., *Critical Readings of John 6.* BibInt 22 (Leiden: Brill, 1977) 129–48; Johnson and Kurz, *The Future,* 203–18 (these pages are from Kurz); Francis J. Moloney, "The Function of John 13–17 within the Johannine Narrative," in Fernando F. Segovia, ed., *"What is John?" Literary and Social Readings of the Fourth Gospel.* SBLSym 7 (Atlanta: Scholars, 1996) 21–41.

23. Gérald Caron, *Qui sont "les Juifs" de l'évangile de Jean?* Recherches 35 (Québec: Bellarmin, 1997). In this the work of J. Louis Martyn and Brown (see n. 5 above), however much contested these days, was more responsible. See Luc Devillers, *La Fête de l'Envoyé. La section johanniques de la fête des Tentes (Jean 7,1–10,21) et la Christologie.* EB (Paris: Gabalda, 2002) 206–13, for a positive reception of Caron's reading of the narrative, but a healthy warning that "un texte n'est pas un jardin clos, une source scellée" (p. 209), and thus must lead the interpreter to ask questions about the history that produced the text.

24. This is one of the largely unaddressed problems that emerges from Johnson and Kurz, *The Future of Catholic Biblical Scholarship,* despite that fact that both of these fine scholars exercise a prophetic role in their work as scholars, teachers, and authors within the Catholic tradition. Both are aware of the problem, and briefly touch on it in the dialogue they carry on to "open the conversation" on pp. 263–87 (especially Johnson). Any human institution, along with its "magisterium," has a tendency to "domesticate" the demands of the biblical tradition. This must always be recognized and challenged. See the wise reflection of Joseph Ratzinger, commenting on the approval of critical biblical scholarship at Vatican II: "A reference to the ecclesial nature of exegesis, on the one hand, and to its methodological correctness on the other, again expresses the inner tension of church exegesis, which can no longer be removed, *but must be simply accepted as tension*" ("Sacred Scripture in the Life of the Church," in Herbert Vorgrimler, ed., *Commentary on the Documents of Vatican II.* 5 vols. [London: Burns & Oates, 1967–69] 3:268). Emphasis supplied.

25. P. J. Rabinowitz. "Whirl without End: Audience-Oriented Criticism," in G. Douglas Atkins and Laura Morrow, eds., *Contemporary Literary Theory* (London: Macmillan, 1989) 94. Good examples of this tendency can be found in the work of Jeffrey L. Staley (see, among many contributions, the important study *Reading with a Passion: Rhetoric, Autobiography, and the American West in the Gospel of John* [New York: Continuum, 1996]) and Werner Kelber (see his "In the Beginning Were the Words. The Apotheosis and Narrative Displacement of the Logos," *JAAR* 58 [1990] 69–98, and "The Birth of a Beginning," *Semeia* 52 [1990] 121–44).

26. See Brown, *John,* 1:vi.

27. *The Community of the Beloved Disciple* appeared in 1979. It was the first book-length fruit of his association with J. Louis Martyn at Union Theological Seminary in New York and his work on the Johannine Epistles.

28. See Brown, *John,* 1:xxxiv–xxxix.

29. See Brown, *Introduction to the Gospel of John,* 62–89. Henceforth *Introduction,* but not to be confused with his 1997 *Introduction to the New Testament.* Brown's original five-stage theory was widely criticized as too complex. He has regularly pointed out that the first two of those "stages" were not literary: the activity of Jesus (Stage One) and the preaching of the first disciples (Stage Two). He has now subsumed these two stages into his new Stage One.

30. On the Beloved Disciple see Brown, *Introduction,* 189–96.

31. Brown, *Introduction,* 81.

32. I have reservations concerning the "newness" of this proposal. Brown claims to have altered his original theory of Five Stages to a newer theory of Three Stages. He suggests that his proposed three stages could be posited for the development of all four gospels. However, there is some sleight of hand here, as Brown has drawn into his new First Stage (the activity of Jesus and the witness of a disciple) what were originally two different preliterary stages. He then has *two* figures playing a crucial role in his present Third Stage: the evangelist and the redactor. When one

adds this up, one returns to the Five Stages of 1966. I have no objection to that. It is Brown's way of making more acceptable what was always (even in 1966), to his mind, a three-stage composition history that produced the Gospel of John. In this, it needs to be said, much objection to the complexity of Brown's original five stages had not really understood its simplicity. See Moloney, "A Presentation and Some Questions," 14.

33. See Brown, *Introduction,* 94–104.

34. Neirynck has many studies that depend upon this theory. See his most extensive treatment of the question in Frans Neirynck, *Jean et les Synoptiques: Examen critique de l'exégèse de M.-E. Boismard.* BETL 49 (Leuven: Leuven University Press, 1979).

35. For an up-to-date survey of both the evidence and scholarly discussion of the relationship between John and the Synoptics across the twentieth century see D. Moody Smith, *John Among the Gospels* (2d ed. Columbia: University of South Carolina Press, 2001). After a thorough and illuminating review, Moody Smith also concludes that the Gardner-Smith/Dodd position should be regarded as the best solution to a complex problem.

36. See Udo Schnelle, "Johannes und die Synoptiker," in Frans van Segbroeck, Christopher M. Tuckett, Gilbert van Belle, and Jozef Verheyden, eds., *The Four Gospels 1992. Festschrift Frans Neirynck.* 3 vols. BETL 100 (Leuven: Leuven University Press, 1992) 3:1799–1814.

37. Brown reaffirms the need to always raise this question in *Introduction,* 94–111. See further Francis J. Moloney, "The Fourth Gospel and the Jesus of History," *NTS* 46 (2000) 42–58.

38. See Brown, *Introduction,* 115–50.

39. Wrongly, in my opinion. See, on this, the comprehensive and persuasive study of Schnelle, *Antidocetic Christology in the Gospel of John: An Investigation of the Place of the Fourth Gospel in the Johannine School,* trans. Linda M. Maloney (Minneapolis: Fortress, 1992).

40. See Brown, *Introduction,* 157–75.

41. See Brown, *Introduction,* 199–206.

42. Brown, *Introduction,* 110–11.

43. Johnson and Kurz, *The Future of Catholic Biblical Scholarship.*

44. Johnson's contributions on Origen and Augustine (*The Future,* 64–118), and Kurz's reading of John 1:1-18 and John 6 with Catholic eyes (ibid. 178–81, 219–36) are stimulating and helpful. The same must be said for their creative suggestions about the need to make Roman Catholics more "at home" in the biblical world. But I do not find that they are "breaking new ground" by devising a uniquely "Catholic" scholarship. Such studies all play an important part in "catholic," not only Roman Catholic, scholarly reflection upon the Sacred Text.

45. Pontifical Biblical Commission, *The Interpretation of the Bible in the Church* (Rome: Libreria Editrice Vaticana, 1993) 85 (in this edition). The rest of the paragraph bears repeating. "It recognizes that one of the aspects of biblical texts is that they are the work of human authors, who employed both their own capacities for expression and the means which their age and social context put at their disposal. Consequently, Catholic exegesis freely makes use of the scientific methods and approaches which allow a better grasp of the meaning of the texts in their linguistic, literary, socio-cultural, religious and historical contexts, while explaining them as well through studying their sources and attending to the personality of each author. Catholic exegesis actively contributes to the development of new methods and to the progress of research." On this see Joseph A. Fitzmyer, *The Biblical Commission's Document "The Interpretation of the Bible in the Church." Text and Commentary.* SubBi 18 (Rome: Biblical Institute Press, 1995) 132–33.

46. Brown, *John,* 1:vi.

47. See, for example, his section on the use of "the Jews" in the gospel (*Introduction,* 157–75), and his rewriting of his earlier study of Johannine theology (pp. 220–77).

48. See, for example, Brown, *Introduction,* 225, n. 19, where he rejects his earlier use of Revelation, and pp. 227, n. 24 and 237, n. 39, where he continues his earlier association of the two "Johannine" documents.

49. See Brown, *Introduction,* 76–77, 108, 161, 237. I have added editor's notes to those pages. Yet it must be recognized that Brown continues to use "replacement" language in his *Introduction to the New Testament,* 344–49.

50. In my opinion this is the case for the clumsy Johannine use of Isaiah 6:9-10 in 12:37-43. See Moloney, *John*, 363–65, 367–68.

51. See C. H. Dodd, *The Interpretation of the Fourth Gospel* (Cambridge: Cambridge University Press, 1953) 290.

52. See *John*, 1:18–23.

53. See *John*, 1:284–91.

54. See *John*, 2:581–604.

55. For a brief description of this school, its methodology, and its weaknesses, with accompanying bibliography, see Hans-Josef Klauck, *The Religious Context of Early Christianity. A Guide to Greco-Roman Religions* (Minneapolis: Fortress, 2003) 2–7. On Bultmann, and subsequent reaction to his groundbreaking work, see D. Moody Smith, "Johannine Studies Since Bultmann," *Word & World* 21 (2001) 343–51.

56. Klauck, *Religious Context*, 5–6. Emphasis supplied. The helpful methodological principles on pp. 4–7 should be read in their entirety.

57. See Brown, *Introduction*, 259–65.

58. Brown, *Introduction*, 263, n. 99.

59. The work of Martin Hengel, *Judaism and Hellenism: Studies in Their Encounter in Palestine During the Early Hellenistic Period* (London: S.C.M. Press, 1974), marked a watershed in these discussions. See also the briefer but lucid treatment of Lee I. Levine, *Judaism and Hellenism in Antiquity* (Peabody, MA: Hendrickson, 1999).

60. Klauck, *Religious Context*, 460.

61. For a well-documented and balanced survey of this tortured question see Klauck, *Religious Context*, 455–61.

62. See Klauck, *Religious Context*, 437–38.

63. Giovanni Filoramo, *A History of Gnosticism* (Oxford: Blackwell, 1990) 11–12. Emphasis supplied.

64. Klauck, *Religious Context*, 459. Klauck elsewhere rightly remarks: "It is, of course, sometimes forgotten that the origin and the essence of a phenomenon are two distinct things" (ibid. 456).

65. See Moloney, *John*, 5–6.

66. Some contemporary Markan scholars are suggesting that the Gospel of Mark, however Jewish its origins, was shaped to speak to a Greco-Roman audience. See, for example, T. H. Kim, "The Anarthrous υἰὸς θεοῦ in Mark 15,39," *Bib* 79 (1998) 221–41; Adela Yarbro Collins, "Mark and His Readers: The Son of God among Jews," *HTR* 92 (1999) 393–408; eadem, "Mark and His Readers: The Son of God among Greeks and Romans," *HTR* 93 (2000) 85–100; Craig A. Evans, "Mark's Incipit and the Priene Calendar Inscription: From Jewish Gospel to Greco-Roman Gospel," *Journal of Greco-Roman Christianity and Judaism* 1 (2000) 67–81; idem, *Mark 8:27–16:20.* WBC 34B (Nashville: Thomas Nelson, 2001) lxxx–xciii.

67. The influence of Gadamer and his "fusion of horizons" *(Horizontsverschmelzung)* has been very influential here. See Hans-Georg Gadamer, *Truth and Method* (New York: Seabury, 1975) 269–74. See also Sandra M. Schneiders, *The Revelatory Text: Interpreting the New Testament as Sacred Scripture* (San Francisco: Harper Collins, 1991; 2nd ed. Collegeville: Liturgical Press, 1999).

68. On the *inevitable* presence of the *persona* of an author in a narrative see Francis J. Moloney, "Adventure with Nicodemus. An Exercise in Hermeneutics," in idem, *"A Hard Saying." The Gospel and Culture* (Collegeville: Liturgical Press, 2001) 259–79.

69. For the same sentiments see the study by Klaus Scholtissek, *In ihm sein und bleiben. Die Sprache der Immanenz in den johanneischen Schriften.* Herders Biblische Studien 21 (Freiburg: Herder, 2000) 23–130. See his summary statement on p. 23: "So reflektiert das JohEv sowohl die Angefochtenheit, Bedrohtheit und Erlösungsbedürftigkeit menschlicher Existenz als auch die Antworten philosophischer und religiöser Gruppen innerhalb der zeitgenössischen Umwelt." See also Dodd, *Interpretation*, 9: "We are to think of the work as addressed to a wide public consisting primarily of devout and thoughtful persons . . . in the varied and cosmopolitan society of a

great Hellenistic city such as Ephesus under the Roman Empire." And see Richard J. Cassidy, *John's Gospel in New Perspective. Christology and the Realities of Roman Power* (New York: Maryknoll, 1992).

70. For a fuller development of the following see Francis J. Moloney, "Where Does One Look? Reflections on Recent Johannine Scholarship," *Salesianum* 62 (2000) 223–51.

71. These first two headings continue to generate scholarly interest on both sides of the Atlantic. See, for example, Michael Labahn, *Jesus als Lebensspender. Untersuchungen zu einer Geschichte der johanneischen Tradition anhand ihrer Wundergeschichten.* BZNW 98 (Berlin and New York: de Gruyter, 1999); Klaus Scholtissek, *In ihm sein und bleiben;* Adele Reinhartz, *Befriending the Beloved Disciple. A Jewish Reading of the Gospel of John* (New York: Continuum, 2001), especially 32–53; Martin Asiedu-Peprah, *Johannine Sabbath Conflicts and Judicial Controversy.* WUNT 2nd ser. 132 (Tübingen: J. C. B. Mohr [Paul Siebeck], 2001). This excellent reexamination of the Jewish forensic background to Johannine conflicts was written in Australia by a very promising young scholar from Ghana.

72. This issue is still vigorously debated, especially under the leadership of Frans Neirynck at Louvain (see n. 33 above). I am personally attracted to the proposal of Labahn, *Jesus als Lebensspender,* 89–99. Depending upon Walter Ong's studies of orality, Labahn suggests that there may have been an oral tradition that grew from the *existing* Synoptic Gospels. The Fourth Evangelist, aware of the existence of gospels of Mark, Matthew, and Luke, draws from the "secondary orality" (Ong's expression) that had developed from them. The relation, nevertheless, is not one of literary dependence. See also Michael Labahn, *Offenbarung in Zeichen und Wort. Untersuchungen zur Vorgeschichte von Joh 6,1-25a und seiner Rezeption in der Brotrede.* WUNT 2nd ser. 117 (Tübingen: J. C. B. Mohr [Paul Siebeck], 2000) 231–76. In this I am unable to accept the position of the fine recent study of Manfred Lang, *Johannes und die Synoptiker. Eine Redaktionsgeschichtliche Analyse von Joh 18–20 vor dem markinischen und lukanischen Hintergrund.* FRLANT 182 (Göttingen: Vandenhoeck & Ruprecht, 1999).

73. The question of dependence on the synoptic tradition and the possibility of a redaction history of the Gospel of John are closely related. This is the ultimate objective of the work of Lang, *Johannes und die Synoptiker.*

74. The work of John Meier, *A Marginal Jew. Rethinking the Historical Jesus.* 3 vols. to date (New York: Doubleday, 1991–2001), is outstanding in this regard. Unlike the older quests for the historical Jesus and the recent work of the Jesus Seminar, Meier always considers the possibility that the Johannine portrait may contain elements that contribute to an understanding of the Jesus of history, and that the latter may have helped to shape the former.

75. See Mary L. Coloe, *God Dwells with Us. Temple Symbolism in the Fourth Gospel* (Collegeville: Litugical Press, 2001); Luc Devillers, *La Fête de l'Envoyé.* Both of these studies approach well-worked Johannine themes and produce refreshingly new results. As well as developing an imaginative appreciation of Johannine literary and theological creativity, Devillers makes an important contribution to the issue of "the Jews" in the gospel and the history of the Johannine community. Some might be surprised that I have not listed ongoing research into the reconstruction of a Johannine Signs Source. For example, Urban C. von Wahlde, *The Earliest Version of John's Gospel. Recovering the Gospel of Signs* (Wilmington: Michael Glazier, 1989), has continued this discussion. However, most Johannine scholars have abandoned their search for this source. The discussion was dealt a deathblow by Gilbert van Belle, *The Signs Source in the Fourth Gospel.* BETL 116 (Leuven: University Press/Peeters, 1994).

76. See Labahn, *Jesus als Lebensspender;* Adeline Fehribach, *The Women in the Life of the Bridegroom. A Feminist-Literary Analysis of the Female Characters in the Fourth Gospel* (Collegeville: Liturgical Press, 1998); Reinhartz, *Befriending the Beloved Disciple.*

77. Many contemporary narrative-critical readings of the Gospel of John, following the groundbreaking work of R. Alan Culpepper, *Anatomy of the Fourth Gospel. A Study in Literary Design* (Philadelphia: Fortress, 1983) 99–148, rightly dedicate attention to this issue. See, among

many, Caron, *Qui sont "les Juifs"?;* Colleen M. Conway, *Men and Women in the Fourth Gospel. Gender and Johannine Characterization.* SBLDS 167 (Atlanta: Scholars, 1999).

78. See Dorothy Lee, *Flesh and Glory. Symbolism, Gender and Theology in the Gospel of John* (New York: Crossroad, 2002); Craig R. Koester, *Symbolism in the Fourth Gospel. Meaning, Mystery, Community* (2d ed. Minneapolis: Fortress, 2003).

79. See Reinhartz, *Befriending the Beloved Disciple;* Fehribach, *The Women in the Life of the Bridegroom.*

80. The German and French titles in the above notes are an indication of how important it is that Johannine scholarship "beyond" Brown be pursued by scholars who, like him, dialogue across the Atlantic—and perhaps even across the Pacific! Despite Johnson's criticism (see *The Future,* 12), this preparedness to dialogue with other scholars across national and confessional boundaries leads to a genuinely "catholic" reading of the Bible. What is ironic is that Johnson's own masterly exegetical work (his commentaries on Luke, Acts, James, 1 and 2 Timothy, etc.) pursues this "catholic" dialogue most effectively.

81. This is not a new discovery. See the important essay of Rudolf Bultmann, "Is Exegesis Without Presuppositions Possible?" in Shubert M. Ogden, ed., *New Testament Mythology and Other Basic Writings* (Philadelphia: Fortress, 1984) 145–53. The original German appeared in *TZ* 13 (1957) 409–17.

82. On this see Moloney, *"A Hard Saying,"* 259–79.

83. See Gadamer, *Truth and Method,* 273: "Understanding . . . is always the fusion of these horizons which we imagine to exist by themselves."

84. On this principle see Pontifical Biblical Commission, "The Interpretation." The whole document is valuable, but see especially pp. 93–94. These pages deal with the formation of the canon, and conclude: "In discerning the canon of Scripture, the Church was also discerning and defining her own identity. Henceforth Scripture was to function as a mirror in which the Church could continually rediscover her identity and assess, century after century, the way in which she constantly responds to the gospel and equips herself to be an apt vehicle of its transmission (cf. *Dei Verbum,* 7)" (p. 94). See Fitzmyer, *The Biblical Commission's Document,* 143–45, and the recent helpful presentation of this document by P. S. Williamson, "Catholic Principles for Interpreting Scripture," *CBQ* 65 (2003) 327–49.

85. See, most recently, the study of Brenda D. Schildgen, *Power and Prejudice. The Reception of the Gospel of Mark* (Detroit: Wayne State University Press, 1999).

86. Barend P. van Heusden, *Why Literature? An inquiry into the nature of literary semiosis* (Groningen: Krips Repro Meppel, 1994; Tübingen: Stauffenberg, 1997) 235. Interestingly, as with biblical studies, there are nowadays increasingly strident debates over the classical musical and literary canons. What privileges Honoré de Balzac over Walt Disney, Wolfgang Amadeus Mozart over the Beatles? See Schildgen, *Power and Prejudice,* 30–33.

The Legacy of Raymond E. Brown and Beyond

A Response to Francis J. Moloney

R. Alan Culpepper

McAfee School of Theology, Mercer University

As a first semester seminarian I took advanced placement tests, waived the survey courses in New Testament, and plunged into an elective course on the Gospel of John. It was the fall of 1967, the year after the publication of the first volume of Raymond Brown's Anchor Bible commentary on John. The professor required that we read it—and the required reading for the first part of the course was far better than for the latter part of the course! Before I finished reading the introduction I was hooked, infected with a contagious fever to study this gospel—a palpably psychosomatic, mantic condition from which I have never recovered. It was not only my introduction to the study of the Gospel of John; it was also my first introduction to advanced critical study of the New Testament, and not incidentally my first encounter with Roman Catholic biblical scholarship. I thought all Roman Catholic scholars were like Father Brown! And over the years I have found that my naïve assumption was more accurate in important respects than the anti-Catholic prejudice of the southern and Baptist heritage of my early years. Several years later I had an opportunity to meet Father Brown, and then after that opportunities to be in seminars and meetings with him. He was unfailingly gracious to me, as he was to others, both in person and in print.

I was intrigued by Brown's approach to the introductory issues, as he maintained a healthy respect for the authority of the gospel while sparing no intellectual effort to interpret the clues to its history, setting, development of the tradition, or its theological contribution. I propose to revisit Brown's contribution to these areas briefly, focusing on ways in which he advanced Johannine scholarship. Hence, rather than a response to Frank Moloney's fine paper, with which I find little to disagree, mine will be a parallel paper, touching on many of the same topics.

40

I. Brown's Contribution to Johannine Scholarship

In order to understand Brown's contribution to Johannine scholarship, it is helpful to look at the state of that scholarship at the time he wrote the Anchor Bible commentary. Brown was fully conscious of the ecclesiastical and critical context in which he worked. His work may be situated, therefore, in the context of four arenas in the 1950s and 60s: (1) the growing openness among scholars from various ecclesiastical traditions to dialogue about the literal meaning of Scripture (*John,* 1:vi), (2) the postwar era of developing dialogue with and between German and British scholarship, (3) the context of the emergence of a new era of Catholic scholarship following *Divino Afflante Spiritu* (1943) and the Roman Pontifical Biblical Commission's "Instruction on the Historical Truth of the Gospels" (1964) during the papacies of Pius XII and John XXIII and the work of the Second Vatican Council,[1] and (4) the beginning of an era of tremendous energy in American New Testament scholarship (evidenced by the transformation of the Society of Biblical Literature, the founding of Scholars Press, and the rise of a generation of scholars that included James Robinson, Robert Funk, Paul Achtemeier, Leander Keck, Moody Smith, and Victor Furnish, among others). It was a time of great confidence in critical scholarship. Brown could write: "Fortunately, we live at a time when a considerable degree of objectivity has been achieved in biblical scholarship" (*John*, 1:vi).

It was also a period of reconsideration of Bultmann's theory of Johannine origins: that the gospel was late, the result of the compilation of sources from divergent backgrounds (including a signs source, a revelatory discourse source, and a Passion-and-resurrection story), that its thought was deeply influenced by Gnosticism, and that it suffered disarrangement and subsequent rearrangement and editing by an ecclesiastical redactor. In John A. T. Robinson's word, it was the era of the "new look" in Johannine studies,[2] and Brown situated his work deftly in the midst of all these crosscurrents. The commentaries Brown cites as major postwar contributions to Johannine scholarship are Hoskyns (1940) and Bultmann (1941), since they were not widely circulated until after the war, as well as Dodd's *Interpretation* (1953), Barrett (1955), and Lightfoot (1956).[3] Brown's contribution is cast in a revealing light when placed alongside these volumes. As Moloney notes, Brown really had no American predecessors, nor is there a Roman Catholic in this list. For an American predecessor one would probably have to go back to B. W. Bacon, though Bacon did not produce a commentary on John.[4]

A. The Composition of John

Following Moloney's lead, I will concentrate on Brown's introduction to the Gospel of John. His approach to the thorny introductory issues and the divergent positions taken by other scholars set the pattern for his later work on the birth and death of the Messiah, so although our focus on this one part of Brown's legacy is arbitrary it may bring to light some broader patterns that characterized his life of scholarship.

Brown dissected the elements of Bultmann's theory and the earlier theories on which it built: accidental displacements, multiple sources, and multiple editions. He was most critical of the theories of accidental displacements, noting that they often serve the interests of the commentator, that it is presumptuous to contend that two millennia later we can see more clearly what the original order was than the redactor could, and that it is unclear how the disarrangements occurred (*John*, 1:xxvi–xxviii; *Introduction*, 43–46). Brown was similarly critical, especially of Bultmann's theory of sources drawn from various venues, of theories of multiple editions that succumbed to "the temptation to reconstruct too exactly the history of the editions" (*John*, 1:xxxiv), and of composite theories that posit multiple sources compiled in stages through multiple editions. Regarding the latter, he warned that "such a composite theory can become quite complicated" (*John*, 1:xxviii).

Following this review of earlier scholarship, and seen in the light of it, Brown's own theory is characteristically balanced. He did not minimize the evidence of the breaks, gaps, repetitions, and inconsistencies in the gospel in order to argue for a unified composition by the evangelist, as others have. Instead, he adapted elements of the earlier theories in a "moderately critical theory of the composition of the Gospel" (*John*, 1:vi) that maintained the continuous development of tradition reaching back to Jesus within a distinct community gathered around an eyewitness to the ministry of Jesus. These controls balanced the more speculative elements of the earlier theories. Sources derived from the eyewitness, but the tradition and indeed the composition of the gospel developed over time. Multiple hands were involved, at least an evangelist and a final editor, but the final editor was a disciple of the evangelist, whose thought and language were shaped by the influence of his teacher and the tradition and community that developed around him. One can identify multiple editions, stages in the composition of the farewell discourse, and perhaps even a displacement at one time of chapters 5 and 6, but overall the gospel makes sense in its present order and form. It is the work of a skilled author, and it generally defies reconstruction of the wording of its sources. On the other hand, while Brown would certainly caution us that he was merely proposing a working hypothesis, the result is a theory of two editions and a redaction. In view of Brown's second thoughts about the viability and usefulness of positing two editions by the evangelist in his *Introduction* (pp. 81–82), one should note that he devoted only one paragraph to stage 4, the "secondary edition by the evangelist," in his commentary (*John*, 1:xxxvi). Brown's modification of his stages in the *Introduction* would have been cleaner, I think, if he had split the third stage so that he could speak of the following four stages: Jesus, the Beloved Disciple, the Evangelist, and the Redactor. The genius of

Brown's original proposal, however, is that the evangelist himself was responsible for the second edition, and the redactor was a close disciple who used the
evangelist's material in the final redaction.[5]

Parenthetically, I have been intrigued that Brown assigns so much material
to the redactor, and on this point the *Introduction* shows that his view remained unchanged. The redactor worked conservatively, setting the material
he added within the gospel rather than reworking the text of the gospel. Brown
also posits that the redactor added two kinds of material to the gospel: first, the
redactor preserved material from the earlier stages. The redactor was responsible for 6:51-58; 3:31-36, 12:44-50, the block of material in chapters 15–17,
and probably also chapters 11–12 (on the basis of the conclusion in 10:42 and
the difference in the use of the term "the Jews" in these chapters). Second, the
redactor added material that had not come from the evangelist: in particular
the prologue and chapter 21, and perhaps some of the passages where John is
similar to Mark. Brown does not address the question of whether these two
kinds of material necessarily come from the same hand or represent two
phases within Stage 5 (*John,* 1:xxxvi–xxxviii) or the second part of stage 3 in
the simplified theory of his *Introduction* (82–85). Nevertheless, the more one
follows Brown's emphasis on the importance of interpreting the final form of
the gospel, "the only form that we are certain has ever existed" (*Introduction,*
111), the more the object of our study becomes the product of the work of the
redactor rather than the work of the evangelist—unless one abandons the distinction between the two altogether.

B. The "New Look" in Johannine Studies

Brown's originality can also be seen by comparing his view of the authorship and composition of the gospel with the "new look" defined by John A. T.
Robinson. At the conference on the four gospels at Oxford in 1957 Robinson
assessed current critical orthodoxy as generally agreeing on the following five
presuppositions:

(1) That the Fourth Evangelist is dependent on sources, including (nor-
    mally) one or more of the Synoptic Gospels.
(2) That his own background is other than that of the events and teaching
    he is purporting to record.
(3) That he is not to be regarded, seriously, as a witness to the Jesus of his-
    tory, but simply to the Christ of faith.
(4) That he represents the end-term of theological development in first-cen-
    tury Christianity.
(5) That he is not himself the apostle John or a direct eyewitness.[6]

Robinson then proceeded to argue that recent work was challenging each of
these presuppositions. (1) C. K. Barrett had reasserted John's knowledge of

the Synoptics, at least Mark, and Eduard Schweizer and Eugen Ruckstuhl, among others, were questioning the cogency of Bultmann's sources on the basis of the consistency of style in the gospel. (2) The discovery of the scrolls ten years earlier had opened for the first time a library of Jewish literature that bore striking resemblance to the language and thought of the gospel—and here Robinson cited Brown's early article on John and the scrolls.[7] (3) In arguing for a "new look" at the value of John for history, Robinson cited C. H. Dodd, Joachim Jeremias, William H. Brownlee, Bo Reicke, and Brown's mentor, William F. Albright. (4) Robinson's argument that while mature, John's theology is nevertheless early and "stands very near to the primitive apostolic witness" foreshadows his own later work in *Redating the New Testament* and *The Priority of John*.[8] (5) Citing Bent Noack's recent book on Johannine tradition, Robinson argued for reclaiming the importance of eyewitness (if not apostolic) testimony at the source of the gospel's tradition.

On the first presupposition (1), regarding John's use of the Synoptics, Brown argues for the independence of the gospel's tradition from the Synoptics, while allowing that there may have been "cross-influences" from Mark and Luke, especially at stage two in the gospel's composition (*John*, 1:xliv–xlvii; *Introduction*, 94–104). If there was any change in Brown's view of this matter, it is slight. Brown does not abandon either the independence of the Johannine tradition or the evidence of cross-influences from the Synoptics. Frank Moloney rightly notes Brown's comment that "it is hard to believe that this community would not sooner or later have become familiar with the kind of gospel tradition accepted by other communities, the kind of tradition that eventually found its way into the Synoptic Gospels" (*Introduction*, 101).

(2) As we have already indicated, one of the major contributions of Brown's commentary is that it asserted the importance of Jewish language and thought for understanding the gospel (*John*, 1:lix–lxiv; *Introduction*, 132–42). While Bultmann had turned to Gnosticism, and Dodd to the Hermetic writings and Philo, Brown for the first time mined the recently discovered Dead Sea Scrolls, while resisting any notion of direct dependence on the scrolls and favoring the importance of the Wisdom tradition for understanding John (see especially *John*, 1:cxxii–cxxv; see *Introduction*, 259–65). Unfortunately, there is no index of ancient sources at the end of the commentary, but Brown's use of the scrolls and other Jewish sources is evident throughout.

(3) In regard to the third presupposition, Brown pays constant attention to the historical value of the gospel (see *John*, 1:xlvii–li; *Introduction*, 104–11). Characteristically, his view here is nuanced and defies being summarized briefly.[9] In response to the new questers Brown lamented their neglect of John. He pointed out areas where John presents valuable historical information indicating that it rests on primitive tradition. At the same time, he treats the question of history by reviewing the formation of the gospel through the various stages he posited, meaning that the scholar must always exercise caution in

using John, or the other gospels, to reconstruct Jesus' ministry and teaching (*John*, 1:l–li). One could argue, therefore, that Brown represents an advance over both the skepticism of Bultmann (and more recently the Jesus Seminar) on the one hand and the conservatism of Dodd, Robinson, and later D. A. Carson on the other hand.[10] Parenthetically, the *Introduction* reflects a slight turn away from historical-critical concerns when, at the end of the section on the gospel's historical value for reconstructing Jesus' ministry, Brown comments: "In my opinion, the main duty of the commentator is not to find out what happened historically but to explain what the writer(s) intended and conveyed to the intended audience by the final gospel narrative" (*Introduction*, 110).

(4) The same general posture can be seen in Brown's assessment of John's theology. He rejects the view that John represents a Hegelian synthesis of the Synoptics and Paul, that the evangelist's work was at variance with orthodox Christian thought and required censorship by an ecclesiastical redactor, that New Testament theology developed in any linear pattern, and any simple retrojection of Johannine thought onto Jesus that overlooks the uniqueness of John's theological contribution. On the other hand, Brown insisted both that John's thought is "highly individual" and that we have no difficulty "fitting John into the mainstream of Christian thought" (*John*, 1:cxxvi; see *Introduction*, 266). In passing, we should note that in the commentary Brown treats ecclesiology, sacramentalism, and eschatology as "crucial questions in Johannine theology" (*John*, 1:cv–ccxxi), but passes over the development of John's christology and John's distinctive views of sin, faith, and the death of Jesus. In the *Introduction* he remedies these omissions by adding sections on christology, the Son of Man, and Wisdom motifs (pp. 249–65), while expanding his discussion of the earlier topics.

(5) As is well known, in the commentary Brown accepted the traditional identification of the Beloved Disciple as John the son of Zebedee (*John*, 1:xcviii–cii) but he rejected it later.[11] Nevertheless, consistent with Robinson's fifth presupposition, the significant issue for Brown was and remained that the gospel's tradition derived from early, eyewitness tradition. Viewing Brown's work against the background of the five points of Robinson's "new look" reveals that while there is certainly an affinity between Brown and the "new look," Brown generally nuanced the points and resisted simplification rather than championing Robinson's cause.

C. Brown's Influence

Having examined Brown's contribution in relation to his predecessors, and his originality in the context of Johannine scholarship of the 1950s and '60s, we may turn to the influence of his view of the origin and composition of the gospel on later scholarship. Brown's theory was influential, though not universally accepted. Schnackenburg, whose first volume appeared in English in 1968, held that the evangelist composed a "basic document" or "basic gospel" that he left unfinished and to which a redactor added additional material, especially the dialogues and discourses of Jesus, but Schnackenburg does not clearly distinguish two editions of the gospel prior to its redaction.[12] Barnabas Lindars has two editions and develops the view that the gospel's sources were homilies rather than positing separate origins for the signs and the discourse material.[13] Robert Kysar adopts the view of two editions and a final redactor.[14] John Painter bases his view on Brown's,[15] and Moody Smith's brief discussion of the issue reflects his indebtedness to Brown and J. Louis Martyn.[16] Among those who remain skeptical of defining stages of composition overly precisely one may list C. K. Barrett, G. R. Beasley-Murray, and Gerald Borchert.[17] It is interesting that Brown's theory of two editions by the evangelist did not garner greater support from other commentators, and in the *Introduction* Brown himself qualifies the importance of a theory of multiple editions by commenting that "for all practical purposes the two-edition theory is not helpful in developing a coherent commentary upon the gospel as a whole" (p. 82; cf. p. 211 n. 55).

One also finds evidence of scholarship moving beyond Brown not by adopting a more persuasive view of the history of the composition of the gospel but by turning away from the issue of composition history and focusing instead on the narrative elements of the finished gospel.[18] D. A. Carson is noteworthy for rejecting both Brown's view of stages in the composition of the gospel and narrative criticism in favor of a conservative approach that defends the gospel's historicity.[19] While narrative criticism of the gospel focuses on a different set of issues, I would insist that it neither disproves Brown's view that the gospel was composed in stages, nor does it mean that the question of the gospel's composition history is unimportant. It simply opens a different angle of vision on the text.

D. The Interpreter as Historian

Brown's reconstruction of the stages of the composition of John and his attention to the development of the gospel tradition and its historical value throughout the commentary invite further comment on his understanding of the relationship of the gospels to the history of Jesus' ministry and the life of the early church. Four observations guide this discussion. First, Brown was primarily concerned with the New Testament texts, not with history. His major volumes are all commentaries (on John, the Johannine Epistles, the birth narratives, and the Passion narratives) and an introduction in which he states that his concern is with the New Testament documents rather than with the history of early Christianity.[20] Second, Brown was always concerned to trace the development of the gospel traditions, and he never shied away from demonstrating either the historicity or the nonhistoricity of specific materials. Third, he insisted that problems of discerning the historical core in John differ in degree but not in kind from those posed by the Synoptic Gospels also. And fourth, Brown's articulation of the problem may have become sharper and more focused in the course of four decades of writing, but one can scarcely argue that it shifts significantly. Brown maintained a tension or dialectic between history and Scripture while maintaining a keen interest in historicity and the development of the tradition.

The following quotations from his major works illustrate and document these observations. In the introduction to the commentary on John, Brown wrote:

> If all of this means that John (and this is true of the other gospels as well) is somewhat distant from a history or biography of Jesus, John xx 30-31 has made it clear that the author's intention was to produce a document not of history but of faith. Yet Sanders [J. N. Sanders, "The Gospel and the Historian," *The Listener* 56 (1956) 753–57] is quite right in insisting that John is deeply historical—historical in the sense in which history is concerned not only with what happened but also with the deepest meaning of what happened. (*John*, 1:xlix)

Wrestling with the differences between the birth accounts in Matthew and Luke, the development of infancy narratives in the early church, and the evangelist's use of these stories as vehicles for faith and theology led Brown to instruct readers of *The Birth of the Messiah* that

> The thesis of inspiration may not be invoked to guarantee historicity, for a divinely inspired story is not necessarily history. Any intelligent attempt to combine an acceptance of inspiration with an acceptance of biblical criticism must lead to the recognition that there are in the Bible fiction, parable, and folklore, as well as history. Nor will it do to argue that the infancy narratives must be historical or else they would not have been joined to the main body of the gospel material which had its basis in history. That argument wrongly supposes that history or biography was the dominant optic of the evangelist, and also that the evangelist could tell whether the stories he included had a historical origin. (*Birth*, 33–34)

Similarly, at the end of an extended section on "the role of history" in the Passion narratives (*Death*, 13–24), Brown wrote:

> While I have a deep respect for historical investigation, I regard an obsession with the historical to be as great an obstruction to understanding the Gospel PNs [passion narratives] as the cavalier assumption that Christians knew nothing about what happened. It is not tautological to insist that the Gospels are primarily evangelistic; to make them dominantly reportorial is a distortion. (*Death*, 24)

Given this critical stance, and his commitment to examine the gospels as theological documents grounded in the traditions of the early church, it is revealing to note how at the end of the day Brown maintained historical continuity through the Gospel and Letters of John. First, Brown maintained continuity from Jesus to the Johannine tradition. In the Preface to the commentary on

John, Brown affirmed "the conviction that the Gospel is rooted in historical tradition about Jesus of Nazareth" (*John,* 1:vi). Whereas Bultmann and German scholarship generally had severed the continuity between Jesus and the Johannine tradition by concluding that the evangelist was not the apostle, that the gospel drew upon various sources, and that it was a late composition, Brown, as we have seen, maintained the continuity by affirming that the Beloved Disciple was an eyewitness (or at least drew on eyewitness testimony), that the evangelist was a close associate of the eyewitness, and that even the later material in the gospel came from the same fund of early tradition.

Second, Brown maintained continuity within the Johannine tradition. John's sources, the evangelist, the redactor, and the author of the epistles can all be traced to the same community, the Johannine school. One cannot drive a wedge between the sources and the evangelist, as though the evangelist had to correct the theology of the sources, or between the evangelist and the redactor. Similarly, the elder of the Epistles represents the traditions of the gospel in his battle with the secessionists for the faith and theological perspectives of the Johannine community.

Finally, whereas others have emphasized the connections between the Johannine writings and the second-century gnostic groups, Brown maintained the continuity between the Johannine writings and the "Great Church." With his characteristic blend of cautions, caveats, and creative insight, Brown suggested that the secessionist adversaries of 1 John "were the bridge by which GJohn gained acceptance among the gnostics" (*Epistles,* 106).[21] Then, for nine pages—Brown was nothing if not thorough—he discussed "the path from the Epistles to the Great Church" (*Epistles,* 106–15). While resisting the conclusion that the author of 1 John was the redactor of the gospel, Brown nevertheless contended that the Elder's interpretation of the Johannine tradition opened the way for its acceptance beyond the Johannine community: "eventually the comment patterned upon GJohn that the epistolary author left behind (known to us as I John) accomplished the purpose for which it was written—it saved the Johannine Gospel, no longer for the elect of the Johannine Community but for the Great Church and for the main body of Christians ever since" (*Epistles,* 115). I hesitate to attribute this emphasis on continuity to Brown's identity as a Roman Catholic biblical scholar, but it is a model for critical biblical scholarship, Catholic and Protestant, in a time when caustic historical conclusions are often based on interpretation that reflects little interest in the theology of the gospels or the life of the church.

II. Moving Beyond Brown

The question that Frank Moloney rightly raises is whether Brown's work will withstand the challenges of changing critical perspectives in New Testament scholarship. Moloney has written a sure-handed survey of the most important new directions in Johannine studies, so there is no need to review the same ground here. In order to set the issue in perspective, however, one might compare the writings of two Roman Catholic Johannine scholars whose work, though they are from different generations, overlapped for slightly over twenty years. I have in mind Raymond Brown and Fernando Segovia.

One of the strengths of Segovia's work has always been his attention to critical methodology and his willingness to follow evolving methodological concerns into new approaches to the Gospel of John. Reflecting on the past twenty years, Segovia observes, "Not only has the discipline changed, but I too have changed as reader and critic."[22] He notes that these decades have witnessed "the collapse and displacement of historical criticism as the controlling paradigm in biblical criticism . . . and the corresponding emergence and development of a number of competing paradigms."[23] Segovia's dissertation, *Love Relationships in the Johannine Tradition* (1978),[24] is a lucid investigation of the development of the Johannine tradition and the relationship between the gospel and 1 John on the basis of historical criticism. Like Brown, Segovia constructed stages in the development of the tradition and related them to the history of the Johannine community. Segovia continued his research on the Johannine Farewell Discourse with the publication of *Farewell of the Word* in 1991, but in this book he notes that his perspective has shifted from diachronic to synchronic, from a redactional to an integrative perspective that requires narrative and rhetorical criticism of the text: "I now see the farewell speech as both an artistic and a strategic whole, with a unified literary structure and development, as well as unified strategic concerns and aims."[25] Recognition of the importance of the role of the interpreter as reader and critic led Segovia, within the next five years, to shift his concern once again, this time from the literary and rhetorical features of the text to the readings of readers, then to cultural, and then post-colonial criticism, a progression that reflects increasing concern with the ideologies of texts and their interpretation.[26] Such a brief survey does not do justice to the methodological reflection with which Segovia has made each of these moves. Nevertheless, it points to the changes we have witnessed in the past quarter-century of Johannine and biblical scholarship, and it sets up the striking contrast between Segovia and Brown. Segovia has consistently focused his work on the Gospel and Letters of John while engaging in the development of new approaches to these texts. In contrast, Brown wrote monumental commentaries on the Gospel and Letters of John and then went on to the birth narratives and the Passion narratives with minimal change in his critical perspective across the span of his career.

I have focused rather narrowly in this paper on Brown's introduction to the commentary on John and the recently published revision of that introduction. We would be remiss if we did not underscore again that Brown's contribution to New Testament studies is far wider than is reflected here. In reading the *Introduction* one is reminded of Brown's gift for clear prose, cutting through obscurity and succinctly stating the key issues. It is fitting that his last book was an introduction, because just as the introduction to the commentary served as my introduction to critical New Testament studies, so many students will continue to be introduced to the study of the New Testament by Brown's writings.

History will judge Brown's work, and it is too soon to attempt more than a risky prediction as to what its judgment will be. On the extremes, history will either judge that Brown represents the pinnacle of the integration of confessional and critical scholarship before the fortress of historical criticism fell to nihilistic post-modern criticisms, or that Brown was the last holdout of a bankrupt historicism that led to increasingly speculative theories about the origin of the gospel and the history of the Johannine community. My guess is that the judgment of history will be more nuanced and balanced than either of these. Because the New Testament writings are historical documents, they will always require historical criticism. Because the New Testament writings are literary, rhetorical, and social documents, they will always require literary, rhetorical, and social criticism. And because we cannot escape our own critical perspectives, these will always have to be held up for scrutiny so that both our own personal, cultural, and confessional perspectives and the ideologies of our readings of the text can be brought into the arena of discussion as well. If this occurs, Brown's work will endure for what it offers for generations of future scholars, while at the same time leaving for them issues and tasks that Brown did not engage. More we cannot ask, and more we cannot ask of our mentor, colleague, and friend.

Notes

1. See Raymond E. Brown, *Biblical Reflections on Crises Facing the Church* (New York: Paulist, 1975); *The Critical Meaning of the Bible* (New York: Paulist, 1981); and *Biblical Exegesis and Church Doctrine* (New York: Paulist, 1985). For full bibliographical data on Brown's work, see Appendix One.

2. John A. T. Robinson, "The New Look on the Fourth Gospel," in *Studia Evangelica*. TU 73 (Berlin: Akademie-Verlag, 1959) 338–50, reprinted in Robinson's *Twelve New Testament Studies*. Studies in Biblical Theology 34 (Naperville, IL: Alec R. Allenson, Inc., 1962) 94–106.

3. E. C. Hoskyns, *The Fourth Gospel* (1940; 2nd ed. edited by George R. Beasley-Murray et al., Philadelphia: Westminster, 1971); C. H. Dodd, *The Interpretation of the Fourth Gospel* (Cambridge: Cambridge University Press, 1953); C. K. Barrett, *The Gospel according to St. John* (1955; 2nd ed. Philadelphia: Westminster, 1978); R. H. Lightfoot, *St John's Gospel* (ed. C. G. Evans; London: Oxford University Press, 1956).

4. See Hoskyns, *The Fourth Gospel*, 38.

5. This point was also noted by George R. Beasley-Murray, *John*. WBC 36 (Waco, TX: Word, 1987) xlii.

6. Robinson, *Twelve New Testament Studies*, 95.

7. Now published in Raymond E. Brown, "The Qumran Scrolls and the Johannine Gospel and Epistles," in idem, *New Testament Essays* (London: Geoffrey Chapman, 1967) 102–31. See Francis J. Moloney's paper, "The Gospel of John. The Legacy of Raymond E. Brown and Beyond," p. 33, n. 1.

8. Robinson, *Twelve New Testament Studies,* 102. Cf. idem, *Redating the New Testament* (Philadelphia: Westminster, 1976), and *The Priority of John* (ed. J. F. Coakley; London: S.C.M. Press, 1985).

9. Note Brown's references to the Roman Pontifical Biblical Commission's "Instruction on the Historical Truth of the Gospels" (1964) in his *The Community of the Beloved Disciple* (New York: Paulist, 1979) 17, n. 19 and 2, n. 26.

10. D. A. Carson, *The Gospel according to John* (Grand Rapids: Eerdmans, 1991).

11. *The Community of the Beloved Disciple,* 33–34. See *Introduction,* 191. For Robinson's response to Brown's change of mind see *The Priority of John,* 107–108.

12. Rudolf Schnackenburg, *The Gospel according to St. John* (trans. Kevin Smyth; New York: Herder and Herder, 1968) 1:72–74.

13. Barnabas Lindars, *The Gospel of John.* New Century Bible (London: Oliphants, 1972) 46–54.

14. Robert Kysar, *John.* Augsburg Commentary on the New Testament (Minneapolis: Augsburg, 1986) 13–14.

15. John Painter, *The Quest for the Messiah* (Edinburgh: T & T Clark, 1991) 42–45.

16. D. Moody Smith, Jr., *John.* Abingdon New Testament Commentaries (Nashville: Abingdon, 1999) 27–29.

17. Barrett, *The Gospel according to St. John,* 25–26; Beasley-Murray, *John,* xliii; Gerald L. Borchert, *John 1–11.* New American Commentary 25A (Nashville: Broadman & Holman, 1996) 42–50.

18. Charles H. Talbert, *Reading John* (New York: Crossroad, 1992); Mark W. G. Stibbe, *John* (Sheffield: JSOT Press, 1993); Thomas L. Brodie, *The Gospel according to John* (New York: Oxford University Press, 1993); Wes Howard-Brook, *Becoming Children of God: John's Gospel and Radical Discipleship* (Maryknoll, NY: Orbis, 1994); Ben Witherington III, *John's Wisdom: A Commentary on the Fourth Gospel* (Louisville: Westminster John Knox, 1995); Francis J. Moloney, *The Gospel of John.* SP 4 (Collegeville: Liturgical Press, 1998).

19. Carson, *The Gospel according to John,* 36, 56, 63–68.

20. Raymond E. Brown, *An Introduction to the New Testament* (New York: Doubleday, 1997) viii.

21. Note that I anticipated this proposal in *The Johannine School.* SBLDS 26 (Missoula: Scholars, 1975) 287.

22. Fernando F. Segovia, "The Tradition History of the Fourth Gospel," in R. Alan Culpepper and C. Clifton Black, eds., *Exploring the Gospel of John* (Louisville: Westminster John Knox, 1996) 179.

23. Ibid.

24. Fernando F. Segovia, *Love Relationships in the Johannine Tradition.* SBLDS 58 (Chico: Scholars, 1982).

25. Fernando F. Segovia, *The Farewell of the Word: The Johannine Call to Abide* (Minneapolis: Fortress, 1991) viii.

26. See Segovia, "The Tradition History of the Fourth Gospel," 183–85; "The Gospel at the Close of the Century: Engagement from the Diaspora," and "Reading Readers of the Fourth Gospel and Their Readings: An Exercise in Intercultural Criticism," in idem, ed., *"What is John?": Readers and Readings of the Fourth Gospel.* SBLSymS (Atlanta: Scholars, 1996) 211–16, 237–77.

Chapter Two

Future Directions
of Johannine Studies

D. Moody Smith

Divinity School of Duke University

Raymond Brown introduced me to Catholic biblical scholarship with his commentary on the Gospel of John.[1] I had been much involved with Bultmann's commentary.[2] In reading and reviewing Brown, I realized we had far more agreement than disagreement (particularly on the composition and order of the Fourth Gospel). I realized also that now there was going to be twice as much to read, probably more. When I was a graduate student we read little but Protestant scholarship. Now there is not only Catholic, but also Jewish New Testament scholarship to read—not to mention agnostic, which is mostly Protestant!

Future directions of Johannine studies? So many have been suggested at this conference I cannot name them. I don't propose to predict the future. I am not a prophet or a prophet's son. But I do think a couple of old issues, in new forms, will continue to occupy us. One of my mentors, Paul Schubert, used to say, as he tried to speak American English, "Vat turns me on is technical history and conzeptual philosophy." (No one ever asked Mr. Schubert what non-conceptual philosophy might be.) Read "theology" for "philosophy" and my interests are the same! More important, history and theology are the areas into which most people's interests fall. What happened? What are we to make of it?

In the scholarly guild we have largely freed ourselves from church and public pressure. But things are now changing in ways that I had not anticipated, and these may not be altogether bad. We may be entering a period in which John becomes the object of public attention and scrutiny as the historical Jesus has been, due largely to the work of the Jesus Seminar. Mel Gibson's film "The Passion of the Christ" has already been the subject of public interest and controversy, even before its release, with articles about it in the *New York Times, The New Republic*, and *The New Yorker*. (Those are only the ones I have read.) The controversy is, of course, about the role played by the Jews in

Jesus' death in the film and in history. Gibson maintains he is only following the gospels, and I have no reason to doubt him. But this is the problem! Without having yet seen the movie I cannot know for sure, but it is a good bet that the role of the Johannine Jews predominates. It is they who argue with Pilate that Jesus must be condemned. And now there has just been released commercially a film entitled "The Gospel of John." I look for it to raise the same or similar issues.[3] These issues are historical and theological.

History and theology have been pivotal aspects or areas in the study of the Fourth Gospel, and they will remain so. In fact, wasn't there once a book called *History and Theology in the Fourth Gospel*?[4] But once we say history or theology the issues are not yet clearly or precisely defined. What is history, or what history does one have in mind? The same might be said of theology: the theology of the gospel or the theological use or impact of the gospel? Interest in history and theology in the Fourth Gospel does not die out, because people keep asking historical or theological questions and looking for commensurate answers. What happened? What does it mean?

Let us look at history first. John purports to be history, or so it was long thought. "We have beheld his glory . . ." (1:14). "We know that his witness is true" (21:24). The most explicitly theological, and christological, of the gospels claims to be historically true.[5] Whatever the *sensus plenior,* this seems to be the *sensus planus.* The apparent claim is related closely to the question of the identity of the witness and/or author, who has written these things or caused these things to be written. It is also related to the question of John's relation to the Synoptics and/or other written sources. John must be true if it is the work of an apostolic witness, but how can John be true if it differs so sharply from the Synoptics? First John even more emphatically insists upon the historical basis of the Johannine witness: "that which was from the beginning, which we have heard, which we have seen with our eyes, which we have looked upon and touched with our hands, concerning the word of life" (1:1); "I am writing you no new commandment, but an old commandment which you had from the beginning . . ." (2:7). Not surprisingly, many of us have been left perplexed. Can a gospel so deeply theological and so different from the others be true historically, or in any other respect? Recently Maurice Casey has argued with some passion that the gospel is not true: not just because it differs from the Synoptics, but because it differs to the detriment of the Jews.[6]

Quite apart from the relation of John to the historical figure of Jesus, another historical question arises. Who are the Jews? It is generally assumed that they are the opponents of Jesus, the representatives of unbelief. But are they real, that is, historical Jews—of Jesus' time or some other time? Which is worse? Or are they literary and theological symbols? Was John written against the Jews—or against the Gospel of Thomas, as Elaine Pagels has quite recently argued?[7] But these do not look like future directions, but mostly like old questions. And they are that. The old questions are the ones that are still put to us by the big, broad world that lies outside Johannine scholarship, and even outside New Testament scholarship, maybe outside theological scholarship, and even outside the world of churches and Christian confessions. Are the claims made about Jesus true? If so, in what sense, and for whom?

Who then were, and are, the Jews? His mortal opponents? Even in John the evidence is not unambiguous. I would simply note that in the public ministry "the Jews" tend to be identified with "the Pharisees," who were apparently the rivals of John a half-century or more after Jesus' death. Yet toward the end, in the Passion narrative, "the Jews" tends to alternate with "the chief priests," and the Pharisees all but disappear. I think this reflects a consciousness, at some level, of a historical difference between Jesus' interlocutors during his ministry and those who had a hand in his condemnation. Moreover, not all Jews are "the Jews," and not even all "the Jews" are the same, as Adele Reinhartz has suggested.[8] Not all "the Jews" are hostile. Some are open to Jesus. Others weep with Mary and Martha, and Jesus, over Lazarus. One of the reasons John fascinates us is that it seems on the face of it so simple or even simplistic, but on closer examination much more complex. It will keep us busy until Jesus returns and the dead arise, if one may allude to the infamous ecclesiastical redactor!

But let me turn back for a moment to the simple or obvious: John's representation of Jesus, whose ministry he purports to narrate. Jesus himself did not actually talk christology the way the Johannine Jesus does. I believe that. Why? Not just because, among other things, I do not want to be expelled from the union, SBL, CBA, SNTS, not to mention the Jesus Seminar. (In fact, I am a dropout from the Jesus Seminar.) More seriously, the "I-words" and related talk set John apart from the Synoptics, which in this respect are much closer to Jesus. (Here it is not just John against Mark, but also against the traditions we designate by Q, M, and L.) But even on this point things are more complex, historically, than they may at first seem.

Let me recall a few examples. As we all know, a number of Jesus' sayings in the Gospel of John have synoptic parallels: "He who loves his life loses it, and he who hates his life in this world will keep it for eternal life" (John 12:25; cf. Mark 8:35; Q 17:33 [Matt. 10:39]). The version found in John not surprisingly sounds Johannine. If we did not have the Synoptics we might think John simply composed it *de novo*. The saying about a prophet's being without honor in his own country (John 4:44) is found not only in all the Synoptics, but in Thomas as well. (Incidentally, when such parallel sayings are not embedded in a narrative they are characteristically found in different locations or contexts in John than in the Synoptics.) On the Synoptic side there is the infamous bolt from the Johannine blue (Matt 11:25-27: ". . . no one knows the Son except the Father, and no one knows the Father except the Son . . ."; cf. Luke 10:21-22). It lacks an exact Johannine parallel (but see John 10:14-15; 17:25-26; 3:35-36), but it does indicate that the broader Jesus tradition contained "christological" sayings.

Where do these christological sayings originate? In the mind of an evangelist, who thought: "I have some great christological ideas! How shall I convince readers to accept them? Put them on the lips of Jesus himself!"? I don't think so. Two factors are worth mentioning. First, if Jesus did not talk this way he seems to have preached and acted in a way commensurate with such speech. Scholars as different as Günther Bornkamm and E. P. Sanders agree that, while he may not have thought of himself as Messiah, Jesus assumed a crucial role as the eschatological prophet of the coming kingdom. Eschatology pivots around him and his message. Sanders concludes: "Christianity, in assigning Jesus a high role, was apparently being true to him."[9] The offense of the kingdom became the offense of christology—particularly in John. I think this road deserves further exploration.

Moreover, along with a number of colleagues I have long thought that words of the Johannine Jesus are Spirit-inspired. I mean this as a phenomenological fact, not a theological judgment. The *paraklētos* is the continuation of the revelation of Jesus (14:26; 16:12-13).[10]

How does this work? There are sayings that are prima facie different from what Jesus of Nazareth might have said. John 14:6: "I am the way, the truth and the life, no one comes to the Father but by me." Here we hear the voice of the exalted Christ, speaking through the Paraclete, and there is no Synoptic parallel. There are other sayings where the situation is more complex. We have already considered the one about loving and hating one's life (12:25). The Johannine Jesus' statement about the destruction of the Temple is another good example.

In John, Jesus says "Destroy this temple and in three days I will raise it up" (2:19). The verb is the aorist imperative and Jesus is addressing "the Jews," who are not yet mortally hostile, but will become so (5:18). The comparable Synoptic version is an accusation against Jesus, that he has said, "I will destroy this temple that is made with hands, and in three days I will build another, not made with hands" (Mark 14:58; cf. 15:29; Acts 6:14). The Johannine version of the saying, now uttered by Jesus himself is, again not surprisingly, pointedly Johannine and opens the way for the narrator's interpretation (2:21): "But he spoke of the temple of his body."

I think E. P. Sanders has convincingly argued that Jesus actually prophesied the destruction of the Temple and expected God to send a new one.[11] In John 2:19 Jesus does just that (cf. Mark 13:2): "Destroy this temple and in three days I will raise it up." The accusation in Mark 14:58, with its reference to three days, already hints at the resurrection of Jesus. Typically, John, I think under the aegis of the Spirit, makes this reference to the resurrection entirely explicit: "He was speaking of the temple of his body." John has taken the tradition of Jesus' saying and christologized it. Jesus is the new temple: "The word became flesh and tabernacled among us" (1:14). I suspect that the Gospel of John, sometimes at those points where it seems most theological, and we say therefore not historical, has some kind of historical basis, as here.

So what about Johannine theology? We should also talk about Johannine ethics. Both are sectarian. Dare I say that at the Raymond Brownfest?[12] But they are, if "sectarian" means insiders are privileged and outsiders are excluded. It is, of course, a matter of definition, as Brown himself sees so clearly. We have spoken of "the Jews." But it is not just "the Jews;" it is the world generally. "If the world hates you, know that it has hated me before it hated you." Johannine theology is the theology of people under siege. Should I say a community? (Community, fellowship, *koinōnia,* is a Johannine word.) The world is divided into insiders and outsiders. The latter are the majority. The Johannine community may not have been a sect, but the gospel and epistles at least display sectarian tendencies. "I am the way and the truth and the life; no one comes to the Father, but by me" (14:6). Most do not come and are condemned. Johannine ethics follows from Johannine theology. The new commandment is to love one another (13:34). This means the disciples' love for other disciples. True, all people will see this mutual love and know that the disciples belong to Jesus, but nothing is said about their being converted. "Do not love the world or the things in the world" (1 John 2:15). "And the world passes away, and the lust of it; but he who does the will of God abides forever" (1 John 2:17). This is really the distinction between the fate of the unbeliever and that of the believer.

It is strange, is it not, that so many readers are attracted to the Christ of this gospel? Understandably, others are put off. The revealer whom God sent to save the world first divides the world. Hasn't the church through the years often followed John's lead? Don't talk to me about ethics, even obedience to God, until you get it right about Jesus! Orthodox belief is getting it right about Jesus. First John certainly seems to think so. John builds walls between people just when such walls need to come down. John's narrative not only invites decision, but demands it. The narrative is so coercive. One can scarcely read it without taking sides.

This gospel is not, however, the work of a literary Philistine or crude theological mind, but of a sophisticated author. Things are carefully staged. Jesus' interlocutors and opponents are not stupid. They just don't understand. The learned Nicodemus doesn't get it. His questions are, of course, quite reasonable. Also, the Jews, who wonder how Jesus can have come down from heaven when they know his parents (6:42), have a point. They just don't know Jesus' true origin (6:45). John has demythologized the Gnostic redeemer myth, if he didn't invent it. John even knows that revelation given in history is ambiguous. When the voice from heaven responds to Jesus (12:28), some believe an angel has spoken to him, but others only hear thunder.

That Jesus' deeds are magnified by John is quite possible; it is also possible that he may know what he is doing. Jesus not only feeds the five thousand, but turns water into wine at a wedding feast (2:1-11). Jesus not only restores sight, but gives sight (9:1-7). One might say he not only restores life but gives life: he raises the dead (11:38-44). Jesus creates sight and life. In each case John may have enhanced the scope and character of a deed with Synoptic parallels. The spectators are often puzzled, even as the reader may be.

Against what background is all this intelligible? Remarkably, the impact of John's gospel may have been pretty much the same as it has moved through nineteen centuries, encountering different cultural settings and people who know nothing of the gospel's origin. The deep dualistic mindset of the author fundamentally shapes the gospel's impact and readers' or hearers' reaction to it for weal or woe. I think Wayne Meeks correctly sensed its basis in the social tension, the hostility, surrounding the origin of this gospel.[13] Here the Qumran sect offers a phenomenological parallel as well as historical influence, direct or indirect. Meeks, like Brown, saw John moving toward Gnosticism rather than originating from it. Brown, of course, saw the gospel falling into Gnostic hands and the author of the First Epistle resisting such Gnosticizing appropriation.[14] As much as I appreciate Brown's understanding of the opponents of 1 John, I cannot help wondering whether the relation to Gnosticism is more deepseated. But we must leave that question aside. Wherever John's roots, in apocalyptic, Jewish sectarianism, or Gnosticism, the work comes to us out of a profoundly troubled and conflicted religious heritage. Perhaps that in itself somehow contributes to its ever-recurring popularity.

It appeals to those who reject the world and want to flee from it, but also to those who want to destroy it, or would see it destroyed in the name of their God. It is thus the gospel of ethereal spiritualists and of fighting fundamentalists. The reader of John, like the gospel itself, walks a narrow line between irrelevance and hatred. These temptations lie on either side. Yet it is all the more important to pay attention to what is said and not said in the gospel.

Against any quasi-Gnostic disparagement or rejection of the world, the Gospel of John affirms that God loved the world (3:16), which, through the Word, he created (1:10). The Johannine Jesus says the world will hate the disciples of Jesus (15:18-19), but not that they should hate the world. (First John 2:15-17 comes close to saying this, as it adjures the reader not to love the world. Moreover, in 1 John 4:9, which seems to echo John 3:16, the object of God's love is not the world, into which the Son was sent, but the believers.) The disciples should love one another (13:34; 15:12; 1 John *passim*), which means initially the fellow disciple, not the neighbor, much less the enemy.

John does not say that God loved the Jews. Of course not. But as we noted, the question of who "the Jews" are may be more complex than at first appears. John does say of the Word, Jesus, that "he came to his own home, and his own people received him not" (RSV 1:11). But Jesus himself is called a Jew by the woman of Samaria (4:9). And John the Baptist declares that he himself had come baptizing so that Jesus "might be revealed to Israel" (1:31). "Israel" is always used positively, but not of the disciples explicitly (as in Gal 6:16). "The Jews" may constitute themselves as such by rejecting Jesus, but Jesus does not tell disciples to hate the Jews. Perhaps significantly, John does not write that "the Jews will hate you," but that the world will. The mortal threat to the disciples (16:2), linked as it is with expulsion from the synagogue, has Jewish opponents in view, but they are not named specifically. (John the evangelist, the narrator, presses "the Jews" into monolithic opposition to Jesus, but the gospel itself reflects a more variegated reality.)

Obviously John portrays a severe tension between Jesus' disciples and "the Jews," but what he does not say, or have Jesus say, may be significant. In John 8 the polemic between Jesus and Jews, characterized—perhaps significantly—as Jews who had believed in him (8:31), is quite sharp and harsh. Yet they are not said to hate Jesus, or he them. It is naturally inferred that their hatred of one another is mutual, but it may be significant that such hatred is not named or enjoined. Jesus himself did not teach people to hate one another. Has the broader Jesus tradition influenced John even at this point? I think so.

The dualistic perspective and roots of John are pervasive, yet finally not determinative. John is not Manichean. All the discourse about the world, and the Jews, evokes the sharpest contrasts, black or white, with little room for grays. Yet as narrative and discourse unfold, and the whole of the gospel is kept in view, things become more complex than they seem at first glance. When the reader moves from gospel to epistles "the Jews" have disappeared, but the sharp dualism has not, and its application has become, if anything, more rigorous. The opponents are no longer "the Jews," but believers who get it wrong about Jesus. There is no ambiguity about them. If anything, dualism has rigidified in the epistles.

Interpretation of the Gospel of John is ultimately not just for ourselves, and not even for the Christian church. It is for anyone who has ears to hear. Mel Gibson's film "The Passion of the Christ," the new film "The Gospel of John," and even the Jesus Seminar have attracted—and will attract—a larger audience for us. We need to stay on message. John's message is that there is a God who loves the world. The statement is astonishing not so much because of its mythological dimension but because of the way it contradicts (or is contradicted by) empirical, observable data. If you can believe that, you can believe anything. Of all John's astonishing statements, this is the most astonishing of all, given the state of the world then and now. Beside it, claims about the descent and ascent of the Son of Man pale in significance. God's command through Jesus is that we love one another. We hear the command as platitudinous, although it is really quite radical. No doubt John had in view the love of disciples for one another. Here is where we may and should engage in *Sachkritik*. The scope of our love is, and must be, expandable, given the scope of God's love. Am I preaching? Not necessarily—just talking about what the gospel implies. Surplus meaning! (I use a phrase introduced into our discussions at this conference.)

Our task as exegetes is to stay on message: on the one hand to show the complexity of the historical issues, on the other to show the clarity of the theological and ethical message. In doing so we shall be true to the intent and heritage of Raymond E. Brown. Like Brown, I assume the intelligibility of the Gospel of John. Its message may require clarification, but there is a literal sense that will be, or can be made, intelligible to the literate modern person.[15] A modern reader may be as perplexed as "the Jews" about how Jesus can claim to be the bread that came down from heaven (6:41) when his father and mother are known (6:42). But this perplexity is a function of the character of the claim, and of the Johannine concept of revelation, not of modernity. Stanley Fish's famous essay "Is There a Text in This Class?" is helpful at this point.[16] He speaks of interpretive communities. The Gospel of John has a wide interpretive community spreading across two thousand years and around at least the Western World—a classic, according to Gadamer's standard? (It may be that the symbols and stories of the gospel are virtually universal in their intelligibility, appeal, and offense.) People may or may not like the Gospel of John, but they can get it. Its extravagant historical and theological claims arouse interest when they are found appalling as well as when they are found appealing. John apparently wants to coerce the reader into deciding whether his book, and Jesus, are true. Otherwise the reader finds himself or herself among "the Jews" who are the unbelievers. Bultmann made that equation, and it is not entirely wrong exegetically, although more must be said historically, and theologically.[17] I don't know about future directions of Johannine study generally, but we must keep thinking about history and theology in John.

"What about literary criticism and theory?" one might reasonably ask. Forty-odd years ago a young scholar wrote a piece entitled *The Composition and Order of the Fourth Gospel: Bultmann's Literary Theory.* The monograph was read by Raymond Brown, who cited it in his commentary and generally agreed with its conclusions. Literary theory? When I was working on that project, literary theory meant proposals about sources, redaction, and rearrangement. We have come a long way since then. We even speak of literary effect, as well as literary cause, reader-response criticism, and communities of interpretation. We have learned how to stay at the (synchronic) level of the transmitted text. As my mentors in these matters, Alan Culpepper and Frank Moloney, have demonstrated, such literary interests do not need to replace older historical and theological interests, but often support them.[18]

Will you indulge me in a couple of ruminations as I reflect back on Bultmann's John commentary and interpretation? It was fantastic in several senses of that word. What would Bultmann have thought and written had he known what we know now? Perhaps he would have presented his elaborate reconstruction of the Gospel of John differently: not as actual literary-historical process, but as his own reading of John—the product of *Sachkritik,* to use his own term. As a literary-historical theory it was the most complex—at least until it was surpassed in that respect by Boismard![19] It could be true, but how could one be sure if it were? I cannot imagine. We are, however, learning more about taking the text on its own terms, and discovering what those terms are.

I began by mentioning Bultmann along with Brown. Both are theologically responsible exegetes, one Lutheran, the other Catholic. The text stands before us. Bultmann wanted to hear the text, but it was his reconstructed text and he was thoroughly implicated in it. Brown also had a theory of the text's composition, but he was willing to stand outside the text to hear, as he himself put it, "what was most likely meant by the first-century author and most likely understood by the first-century audience."[20]

We may need to say more, but we should not strive for any less. Brown remains a model of exegetical focus. Like Bultmann, he too was totally invested in the task of understanding the text. Yet because he remained outside the text he was in a better position to hear it. I can think of no exegete, Protestant or Catholic, in the latter half of the twentieth century who performed this task more faithfully and carefully than Raymond E. Brown. Who was the most influential Protestant exegete in the latter part of the twentieth century? In North America, Raymond E. Brown. But he was a Catholic priest! Nevertheless, I vote for Brown.

Notes

1. Raymond E. Brown, *The Gospel According to John.* AB 29, 29A (Garden City, NY: Doubleday, 1966, 1970); reviewed by D. Moody Smith, "A Major New Commentary on John," *Interpretation* 21 (1967) 469–75.

2. D. Moody Smith, Jr., *The Composition and Order of the Fourth Gospel: Bultmann's Literary Theory.* Yale Publications in Religion 10 (New Haven: Yale University Press, 1965), was an analysis of Rudolf Bultmann's work, principally his *Das Evangelium des Johannes.* KEK II/15 (Göttingen: Vandenhoeck & Ruprecht, 1941, with 1957 *Ergänzungsheft*). The commentary was subsequently translated as *The Gospel of John: A Commentary* by G. R. Beasley-Murray, R. W. N. Hoare, and John K. Riches (Philadelphia: Westminster, 1971), thirty years after its original publication. My interest in Bultmann's work has continued: D. Moody Smith, "Johannine Studies since Bultmann," *Word and World* 21 (2001) 343–51.

3. Since delivering this paper I have seen the film, produced by a Toronto-based company, with New Testament colleagues Peter Richardson, Adele Reinhartz, and Alan Segal, among others, as historical advisers. The film incorporates the entire text of the Fourth Gospel in the Good News translation of the American Bible Society. Since it includes the entire Gospel of John, nothing more or less, it does not involve the producers in the difficult task of deciding what is historical and what not. I was surprised by the quality of the cinematography, and would not have thought that the Gospel of John could be transformed into as engaging a film.

4. J. Louis Martyn, *History and Theology in the Fourth Gospel,* has recently appeared in a new edition (3rd ed. Louisville: Westminster John Knox, 2003). The original edition was published in 1968.

5. Whether John's truth claims apply primarily, if at all, to history, or whether they may be seen as merely conventional is debatable. See the finely nuanced paper of Andrew T. Lincoln, "'We Know that His Testimony is True': Johannine Truth Claims and Historicity," presented at the Annual (2003) Meeting of the Society of Biblical Literature, in the Consultation on John, Jesus, and History, as well as his article "The Beloved Disciple as Eyewitness and the Fourth Gospel as Witness," *JSNT* 85 (2002) 3–26. My own view is that the plain sense of the Johannine statements involves historical truth claims, but I agree with Lincoln that this is the beginning of the problem, not the end.

6. Like Lincoln, I am aware of the sharpness of the truth question as it is posed by Maurice P. Casey, *Is John's Gospel True?* (London: Routledge, 1996). Casey answers that it is not (historically and in other ways). His negative answer is related to the gospel's alleged or apparent anti-Jewishness and to his view that wherever John differs from the Synoptics it departs from historical reality and reliability.

7. Elaine Pagels, *Beyond Belief: The Secret Gospel of Thomas* (New York: Random House, 2003). Pagels argues that "John probably knew what the Gospel of Thomas taught—if not its actual text," (p. 39). She then remarks that "What first impressed scholars who compared these two gospels is how similar they are." She then notes that Helmut Koester, *Ancient Christian Gospels* (Philadelphia: Trinity Press International, 1990), 86–128, "has noted such similarities in detail, and concludes that these two authors drew upon common sources" (40). Koester does not discuss Thomas and John throughout pp. 86–128, however, but only on pp. 113–24, and again on pp. 259–67, where he brings in other Gnostic texts. As Pagels notes, Koester does not think John knew Thomas, but that they have a common ancestor, which seems to me more likely. Pagels' position looks a little like Bultmann's view that John used Gnostic conceptuality and terminology to produce a decidedly non-Gnostic, even anti-Gnostic gospel, except that where Bultmann favors the Fourth Evangelist, Pagels favors Thomas. One might have thought it odd that the Gnostic Thomas seems to be based on Synoptic sayings and shows so little, if any, knowledge of John, the most gnosticizing of the canonical gospels. Pagels' thesis would then explain this odd fact: John is later. Of course, the question of which is earlier has usually been decided in favor of John. Strangely, Pagels seems not to mention Thomas' sharpest divergences: Thomas is not a narrative and does not mention Jesus' death.

8. Adele Reinhartz, *Befriending the Beloved Disciple: A Jewish Reading of the Gospel of John* (New York and London: Continuum, 2001), certainly does not minimize John's hostility to "the Jews" as opponents of Jesus—quite the contrary. Yet her reading of the gospel has made me more aware of a lack of uniformity in John's representation of people he must know are Jewish. "The Jews" may be portrayed as Jesus' enemies, and vice versa, yet in the gospel not all the *Ioudaioi* actually are.

9. E. P. Sanders, *Jesus and Judaism* (Philadelphia: Fortress, 1985) 333. Cf. Günther Bornkamm, *Jesus of Nazareth*, trans. Irene and Fraser McLuskey, with James M. Robinson (London: Hodder and Stoughton, 1960) ch. 8, "The Messianic Question," 169–78, in which Bornkamm holds that the status of Jesus is to be inferred from his words and deeds rather than derived from any claim he might have made.

10. See D. Moody Smith, "John's Quest for Jesus," in David E. Aune, Torrey Seland, and Jarl Henning Ulrichsen, eds., *Neutestamentica et Philonica: Studies in Honor of Peder Borgen.* NTSupp 106 (Leiden: Brill, 2003) 233–53.

11. *Jesus and Judaism,* 61–76.

12. See Raymond E. Brown, *The Community of the Beloved Disciple* (New York: Paulist, 1979) 14–17, 89–91, where Brown rejects the characterization of the Johannine community as a sect.

13. Still of fundamental importance is Wayne A. Meeks, "The Man from Heaven in Johannine Sectarianism," *JBL* 91 (1972) 44–72.

14. A position first set forth in *Community of the Beloved Disciple* in 1979 (see especially 95–144) and given full exegetical defense in Brown's commentary, *The Epistles of John.* AB 30 (Garden City, NY: Doubleday, 1982), especially 47–68, 69–115.

15. See Raymond E. Brown, *An Introduction to the New Testament.* ABRL (New York: Doubleday, 1997) 35–40.

16. See Stanley Fish, *Is There a Text in This Class? The Authority of Interpretive Communities* (Cambridge: Harvard University Press, 1980). The foundational essay is on pp. 303–21.

17. I have tried to say some of those things in this essay and elsewhere, as have many others. See D. Moody Smith, "Judaism and the Gospel of John," in James H. Charlesworth, ed., *Jews and*

Christians: Exploring the Past, Present, and Future (New York: Crossroad, 1990) 76–99; idem, "John," in John Barclay and John Sweet, eds., *Early Christian Thought in its Jewish Context* (Cambridge: Cambridge University Press, 1996) 96–111. In the latter I argue that the Johannine Jesus' opposition to "the Jews," while a reflection of a bitter parting of the ways between Jesus and those who considered themselves Jews no longer, has not only a close connection but a common ground. Indeed, the depiction of Judaism that can be derived from John is not a caricature so much as the depiction of an emergent theological contrariety.

18. See R. Alan Culpepper, *Anatomy of the Fourth Gospel: A Study in Literary Design* (Philadelphia: Fortress, 1983). Now twenty years old, Culpepper's book remains a classic. Francis J. Moloney's contributions culminate in his commentary *The Gospel of John*. SP 4 (Collegeville: Liturgical Press, 1998), which consolidates his earlier commentary, published in three volumes over a five-year period by Fortress: *Belief in the Word. Reading John 1–4* (1993); *Signs and Shadows. Reading John 5–12* (1996); *Glory not Dishonor. Reading John 13–20(21)* (1998). For his excellent succinct statement see Raymond E. Brown, *An Introduction to the Gospel of John*, ed. Francis J. Moloney (New York: Doubleday, 2003) 30–39, "Narrative Approaches to the Fourth Gospel."

19. See Marie-Emile Boismard, André Lamouille, and Gérard Rochais, *L'Evangile de Jean: Commentaire*, the third volume of his *Synopse des quatres Evangiles en Francais* (Paris: Cerf, 1977). I have presented and discussed Boismard, as well as Frans Neirynck's critique of his position, in D. Moody Smith, *John Among the Gospels* (rev. ed. Columbia, SC: University of South Carolina Press, 2001) 141–58.

20. *Introduction to the Gospel of John*, 111.

Part II
Historical Context and the Gospel of John

Chapter Three

The Whence and Whither
of the Johannine Community

Robert Kysar

Emory University

A description of either the whence or the whither (the origin or the future) of the idea of the Johannine community in scholarly research is not a simple matter and is most certainly fraught with dangers. Contemporary biblical scholarship is deeply embedded in its culture and is, therefore, most often the result of a complex of influences, many of which are elusive. To make matters worse, the future of biblical studies is far from determined. Moreover, the task cannot be done without betraying the presuppositions and social setting of the investigator. Notwithstanding these difficulties, we plunge ahead.

The Whence of the Johannine Community

In modern interpretation the rise of the importance of the communities behind and implied within the biblical documents was a gradual but natural one. For instance, D. Moody Smith discusses the differences between John and the Synoptics and then proposes that those differences can hardly be attributed simply to unique personal, literary, or theological views. Rather they "seem more a function of a different set of historical circumstances and problems." He concludes: "[i]t is not a matter of chance that in recent years considerable attention from various quarters or perspectives has been devoted to the question of the Johannine Christianity and the nature and shape of the community or church that produced the Fourth Gospel."[1]

The Beginnings of the Community Hypothesis

A number of movements in biblical interpretation in the nineteenth and twentieth centuries gave birth to this keen interest in community. We might note, for instance, the acceleration of the importance of the historical contexts out of which the biblical documents arose. History of religions methods emphasized the significance of the setting of the author and the original readers. Equally important is the rise of theories involving the so-called "schools" in Pentateuchal criticism[2] and the community's role in the Psalms,[3] as well as elsewhere.[4]

However, in large part, I think, form and redaction criticisms were most instrumental in leading us to the quest for the community related to a passage. Rudolf Bultmann, for instance, writes: "The proper understanding of form-criticism rests upon the judgement that the literature in which the life of a given community, even the primitive Christian community, has taken shape, springs out of quite definite conditions and wants of life."[5] Likewise, the redaction-critical studies of the Synoptic Gospels, of course, assigned a major role to the community within which and for which the redaction was done.[6]

Still, the beginnings of the study of the Johannine community are difficult to identify. The rise of interest in the development of the Fourth Gospel through several stages implied some sort of setting for each stage, but prior to the 1960s scholars, it seems, never posited or pursued the idea of a single community behind the process.[7] Others, however, suggested that the Fourth Gospel implies the existence of a group of Christians and not one author.[8] In contrasting the Hermetic literature and the Gospel of John in 1963, C. H. Dodd writes: "in the Fourth Gospel the whole process of initiation takes place within a body of 'friends' of Jesus. The corporate character of the transaction is essential. It is only in the body that the individual finds eternal life."[9] The concept of "a body of 'friends' of Jesus" clearly approaches something like a Johannine community. John Ashton points out, too, that Klaus Haacker conceived of an "institution" or "founding" of salvation behind the gospel that Haacker thought of as a community.[10]

Certainly the concept of the "Johannine School" contributed to widening the interest in composition from one person and seems to be the clearest predecessor to the Johannine community. R. Alan Culpepper traced the origins of the Johannine school from the seventeenth century and argues that by the 1860s the basic features of the Johannine school had been proposed. He concludes his quest for the origins of the idea of a school of John, observing that by 1974 many scholars used the idea, but in sundry different ways. He suggests that the Johannine community shared many of the features of an ancient school, thus offering the school concept as the very nature of the community.[11]

Whether or not the school concept epitomizes the community behind the Fourth Gospel, perhaps it limits too severely the nature of that community. Raymond E. Brown correctly distinguishes between the concepts of school and community. Recognizing that he understands "school" differently than Culpepper, he writes: "the community was not the author of the Gospel. I envision 'school' in a much more restricted sense of a special group (all of them disciples of the [beloved disciple])."[12] The concept of school provides us with a number of important features of the community, but it is not to be equated with the whole of the community.

Notwithstanding Culpepper's equation of school and community, it appears that in 1977 Adolph Bühner was the first to use the expression "the Johannine community" in the sense it is used today.[13] John Ashton correctly observes that this expression "conceals a major shift of emphasis, a radical change of direction in Johannine research."[14]

One other factor—perhaps most important of all—should be considered part of the origin of the community concept in Johannine studies. The hypothesis of such a community is deeply embedded in the modern historical critical method of biblical studies and would never have arisen had it not been for the character of that method. Historical criticism, of course, supposes the importance of history and goes so far as to claim that the meaning of any text is dependent on the historical occasion for and in which it was written. There is no way to discern and claim meaning for a text without first knowing what the author(s) intended by it when it was written or spoken. The assumption is that meaning is embedded in the text itself, deposited there by the historical act of its composition. Therefore the historical critical method was destined to go behind the text itself to try to discover the settings out of which biblical documents were written. As it developed it went further and further in elaborating those settings and occasions for the writings. Hence we cannot speak of the whence of the community interpretative method without reference to the modernist view of history and meaning. (And to this subject we will return below.)

The Contemporary Origin of the Community Concept

With these introductory observations in place, we turn to the more specific question of the origin of the centrality of the Johannine community as an interpretative tool in the second half of the twentieth century. For the sake of time I propose to remind you of the whence of the community concept by means of summaries of four originating events.

The First Originating Event: Raymond E. Brown. The first and doubtless clearest initiating event in the recent and phenomenal reconstruction of the Johannine community is found in fragmentary form in the first volume of Raymond Brown's commentary. In his discussion of the composition of the gospel Brown sketches as a "working hypothesis" his now-famous five stages in the production of the document. He only hints at different events or conditions in the community for whom the gospel was intended, although he specifically claims that the secondary editing was in response to objections from various groups (including Jewish Christians who were still in the synagogue).[15] In discussing the purpose of the writing Brown devotes a good deal of attention to "Argument with the Jews," in which he addresses the polemic use of the expression "the Jews" and explains it as occurring during a period when there was tension between the church and the synagogue. Later he mentions a hypothetical group of "crypto-Christians" who believed in Jesus but remained in the synagogue after most had left or been expelled from their religious community.[16] Elsewhere in his consideration of the date of the gospel Brown suggests that the Christians' expulsion from the synagogue was a result of the formal excommunication propagated by the Council of Jamnia toward the end of the first century C.E. That event, he argues, determines the latest possible date for the final stage in the composition of the gospel.[17] Finally, he attempts to correlate the hypothesis of John as the author of the gospel with his proposal for its developmental composition.[18]

This first publication of his view of the Johannine community in 1966 was, of course, to become much more detailed and explicit in his book, *The Community of the Beloved Disciple: The Life, Loves, and Hates of an Individual Church in New Testament Times,* published in 1979. Brown then completed his reconstruction of the history of the community in his commentary on the Johannine epistles (published in 1982), where he incorporated a later period in the community's life when (among other things) the church divided over its interpretation of the gospel.[19] Still later he was to explore the history more fully and argue that crises in the community account for features of the gospel (e.g., its realized eschatology).[20]

What is worth noting about his proposal is the way in which it is wrapped up in the other introductory issues involved in the Fourth Gospel. His appeal to a single community to which the gospel was directed attempts to take into account the peculiar features of the document by references to several events in the community's life. *Consequently, the community concept grew out of Brown's efforts to explicate the peculiarities of the gospel.*

The Second Originating Event: J. Louis Martyn. The same is true, of course, of the second crucial event in the rise of the Johannine community, namely, J. Louis Martyn's proposal that the expulsion of the Johannine Christian Jews from their synagogue home was the community's definitive experience. In 1968 (between the publication of the two volumes of Brown's commentary) Martyn published the first edition of *History and Theology in the Fourth Gospel,* now available in its third revised edition. Without a doubt this remarkable study is one of the grand achievements of Johannine research in the twentieth century. However, we need only mention two of its contributions to the concept of the Johannine community as such.

The first is Martyn's proposal that at least portions of the Fourth Gospel are to be read on two levels: first, the report of Jesus' words and activities in his own time and, second, the experience of the community at the time of the writing of the gospel. The evidence of this two-layer narrative is found most especially in chapter 9 and the three occurrences of the expression "expel from the synagogue," ἀποσυνάγωγος—9:22, 12:42, and 16:2. While chapter 9 represents the rejection of the Christian Jews, chapters 5 and 7 as well as 10:20 reflect the time during which the controversy between the Jews and the Jewish Christians continued after the synagogue expulsion. Martyn taught many of us how to read the gospel in the light of the community's traumatic banishment from their religious home and addressed the troublesome, anachronistic-sounding references to expulsion from the synagogue.

The second of Martyn's many contributions was his meticulous research into the history of Jewish-Christian relations in the first and second centuries and in particular the reformulation of Twelfth Benediction, which he believes was the occasion for the division between synagogue and church. According to Martyn this liturgical prayer was revised specifically to identify those within a synagogue who were adherents to Christianity and others who held distorted views of Jewish faith and practice—the *Nazarenes* and the *Minim*.[22]

The impact of Brown's and Martyn's nearly simultaneous proposals of an expulsion from the synagogue was revolutionary.[23] The two of them did not entirely agree on the details of the split, but together they laid the foundation for making the experience of the Johannine community the key to the interpretation of the Fourth Gospel—a foundation that has sustained much of Johannine studies, especially in North America.[24]

The Third Originating Event: Wayne A. Meeks. As important as the contributions of Brown and Martyn are, the publication of Wayne A. Meeks's article, "The Man from Heaven in Johannine Sectarianism,"[25] must be mentioned as the third of the crucial events in the genesis of the contemporary concept of the Johannine community.[26] Using the methods of a sociology of knowledge, Meeks examines the descent/ascent motif in John and proposes that it comprises a myth by which the Johannine Christians understood and strengthened their status as a sectarian counter-culture group. Meeks's provocative study did much to fashion a view of the Johannine community that—to varying degrees—dominated scholarship for years to come. While the war waged over the use of the term "sect" or "sectarian" to describe the community,[27] the view of the Johannine Christians as a minority group in their culture and their emphasis on the in-group/out-group distinction became nearly a basic assumption of later scholarship. Equally important, I think, Meeks's ingenious proposal was the spark that ignited a wide range of social-scientific investigations of the reconstructed Johannine community.

The Fourth Originating Event: The Discoveries at Qumran. The proposal that we understand the Johannine community as a sect is linked with the impact of the Dead Sea Scrolls. This event offered Johannine scholars a model of religious communities in the first century C.E. Early on, there were efforts to find parallels between the Gospel of John and the views of the Qumran community, the most prominent doubtless being the dualistic use of light and darkness,[28] and some extravagant claims were made for the scrolls as providing a background for the Fourth Gospel.[29] Gradually we have come to appreciate the scrolls without exaggerating their importance, not least because they afford us a glimpse of a Jewish community contemporaneous with the rise of Christians churches.

What we learn about the Qumran community invites us to think of the earliest of the Christian churches in similar ways. In particular "[t]he discovery of the Dead Sea Scrolls revealed a . . . Jewish sect in first century Palestine that expressed itself in much of the same dualistic, exclusivistic, and 'inward' terminology as John."[30] We no longer need to explain the thought of the Fourth Gospel by invoking Hellenistic thought, for we now know there were heterodox forms of Jewish sectarianism contemporaneous with the birth of Christianity. Another door to the picturing the Johannine community was opened.

Some Conclusions. In these publications and discoveries, the concept of the experience of the community behind the Fourth Gospel functioned in a definitive way. In each case, community experience was understood to be the key that unlocked the puzzles of the gospel—both its theological themes and the language it uses to tell its story of Jesus.[31] Moreover, by means of the experience of the Johannine community scholars were able to address (if not solve) the problem of the gospel's attitude toward "the Jews."

These four pivotal events (along with others) formed a magnetic force in Johannine scholarship. The six years between 1966 and 1972 were to set in motion a deluge of studies that took the community as their focus.[32] A wave of studies seemed to offer ever stronger evidence for the likelihood of a community in trauma, struggling to redefine itself over against Judaism. As one of the accomplishments of the research for the decade, 1963–1973 I claimed that "[c]ontemporary Johannine criticism has confirmed that the Gospel is a community's document," that John was "an occasional writing," and that John "cannot be read meaningfully apart from some understanding of the community out of which and to which it was written."[33]

Sparked by Meeks's work, the concept of the Johannine community also generated a number of social-scientific studies and contributed significantly to the rise of that discipline. Cases in point include Jerome H. Neyrey's investigation of Johannine christology and Norman Peterson's study of language and characterization in John.[34] Significantly, the concept of the "Johannine community" became a primary basis for one of the new approaches to biblical interpretation.[35]

If this brief summary reminds us of some of the essentials in the whence of the Johannine community, what can we say with any confidence about the future—the whither—of the concept?

The Whither of the Johannine Community

Notwithstanding the popularity of the supposition that the Fourth Gospel was a literary reflection of a real-life religious community in the late first century C.E., like nearly every biblical theory, this one never went unquestioned.[36] That is the nature of our discipline. Still, any effort to speak now of what the future holds for Johannine scholarship and more specifically for the concept of the Johannine community as an interpretative principle is difficult, if not impossible. None of us can foretell what the future holds for scholarship. One can only speculate, and so I claim nothing more for my remarks than that they have some bases in what I see as current trends.

I wish to speak of the whither of this concept in two different voices. In the first I will raise some doubts that appear serious to me, and in the second I will identify some of the challenges that may face the future of the concept.

Doubts Likely in the Whither-of-the-Johannine-Community Concept

The most serious problem with the historical reconstruction on which the whole idea of the Johannine community is based includes at least two parts.

The first problem has to do with the evidence for such a hypothetical construction as the Johannine community.[37] The emphasis on community raises some of the same questions as those recently cited against Bultmann's form-critical method. One of those has to do with the relationship between the individual and the community. How are we to determine that the community alone and not some individual or individuals is reflected in the language and story of the gospel? Surely the literary style of the documents hints that the author was a literary person skilled in writing.[38] If this is the case, can we say that the gospel as a whole *always* expresses the community's experience?[39]

Most likely scholars who embrace the current reconstruction of the Johannine community will be forced to face a number of other critical questions, one of which may be "what constitutes evidence for such a group?" Understandably, the evidence we most often use to support the idea consists of particular texts that seem to need elucidation and can be better understood (at least in the opinion of some) by reference to the community behind the texts.

Certainly one such bit of evidence is the triple reference to expulsion from the synagogue. But is it really possible for us to determine what those references originally meant? How would we do that? Do they necessarily refer to *an event that has already happened?* We move quickly to go beyond the texts themselves to say that they must mean the Christians have in the past been expelled. Why could they not just as well have to do with a skepticism about the continued life of the Christians in the synagogue rather than an event that has already occurred or even would ever occur? Actually, perhaps we should wonder if all the possible meanings of 9:22, 12:42, and 16:2 could be reduced to one and only one reference. On what basis do we make the supposed expulsion a blanket explanation for the rest of the Johannine story?[40]

How do we know that the hostile relationship with the Jews we see reflected in the gospel is the result of a community's suffering exclusion from their synagogue? Indeed, the meaning of the expression "the Jews" continues to puzzle scholars and seems finally irresolvable.[41] Moreover, why are we so quick to dismiss the possibility that the authors of the gospel were themselves prejudiced against the Jews? Whereas for centuries we might attribute something of this sort to an individual author, now we hasten to attribute it to a community's experience. Are we hesitant to admit that there is indeed evidence of an anti-Jewish prejudice in a good deal of the New Testament?[42]

Furthermore, does the descent-and-ascent motif necessarily have to be an expression of the community's own isolation and sectarian relationship with its society? Meeks himself cautions, "I do not mean to say that the symbolic universe suggested by the Johannine literature is *only* the reflex or projection of the group's social situation."[43] If it is not only such a projection but something else, what is to say that the "something else" and not the community created this myth? Is there any way by which we can really determine from where the author(s) of the gospel derived this myth? Are myths not themselves sometimes created for all sorts of reasons and sometimes even unconsciously? Moreover, we need to ask whether the sociology of knowledge produces reliable insights into social belief structures of groups in the past or becomes a kind of self-predicting analysis that is likely to find what it was looking for.

Finally, is there extra-biblical evidence that would point us in the direction of the experience of a community behind this gospel? There does not seem to be any indication of the existence of a community like the one scholars have proposed and now take for granted. Unfortunately, there are no literary citations for the existence of such a community. How about the proposed implementation of the Twelfth Benediction to separate Christians from Jews? In spite of Martyn's admirable efforts to demonstrate the reformulation of this prayer in the first century there are numerous reasons to question that it was used in the first century, much less that it included Christians.[44]

If the effort to determine what constitutes evidence for the Johannine community becomes widely questioned I fear the methodology on which it is based will prove in and of itself enough to fatally weaken the community interpretation. To be candid, I must admit that I am not sure what sort of evidence would be convincing and that, for me, the evidence used as the foundation for the community interpretation has become increasingly fuzzy.[45] How does one go about demonstrating the existence of a particular body of Christians? Moreover, even if we could identify what evidence is admissible in this matter, we must then further ask: how much evidence is enough?

The problem is further aggravated when we ask how we might go about testing the veracity of the proposed Johannine community. Some will maintain (as I do) that there is no possible way to verify the proposal. One of the most frequent tests for a hypothesis in our discipline is to ask, "Does it illumine what was unclear?" The case I myself have made several times in favor of the Johannine community and the expulsion of the Johannine Christians from their synagogue home is the way in which it seems to shed light on so many issues in the gospel. In 1984 I wrote, "Martyn's hypothesis has received extensive support from a number of studies, many of which are independent of his work and approach the question from a variety of different directions." These studies, I suggested, offer confirmation of the community's expulsion from the synagogue and the gospel's witness to its ongoing dialogue with the Jews.[46]

However, is it the case that a supposition that seems to give meaning to specific passages is necessarily true? Is it not possible that a faulty supposition might do the same? *Simply because a hypothesis illumines the possible meaning of a passage does not necessarily prove that the hypothesis is true.* To be sure, the theory of the community's expulsion from the synagogue makes the reason for the gospel's sectarian attitude clearer; however, that attitude could also have been the result of many other experiences. This sectarianism may have been a result, for instance, of exposure to certain Gnostic-like (or pre-Gnostic-like) Christian views.

If, in the future, the case for a Johannine community (and its history as we now conceive it) is severely weakened by examinations of the nature of the evidence for it, the hypothesis will likely become indefensible at best. If there is no way of testing the hypothesis, how can we possibly continue to embrace it as even a "likelihood"?[47]

Likely Future Challenges to the Johannine Community Hypothesis

In addition to the questions that are liable to face the community concept, there are a number of explicit challenges that defenders of the hypothesis face already or will soon face. First and most threatening among them, I think, is *the decline of historical criticism.* In recent years scholarship has begun to show signs of a significant shift away from dependence on the concept of a reconstructed Johannine community. Consequently the whither of the concept of the Johannine community is intertwined with the whither of postmodernism.

The historical critical method has for some time been attacked and threatened from many sides. The first major attack of the twentieth century came from Karl Barth and others who attempted to restore a commitment to Scripture as the means of the Word of God.[48] In a sense that attack, in different forms, continues today within believing communities who find historical criticism counterproductive.[49]

Still, today the threat to the concept of the Johannine community is due more directly to the objections confronting the study of history in general and not just historical criticism. The waves of what some are calling postmodernism have gradually washed away the assumptions on which the study of history was founded during the Enlightenment. The challenge of postmodernist thinkers raises new questions about the validity of much that we take to be knowledge of the past. Simply put, postmodernists claim that it is sheer pretense to suppose that any of us can examine the evidence for the past and come up with an objective, unbiased, and true picture of what took place. The Bible and Culture Collective puts it this way in *The Postmodern Bible:*

Biblical scholars have been slow to awaken from the dream in which positivist science occupies a space apart from interest and values, to awaken to the realization that our representation of and discourse about what the text meant and how it means are inseparable from what we *want* it to mean, from how we *will* it to mean.[50]

Postmodernism urges us to admit that writing history is an ideological act. That is to say, it calls us to acknowledge that historians impose their meaning (or meanings) on the past, and there is no possible way to "prove" that a recitation of history is "true." Finally, therefore, history and fiction are essentially the same, insofar as what we claim is history is anything more than our biases imposed on the past. To be sure, events in the past happened, but they are irretrievably lost to us. Fred W. Burnett suggests that

[T]he practice of writing history is ideological production in three minimal ways. First, meanings are imposed on the past by "outsiders" and nonparticipants in the events that are represented. Second, imaginary causal links and explanatory relationships, particularly among past personages, are made by the historian. . . . Finally, the models that historians use are socially inscribed and are, therefore, value-laden. . . . *any* historical account could be written otherwise by historians who are inscribed in different power and socio-economic relationships.[51]

Obviously, if postmodernism prevails it will mean the death of the historical critical method of biblical interpretation and all the historical reconstructions that were results of the method, including those involving the Johannine community. We are again confronted with what the future holds for biblical criticism, and our speculations remain just that.

The weakening of the historical critical method entails the increasing popularity of other interpretative methods. Therefore the second challenge to the community thesis is clearly *the rise of these new methods of interpretation.*

Some of the newer methods have built upon the assumptions of historical criticism, the best examples of which are certain of the social-scientific methods. In these cases the history pertinent to the interpretation has been widened and redefined.[52] However, along with the advent of these new historical studies has also come the flood of studies done within what we call the new literary criticism. As the future of the concept of the Johannine community is entangled with the future of postmodernism, so too is the whither of the new literary criticism determinative for that of the Johannine community hypothesis. Of course, literary criticism has taken many different forms in the past decades, so that generalities about its relation with the concept of the Johannine community are impossible. There are a good number of interpreters who choose to practice both a literary and a historical criticism and find no conflict between them. However, I want to speak only of what might be called the more radical views propagated by some of the literary critics. These are views totally incompatible with historical criticism.

Some literary critics have been explicit in their challenge to historical criticism, and the greatest of these challenges, in my opinion, is the question of the *locus of meaning*. The distinction between the text as a window and as a mirror is now well known[53] (and perhaps overused), but it entails the issue I think is vital. Of course, the meaning of a text for the historical critics lies in the occasion behind the text, so that they are required to pick up clues in the text and its larger literary context regarding the events that shaped the text itself. Some literary critics, however, argue that the meaning of any text is found and discernible in the text itself without reference to the history behind it.[54]

More radical is the insistence that meaning is not behind or even in the text but only in the reader's experience of the text, making its historical setting and even the author's original intent irrelevant to its meaning. The so-called "intentionality fallacy" nicely summarizes the revolutionary character of this new literary enterprise.[55] The reader "creates" the meaning of a text. The Bible and Culture Collective summarizes the point this way:

> Meaning is not in the past (when the text was produced) or in the text as an object, but meaning is produced in the reader's present when the text is read. . . . For reader-response critics meaning is not a content in the text which the historian simply discovers; meaning is an experience which occurs during the reading process.[56]

A further contribution of the new criticisms is to deny the long-held assumption that any and every text has but one "true meaning," that is, the meaning the author intended to express. Scholarship in the era of historical criticism fostered such a view and many of our discussions revolved around the argument that *our* interpretation uncovers the text's real meaning, what Fernando Segovia has characterized as "discussion by means of attack and dismissal." Against such a monolithic assumption concerning meaning, the new criticism has fostered the opposite view, namely, that a text means differently as it is interpreted by different readers.[57] In large part, the reader's social location determines meaning, and as that location varies, the meaning of a text also varies.[58]

In effect, as with a work of art, the text's meaning does not depend on the originator's intent at the time of its creation but means for the readers—meanings that vary among those who experience the work. This admission is both radical and far-reaching. It puts aside much of what has been characteristic of the scholarly search for the meaning of John and in particular the role of the proposed Johannine community.

The still-debatable question of whether meaning is in the text or in the reader's experience of the text alone does not really matter for our purposes. What does matter is that what a passage means is *not* determined by what is behind the text, that is, by what its author meant or by the historical setting in which it was written. If such interpretative methods as exemplified in this kind of literary criticism become widely accepted, the whither of the concept of the Johannine community is not bright.

Between the Whence and the Whither

The whence of the hypothetical reconstruction we call the Johannine community and its use in critical studies surely marks one of the great achievements of the last four decades of the twentieth century. It offered those of us who struggle to understand the Fourth Gospel a remarkably useful hypothesis on which to proceed. No student of Johannine interpretation can deny its success within its historical and cultural setting.

Currently the Johannine community still remains a central theme in studies of John. However, the reconstruction of the Johannine community is based on both historical and interpretative methods now under siege and being dismantled piece by piece. What do we do, living and working in the interim between the whence and the whither (whatever it proves to be)? It seems clear that the current state of biblical study calls for new critical assessment and analysis of those hypotheses we have come to regard as true. The cultural and scholarly atmospheres have changed since the originators of the contemporary concept of the Johannine community offered up their best work. That does not mean, I think, that we should all abandon and denounce the whole enterprise to which Brown, Martyn, Meeks, and many others contributed so brilliantly. It does mean that each one of us is called to take another look at the thesis and determine its worth for our work in the immediate future. However, it is equally clear that each of us is responsible for trying our best to keep our work up to date and relevant. That means, I think, that none of us can naïvely and casually invoke the hypothesis without serious critical judgement. Still, if postmodernism means anything, it means an openness to a variety of points of view. I hope biblical scholars will continue to work together with mutual respect and in genuine dialogue during this time of transition in our culture.

My own view is that there is now sufficient evidence in these early years of the twenty-first century to indicate that the whither of the Johannine community is likely to include its demise. Gather the evidence that points toward what is to come about in biblical studies in this century, and the sum points clearly away from historical reconstructions such as those we call the Johannine community. My own sense is that scholarship will recognize the weaknesses in the historical critical method we inherited, turn increasingly to the newer interpretative methods, and seek fresh ways of reading Scripture. We will increasingly concentrate attention on the text itself, I believe, without efforts to find the history behind the text. Still, should the whither of the Johannine community entail abandonment and rejection, we can and ought to continue to be grateful to those figures who contributed to its origin.

In all events, scholarly discernment always comes as a result of vigorous and sustained discussion within the guild. I hope that such a discussion continues among us, for (whatever its outcome) such communal scholarly pursuit honors the one whose devotion to both the church and learning we acknowledge in these meetings, Raymond E. Brown.

Notes

1. D. Moody Smith, "Johannne Studies," in Eldon Jay Epp and George W. MacRae, s.j., eds., *The New Testament and Its Modern Interpreters.* The Bible and Its Modern Interpreters, general ed. Douglas A. Knight (Atlanta: Scholars, 1989) 281.

2. C. R. North, "Pentateuchal Criticism," in H. H. Rowley, ed., *The Old Testament and Modern Study: A Generation of Discovery and Research* (Oxford: Oxford University Press, 1951) 57.

3. A. R. Johnson, "The Psalms," *The Old Testament and Modern Study,* 165–67.

4. For instance, Krister Stendahl, *The School of Matthew and Its Use of the Old Testament* (Philadelphia: Fortress, 1968).

5. Rudolf Bultmann, *The History of the Synoptic Tradition,* trans. John Marsh (Oxford: Basil Blackwell, 1963) 4.

6. Willi Marxsen acknowledges that redaction criticism inquires "into the situation of the community in which the Gospels arose. . . . Our concern is . . . with what is typical in the community in its views, its time, perhaps its composition." But he goes on to stress the "individualistic trait oriented to the particular interest and point of view of the evangelist concerned" in idem, *Mark the Evangelist: Studies on the Redaction History of the Gospel,* trans. James Boyce, Donald Juel, William Poehlmann, and Roy A. Harrisville (Nashville and New York: Abingdon, 1969) 24. Julius Schniewind is credited with having declared that the gospels are "kerygma of a definite situation and task." See Günther Bornkamm, Gerhard Barth, and Heinz Joachim Held, *Tradition and Interpretation in Matthew.* NTL (Philadelphia: Westminster, 1963) 12.

7. See the review of scholarship in Wilbert Francis Howard, *The Fourth Gospel in Recent Criticism and Interpretation* (rev. ed. C.K. Barrett; London: Epworth, 1955), e.g., 53–69.

8. Ibid. 27.

9. C. H. Dodd, *The Interpretation of the Fourth Gospel* (Cambridge: Cambridge University Press, 1963) 422.

10. John Ashton, *Understanding the Fourth Gospel* (Oxford: Clarendon, 1991) 194. Klaus Haacker, *Die Stiftung des Heils: Untersuchungen zur Struktur der johanneischen Christologie.* Arbeiten zur Theologie 1/47 (Stuttgart: Calwer Verlag, 1972).

11. R. Alan Culpepper, *The Johannine School: An Evaluation of the Johannine-School Hypothesis Based on an Investigation of the Nature of Ancient Schools.* SBLDS 26 (Missoula: Scholars, 1975) 1–38. The continued use of this hypothesis is witnessed in Martin Hengel, *The Johannine Question* (London: S.C.M. Press; Philadelphia: Trinity Press International, 1989), e.g., 104–105, and Udo Schnelle, *Antidocetic Christology in the Gospel of John: An Investigation of the Place of the Fourth Gospel in the Johannine School,* trans. Linda M. Maloney (Minneapolis: Fortress, 1992).

12. Raymond E. Brown, *An Introduction to the Gospel of John,* ed. Francis J. Moloney. ABRL (New York, NY: Doubleday, 2003) 197.

13. Jan Adolph Bühner, *Der Gesandte und sein Weg im vierten Evangelium: Die kultur- und religionsgeschichtliche Grundlagen der johanneischen Sendungschristologie sowie ihre traditionsgeschichtliche Entwicklung.* WUNT 2nd ser. 2 (Tübingen: J. C. B. Mohr [Paul Siebeck], 1977) 1.

14. John Ashton, "Introduction: The Problem of John," in idem, ed., *The Interpretation of John.* Studies in New Testament Interpretation (2nd ed. Edinburgh: T & T Clark, 1997) 12.

15. Raymond E. Brown, *The Gospel According to John.* 2 vols. AB 29, 29A (Garden City, NY: Doubleday, 1966).

16. Ibid. lxx–lxxiv.

17. Ibid. lxxxv–lxxxvi, but see *Introduction to John,* 213. Earlier in the discussion (207–10) he lists a series of arguments for taking a post-70 date as the *terminus post quem* for the dating of the composition of John. For him among the most conclusive was the discovery of the Bodmer Papryi II and XV ($\mathfrak{P}^{66}$ and $\mathfrak{P}^{75}$).

18. Brown summarizes and critiques Georg Richter's proposed reconstruction of the history of the Johannine community in *The Community of the Beloved Disciple: The Life, Loves, and Hates of an Individual Church in New Testament Times* (New York: Paulist, 1979). The reference is to Richter, "Präsentische und futurische Eschatologie im 4. Evangelium," in Peter Fiedler and Dieter Zeller, eds., *Gegenwart und kommendes Reich: Schülergabe Anton Vögtle zum 65. Geburtstag* (Stuttgart: Katholisches Bibelwerk, 1975) 117–52.

19. *The Epistles of John.* AB 30 (Garden City, NY: Doubleday, 1984), e.g., 70–71, 94–97. Brown also identified what he called the "Johannine School" within the larger community. This group consisted of "the tradition-bearers and interpreters . . . who are vehicles of the Paraclete, the only teacher" (96–97).

20. Brown, *Introduction to John,* 183.

21. Martyn, *History and Theology in the Fourth Gospel,* was originally published by Harper & Row in 1968, then revised and enlarged in a 1979 edition from Abingdon Press. In 2003 Westminster John Knox issued the third edition as part of their "New Testament Library."

22. For an excellent survey of Martyn's contributions in the context of twentieth-century Johannine scholarship see D. Moody Smith, "The Contributions of J. Louis Martyn to the Understanding of the Gospel of John," in Martyn, *History and Theology in the Fourth Gospel.* NTL (3rd ed. Louisville: Westminster John Knox, 2003) 1–23. See also J. Louis Martyn, *The Gospel of John in Christian History: Essays for Interpreters.* Theological Inquiries: Studies in Contemporary Biblical and Theological Problems, ed. Lawrence Boadt, c.s.p. (New York: Paulist, 1978) 90–121.

23. Nearly twenty-nine years ago I pronounced the theory of the expulsion from the synagogue the most promising proposal for the concrete setting for the Gospel of John, and I dared even to call the new understanding of the setting for John resulting from the theory "the lasting contribution of the last quarter of the twentieth century to Johannine scholarship." Kysar, *The Fourth Evangelist and His Gospel: An Examination of Contemporary Scholarship* (Minneapolis: Augsburg, 1975) 149–56.

24. Another influential voice in the emergence of the Johannine community concept is Klaus Wengst, *Bedrängte Gemeinde und verherrlichter Christus: Der historische Ort des Johannesevangeliums als Schlüssel zu seiner Interpretation.* BTS 5 (Neukirchen-Vluyn: Neukirchener Verlag, 1981).

25. Wayne A. Meeks, "The Man from Heaven in Johannine Sectarianism," *JBL* 91 (1972) 44–72; reprinted in Ashton, *The Interpretation of John,* 169–206. Meeks's method continues to influence scholarship today. See, for instance, James F. McGrath, *John's Apologetic Christology: Legitimation and Development in Johannine Christology.* SNTSMS 111 (Cambridge: Cambridge University Press, 2001).

26. I bypass the work of Oscar Cullmann on this subject partly because it proved to be less influential than the three discussed above and because Cullmann's argument is less complete and convincing. See his *The Johannine Circle,* trans. John Bowden (Philadelphia: Westminster, 1976). For critiques of Cullmann and Meeks see Brown, *The Community of the Beloved Disciple,* 176–78 (as well as his review mentioned on p. 38, n. 57) and Kysar, *The Fourth Evangelist,* 182–84 and (more briefly) "The Fourth Gospel: A Report on Recent Research," *ANRW.* Principat 2/25, ed. Hildegard Temporini and Wolfgang Haase (Berlin: Walter de Gruyter, 1984) 2424 and 2444–45.

27. See, for instance, Brown, *The Community of the Beloved Disciple,* 88–91.

28. See, for instance, James H. Charlesworth, ed., *Qumran and John* (London: Chapman, 1972) and Herbert Braun, *Qumran und das Neue Testament*. 2 vols. (Tübingen: J. C. B. Mohr, 1966).

29. In 1968 A. M. Hunter spoke of the dangers of "Scrollomania" but, nonetheless, went on to say that "what makes their discovery important is that, for the first time, they give us a body of thought which may provide an actual background for the Fourth Gospel," in *According to John: The New Look at the Fourth Gospel* (Philadelphia: Westminster, 1968) 27.

30. David Rensberger, *Johannine Faith and Liberating Community* (Philadelphia: Westminster, 1988) 19–20. I am indebted to Professor Rensberger for the suggestion that the rise of the concept of Johannine community in scholarship was due, in part at least, to the discoveries at Qumran.

31. For a contemporary example see David Ihenacho, *The Community of Eternal Life: The Study of the Meaning of Life for the Johannine Community* (Lanham, MD: University Press of America, 2001).

32. See *Interpretation* 31 (1977). Those articles were reprinted in James Luther Mays, ed., *Interpreting the Gospels* (Philadelphia: Fortress, 1981) 247–306.

33. Kysar, *Evangelist,* 269–70.

34. Jerome Neyrey, *An Ideology of Revolt: John's Christology in Social-Science Perspective* (Philadelphia: Fortress, 1988) and Norman Peterson, *The Gospel of John and the Sociology of Light: Language and Characterization in the Fourth Gospel* (Valley Forge, PA: Trinity Press International, 1993).

35. See Brown's own review of "Recent Reconstructions of Johannine Community History" in *The Community of the Beloved Disciple, 171–82*. The impact of concepts of community on theories of composition, already present in Brown's commentary, is represented in such studies as Urban C. von Wahlde, "The History and Social Context of the Johannine Community," *Int* 49 (1995) 379–89.

36. E.g., Schnelle, *Antidocetic Christology,* especially 25–36.

37. Luke Timothy Johnson, *The Real Jesus: The Misguided Quest for the Historical Jesus and the Truth of the Traditional Gospels* (San Francisco: HarperSanFrancisco, 1996) 100.

38. See Samuel Byrskog's recent review of Bultmann's *History of the Synoptic Tradition* in *JBL* 122 (2003) 549–55. He writes, "the tradition ultimately reflects a manifold communication of how the past was envisioned in the oral histories of various individuals" (551); see also 554.

39. Brown claims there is "no sharp distinction between community and personal union with Jesus" (*Introduction to John,* 226; see also 229).

40. See the work of Adele Reinhartz, e.g., "The Johannine Community and Its Jewish Neighbors: A Reappraisal," in Fernando F. Segovia, ed., *What Is John? Volume II. Literary and Social Readings of the Fourth Gospel.* SBLSymS 7 (Atlanta: Scholars, 1998), 121–30; "'Jews' and Jews in the Fourth Gospel," in Reimund Bieringer, Didier Pollefeyt, and Fréderique Vandecasteele-Vanneuville, eds., *Anti-Judaism and the Fourth Gospel: Papers of the Leuven Colloquium.* Jewish and Christian Heritage Series 1 (Assen: Van Gorcum, 2001) 352–53; *Befriending the Beloved Disciple: A Jewish Reading of the Gospel of John* (New York: Continuum, 2001) 40–48.

41. See the recent and thorough collection *Anti-Judaism and the Fourth Gospel,* cited in the previous note, and Manfred Diefenbach, *Der Konflikt Jesu mit den "Juden" : Ein Versuch zur Lösung der johanneischen Antijudaismus. Diskussion mit des antiken Handlungsverständnisses.* NTAbh n.s. 41 (Münster: Aschendorff, 2002).

42. See N. A. Beck, *Mature Christianity: The Recognition and Repudiation of the Anti-Jewish Polemic of the New Testament* (Selinsgrove: Susquehanna University Press, 1985), especially 250–51.

43. Meeks, "The Man from Heaven," 194 (italics in original).

44. See the following: Reuven Kimelman, "*Birkat Ha-Minim* and the Lack of Evidence for an Anti-Christian Jewish Prayer in Late Antiquity," in E. P. Sanders, ed., *Jewish and Christian Self-*

Definition. Aspects of Judaism in the Greco-Roman Period 2 (Minneapolis: Fortress, 1981) 244; S. T. Katz, "Issues in the Separation of Judaism and Christianity After 70 C.E. A Reconsideration," *JBL* 103 (1984) 43–76; and more recently Pieter W. van der Horst, "The *Birkat Ha-Minin* in Recent Research," *ExpTim* 105 (1994) 367–68. Brown himself seems to have agreed with Kimelman's conclusions, even though he still endorsed the idea of some kind of break from the synagogue: *Introduction to John,* 213. See Moloney's "Editor's Note" on p. 68 in that volume.

45. Edward Klink of the University of St. Andrews kindly suggested that I look at Richard Bauckham, ed., *The Gospels for All Christians: Rethinking the Gospel Audiences* (Grand Rapids: Eerdmans, 1998) which raises some additional issues concerning our topic. Unfortunately, I was not able to acquire and use it before the manuscript was due.

46. Kysar, "The Fourth Gospel: A Report on Recent Research," 426.

47. I offer my own view of the gospel as evidence of such a movement away from, in particular, the theory espoused by Martyn in "The Expulsion From the Synagogue: A Tale of a Theory," forthcoming.

48. See the helpful article by Thomas E. Provence, "The Sovereign Subject Matter: Hermeneutics in the *Church Dogmatics*," in Donald K. McKim, ed., *A Guide to Contemporary Hermeneutics: Major Trends in Biblical Interpretation* (Grand Rapids: Eerdmans, 1986) 241–62.

49. Examples include Hans W. Frei, *The Eclipse of Biblical Narrative* (New Haven: Yale University Press, 1974); Brevard S. Childs, *Biblical Theology in Crisis* (Philadelphia: Westminster, 1970); Ferdinand Hahn, "Problems of Historical Criticism," in idem, *Historical Investigation and New Testament Faith: Two Essays* (Philadelphia: Fortress, 1983); Arthur Wainwright, *Beyond Biblical Criticism: Encountering Jesus in Scripture* (Atlanta: John Knox, 1982). The assault took on a new tone in 1973 with Walter Wink's now famous (or infamous) declaration, "Historical biblical criticism is bankrupt" in his *The Bible in Human Transformation: Toward a New Paradigm for Biblical Study* (Philadelphia: Fortress, 1973) 1.

50. The Bible and Culture Collective, *The Postmodern Bible* (New Haven: Yale University Press, 1995) 14 (italics in original). See also Tania Oldenhage, *Parables for Our Time: Rereading New Testament Scholarship After the Holocaust.* AAR Culture Criticism Series (New York: Oxford University Press, 2002).

51. This whole paragraph is indebted to Fred W. Burnett, "Historiography," in A. K. M. Adam, ed., *Handbook of Postmodern Biblical Interpretation* (St. Louis: Chalice, 2000) 110–11, at 111.

52. As an example of how radically social-scientific studies have revised historical criticism see Bruce J. Malina's review of D. Moody Smith, Jr., *John.* Abingdon New Testament Commentaries (Nashville: Abingdon, 1999) in *RBL* 12 (2002), n.p. [10 December 2002], online at: http://www.bookreviews.org.

53. R. Alan Culpepper, *The Anatomy of the Fourth Gospel: A Study in Literary Design.* Foundations and Facets, New Testament (Philadelphia: Fortress, 1989) 3–4. See also Paul Ricoeur, "The Hermeneutical Function of Distanciation," in John B. Thompson, ed. and trans., *Paul Ricoeur: Hermenetuics and Human Sciences: Essays on Language, Action and Interpretation* (Cambridge: Cambridge University Press, 1981) 131–44.

54. Although the lines are blurred, structuralism and narrative criticism assume that meaning is in the text. At least, as Mark Allan Powell has written, these critical methods "focus on ways in which the text determines the reader's response rather than on ways in which the reader determines meaning" (as reader response criticism supposes): *What Is Narrative Criticism?* Guides to Biblical Study, New Testament Series, ed. Dan O. Via, Jr. (Minneapolis: Fortress, 1990) 18.

55. See, e.g., Elizabeth Struthers Malbon's discussion of the difference between redaction and narrative criticisms, "Narrative Criticism: How Does the Story Mean?" in Janice Capel Anderson and Stephen D. Moore, eds., *Mark and Method: New Approaches in Biblical Studies* (Minneapolis: Fortress, 1992) 35.

56. *The Postmodern Bible,* 42.

57. See, e.g., Fernando F. Segovia, "Introduction," in R. Alan Culpepper and Fernando F. Segovia, eds., *The Fourth Gospel from a Literary Perspective. Semeia* 53 (Atlanta: Scholars,

1991) 16. Segovia writes: "the meaning of the text is now located within a much wider spectrum ranging from the reader as member of an interpretative community to the interaction between reader and text. . . . As such the focus of attention shifts to the reader and to the process of negotiation between text and reader in the construction of meaning . . . . Consequently, *the former search for a sole and objective meaning yields to an acceptance of a plurality of meanings,* while the former mode of discussion by means of attack and dismissal gives way to an emphasis on the social location of the various readers of the text." (Italics supplied.)

58. See the excellent collection of essays in Fernando F. Segovia and Mary Ann Tolbert, eds., *Reading from this Place.* 2 vols. (Minneapolis: Fortress, 1995).

Community, History, and Text(s)

A Response to Robert Kysar

Hans-Josef Klauck
University of Chicago

A. The basic question: referentiality

First I want to thank Robert Kysar for his challenging reflections on "The Whence and Whither of the Johannine Community." In the first part of his fine contribution he has traced the rise of this concept and shown why it has enjoyed and still enjoys such popularity in biblical scholarship. Then, in the second part, he has summarized some basic shifts in our ways of approaching texts and history that could in the end prove devastating for any further defense of the very existence of a Johannine community.

I basically agree with his description of the genealogy of the community theory, and I share some of his doubts concerning its future. Even some of my experiences are quite similar to his. I remember quite well that I was just fascinated when, as a young scholar, I read for the first time the relevant studies of J. Louis Martyn, Raymond E. Brown, and Klaus Wengst, which had been published between 1968 and 1981.[1] I even gave a successful seminar for my doctoral students on these topics in the summer of 1984.[2] Since then I have come to doubt more and more if these evolved reconstructions can really bear close scrutiny and, even more importantly, if they can serve as a key for establishing the true meaning of the Johannine texts—if such a true meaning exists at all. We all have felt by now the impact of new, text-centered methodologies and postmodern theory,[3] but not all of us are willing simply to throw historical criticism overboard.

But what can we do now? By way of response I propose to take up a question I consider basic and show some very modest ways to find partial answers at least. The basic question is about referentiality of texts. Do texts only refer to themselves and function as a closed system (structural and narrative criticism)? Do they, beyond that, only refer to other texts and textual worlds (intertextuality)? Do they, if they open up at all, only open up to the readers who create the meaning (reader-response criticism, reception history, and, in some ways, rhetorical criticism, too)? Or do they refer also to extratextual realities, events, figures, social structures, and so on? Do they, in other words, refer to their historical context (historical criticism; social science approach)?[4] And what does that imply? Do we need this knowledge at all, or are we better off without?

B. Partial answers: some texts

All this partly depends on the genre of the texts we have to deal with, I would say. There is a group of texts whose external referentiality is usually admitted, namely letters, especially documentary letters, as we know them in the thousands from ancient papyri. Michael Trapp, the editor of a new anthology of Greek and Latin letters published in 2003, writes in the introduction that there is a certain "degree of fictionalizing involved in the various letters in this collection,"[5] but that documentary letters especially are "of huge value to the historian, affording a ground-level view of aspects of ancient life."[6] The act of reading such letters today he describes as follows: "we listen in to fragments of ancient conversations, filling in the gaps in our contextual knowledge as best we may, drawn in and at the same time tantalized by the incomplete hints and allusions that correspondents in the know can safely limit themselves to."[7]

1. 2 John and 3 John

The same could be said of reading 2 John and 3 John, too. That these two short documents with their close correspondence to the ancient letter format were fictions is rarely defended.[8] Most scholars accept them at face value. But if it is true that there are "incomplete hints and allusions" to extratextual figures and events there, we have to fill "in the gaps in our contextual knowledge as best we may," and we will be "tantalized" by the incompleteness of the information we get. In 3 John we hear about the elder, Gaius, the brothers and Diotrephes, and, most interesting, a community (ἐκκλησία) is mentioned twice: the community of the elder in v. 6 and the community of Diotrephes, as it seems, in vv. 9-10. In 2 John the community is found disguised as the "elect lady and her children," addressed by the elder in v. 1, and as "the children of your elect sister," who send their greetings in v. 13. Community matters also seem to form the context of the order in v. 10: "Do not receive into the house or welcome anyone who comes to you and does not bring this teaching," especially if we keep in mind that house churches would have been the natural place for teaching.[9] In a true letter the warning in v. 7 ("Many deceivers have gone out into the world") should refer to a real danger, too. That is not to deny its apocalyptic overtones, and I admit that even here processes are involved that we might call fictitious, since (to quote Michael Trapp again) "letter writers select what they are going to say and what they are not going to say, and choose how they are going to slant what they do say, and thus construct a personalized version of the reality they are referring to,"[10] and they also "construct and project a *persona*," which might be very different from "their character as perceived by others than their correspondent of the moment."[11] But this is a matter of "degree of fictionalizing involved,"[12] not one of principle. In principle, letters are not simply self-referential, but refer to an external context, too.

Looking, therefore, at the context of 2 John and 3 John could give us some clues for the existence of communities where these texts were produced, read, and kept—otherwise we would not know them. There is even some materiality involved here, since our electronic versions in Bible Works are finally based on some scraps of papyrus from the late first or early second century C.E. We must be modest in our expectations, of course. We might not be able to say very much about the shape and history of these communities, and by trying to construct their profile we have not yet fully explained our two short documents, but only begun to do so. But we are dealing with a principle here, not with the details.

Even if this might seem a rather bold move, my thesis now is that this principle of external referentiality also holds true to a slighter degree for other writings of the Johannine corpus. Let us look first at 1 John.

2. 1 John

Our task would be easier if we could deal with 1 John as another example of a documentary letter. But this is not possible. The most distinctive features of the letter format, an epistolary opening (prescript) and closing (greetings, visit talk), are completely missing. The question of the genre of 1 John is not yet really solved. In my opinion the peculiar form of the opening and closing of 1 John is to be explained as conscious imitation, *mimēsis,* of the beginning and the ending of the Gospel of John, that is, in other words, by intertextuality. But that is disputed, I know.

This leaves us with some features in the body of the text that seem to hint at a real process of communication as its *Sitz im Leben:*

- the distinction between "we" and "you" (plural) in 1:5 and frequently elsewhere; between "I" and "you" in 2:1 and at several other places;
- the address "children" (τεκνία) in 2:1, 12, 28; 3:7, 18; 4:14; 5:21; παιδία in 2:14, 18) or "beloved" (in 2:7; 3:2, 21; 4:1, 7, 11; cf. ἀδελφοί in 3:13);
- the references to the act of writing: "I write these things to you" in 5:13 (cf. 2:1, 7-8, 12-14, 21, 26);

- the inclusive "we" of passages like 3:1-2 ("now we are children of God") or the "slogans" of 1:6-10 ("If we say that we have communion with him . . .").

Besides that, we should not forget the obvious correspondence in idiom and topics of 1 John especially with 2 John, to a lesser degree also with 3 John, which means with letters of the more documentary type.[13] I am therefore not convinced by the thesis of Hansjörg Schmid, who defines the genre of 1 John as "foundational manifest," more fictional than factual in character and relatively autonomous, i.e., not bound to any context or situation.[14] He therefore employs a mixture of intertextuality, constructivism, systemic theory, and speech-act theory to explain the text—in my eyes a rather breathtaking combination. A key issue is the interpretation of 1 John 2:19: "They went out from us, but they did not belong to us; for if they had belonged to us, they would have remained with us." I still feel that this sentence is best understood as referring to a real schism in a community, with one group—perhaps even the group of the author—going their own way.[15] There are enough textual elements and theoretical considerations that help to defend this position.

3. The Fourth Gospel

We come to the Gospel of John, which is a narrative, to be sure, but is it also a purely fictitious one? Not everything, but quite a bit depends on the genre of the gospel. A strong argument has been made in recent discussion for understanding the gospels as specimens of Hellenistic biography.[16] As such they would belong to the large realm of historiographic writings, and this type of text by definition cannot be completely self-referential, but will refer to extratextual events and persons.

I do not want to decide this very sensitive generic question here and now, since there is still one other argument: Even pure fiction, at least in antiquity, cannot do without a minimum of external referentiality, as we can see when looking at the Hellenistic-Roman novels. Otherwise articles like "Hellenistic History in Chariton of Aphrodisias" (the author of the novel *Callirhoe*)[17] or a book with the title *Fiction as History*[18] could not have been written. Let us for a moment assume that the Fourth Gospel was a piece of pure fiction, like Chariton's *Callirhoe*. Even then nobody would maintain that Pontius Pilate in John 18–19 was a purely fictional character. In his case we not only know other texts that prove his existence but we also have a famous inscription, found at Caesarea, with his name and his office *(praefectus)*.[19] And stone beats text, as we have learned by the case of the James ossuary. We might add: stone, even if faked, beats text, even if true.

But this, of course, does not yet lead us to a Johannine community. I will not come back to the much discussed expulsion from the synagogue,[20] especially not since two other excellent contributions on this controversial issue are found in this volume. I will focus instead on another detail that I find quite instructive. In the Fourth Gospel we meet Jews secretly believing in Christ without confessing him publicly, "for they loved human glory more than the glory of God" (John 12:43). These "crypto-Christians" play an important role in descriptions of the Johannine community. It is much to the credit of Martyn that he looked for additional evidence, and he found it in the Pseudo-Clementines.[21] There the relevant passages belong to a section (*Rec.* 1.27-71) that might come from an earlier Jewish-Christian source of around 200 C.E. that does not share John's criticism of these people.[22] We might add Epiphanius, who knew such secret Jewish Christians, too.[23] This phenomenon, then, does not seem to be a product of the historical imagination of some exegetes without conclusive evidence in the texts.

Again, our aims should be more modest than they have been before. But a more general summary like the following one, which I take from Helen C. Orchard's study, *Courting Betrayal,* still seems to have some foothold in the text itself: "The historical context of the Gospel of John was that of a community in crisis, experiencing persecution and alienation from both Jewish and Roman sources. This resulted in the group developing a sectarian attitude, with victimization being both a frequent experience and a contributing factor to shaping its identity."[24] Or looking for a Johannine trajectory in early Christianity could perhaps be a more valid approach that integrates some elements of the community theory.

4. The Acts of John

It would be helpful for this project if we could somewhat expand the corpus of Johannine writings. Here I am not thinking of Revelation, but of the Acts of John, which have so far not been used very often for this task.[25] Unfortunately this writing has been transmitted to us only in a fragmentary state. In its full form, including the "gnostic" chapters 94–102 and 109, it might have been composed as early as 150 C.E. somewhere in Asia Minor, though probably not in Ephesus.[26] This brings us, in time and place, rather close to the canonical *Corpus Johanneum.* A comparison could develop in two directions:[27]

The "gnostic" section in chapters 94–102 clearly refers to the Fourth Gospel, but does so by flatly rejecting its teaching. At the very hour of the crucifixion John meets the Lord in a cave on the Mount of Olives. The Lord shows him a cosmic cross of light and tells him: "This is not the cross of wood which you will see when you go down (to the city); neither am I he who is upon the cross" (99). "I have suffered none of the things which they will tell of me . . . . You hear . . . that I was pierced, yet I was not wounded . . . that blood flowed from me, yet it did not flow" (101). This is part of a fully developed docetic reading of the Passion story. If Raymond Brown's reconstruction of the christology of the opponents in 1 John is approximately right, then their thinking might have taken exactly this turn in the decades between 1 John and Acts of John.[28]

The program of the main body of the narrative could be summed up by the slogan "Claiming Ephesus for John."[29] John, not Paul, is chosen "for the apostleship among the Gentiles" (112). He is blinded for a while by the Lord to prevent him from marrying (113). He seeks the confrontation with Artemis of Ephesus (37) and wins it by destroying her temple (42), which is more than Paul ever did. No trace of Paul's mission is found in Ephesus; it is John who introduces Christianity to this city. This corresponds to the general observation that Ephesus in the second century more and more becomes John's city, but the antagonism in this case is nevertheless remarkable. It looks as if a group, focused on John, aggressively tries to defend its identity and establish its authority—traces of a Johannine trajectory?

Looking back at this section, I can only quote approvingly Richard Pervo: "Investigation of 'the Community of the Beloved Disciple' might well take into account the communities visible in such texts of later Johannism as these Acts."[30] That is another example of the fact that dealing with texts—of course not only with canonical ones—is our main business as exegetes, and as long as we focus on that, there might be a chance that we will find convincing answers.

C. An open end: history

It is time to come to an end. There are theoretical discussions also going on in modern historiography.[31] If I have understood them correctly, historians no longer pretend that they can reconstruct the past. What they do is construct history. The past can never be repeated or revived, but textual and material remains of the past may be used to construct meaningful narratives that help us to a better understanding of the situation we find ourselves in. That implies that the present time we live in will always have an impact on the way we look at our data and on the kind of questions we ask. But we have no choice; we have to do this task. The adequacy and inadequacy of our constructions of history are negotiated by the academic community (please note that I avoid speaking of "truth" and "decided," but choose "adequacy" and "negotiated" instead).

That is exactly what we are doing just now, in discussing the rise and potential fall of an influential and respectable model in our field, i.e., the construction of the history of the Johannine community. That leads us back to the main paper, to respond to which has been my privilege. In the end, you see, our evaluations of this issue, Robert Kysar's and mine, are not very far apart.

Notes

1. J. Louis Martyn, *History and Theology in the Fourth Gospel* (New York: Harper & Row, 1968; 3rd ed. Louisville and London: Westminster John Knox, 2003); Raymond E. Brown, *The Community of the Beloved Disciple: The Life, Loves, and Hates of an Individual Church in New Testament Times* (New York: Paulist, 1979); Klaus Wengst, *Bedrängte Gemeinde und verherrlichter Christus: Der historische Ort des Johannesevangeliums als Schlüssel zu seiner Interpretation.* Biblisch-theologische Studien 5 (Neukirchen-Vluyn: Neukirchener Verlag, 1981; 3rd ed. as *Bedrängte Gemeinde und verherrlichter Christus: Ein Versuch über das Johannesevangelium* [München: Kaiser, 1990]); see, as an early, perceptive criticism of Wengst, Joachim Kügler, "Das Johannesevangelium und seine Gemeinde—kein Thema für Science Fiction," *BN* 23 (1984) 48–62; Martyn's "dramatization" of John 9 is critically reviewed by Colleen M. Conway, "The Production of the Johannine Community: A New Historicist Perspective," *JBL* 121 (2002) 479–95; see also Thomas L. Brodie, *The Quest for the Origin of John's Gospel: A Source-Oriented Approach* (New York and Oxford: Oxford University Press, 1993) 15–21, and Tobias Hägerland, "John's Gospel: A Two-Level Drama?" *JSNT* 25 (2003) 309–22.

2. At the University of Würzburg, Germany. We started, by the way, with Wilhelm Baldensperger, *Der Prolog des vierten Evangeliums: Sein polemisch-apologetischer Zweck* (Freiburg: J. C. B. Mohr, 1898), and its review by William Wrede, *Göttingische gelehrte Anzeigen* 162 (1900) 1–26. We used the German edition of Brown's book: *Ringen um die Gemeinde: Der Weg der Kirche nach den Johanneischen Schriften* (Salzburg: Müller, 1982), and, besides Martyn and Wengst, we also read Oscar Cullmann, *Der johanneische Kreis: Sein Platz im Spätjudentum, in der Jüngerschaft Jesu und im Urchristentum. Zum Ursprung des Johannesevangeliums* (Tübingen: J. C. B. Mohr, 1975).

3. See, in relation to our topic, Jeffrey L. Staley, "What Can a Postmodern Approach to the Fourth Gospel Add to Contemporary Debates About Its Historical Situation?" in Robert T. Fortna and Tom Thatcher, eds., *Jesus in Johannine Tradition* (Louisville and London: Westminster John Knox, 2001) 47–57; still from within the historical paradigm, the community model is also criticized by Richard Bauckham, "The Audience of the Fourth Gospel," ibid. 101–11; he sees the Gospel of John addressed not to individual communities, but to the whole church and even to non-Christian readers; cf. idem, ed., *The Gospels for All Christians: Rethinking the Gospel Audiences* (Grand Rapids: Eerdmans, 1998).

4. The social-science approach (see, e.g., Jerome Neyrey, *An Ideology of Revolt: John's Christology in Social-Science Perspective* [Philadelphia: Fortress, 1986]) would also be affected by a decline of historical criticism. It relies on data from the past (texts, artefacts, inscriptions) to be able to construct social values like honor and shame and social structures like patronage. Where else could it get these concepts from? I have the impression that this is rarely seen or admitted.

5. Michael Trapp, *Greek and Latin Letters: An Anthology with Translation.* Cambridge Greek and Latin Classics (Cambridge: Cambridge University Press, 2003) 3.

6. Ibid. 10.

7. Ibid. 11.

8. For some exceptions see the discussion in Hans-Josef Klauck, *Der zweite und dritte Johannesbrief.* EKKNT 23/2 (Zürich: Benziger; Neukirchen-Vluyn: Neukirchener Verlag, 1992) 21.

9. For house churches in 2 John and 3 John cf. now the valuable discussion in Roger W. Gehring, *Hausgemeinde und Mission: Die Bedeutung antiker Häuser und Hausgemeinschaften—von Jesus bis Paulus.* Bibelwissenschaftliche Monographien 9 (Giessen and Basel: Brunnen, 2000) 468–77. English: *House Church and Mission: The Importance of Household Structures in Early Christianity* (Peabody, MA: Hendrickson, 2004) 281–87.

10. Trapp, *Greek and Latin Letters*, 4.

11. Ibid.

12. Ibid. 3.

13. Detailed lists are found in Hans-Josef Klauck, *Die Johannesbriefe*. EdF 276 (2nd ed. Darmstadt: Wissenschaftliche Buchgesellschaft, 1995) 111–16.

14. Hansjörg Schmid, *Gegner im 1. Johannesbrief? Zu Konstruktion und Selbstreferenz im johanneischen Sinnsystem*. BWANT 159 (Stuttgart: Kohlhammer, 2002), especially 34, 46, 56; more careful is in this respect is Terry Griffith, *Keep Yourselves from Idols: A New Look at 1 John*. JSNTSup 233 (Sheffield: Sheffield Academic Press, 2002), though he, too, opts for a non-polemical reading of 1 John.

15. This position is misrepresented in L. J. Lietaert Peerbolte, *The Antecedents of Antichrist: A Traditio-Historical Study of the Earliest Christian Views on Eschatological Opponents*. JSJSup 60 (Leiden, New York, and Köln: Brill, 1996) 98, n. 2; that the author of 1 John may have used Deut 13:13-14 for his description does not imply that his opponents are fictitious; otherwise Peerbolte produces a fine exegesis of the disputed passage 1 John 2:18-27.

16. I mention only Charles H. Talbert, *What is a Gospel? The Genre of the Canonical Gospels* (Philadelphia: Fortress, 1977); Richard A. Burridge, *What are the Gospels? A Comparison with Graeco-Roman Biography*. SNTSMS 70 (Cambridge and New York: Cambridge University Press, 1992); Detlev Dormeyer, *The New Testament among the Writings of Antiquity*, trans. Rosemarie Kossov, ed. Stanley E. Porter. The Biblical Seminar 55 (Sheffield: Sheffield Academic Press, 1998) 214–43; Dirk Frickenschmidt, *Evangelium als Biographie: Die vier Evangelien im Rahmen antiker Erzählkunst*. TANZ 22 (Basel and Tübingen: A. Francke, 1997).

17. See Christopher P. Jones, "Hellenistic History in Chariton of Aphrodisias," *Chiron* 22 (1992) 91–102; on a more theoretical level see Tore Wigren, "Narratives and References," *Studia Theologica* 56 (2002) 164–91.

18. Glen W. Bowersock, *Fiction as History: Nero to Julian*. Sather Classical Lectures 58 (Berkeley: University of California Press, 1994).

19. See, with a new reconstruction, Géza Alföldy, "Pontius Pilatus und das Tiberieum von Caesarea Maritima," *Studia Classica Israelica* 18 (1999) 85–108.

20. Robert Kysar, "The Expulsion from the Synagogue: A Tale of a Theory," forthcoming; see especially Adele Reinhartz, "The Johannine Community and Its Jewish Neighbors: A Reappraisal," in Fernando F. Segovia, ed., *"What is John?"* vol. 2: *Literary and Social Readings of the Fourth Gospel*. SBLSymS 7 (Atlanta: Scholars, 1998) 111–38, and cf. on the closely connected issue of anti-Judaism in John the exhaustive treatment in Reimund Bieringer, Didier Pollefeyt, and Frédérique Vandecasteele-Vanneuville, eds., *Anti-Judaism and the Fourth Gospel: Papers of the Leuven Colloquium, 2000*. Jewish and Christian Heritage Series 1 (Assen: Van Gorcum, 2001).

21. J. Louis Martyn, "Clementine Recognitions I,33-71, Jewish Christianity, and the Fourth Gospel," in Jacob Jervell and Wayne A. Meeks, eds., *God's Christ and His People: Studies in Honour of Nils Alstrup Dahl* (Oslo, Bergen, and Tromsö: Universitetsforlaget, 1977) 265–95.

22. See F. Stanley Jones, *An Ancient Jewish Christian Source on the History of Christianity: Pseudo-Clementine Recognitions 1.27-71*. SBLTT 37 (Atlanta: Scholars, 1995).

23. Ibid. 165.

24. Helen C. Orchard, *Courting Betrayal: Jesus as Victim in the Gospel of John*. JSNTSup 161 (Sheffield: Sheffield Academic Press, 1998) 264. On the community see also 65–95 and 94–149; the qualification "sectarian attitude" in this quotation would certainly need special discussion, which cannot be done here; I am a bit skeptical about importing the modern notion of "sect" into the Johannine writings, but I must admit that the "sectarian" reading of John in Robert H. Gundry, *Jesus the Word according to John the Sectarian: A Paleofundamentalist Manifesto for Contemporary Evangelicalism, Especially Its Elites, in North America* (Grand Rapids: Eerdmans, 2002), is in its own way challenging, provocative, and also rewarding. On a community in distress see also Andrew T. Lincoln, *Truth on Trial: The Lawsuit Motif in the Fourth Gospel* (Peabody, MA: Hendrickson, 2000) 265–332.

25. A welcome exception is Richard J. Pervo, "Johannine Trajectories in the *Acts of John*," *Apocrypha* 3 (1992) 47–68.

26. See Pieter J. Lalleman, *The Acts of John: A Two-Stage Initiation into Johannine Gnosticism*. Studies on the Apocryphal Acts of the Apostles 4 (Leuven: Peeters, 1998) 245–70.

27. For text and commentary see Eric Junod and Jean-Daniel Kaestli, *Acta Johannis,* vol. I: *Praefatio—Textus;* vol. II: *Textus alii—Commentarius—Indices.* CCSA 1–2 (Turnhout: Brepols, 1983).

28. Cf. Lallemann, *Acts of John,* 246–53.

29. See Trevor W. Thompson, "Claiming Ephesus: The Apocryphal John and the Canonical Paul," Term Paper at the University of Chicago, Spring Quarter 2003. The author has graciously allowed me to make use of some of the fine insights of his unpublished paper.

30. Pervo, "Trajectories," 68.

31. See Paul Ricoeur, *Time and Narrative,* vols. 1–3, trans. Kathleen McLaughlin and David Pellauer (Chicago: University of Chicago Press, 1984–88); Christoph Conrad and Martina Kassel, *Geschichte schreiben in der Postmoderne: Beiträge zur aktuellen Diskussion.* UB 9318 (Stuttgart: Reclam, 1994); Volker Sellin, *Einführung in die Geschichtswissenschaft.* Sammlung Vandenhoeck (Göttingen: Vandenhoeck & Ruprecht, 1995); Hans-Jürgen Goertz, *Umgang mit Geschichte: Eine Einführung in die Geschichtstheorie.* Kulturen und Ideen 555 (Reinbek bei Hamburg: Rowohlt, 1995); Jörn Rüsen, *Zerbrechende Zeit: Über den Sinn der Geschichte* (Köln: Böhlau, 2001).

Chapter Four

Methodological Considerations in the Study of John's Interaction with First-Century Judaism

Rabbi Burton L. Visotzky

Jewish Theological Seminary, New York

Rabbi Yohanan taught that when the living quote the teachings of a scholar who has died, the departed scholar's lips whisper in the grave.[1] I offer my contribution in memory of my teacher, our teacher, Raymond E. Brown, in the hope of continuing a conversation we began almost three decades ago. It is my prayer that in our exchange here we yet can hear Ray whispering.

I. Disclosure

I first studied the Gospel of John as a student of Father Raymond E. Brown, in the fall of 1976, during my senior year in rabbinical school. In the years that followed my ordination I worked toward a Ph.D. in Rabbinics and became (in 1980) a visiting faculty member at Union Theological Seminary, where Ray and J. Louis Martyn became close colleagues whom I helped with teaching and supervising the dissertations of their doctoral students. It is important that my biases favoring my friends and mentors be set out at the beginning, for it was under the sway of Professors Brown and Martyn that I cut my teeth on New Testament studies before moving on to Patristics as the cognate literature for my own work in Rabbinics.

In the spirit of full disclosure I offer a bit more about who I am, so that the remarks that follow may be put in context. I am a Jew, born in Chicago of Illinois, but brought up in New York City at the feet of the descendents of Gamaliel, educated according to the strict manner of the law of our fathers, being zealous for God, as you all are this day. Circumcised on the eighth day, of the people of Israel, of the tribe of Levi, a Hebrew born of a Hebrew; as to the law, a Pharisee. Brethren, I am a Pharisee, a son of Pharisees.[2] I am also a

Conservative rabbi and the Nathan and Janet Appleman Professor of Midrash and Interreligious Studies at the Jewish Theological Seminary.

I do not think that one can study the Gospel of John without regular recourse to the literatures and artifacts of first-century Judaism. This is not nearly as simple an undertaking as it might first seem, despite John's own Jewish proclivities,[3] and the title of my paper is meant to signal the need for a hermeneutic of suspicion when combining the terms Gospel of John and Judaism in a sentence. In the last few decades it has been far more in vogue to link John with *anti*-Judaism. In those decades the gospel itself has served as prime, if not probative, evidence of first-century Judaism's persecution of early Christianity. This religiously sensitive issue, post-Holocaust and post-Vatican II, of necessity colors everything I and probably almost anyone else could say about John and Judaism.

II. Four-Level Drama

In short, Jews read John differently than do Christians. I suspect that in his own community Jews read John's gospel differently than did those who came from pagan families. I will not rehearse here decades (and more) of scholarship on John. I would like to offer the observation that the Gospel of John is a four-level drama. The *first level* is the story of Jesus, his ministry, and his crucifixion. The *second level* is the story of John's own community, whoever they were, expressed through the first level but peeping through on its own here and there. For them the drama of level one went beyond Jesus' crucifixion to his resurrection and divinity. Thus far I agree with the perspicacious observations of Louis Martyn. But when Lou wrote his *History and Theology in the Fourth Gospel* he only acknowledged these two levels of the drama. As we will see, Professor Martyn's own moral probity combined with his tightly focused scholarship to produce difficulties for subsequent readers of his theory, as well as for the gospel seen through the lens of Martyn's hermeneutic.

The *third level* of John's gospel drama is that of the received text of the New Testament, and its interpretations and uses throughout the ensuing centuries. This is not the place to rehearse the sorry history of anti-Semitism caused and/or abetted by readings of the Fourth Gospel. Nevertheless, this history needs to be acknowledged by any modern interpreter of John. Anyone who reads the gospel stands as part of a long chain of tradition. Denying that Johannine interpretation has either been anti-Semitic or served anti-Semitism is exactly that, a case of denial.

I think that for the last fifty years there has been general agreement that this denial is as unhealthy as the anti-Semitism itself. This leads me to the *fourth level* of the drama. On this level *we* are the players in the drama. As readers and exegetes we acknowledge the complexities of New Testament interpretation. As scholars we recognize that all interpretation has a history, and not necessarily one of which we are proud.

Yet when I confronted Professor Martyn with the probability that his reading of the two-level drama might further rather than diminish anti-Semitism, Lou's response in essence was: let the chips fall where they may. I think that Martyn believed his job as an historian was to tell it "like it really was" and that should be sufficient. He did not reckon with Level Three, the long, sorry, anti-Semitic history of Johannine interpretation. Reading some of the polemic that has erupted subsequent to his innocent theory regarding the *Birkat HaMinim* (on which more below), one can only regret that Professor Martyn did not attend more to what I have designated as Level Three of the drama, the history of interpretation, along with Level Four, our own roles in the drama.

His colleague, Father Raymond E. Brown, was more attentive to the history of interpretation and the uses and abuses of modern hermeneutics. Perhaps it was Ray's training as a Roman Catholic or his sensitivities to what I might term Vatican II issues, but from the time of his *Community of the Beloved Disciple* up to his death he knew only too well how historical exegesis required moral exhortation to prevent abuse. Ray preached before Easter every year at Corpus Christi Church, conveniently located one block from both Union and Jewish Theological Seminaries, regarding the dangers of anti-Semitism inherent in unassisted interpretation of the gospel. Not so very long ago (April 1995) Ray wrote in the Jesuit weekly, *America,* exhorting his readers about the dilemma of the gospel and the necessity for Catholics to read it with an open and inclusive heart. Even from the grave, in his recent posthumously published *Introduction,* Ray speaks the warning, "in proclaiming John preachers must be careful to caution hearers that John's passages cannot be used to justify any ongoing hostility to Jewish people . . . ."[4] Father Brown accepted the exegesis of Professor Martyn, yet he appreciated what the possible implications of that interpretation could be for current Jewish-Christian relations.

If I might quibble with the gospel (8:39, 44) and class myself as a child of Abraham, I wish to speak for a few moments more about my problems with Abraham, Martyn, and John, before going on to lay out my methodological cautions, my quibbles with certain of Professor Brown's uses of Jewish sources, and finally, my revisitation of the issue that was so central to Lou Martyn's reading of John—the question of *aposynagōgos.*

III. Martyn and Brown on John

Even before the publication of *History and Theology,* a school of thought had been founded on Morningside Heights regarding the role of the Jews in the Fourth Gospel. In retrospect Ray Brown's stance on the issue in the John commentary makes clear that he and Lou Martyn were of like minds early on. Although Brown does not burden the line-by-line commentary with extended exegeses *ad loc* regarding the *aposynagōgos,* in his Introduction to the Anchor *Commentary*[5] Brown makes clear his association of the *Birkat HaMinim* with the *aposynagōgos*. J. Louis Martyn, in his treatment of the same, took the *Birkat HaMinim* and ran with it all the way to a theory of Jewish persecution of the Johannine church at the time of the writing of the gospel.

Both scholars, depending upon this association with a prayer presumably canonized at Yavneh in the mid-80s to early 90s of the first century, opted for a reasonably early date for the gospel. This dating ran to the earliest of the dates Brown had suggested in his *Introduction,* where he allowed for a latest dating of 100–110 C.E.[6] Father Brown published his first volume of *John* in 1966, and Professor Martyn published his *History and Theology* in 1968. By 1979, when Brown published *The Community of the Beloved Disciple,* the *Birkat HaMinim* theory itself had become gospel.[7]

The Brown/Martyn early dating allowed them to suggest that it was the *Jewish* community that initiated the break between Christianity and Judaism. According to this theory, thanks to the universal power of the Yavnean rabbis a ban was placed upon Christian attendance in the synagogue. It was assumed that Christians could not bear to hear themselves cursed in the daily prayers nor, understandably, curse themselves. Evidence from Justin and later Church Fathers was brought in support of the Brown/Martyn hypothesis. The way was opened for seeing not only Jesus (Level One of Martyn's drama) as a victim of the Jews, but John's own community (Level Two of the drama) equally victimized. Brown was, I repeat, careful to couple his historical exegesis with modern moral exhortation, exculpating modern Jews from responsibility, and ancient Jews from guilt, but not from responsibility.

IV. The Jewish Reaction and the Subsequent Christian Amen

I believe the first reply to the thesis was by Reuven Kimelman in 1981, closely followed by William Horbury in 1982 (who, however inclined away from Kimelman's position and towards Martyn's), and then by Steven Katz in 1984.[8] It comes as no surprise, especially in hindsight, that Jews would run to defend their rabbis from charges of persecuting the church through the vehicle of their liturgy. Indeed, both aforementioned Jewish scholars made a case against a broad ban of Christians through the vehicle of the *Birkat HaMinim*. Manuscripts were cited, linguistics and philology offered in evidence; in general the approach was: well, yes, there might have been one community where Jews and Christians might not have gotten along well, but it was not John's community who were the target of the *Birkat HaMinim,* and it was not the rabbis who were chasing the Johannine Christians out of their synagogues. The apologetic tone is very strong in these writings, even when they are read two decades later. The basic thrust of the early arguments is something like that of a New York waiter whose eye one has finally managed to catch, who replies, after all, "not my table." Not my rabbis, not Christianity at large or even, necessarily, the Johannine community—not us, not our ancestors, not your church, not my table.

The last five years or so have seen a resurgence of interest in the *Birkat HaMinim,* "the Jews," and John's gospel.[9] On the whole, distancing from Martyn's linkage of *Birkat HaMinim* to *aposynagōgos* has continued apace, but now with Christian scholars joining the chorus. The theological implications of Martyn's findings, the history of abuse of Judaism with John as justification, and some serious second thoughts about the history of the period itself have been responsible for this reassessment of the Martyn hypothesis. In particular I think there has been a vast overestimation of the power and importance of the Yavnaen rabbis in the late first century. While this inflated sense of the importance of the rabbis is, I admit, shared by my rabbinical students and most of my rabbinic colleagues, it is, for better or worse, a fantasy. Martyn and others presumed that the rabbis at Yavneh could make a decree that would affect Jewry worldwide. But the rabbis of Yavneh were a small, politically divided, largely impotent group who only had power over a tiny minority of Palestinian Jewry in the late first century, and had little power even in the years beyond.[10]

Add to this the growing consensus that the explicitly anti-Christian portion of the *Birkat HaMinim* was most probably added to the prayer only in the fourth century.[11] This is in keeping with my own general feeling that rabbinic Jews, at least, tended to ignore Christianity in its early centuries, perhaps in the hope that if they did so long enough, it would just go away. Only after the church became the empire did the rabbis finally hear the bell tolling.[12] This does *not* mean that Jews did not throw Christians out of some synagogue, or that the Johannine community did not take that move rather badly. It simply means "not my table."

V. On the Uses of Rabbinic Literature to Illuminate the New Testament

Father Brown was careful to caution his readers against what Lou Martyn so aptly called "raiding Rabbinics" rather than reading.[13] In his posthumous volume Brown is much more cautious about the use of Rabbinics, stating, "none of the extant documents was written before the second century, so it is very difficult to evaluate the light they cast on the NT."[14] Here, too, my own "amen" to Father Brown's caution is tinged with a bit of what I have already described as "not my table." To deny the usefulness of Rabbinics in illuminating John's gospel is a form of apologetics by denial. So allow me to be more careful in spelling out the problems inherent in the use of rabbinic literature to illuminate the NT, and then cautiously suggest some possible ways in which rabbinic literature might prove useful to NT scholars.

As Brown said, *all* of rabbinic literature postdates the redaction of the NT. The reliability of attributions even within the earliest, Tannaitic layer of the literature is spotty.[15] What this means for me is that the earliest dating we can afford to any rabbinic tradition will be no earlier than the redaction of the Mishnah, ca. 200 C.E. The only exception to this rule would be cases in which the material is paralleled in earlier materials: e.g., the Apocrypha, Philo, Josephus, the Dead Sea Scrolls, and the works of the Apostolic Fathers.[16] Of course, if one has parallel traditions in those literatures one hardly needs to turn to Rabbinics for a later "trajectory."

Some argue that there is the possibility of dating an idea or concept in rabbinic literature to a given early generation rather than to a specific named rabbi. So, for instance, one might not trust the reliability of a given attribution but one could, on the basis of parallels within and outside of rabbinic literature, note that such and such idea or concept was appropriate to, say, the first generation of Tannaim (70–95 C.E), or the second generation (95–120), etc.[17] I am more dubious than my colleagues about the reliability of such an approach, but to the extent it may be reliable, it might be helpful in finding some parallels to the NT within the first generation of Tannaitic literature and drawing some conclusions. Still, the undertaking is better off if buttressed by parallels from outside the rabbinic corpus, in which case, see above.

Stipulating from the outset that the rabbinic "background" one is seeking is more likely to be contemporary with Patristic commentary on or use of a New Testament passage is a more useful way of viewing the potential of rabbinic material.[18] In other words, the rabbinic text may be seen as a form of later commentary on or reaction to a New Testament passage, either as it appears in the NT or as it was used in a later generation by the Church Fathers. This, of course, forces NT scholars to use the rabbinic material with much more caution (although it is a boon to Patristics scholars). Acknowledging that a rabbinic "parallel" may be no more authoritative than a comment by John Chrysostom or Jerome still grants the rabbis a great deal of hermeneutic usefulness, but denies them the role of providing authentic background.

It is in this light that rabbinic literature can serve as a hermeneutical heuristic, a fertile ground for ideas and directions for NT exegesis, as opposed to providing a Q.E.D. parallel or proof of an historic circumstance. Using rabbinic literature as a form of exegetical NT commentary, as it were, and/or as a template for searching other, earlier, non-rabbinic but nonetheless Jewish material,[19] is the most that the historic constraints of the literature should allow.

One final caution regarding the use of rabbinic literature has to do with the fluidity of rabbinic textual transmission. The Torah text was stabilized from a reasonably early stage. Next in line of stability were rabbinic halakhic texts such as the Mishnah.[20] Talmudic texts, which combine legal passages with *aggada,* are less stable. The least stable texts are those that are regarded as almost purely aggadic, and the later in time these texts date from (up to the advent of printing) the less reliable the accuracy of their scribal transmission. It is well known that many if not most rabbinic texts may have an oral *Vorlage,* considerably exacerbating the reliability of transmission. The most fluid of texts in rabbinic transmission are liturgical texts that were only "canonized" at a relatively late date.[21] The *Birkat HaMinim,* the text and date of which were central to Martyn's thesis, is on exceptionally thin ice in the form in which Martyn quotes it.[22]

VI. Some Uses of Rabbinic Literature in Brown's *John* Commentary

Necessary caveats having been sounded, I turn now to some notes on Brown's use of rabbinic parallels in the opening chapters of the Gospel of John. I offer some select examples here, based primarily on the cautions stated above and my years of dialogue with Father Brown. I note that Ray was hardly the first to offer rabbinic parallels, but I engage his work in particular for four reasons: (1) it is Father Brown whose memory is being honored by this volume, (2) his *John* commentary remains a monument of New Testament scholarship, (3) he was my teacher, and (4) he paid me the extraordinary honor of becoming my student and sitting in my Introduction to Rabbinic Literature class at Union Seminary.

John 1:1, *Ho Logos.* Strack-Billerbeck (StB) *ad loc* points the way here with a long excursus on the *Memra.* Brown, in his "Appendix II: The Word,"[23] appropriately cites StB and still more appropriately cites the *logos* role in Wisdom of Solomon and other pre-rabbinic texts. Yet Brown neglects to cite an early rabbinic text, *Mishnah Pirqe ʾAbot* 5:1, "By ten utterances *(maʾamarot)* was the world created," and the adumbrations of this tradition in later rabbinic literature. This Hebrew text may well predate the use of the Aramaic Targumic *memra* here.

Since we have the nexus of word with creation, this is an important parallel to further expand the variety of ideas alongside the Hellenistic *logos.* If I may, as a heuristic, cite a ninth-century (!) rabbinic text; *Pirqe Rabbi Eliezer* 3 notes that before creation only God and "God's great name" existed. I do not think that our rabbinic author is conscious of John's usage—or, likely, of Hellenistic usage of the *logos.* Most likely he is reflecting the targumic *memra* traditions.[24] Nevertheless, the parallels to both *ʾAbot* and *Pirqe Rabbi Eliezer* are useful, not as background but as a means to understand the full range of possibilities in the history of ideas stemming from the Johannine text.

John 2:19, "Destroy this Temple." Brown[25] cites a tradition of Rabbi Zadok having fasted for forty years so that his act of piety might prevent the destruction of the Temple. Brown is canny here in pointing to a rabbinic tradition that shares Jesus' "prediction" of the Temple's destruction and roughly dates to the same era (70 C.E. minus forty years of fasting yields a beginning date of Zadok's concern for the destruction of the Temple about 30 C.E.).

The illumination of rabbinic concerns for the Temple is useful, as even within the rabbinic community there were complicated attitudes toward the late Second Temple and the corrupt priesthood therein. However, the reliability of the Zadok traditions is unsound. The two citations Brown offers are from the Babylonian Talmud and *Lamentations Rabbah,* the former early sixth century and the latter likely fifth or sixth century.[26] Further, the tradition itself is part of either a foundation legend regarding the academy at Yavneh, or an anti-Yohanan ben Zakkai tradition promulgated by the Gamalielites. In either case the dates of the tradition (both the forty years and the era of redaction) render useless this testimony regarding the 30s of the first century.

John 3:1, 9, "Nicodemus." Brown[27] identifies Nicodemus variously as "a member of the Jewish Sanhedrin" and as holding "the office of teacher of Israel." I argued with Ray about his identification of Nicodemus as a member of the Sanhedrin, which is how Brown translates *archōn tōn Ioudaiōn.* Ironically, my argument stems from that other Nicodemus mentioned in rabbinic sources (see StB *ad loc*). Very often the "rabbinic" Nicodemus is grouped with two other men, Ben Tzitzit HaKeset and Ben Kalba Savua, and together the three make up a set of archetypal rich men. They are called *gedolei hamedinah* or *gedolei yerushalayim,* literally great men of the city or of Jerusalem. What this means is that these men are heavy hitters, men of clout, donors, movers and shakers. I would suspect that this is what lies behind *archōn tōn Ioudaiōn* in John. They are not members of the Sanhedrin, but rather the rich and powerful men who stood behind those public figures. As such, Nicodemus' emergence from the darkness into the light[28] is all the more significant.

John 3:13-14, "No one has gone up into heaven . . . just as Moses . . . so the Son of Man." Brown, *ad loc,* appropriately quotes from Wis 16:6-7 as well as *Barn.* 12:5-6. He does not quote the *Mishnah RH* 3:8, which offers a close parallel to Barnabas.[29] I admit that the Mishnah text is problematic enough as a parallel to Barnabas, let alone John. Yet it opens the door to another parallel, as well as a particular rabbinic analogical exegetic method John may be employing here.

The parallel draws upon Prov 30:4, "Who has ascended to heaven and come down?" The fifth-century *Pesiqta de Rab Kahana* variously comments on the verse, "'Who has ascended to heaven?' This refers to God . . . to Elijah . . . to Moses." The original Proverbs verse continues, "What is his name or his son's name?" which would be a most apposite allusion for John with his high christology. If I may return for a moment to the *Pesiqta,* the rabbinic midrash answers the question, "what is his son's name?" with the verse (Exod 4:22), "Israel is my firstborn." I certainly do not wish to imply that this rabbinic reading is background for John, but it is likely that some christological reading of Proverbs is the impetus for the rabbinic interpretation.[30]

The form of the analogy in John is a classic rabbinic *mah . . . af* construction: just as in the case of X, so too in the case of Y. But this construction also includes the possibility of *qol wahomer* construction—if in the case of X, how much more so in the case of Y. In John, this form of contrast would instruct the listener that Jesus is superior to Moses, *a fortiori.* Of course, my very quotation of the Latin name of this device lets us know that one need not depend upon Rabbinics to reason from minor to major. Any locus within the Hellenistic world suffices for such an analogical construction.

John 4:10-11, "living water . . . well (cistern)." Cf. John 7:38 and Brown's *Commentary.*[31] Brown quotes the distinction between the well and the cistern but could have exploited it aptly with a quote from *Pirqe ʾAbot* 2: 8, in which Yohanan ben Zakkai describes his students. "Eliezer ben Hyrcanus is a limed cistern which never loses a drop"—that is to say, he is a master of tradition. "Elazar ben Azariah is an overflowing fountain"—a wellspring of original thought. In an early commentary on this passage *ʾAbot de Rabbi Nathan* comments that Elazar is "a running stream and an overflowing fountain, the waters of which rise up and go forth, to fulfill that which is written, 'Your streams will gush forth in rivulets in the public square' (Prov 5:16)."[32] I grant that the *ʾAbot de Rabbi Nathan* formula sounds more like Matthew than John, but it remains apposite. I note that Elazar and Eliezer are contemporaries of the gospel even as I note that the likely final redaction date of *ʾAbot de Rabbi Nathan* is as late as the eighth century.

Father Brown cites a different Tannaitic text in parallel to the passages being discussed, the early-third-century Tannaitic commentary *Sipre Deuteronomy*. He regrettably only cites a small part of the passage. Reasons of space and time preclude my full citation of the passage here,[33] but for the comment that, even with a third-century redaction date, the discussion is illuminative of the mindset of first-century Jews, as the water metaphor stretches back into the Hebrew Bible itself.

John 4:18, "five husbands." Brown follows StB in his comment, "Jews were only allowed three marriages." This is wrong. The rabbinic law limiting marriages only applies when the previous husbands have died during the marriage, in which case the wife qualifies as a "killer wife" and is prevented from marrying further. In point of fact, a very famous rabbi disregarded the law to marry the woman he desired.[34] Our passage simply points to the woman as a liar, but not necessarily "markedly immoral" as Brown construed her.

John 6:3, "Jesus . . . sat down." Brown, *John* 232, suggests: "Jesus, like the rabbis, usually sat down to teach." Yet there is a Tannaitic source in *b. Megillah* 21a that contends: "up to the time of Rabban Gamaliel Torah was taught only while standing."

John 6:5, "loaves and fishes." Brown, *John* 233, cites Num 11:1-22 as background to this Johannine passage. See *Sipre Numbers* (#95) and its parallel in *Sipre Deuteronomy* (#31) on the Numbers passage, where Rabbi Akiba and his disciple Shimeon ben Yohai disagree as to whether the passage indicates a lack of faith in God (can You gather enough?) or a lack of faith in Israel (even if You do gather, they'll still murmur). Even were we to date these traditions to the quoted rabbis, they would postdate the gospel. Nevertheless, this rabbinic tradition regarding either the doubts of Moses about God or the complaints of the Jews illuminates John's general anti-Jewish discourse.

John 6:50, "bread from heaven." Brown, *John* 280, 293–94, cites Peder Borgen and Aileen Guilding on modes of Jewish discourse and the triennial

lectionary cycle. In the recent *Introduction*[35] Brown gently backs away from
Borgen and then continues, "even more open to challenge is the contention of
Aileen Guilding that the discourses . . . are closely related to the themes of
the readings assigned to be read in the synagogues at these feasts." This is a
welcome retreat since the triennial Torah reading cycle was not fixed, but varied from locale to locale. It was possibly even introduced after the first century. Most modern Rabbinics scholars today would be very wary of resting too
much on a triennial lectionary theory, a shift in view from the time of the writing of the Commentary (1966).

   John 6:63, "spirit . . . flesh." See now my article, "The Priest's Daughter
and the Thief in the Orchard."[36]

   John 7:37, "the last and greatest day of the festival." Brown, *John* 320,
suggests the Seventh Day of Sukkot. This is certainly correct. In the rabbinic
calendar this day is called Hoshanna Rabba.

   John 8:13, "I know where I came from and where I am going." See *Pirqe
ʾAbot* 3:1, attributed to the mid-first-century Akaviah ben Mehallalel, "Look
at three things and you will not come into the hands of sin: know where you
came from and where you are going, and before whom you will give accounting. Where you came from? A putrid drop [of sperm]. Where you are
going? To that place of dust, worms, and maggots [the grave]. Before whom
will you give accounting? Before the King of the king of kings, the Blessed
Holy One."

   Akaviah dates before John (and possibly before Jesus), and this section of
ʾAbot is early, likely late first or early second century. Is this background to
John? Possibly, in which case Jesus replies to Akaviah's dour teaching with
his own message of salvation. But following the method of dating to redaction
era outlined above, this section of ʾAbot could be treated as a response to the
message of John, and so read as an anti-Christian polemic. It is equally likely
we are looking at a series of standard philosophical queries or school exercises in which Akaviah gives the Stoic/Cynic answer and John's Jesus his own
unique twist to the question—which is to say the two statements may well
exist independently of one another.

   John 8:20, "the Temple treasury." Brown writes,[37] "the treasury was a stor-
age chamber and hence Jesus would not be inside it." Yet Brown also points to
the parallel usage in Mark 12:41; StB ad Mark, ibid. (and see Billerbeck's
comments on Matt 26:57) correctly points to the *lishkat hagazit,* the Court or
Chamber of Hewn Stone, as the site of the treasury. *Mishnah Sanhedrin* 11:2
reads, "The Great Court was in the Chamber of Hewn Stone, from which
Torah went forth to all Israel." *Mishnah Middot* 5:4 reads, "The Chamber of
Hewn Stone—there sat the Great Sanhedrin of Israel and judged the priests."
If this identification is correct (although *Mishnah Middot* is considered old, it
remains post-destruction), Jesus' teaching in this scene is not only public, but
in the very seat of the Sanhedrin.

John 9:41, "if only you were blind then you would not be guilty of sin, but now that you claim to see, your sin remains." Father Brown comments regarding "a sin unto death." This is close, but I think not entirely on point. Rather, this passage seems to be making a distinction found in rabbinic law, based on Torah passages (Num 15:22-31), between sins done in ignorance *(shogeg)* and sins done with malice aforethought *(mezid).*[38]

VII. *Aposynagōgos* and the Dating of John, Reconsidered

I haven't forgotten about the *aposynagōgos* passage, I just saved the best for last. The term appears in three places in John and nowhere else in the NT. The three passages (in Brown's translation) read:

> *9:22* . . . they were afraid of the Jews, for the Jews had already agreed that anybody who acknowledged Jesus as Messiah would be put out of the Synagogue *(aposynagōgos ginētai).*
> *12:42* Nevertheless, there were many, even among the Sanhedrin *(ek tōn archontōn),* who believed in him. Yet, because of the Pharisees they refused to admit it, or they would have been put out of the synagogue *(aposynagōgoi genōntai).*
> *16:2* They are going to put you out of the Synagogue *(aposynagōgous poiēsousin hymas).* In fact, the hour is coming when the man who puts you to death will think that he is serving God!

In his 1966 *Commentary* to this final *aposynagōgos* passage Brown is most explicit in his embrace of Martyn's two-level drama/*Birkat HaMinim* theory, "this killing of Christians is associated with expulsion from the Synagogue. Therefore, it seems likely that the writer is thinking of Jewish persecution of Christians rather than of Roman persecution."[39] I have already discussed the Martyn/Brown theory and the Jewish and then Christian reactions to it. In the just published *Introduction,* Francis Maloney includes the following *Editor's Note:* "Once widely accepted in Johannine studies as the crucial piece of external evidence to guide the dating and the theological perspective (especially as regards "the Jews") of the Gospel, it is increasingly accepted that there is no need to invoke the *Birkat ha-minim* or synagogue blessing (really a curse) against deviants as was frequently done in the past. The idea that it was a universal Jewish decree against Christians is almost certainly wrong and the dating of that blessing to A.D. 85 is dubious."[40]

This is most welcome. I would add to Father Maloney's remarks that the delinking of the *Birkat HaMinim* from the *aposynagōgos* passages in the gospel also puts the dating of John back into play. In very large measure it was that link that had caused scholars to lean toward the earlier (85–90s C.E.) of the termini for the gospel. Brown reiterates the broader range of dating at the end of his just published *Introduction,*[41] "I find that the span of time during which the final form of the Fourth Gospel may have been written is, at its outermost limits, A.D. 75–110, but the convergence of probabilities points strongly to a date between 90–110."

While Ray Brown certainly also has the Johannine Epistles in mind, he writes regarding the *aposynagōgos* (note that he does not mention the *Birkat HaMinim*),

> If the Johannine writers and many of the Johannine Christians were of Jewish birth, their generalizing use of "the Jews" for those hostile to Jesus indicates a deep alienation from their ancestral people. . . . Being expelled from synagogues and using "Jews" as a designation for others may have had the civil effect that the Roman tolerance of Jewish religious observance no longer applied to them, and that could have left them open to Roman investigation and persecution such as that experienced under Pliny in Asia Minor ca. A.D. 110. That is one way to explain the charge that those who put Jesus' followers out of the synagogue were putting them to death (16:2).[42]

I would like to run with this possibility by suggesting that we consider that the gospel itself may date to the latest period possible, ca. 110 C.E. The background to the persecutions reported in the gospel would be then, as Ray Brown suggested, the Trajanic persecutions such as those reported in Pliny's *Letters* X, 96-97. There we are dealing with the anonymous denunciation of Christians to the Roman authorities, which resulted in torture or death for those who "acknowledged Jesus as Messiah" or "believed in him."

If it were the case that these Christians were easily distinguished from the Jewish community, I am embarrassed to say that I think some Jews might have simply sat silent and watched the Christians being persecuted. Perhaps, worse, they even might have cheered from the sidelines, thinking that these Christians were only getting what they deserved for their troublesome beliefs. As it was, however, it was difficult for the Romans to distinguish Jews from Jewish-Christians and perhaps even pagan-born Christians. To the pagan Romans they all looked the same. This means that synagogue Jews were being arrested and tortured for the "crime" of being Christian, a situation sure to dismay members of the Jewish communities of Asia Minor (Pliny is in Bithynia) and elsewhere.

I think it was just this problem—that Jews who did *not* believe in Jesus were being persecuted as Christians—that led the Jewish community to distance themselves from believing Christians in whatever ways they could. While I doubt very much that the *Birkat HaMinim* came into the picture, I suspect that the types of ban reported in later rabbinic literature may have been invoked,[43] and that some desperate Jews may not have been beyond anonymous denunciations.

As evidence for this hypothesis I offer a text from the *Tosefta,* an early third-century rabbinic document. My own methodology should invalidate this evidence, but I will let it speak for itself in this context because: (a) my own Rabbinics teacher, Professor Saul Lieberman,[44] dated it to the Trajanic persecutions; (b) the rabbi invoked dates from the late first to early second century; and (c) I am wary of rejecting this text due to a "not my table" bias. I quote the passage at length since so much of it is apposite to the *aposynagōgos* discussion.

> Rabbi Eliezer was once arrested for heresy/Christianity *(minut)*.[45] He was brought up to the tribunal *(bēma)* for judgment.[46] That governor *(hēgemōn)* said to him, "Does an elder like you occupy himself with such idle things?" He replied, "I put my faith in the judge."
>
> That governor thought that Rabbi Eliezer was referring to him, while Eliezer only had his Father in Heaven in mind. The judge said, "Since you have put your faith in me, so I opine: Is it possible that these gray hairs[47] would err in such idle matters? *Dimissus,* behold you are released."
>
> When he was released from that tribunal, R. Eliezer was troubled that he had been arrested for heresy/Christianity *(minut)*. His disciples came to comfort him, but he was not amenable. Rabbi Akiba entered and asked him, "May I say something that you might not be upset?" He said, "Speak." Rabbi Akiba said, "Perhaps one of the heretics/Christians *(minim)* spoke some heresy which pleased you?"
>
> Rabbi Eliezer replied, "By heavens, you've reminded me! Once I was walking on the high road *(istratia)* of Sepphoris and James of the village of Sikhnin[48] found me. He related to me a matter of heresy/Christianity *(minut)* in the name of Jesus ben Pantiri,[49] and the matter pleased me. So I was arrested for heresy/Christianity *(minut)* because I transgressed the words of Torah, 'Keep yourself far away from her, do not come near the doorway of her house (Prov 5:8) For many are those she has struck dead, etc. (Prov 7:26)'"
>
> Rabbi Eliezer used to say, "A person must always flee from the hateful *(ki'ur)* and all that resembles the hateful."[50]

If we allow for a dating of this episode (if not the text in which it is found) to the time of the Trajanic persecutions we see that even prominent rabbis could be arrested on charges of Christianity. Rabbi Eliezer, by replying evasively, was able to beat the rap. One sees in this narrative that it is the predilection of the rabbis—which they represent as "words of Torah"—to stay far away from Christianity.

This rabbinic text can serve as a heuristic model for the types of avoidance the Trajanic persecution set between Jews and Christians in synagogues throughout the Roman empire. There did not need to be a formal prayer cursing the Christians; the Jews shunned them for fear of being tarred by association with them. In the face of Roman torture the avoidance reaction of the Jews is somewhat understandable. The fury of the Christians at being turned out (or, perhaps, even turned in) is equally understandable in this context.

Jesus' words make sense to a community undergoing Roman persecution and Jewish abandonment.

J. Louis Martyn and Raymond Brown were correct; there is a two-level drama in John: that of Jesus and that of the Johannine community. Yet it is sensitivity to levels three and four—the long history of (mis)interpretation of the Fourth Gospel and our own current biases—that allows us to fully understand those earlier levels of drama and suggest new ways for understanding their historic setting.

Notes

1. Cf. *b. Yebamot* 97a, *Sanhedrin* 90b.

2. Cf. Acts 22:3, Phil 3:5, and Acts 23:6, with apologies to Paul.

3. See, e.g., Raymond E. Brown, *An Introduction to the Gospel of John*. ABRL (New York: Doubleday, 2003) 160, quoting Pierre Grélot, *Les Juifs dans L'Evangile selon Jean. Enquête historique et réflexion théologique*. CahRB 34 (Paris: Gabalda, 1995).

4. Brown, *Introduction* (2003) 168. Note: This volume was first delivered 21 August 2003, after I had begun drafting this essay.

5. Raymond E. Brown, *The Gospel According to John*. AB 29-29A (Garden City, NY: Doubleday, 1966) lxxiv–lxxv.

6. Brown stands by this dating in both editions of the Introduction (1966, 2003). I will return to this late date below.

7. Brown (and Moloney?) cautiously back(s) away from insistence on *Birkat HaMinim* as a universal ban and recognize(s) that "most contemporary Johannine scholars . . . increasingly insist that this expulsion may have been a very local experience, and should not be linked to the insertion of the *Birkat ha-minim* into the Jewish prayer." Brown, *Introduction* (2003) 172, n. 56. Brown cites Pieter Van der Horst, "The Birkat Ha-Minim in Recent Research," *ExpT* 105 (1994) 367–68. Nevertheless, Brown does not entirely modify his early dating (90s C.E.) of the gospel: see ibid. 213, but see also p. 172 (ca. 90–110) and below.

8. Another Jewish voice in the mix early: Lawrence Schiffman, "At the Crossroads: Tannaitic Perspectives on the Jewish-Christian Schism," in E. P. Sanders, ed., *Jewish and Christian Self-Definition*. 2 vols. (Philadelphia: Fortress, 1981) 2:115–56. Among early Christian reactions to Martyn see Sean Freyne, "Vilifying the Other and Defining the Self: Matthew's and John's Anti-Jewish Polemic in Focus," 117–43, and Wayne A. Meeks, "Breaking Away: Three New Testament Pictures of Christianity's Separation from the Jewish Communities," 93–115, in Jacob Neusner and Ernest Frerichs, eds., *To See Ourselves as Others See Us: Christians, Jews, and "Others" in Late Antiquity* (Chico: Scholars, 1985), and see now Pieter van der Horst, "The Birkat Ha-Minim in Recent Research," *ExpT* 105 (1995) 363–68, for a survey of recent views. Van der Horst points out that Peter Schaefer was also quick to dispute the Martyn thesis.

9. See, *inter alia*, Stephen Motyer, *Your Father the Devil? A New Approach to John and "The Jews"* (Carlisle, UK: Paternoster Press, 1997); Adele Reinhartz, "The Johannine Community and its Jewish Neighbors: A Reappraisal," in Fernando F. Segovia, ed., *What Is John?* (Atlanta: Scholars, 1998) 2:111–38, eadem, *Befriending the Beloved Disciple: A Jewish Reading of the Gospel of John* (New York: Continuum, 2001), and eadem, "'Jews' and Jews in the Fourth Gospel," in Reimund Bieringer, Didier Pollefeyt, and Fréderique Vandecasteele-Vanneuville, eds., *Anti-Judaism and the Fourth Gospel: Papers of the Leuven Colloquium, 2000*. Jewish and Christian Heritage Series 1 (Assen: Van Gorcum; Louisville: Westminster John Knox, 2001) 213–227 (and see the entire volume); Colleen Conway, "The Production of the Johannine Community: A New His-

toricist Perspective," *JBL* 121 (2002) 479–95, and the recent review of Reinhartz, *Befriending the Beloved Disciple,* by Derek Tovey (*JBL* 121 [2002] 568–70).

10. See especially Seth Schwartz, *Imperialism and Jewish Society, 200 B.C.E. to 640 C.E.* (Princeton: Princeton University Press, 2001), as well as Catherine Hezser, *The Social Structure of the Rabbinic Movement in Roman Palestine.* TSAJ 66 (Tübingen: J. C. B. Mohr [Paul Siebeck], 1997) and Lee Levine, *The Rabbinic Class of Roman Palestine* (New York: JTS, 1989).

11. See Van der Horst, "The Birkat Ha-Minim," and now Brown, *Introduction* (2003) 172, n. 56.

12. See now Adam Becker and Annette Yoshiko Reed, eds., *The Ways that Never Parted.* TSAJ 95 (Tübingen: J. C. B. Mohr [Paul Siebeck], 2003), *passim.*

13. Brown, *John* (1966) lxi–lxii., *Introduction* (2003) 132–39.

14. Ibid. 138.

15. Students of Morton Smith, especially Jacob Neusner and his students, effectively undermined that reliability two decades ago. But for subsequent attempts to use Rabbinics for positivist history see Richard Kalmin, *Sages, Stories, Authors, and Editors in Rabbinic Babylonia* (Atlanta: Scholars, 1994) and idem, *The Sage in Jewish Society of Late Antiquity* (New York: Routledge, 1999) and, under the rubric of "new historicism," the recent work of Daniel Boyarin, *Carnal Israel: Reading Sex in Talmudic Culture* (Berkeley: University of California Press, 1993), and idem, *Dying for God: Martyrdom and the Making of Christianity and Judaism* (Palo Alto: Stanford University Press, 1999).

16. Under other circumstances I would include verification of early dating by parallel with NT passages as well, but in this instance it would be tautology.

17. Recent work of Richard Kalmin and, to a much more cautious degree, David Kraemer, *The Mind of the Talmud: An Intellectual History of the Bavli* (New York: Oxford University Press, 1990), and idem, *Reading the Rabbis: The Talmud as Literature* (New York: Oxford University Press, 1996), take this tack.

18. See my comments in my "Trinitarian Testimonies," *USQR* 42 (1988) 73–85, reprinted in Burton Visotzky, *Fathers of the World: Essays in Rabbinic and Patristic Literatures.* WUNT 80 (Tübingen: J. C. B. Mohr [Paul Siebeck] 1995).

19. E.g., Apocrypha, Philo, Josephus, Dead Sea Scrolls, etc.

20. Although differences are to be found between the Mishnah as preserved by the Babylonian Talmud and that in the Palestinian Talmud.

21. See Lawrence Hoffman, *The Canonization of the Synagogue Service* (Notre Dame, IN: University of Notre Dame Press, 1979)

22. See above at n. 11, and in general the discussion in Reuven Kimelman, "*Birkat HaMinim* and the Lack of Evidence for an Anti-Christian Jewish Prayer in Late Antiquity," in E. P. Sanders, ed., *Jewish and Christian Self-Definition* (Philadelphia: Fortress, 1981) 2:226–44.

23. Brown, *John* (1966) 519–24.

24. See Avigdor Shinan, *The Embroidered Targum* (Hebrew) (Jerusalem: Magnes, 1993).

25. *John,* 122.

26. Hermann J. Strack and Günter Stemberger, *Introduction to the Talmud and Midrash* (Minneapolis: Fortress, 1992), s.v. For Rabbi Zadok see Jack N. Lightstone, "Sadoq the Yavnaen," in W. S. Green, ed., *Persons and Institutions in Early Rabbinic Judaism* (Missoula: Scholars, 1977) 49–148.

27. Brown, *John,* 128–30, 137.

28. See ibid. 130, on v. 2.

29. See my comments in *Fathers of the World,* 12–14.

30. See the commentary in Bernard Mandelbaum, *Pesikta de-Rav Kahana.* 2 vols. (New York: JTSA, 1962) 8, ad loc.

31. Brown, *John,* 170 and again at 320–23.

32. Solomon Schechter, ed., *Avot de-Rabi Natan* (Vilna, 1887; repr. with additional material New York and Jerusalem: JTSA, 1997) A ch. 14, p. 58.

33. See Reuven Hammer, *Sifre: A Tannaitic Commentary on the Book of Deuteronomy* (New Haven: Yale University Press, 1986) on #48. The same limits of space may have accounted for Brown's truncated quotation.

34. See Mordechai A. Friedman, "Tamar, A Symbol of Life: The 'Killer Wife' Superstition in the Bible and Jewish Tradition," *AJSRev* 15 (1990) 23–61. For the famous rabbi see ibid. 36–39.

35. Brown, *Introduction* (2003) 139, at nn. 78–79.

36. Burton L. Visotzky, "The Priest's Daughter and the Thief in the Orchard: The Soul of Midrash Leviticus Rabbah," in Wiles, Brown, and Snyder, eds., *Putting Body and Soul Together: Essays in Honor of Robin Scroggs* (Valley Forge, PA: Trinity Press International, 1997) 165–71.

37. Brown, *John* (1966) 342, on v. 20.

38. See my article, "Mortal Sins," *USQR* 44 (1990) 31–53, republished in *Fathers of the World*.

39. Brown, *John* (1966) 691.

40. Brown, *Introduction* (2003) 68, n. 65.

41. Brown, *Introduction* (2003) 215.

42. Brown, *Introduction* (2003) 168–69.

43. See Brown, *John,* 375, on John 9:22.

44. Saul Lieberman, "Roman Legal Institutions in Early Rabbinics and the Acta Martyrum," *JQR* 35 (1944) 57–111. Our passage is discussed on pp. 76–80. The article was reprinted in idem, *Texts and Studies* (New York: Ktav, 1974). See also R. T. Herford, *Christianity in Talmud and Midrash* (London: Williams and Norgate, 1903) 137–45.

45. *t. Hullin* 2:24 (Moses S. Zuckermandel, ed., *Tosefta* [Jerusalem: Bamberger et Wahrmann, (1937)] 503, lines 18-30). Cf. *Eccl. Rabba* 1:8 and *b. AZ* 16b. I generally follow the translation of Lieberman, "Roman Legal Institutions."

46. This includes the possibility of forced testimony under torture. See Lieberman, "Roman Legal Institutions," n. 99.

47. Following Lieberman's sensible emendation, ibid.

48. Heb. *Yakov Ish Kfar Sikhnin.*

49. The "Panther," a crude reference to Jesus' parentage. See my "Mary Maudlin Among the Rabbis," in *Fathers of the World,* 90, n. 13.

50. Note that the parallel in *Eccl.R.* asks, "How far [must one flee]?" The answer: Four cubits—the distance one keeps from those under a ban.

Additional References

Alexander, Phillip. "Rabbinic Judaism and the New Testament," *ZNW* 74 (1989) 237–46.

Becker, Adam, and Annette Yoshiko Reed, eds. *The Ways that Never Parted.* TSAJ 95. Tübingen: J. C. B. Mohr [Paul Siebeck], 2003.

Brown, Raymond E. *The Community of the Beloved Disciple.* New York: Paulist, 1979.

———. "Not Jewish Christianity and Gentile Christianity But Types of Jewish/Gentile Christianity," *CBQ* 45 (1983) 74–79.

———. *The Death of the Messiah.* 2 vols. ABRL. New York: Doubleday, 1994.

———. "The Narratives of Jesus' Passion and Anti-Judaism," *America* 172:11 (April 1, 1995) 8–12.

———. "The Babylonian Talmud on the Execution of Jesus," *NTS* 43 (1997) 158–59.

Fiebig, Paul. *Rabbinische Wundergeschichten des neutestamentlichen Zeitalters in vokalisiertem Text.* Berlin: Walter de Gruyter, 1933.

Horbury, William. "The Benediction of the *Minim* and Early Jewish-Christian Controversy," *JTS* 38 (1982) 19–61; reprinted in idem, *Jews and Christians In Contact and Controversy*. Edinburgh: T & T Clark, 1998, 67–110, with some update of his position on pp. 8–14.

Joubert, S. J. "A Bone of Contention in Recent Scholarship: The 'Birkat Ha-Minim' and the Separation of Church and Synagogue in the First Century A.D.," *Neot* 27 (1993) 351–63.

Katz, Steven, "Issues in the Separation of Judaism and Christianity after 70 C.E.: A Reconsideration," *JBL* 103 (1984) 43–76.

Moloney, Francis J. "'The Jews' in the Fourth Gospel: Another Perspective," *Pacifica* 15 (2002) 17–37.

Martyn, J. Louis. *History and Theology in the Fourth Gospel*. New York: Harper, 1968.

Pagels, Elaine. *The Johannine Gospel in Gnostic Exegesis: Heracleon's Commentary on John*. Nashville: Abingdon, 1973.

———. *The Origin of Satan*. New York: Random House, 1995.

Reinhartz, Adele. "On Travel, Translation and Ethnography: Johannine Scholarship at the Turn of the Century," in Fernando Segovia, ed., *What is John?* 2 vols. Atlanta: Scholars, 1996–98, 2:249–56.

Strack, Hermann J., and Paul Billerbeck. *Kommentar zum Neuen Testament Aus Talmud und Midrasch*. Vol 2: *Das Evangelium nach Markus, Lukas und Johannes, usw.* Munich: Beck, 1924.

Thomas, J. C. "The Fourth Gospel and Rabbinic Judaism," *ZNW* 83 (1991) 159–82.

Visotzky, Burton. "Prolegomenon to the Study of Jewish-Christianities in Rabbinic Literature," *AJSRev* 14 (1989) 47–70; reprinted in idem, *Fathers of the World: Essays in Rabbinic and Patristic Literatures*. WUNT 80. Tübingen: J. C. B. Mohr [Paul Siebeck], 1995.

———. "Der Feind heisst Satan: Elaine Pagels verfolgt die Geschichte des Teufels," *Die Zeit*, 3 November 1995, 13–14.

———. "Horbury's *Jews and Christians in Contact and Controversy*," *JBL* 119 (2000) 780–82.

John and Judaism

A response to Burton Visotzky

Adele Reinhartz

Wilfrid Laurier University

To my regret, I did not have the privilege of studying with Ray Brown in person. Nevertheless, like many of my peers, I consider myself his student. His Anchor Bible commentary was my constant companion at the outset of my study of the Gospel of John in the 1970s, and it remains the commentary I consult most frequently.[1] My copy of *The Community of the Beloved Disciple* is so well-thumbed that I have had to buy a replacement.[2] Ray Brown's exhaustive analyses of the birth and death of the Messiah informed my own thinking on the Infancy and Passion narratives and have been the foundation for graduate seminars on these subjects.[3] While we cannot know another fully through his or her writings, I have a strong sense of relationship with Ray Brown that by grace of the written word transcends the boundaries of life and death. For this reason I dedicate this brief essay to Ray Brown, my teacher.

Like Professor Visotzky, I begin with disclosure. I too am Jewish, but born and raised in Toronto, in a neighborhood populated largely by immigrants. Some, like my family, were Holocaust survivors from Poland, but most were Calabrians from southern Italy, devout and very public Catholics. It was from these children, my constant companions, that I first heard the "good news" that Jesus had come to save my soul. At age nine I had no interest in salvation, which was a concept that never crossed the minds or lips of my secular parents. But even stranger to my young mind was the notion that a person could be both man and God. This skepticism did not prevent me from envying the white dresses and joyous celebrations that my Italian girlfriends enjoyed on the occasion of their first communion. Nevertheless, I could not grasp the Son of God notion, and the questions I persisted in posing to my Catholic friends prepared me well for the discussions with Catholics and other Christians that I enjoy to this day.

My comments in these pages are not a critique of Professor Visotzky's paper but rather reflections upon it. I am in fundamental agreement with his overall approach to the relationship between John and Judaism, and fascinated by the ways in which someone familiar with yet outside the daily cut and thrust of Johannine scholarship views one of its most contentious issues.

Visotzky observes—correctly, in my view—that one cannot study John without regular recourse to the literatures and artifacts of first-century Judaism. He links this necessity to the fraught relationship between John and Judaism that many Johannine scholars, myself included, discuss in terms of anti-Judaism.[4] Whether or not we acknowledge it, the shadow of anti-Judaism within the gospel and the history of its interpretation hangs over much of our scholarly work on this text.[5]

For a Jewish scholar, the gospel's anti-Judaism is the heart of the matter. Yet there are other good reasons for Johannine scholars to draw upon Jewish texts and for scholars of Second Temple and Rabbinic Judaism to study the Fourth Gospel. Some of these are evident in Visotzky's brief discussions of the parallels between rabbinic literature and the Gospel of John. These examples suggest that the authors of the Fourth Gospel, or, put more generally, the men and women who participated in the development of early Christianity, may have brought a familiarity with Jewish legal and exegetical traditions to their Jesus narratives.[6] I agree entirely with Visotzky's methodological caution in this regard. The mining of rabbinic sources, all of which postdate the New Testament, for the background to the earliest period in Christian history is a dangerous occupation, to be undertaken only when the rabbinic source is also paralleled in a first-century Jewish source such as the writings of Josephus or the Genesis apocryphon. Visotzky offers the reverse as a possibility: Some rabbinic texts may have developed in response or reaction to the New Testament or early Christian tradition. This suggestion coheres well with the work of Yisrael Yuval, who has argued for the profound and formative influence of Christianity on the development of medieval Judaism as well as such liturgical texts as the Passover Haggada.[7] This is a provocative suggestion that may well prove fruitful with further study.

There are at least three other reasons why the Gospel of John must be studied in relationship to ancient Jewish texts. One has to do with the nature and purpose of the Fourth Gospel itself. Whether we see John as a missionary text or as an inner-church document intended to strengthen the faith of its readers (cf. 20:30-31), the gospel is also testimony to the attempts of a group of believers in Jesus to work out their identity vis-à-vis Judaism and the Jews among whom they probably lived. Thus the interpretation of the Hebrew Scriptures and the theological significance of Torah and Temple are central to this gospel.

Second, insofar as this gospel is a story about Jesus it is legitimate to ask whether it can be used in the quest for the historical Jesus, and particularly the attempt to situate Jesus within a specific Jewish context.[8] Jewish texts such as the Dead Sea Scrolls and archaeological remains in Sepphoris, Jerusalem, and elsewhere help us to fill out that context.

Finally, there is the question of the Gospel of John as a potential source of knowledge of first-century Judaism. For example, John 8, infamous as the chapter within which Jesus tells the Jews that they have the devil as their father, conveys the absolute monotheism of first-century Palestinian Jews and their self-understanding as children of Abraham and of God.[9]

Detailed development of these points must be left to other occasions. Permit me now to focus on the most contentious issue in Johannine studies today: the theory that Jews persecuted the Johannine Christians by expelling them from the synagogue. In his study of the Johannine community Ray Brown accepted both the methodology and the conclusions that J. Louis Martyn developed in his *History and Theology in the Fourth Gospel*.[10] Brown, like Martyn, viewed the gospel as a two-level drama, the first level consisting of the story of Jesus set in the early decades of the first century and the second pertaining to the experience of the Johannine community at the end of the first century. Fundamental to this way of reading was the assumption that the gospel's story of Jesus encodes the actual experience of the later community. Martyn derived support for this approach from the fact that certain features of the narrative would have been anomalous at the time of Jesus but were quite in keeping with the changing historical circumstances several decades later. The prime examples are the three expulsion passages (9:22, 12:42, and 16:2), in which the narrator or Jesus states that people who professed belief in Jesus as the Messiah were excluded from the synagogue. Such an act would have been unthinkable in Jesus' own lifetime but was plausible, so Martyn argued, in the last decade or so of the first century.[11]

Upon this foundation was built one of the most influential hypotheses in New Testament scholarship: that at some point in the late first century C.E. the Jews expelled the Johannine community from the synagogue, that is, from the Jewish community at large. Although some scholars have now begun to distance themselves from that view,[12] it still appears in most introductory textbooks and in many lecture rooms in our universities and seminaries.[13] This theory, along with the two-level reading strategy that undergirds it, has become virtually axiomatic in Johannine scholarship. But, as I learned from Visotzky's paper, Martyn's formulation does not fully satisfy him. Neither does it satisfy me.

In my own work I have suggested that the gospel in fact has three narrative levels. These I refer to as the historical tale, that is, the story of a person named Jesus who lived in the land of Israel in the early decades of the first century C.E.; the ecclesiological tale, that is, the story of the (hypothetical) Johannine community that existed at the end of the first century C.E., perhaps in Ephesus; and the cosmological tale, the story of God who sent his Son into the world and then called him back out again. The three levels are interrelated: the ecclesiological tale lies under the surface of the historical tale, and both are situated within the all-encompassing framework of the cosmological tale.

Lately, however, I have come to question this three-level theory. It now seems to me that in fact Martyn and others are correct to see only two levels within the gospel narrative itself. But in my view the ecclesiological level, that is, the story of the community, is not one of these two levels. What the gospel presents is a historical tale—a story of Jesus—set within a cosmological meta-narrative: God's creation of and love for the world. The notion that the gospel also tells the history of the community now strikes me as a construct that belongs to the history of interpretation and not to the gospel narrative as such. There is in fact nothing explicit and, I would argue, nothing at all in the gospel to support the assumption that the gospel encodes the community's experience or the methodological approach of reading the community's history out of the gospel. This is not to discount the possibility that the gospel was written in a way that would resonate with the experience of its first readers. It is plausible, and perhaps likely, that the author(s) meant their original readers to see their own experiences as being similar to and/or in continuity with those of Jesus and his earliest followers as described in this gospel. Yet it is important to remember that what I have called the ecclesiological tale is derived from a reading strategy and is not explicit in the text itself. There is no direct evidence either internal to the gospel or external to it for the existence of a "Johannine community" and its specific experiences in relationship to Jews, Gentiles, or others.

This history of interpretation, including but not limited to the expulsion theory, corresponds to what Visotzky calls the third level of the Johannine drama. The fourth level is the story of our own individual, personal encounters with the text. At this fourth level our individual identities, affiliations, and experiences, perhaps influenced by the interpretive communities to which we belong, may lead us in different directions. A non-Christian academic may be able to dismiss this gospel, whereas a Christian pastor may struggle mightily to find a way to preach it.[14]

Anti-Judaism is central to all of these narrative levels—my first two and Visotzky's last two. In the historical tale the Jews are cast as the archenemies of Jesus and his disciples. In the cosmological tale they are identified with the forces of death and darkness that strive against Jesus as the divine Word and Light but fail to overcome him. Anti-Judaism also runs either as a thread or as a challenge through the history of this gospel's interpretation, and each of us must contend with or against it in our own encounter with this text. Anti-Judaism is therefore inherent in the gospel itself and a potential in our own readings, but it is also a factor in the history of interpretation.

Of particular concern are the anti-Jewish undercurrents to the expulsion theory. Yet the anti-Semitic potential of the expulsion theory is not nearly as clear to many Johannine scholars as it is to Visotzky and myself. In fact, many

Johannine scholars believe that the expulsion theory is actually an antidote to anti-Judaism. Two not entirely compatible points are often made. One is that we must see the Johannine believers as Jews, not yet Christians. Doing so will allow us to recognize that the conflict the gospel portrays is a benign and innocent squabble between family members, a family feud. While family members may insult each other and call each other names—such as "children of the devil" perhaps—they do not genuinely hate each other, do they?[15] The second view, often held also by those who propound the first view, is that the gospel's highly negative portrayal of and talk about the Jews are an understandable reaction to the experience of the persecution and expulsion experienced at Jewish hands.[16]

While some may see the expulsion theory as a useful approach to the anti-Judaism question, it may in fact be a way of avoiding it or, even more troubling, of excusing it. In the first place, it is not the case that a family feud is necessarily benign; the fact that all or most of the parties to the supposed dispute between the Johannine Christians and the Jews among whom they lived were Jews in one sense or another does not in itself absolve the gospel of anti-Judaism. Anyone who has read the gospel in Greek will have been struck by the frequent occurrence of the word *ioudaios,* seventy times in fact, many of them negative. Any reader who is not sensitive to issues of anti-Judaism may well develop negative attitudes and feelings toward these Jews, children of the devil (cf. 8:44), who always desire to kill and persecute Jesus. In this sense the gospel is anti-Jewish no matter what the ethnic or religious affiliation of the characters might be.

Second, to use the expulsion theory as a way of explaining the gospel's statements about Jews and Judaism is in itself an anti-Jewish move. It accuses the Jews of persecution of Christians. It may well be true that some Jews persecuted some Christians. If we take Paul at his word we can hardly deny that this occurred. But the Gospel of John does not provide evidence for such persecution, despite the two-level readings offered by Martyn, Brown, and others since them. Further, it implies that to malign the Jews is excusable if it is a response to persecution. Understandable it is, perhaps, but excusable?

Both Martyn and Brown initially believed that the historical conclusions based on the two-level reading of the gospel had external confirmation in the history of Jewish liturgy, specifically in the *Birkat HaMinim*. According to this theory the "blessing upon the heretics" was intended to expose Jewish believers in Jesus, on the assumption that they would feel unable to lead the synagogue in prayers that contained a curse against themselves.[17] Since 1981 many Johannine scholars accept Reuven Kimelman's point that there is no evidence for a curse on Jewish Christians in the late first century.[18] Yet the expulsion theory continues to hold sway, though with more hesitation, and perhaps with the caveat that this was a local Jewish persecution and not a universal decree emerging from the sort of central Jewish authority for which we have no evidence at all in this time, if ever.[19] Brown does not view *Birkat HaMinim* as central to his construction of the history of the Johannine community.[20] But Martyn himself continues to argue that *Birkat HaMinim* is integral to this theory.[21]

My own critique of the expulsion theory rests on exegetical rather than historical grounds. First, it must be noted that Martyn's theory is based on a two-level reading only of the three expulsion passages. If we apply the two-level reading method to the gospel as a whole we no longer come up with a coherent picture of the relationship between Johannine Christians and the Jews.[22] Second, as I have already indicated, there is no internal evidence that the gospel was intended to encode the story of a community. Rather, there are explicit indications, particularly in the gospel's emphasis on the truth and authenticity of its witness (19:35), that it was meant to be read precisely as a story of Jesus. The fact that expulsion from the synagogue may have been anachronistic to Jesus' time does not mean that the original readers would have viewed it as such.[23]

In discounting the expulsion theory, however, we are left with the challenge of speculating as to why the gospel alleges this form of persecution. There is almost no evidence upon which to base an alternative theory, but I have of course not refrained from giving this some thought. In my previous work I have made two suggestions. One is that the background of the gospel entails a situation in which Jews and Johannine Christians no longer saw themselves as belonging to the same community. The expulsion passages may therefore provide an etiology for this situation, tracing it back to the time of Jesus and the Jews' inability to tolerate those among their number who profess Jesus as the Messiah. A second possibility is that, at a time when a Johannine community was still in the process of defining its identity with respect to Judaism, leaders of that community may have been warning members indirectly not to "backslide" into Judaism by painting Jews as persecutors and murderers, as in Heb 10:29.

In his paper Visotzky proposes yet another possibility. Once we no longer have to figure *Birkat HaMinim* into the mix we also no longer have to date the gospel in the ninth decade of the first century, the supposed date of *Birkat HaMinim*.[24] A somewhat later dating, to the first decade of the second century, would place the gospel more firmly into the period of Roman persecution of Christianity. He suggests that many Jews may have been mistaken for Christians and hence subject to persecution. In this context Jews would have distanced themselves from Christians and perhaps even stood by quietly as their Christian neighbors were persecuted.

To support this argument Visotzky points to a number of rabbinic stories that lend themselves to this interpretation. The appeal to post-New Testament sources contravenes his own methodological guidelines as articulated earlier in his article, given that the rabbinic stories postdate the gospel materials by several centuries. In this case, however, the violation is not grave, because the rabbinic stories are meant to be illustrative and not definitive. Visotzky recognizes the absence of contemporaneous evidence for his hypothesis. But one may suggest that his position may have some tenuous and indirect support from Caiaphas' comment that "it is better for you to have one man die for the people than to have the whole nation destroyed" (11:50). Caiaphas' words are taken by the gospel narrator as a prophecy of Jesus' death (11:51). But if we momentarily accept Visotzky's hypothesis, perhaps Caiaphas' words can be read in a different way altogether: that Jews should not speak out in Jesus' defense if Rome seeks his death, for it is better that he be sacrificed than that they die on suspicion of being his supporters (it may have been this fear that led Peter to deny three times that he was Jesus' disciple). This reading not only supports Visotzky's idea but it also recasts Rome as the prime mover behind Jesus' execution, displacing the Jews and/or their leadership from this distasteful role. The fact that this interpretation is appealing, however, does not make it correct. While I find Visotzky's hypothesis intriguing, I would appreciate more evidence before subscribing to it.

These reflections lead directly to the issue of apologetics. Visotzky comments correctly that Jewish writing about *Birkat HaMinim* and, one might add, other aspects of New Testament interpretation often has more than a faint whiff of apologetics. He himself does not rule out the possibility that Jews behaved in less-than-neighborly ways when Christians were targeted by Romans. But it is not only Jewish interpreters who are guilty of apologetics. In fact, apologetics runs through the entire history of New Testament exegesis. When scholars use the expulsion theory to excuse the Gospel of John's negative comments about Jews they are being apologetic; presumably the same could be said about any scholar, Jewish or not, who argues against theories in which Jews are painted as persecutors.

But are apologetics to be avoided at all costs? I would suggest that in our scholarship we often act out a chicken-and-egg conundrum. As a Jew I am repelled by and concerned about anti-Judaism within the gospel and I am sensitive to the anti-Semitic potential in the history of interpretation. If I have the scholarly tools to investigate the question, I will do so and, more likely than not, propose a different solution. Is this apologetic? Perhaps, but does it invalidate the exercise, or the solution? I do not think so. While it is important that we be aware of our own biases, it is also possible that these very biases may—in some cases—spur us on to new insights and discoveries.

So we have come full circle to disclosure. We can see that disclosure is valuable not just for its own sake, but because it allows us and others to be aware of the concerns we bring to our scholarship. These may be idiosyncratic, or they may be concerns that others should share as well. I conclude with thanks to Rabbi Professor Burton Visotzky for prompting my reflections on these important issues and, of course, to Ray Brown. The richness of Father

Brown's work continues to inform our discussions and understanding of this most enigmatic of gospels, and to live on in our ongoing engagement with his work and our dialogue with one another.

Notes

1. Raymond E. Brown, *The Gospel According to John.* AB 29-29a (Garden City, NY: Doubleday, 1966).

2. Raymond E. Brown, *The Community of the Beloved Disciple* (New York: Paulist, 1979).

3. Raymond E. Brown, *The Birth of the Messiah: A Commentary on the Infancy Narratives in the Gospels of Matthew and Luke.* ABRL (New, updated ed. New York: Doubleday, 1993); idem, *The Death of the Messiah: From Gethsemane to the Grave: A Commentary on the Passion Narratives in the Four Gospels.* ABRL (New York: Doubleday, 1994).

4. For a range of opinions on this important topic see Reimund Bieringer, Didier Pollefeyt, and Fréderique Vandecasteele-Vanneuville, *Anti-Judaism and the Fourth Gospel* (Louisville: Westminster John Knox, 2001).

5. For recent treatments of the topic of anti-Judaism in the New Testament see Paula Fredriksen and Adele Reinhartz, *Jesus, Judaism, and Christian Anti-Judaism: Reading the New Testament after the Holocaust* (Louisville: Westminster John Knox, 2002).

6. Peder Borgen, *Bread from Heaven : An Exegetical Study of the Concept of Manna in the Gospel of John and the Writings of Philo* (Leiden: Brill, 1965).

7. Israel Jacob Yuval, *Shene Goyim Be-Vitnekh: Yehudim Ve-Notsrim—Dimuyim Hadadiyim* (Tel-Aviv: Alma/Am Oved, 2000).

8. Cf. Paula Fredriksen, *Jesus of Nazareth, King of the Jews: A Jewish Life and the Emergence of Christianity* (New York: Knopf, 1999).

9. Adele Reinhartz, "John 8:31-59 from a Jewish Perspective," in John K. Roth and Elizabeth Maxwell-Meynard, eds., *Remembering for the Future 2000: The Holocaust in an Age of Genocides* (London: Palgrave, 2001) 787–97.

10. J. Louis Martyn, *History and Theology in the Fourth Gospel.* New Testament Library (3rd ed. Louisville: Westminster John Knox, 2003). The earlier editions were published in 1968 and 1979.

11. Ibid. 47.

12. Gail R. O'Day, *The Word Disclosed: Preaching the Gospel of John* (rev. and expanded ed. St. Louis: Chalice, 2002).

13. John Muddiman, "The Gospels," in John Barton, ed., *The Biblical World* (London: Routledge, 2002) 163–64.

14. Robert Kysar, *Preaching John.* Fortress Resources for Preaching (Minneapolis: Fortress, 2002).

15. This view is expressed in M. C. de Boer, "The Depiction of 'the Jews' in John's Gospel: Matters of Behavior and Identity," in Bieringer, et al., eds., *Anti-Judaism and the Fourth Gospel* (Assen: Van Gorcum, 2001) 264.

16. Barnabas Lindars, "The Persecution of Christians in John 15:18–16:4a," in William Horbury and Brian McNeil, eds., *Suffering and Martyrdom in the New Testament: Studies Presented to G.M. Styler by the Cambridge New Testament Seminar* (Cambridge: Cambridge University Press, 1981) 49.

17. Martyn, *History and Theology in the Fourth Gospel,* 64.

18. Reuven Kimelman, "Birkat-Haminim and the Lack of Evidence for an Anti-Christian Jewish Prayer in Late Antiquity," in E. P. Sanders, Albert I. Baumgarten, and Alan Mendelson, eds., *Jewish and Christian Self-Definition:Aspects of Judaism in the Greco-Roman Period* (Philadelphia: Fortress, 1981).

19. R. Alan Culpepper, "The Gospel of John and the Jews," *RevExp* 84 (1987) 273–88.

20. Raymond E. Brown, *An Introduction to the New Testament.* ABRL (New York: Doubleday, 1997).

21. Martyn, *History and Theology in the Fourth Gospel,* 47, 61–65.

22. Believe me, I have tried. Cf. Adele Reinhartz, "Women in the Johannine Community," in Amy-Jill Levine, ed., *A Feminist Companion to John* (Sheffield: Sheffield Academic Press, 2003) 14–33.

23. For my detailed arguments against the expulsion theory see Adele Reinhartz, "The Johannine Community and Its Jewish Neighbors: A Reappraisal," in Fernando F. Segovia, ed., *"What Is John?" Literary and Social Readings of the Fourth Gospel.* SBLSymS (Atlanta: Society of Biblical Literature, 1998) 111–38.

24. Martyn, *History and Theology in the Fourth Gospel,* 61–62, n. 75.

Chapter Five

Qumran Literature and the Johannine Writings

Joseph A. Fitzmyer, S.J.

Catholic University of America

Raymond E. Brown, s.s., whom we are honoring during this international conference, was one of the scholars who early exploited the data of Qumran literature for the interpretation of the Gospel according to John. Even as a graduate student at the Johns Hopkins University he published a two-part article entitled "The Qumran Scrolls and the Johannine Gospel and Epistles" in the *Catholic Biblical Quarterly* in 1955.[1] Although Brown was already very interested in the study of the Johannine writings, he was influenced also by his mentor, Prof. William Foxwell Albright, who about the same time contributed a chapter to the Festschrift for C. H. Dodd entitled "Recent Discoveries in Palestine and the Gospel of St John."[2]

The year 1955 was significant for Johannine research, because two other articles appeared then on Qumran and the Johannine writings, one in French by François-Marie Braun,[3] the other in Spanish by Marie-Emile Boismard.[4] Oscar Cullmann, too, wrote then on a broader topic, the beginnings of Christianity, but he also dealt with the Johannine Gospel.[5] Brown, however, was not the first to discuss the relation of Qumran literature to Johannine writings, because a year earlier (1954) Lucetta Mowry had done so.[6] In any case, Brown's article in the *Catholic Biblical Quarterly* was a major contribution to the early study of this important topic and was in the vanguard of a long line of studies that have appeared during the following decades.[7] One of the last things Brown wrote before he died in 1998 was a short contribution on the Gospel and Letters of John for the *Encyclopedia of the Dead Sea Scrolls*.[8] It was posthumously published in 2000, but it represents his mature thinking on the topic. His monumental commentaries on the Fourth Gospel and the Johannine Epistles applied all that research to individual passages in those writings.[9]

The importance of Qumran literature for the study of the New Testament is widely recognized, because it provides firsthand information about a Palestinian

Jewish sect that thrived in the last two pre-Christian centuries and in two-thirds of the first century of the Christian era. Part of the Essene community was thus contemporary with Jesus of Nazareth, and the literature it read and in part composed is now available to modern interpreters of the New Testament. Coming from a time that precedes the writing of the Greek gospels and the later books of the New Testament, this literature provides a valuable Palestinian Jewish matrix for the emergence of the earliest Christian writings. Before 1947, when the first cave of Qumran was discovered, no one would ever have suspected that within the following decade ten other caves would yield some 820 scrolls and fragmentary texts that have cast abundant light on the Jewish background of early Christianity. As Martin Hengel has put it, "The Qumran discoveries are a landmark for a new assessment of the situation of the Fourth Gospel in the history of religion."[10]

Traditionally, the author of the Fourth Gospel has been taken to be the apostle John, son of Zebedee, "the disciple whom Jesus loved" (John 19:26). Today, however, most interpreters would distinguish the evangelist not only from the son of Zebedee but even from the Beloved Disciple (who was undoubtedly the source of the Johannine tradition about Jesus), and some would even distinguish the evangelist from the author of the Johannine epistles. Indeed, it is often suggested that a Johannine school of writers is responsible for these four New Testament writings.[11] Although some interpreters in the nineteenth and early twentieth centuries considered the Fourth Gospel to have been composed in mid-second century (e.g., Ferdinand Christian Baur, *ca.* 170 C.E.; Alfred Loisy, *ca.* 150 C.E.) and some have more recently sought to date it very early, even before 70 C.E.,[12] the commonly-used date is *ca.* 90–95 C.E., almost a quarter of a century after the Roman destruction of the Qumran commmunity center. The Johannine Epistles probably date from about a decade later. Whereas elements in the Johannine writings had been considered to be derived from Greek philosophical thinking, those items are more normally recognized today as rooted in a Palestinian matrix, and some even argue that the Fourth Gospel has a (southern) Palestinian origin.[13]

Although there is no quotation of any Qumran text in either the Johannine gospel or epistles and no hint in them of any knowledge of the Qumran community, many interpreters over the last fifty years have called attention to expressions and ideas in the Johannine writings that have parallels in or are similar to phrases in Qumran literature[14]—so much so that in the early 1960s Samuel Sandmel's presidential address at the annual meeting of the Society of Biblical Literature was entitled "Parallelomania,"[15] and in it he cautioned about parallels, source claims, and derivations. For parallels in literature are legion, and one encounters at times the famous dictum of E. R. Goodenough: a parallel by definition consists of straight lines in the same plane that never meet, however far extended in any direction. Still, that definition is derived from Euclidean geometry and is being applied analogously to literary studies.

To repeat the dictum as if it closes the discussion or absolves one from investigating the literary relationship of writings is only a form of obscurantism, something little better than parallelomania or pan-Qumranism. It enables one to avoid asking when a *literary* parallel might prove to be a "contact." Consequently, it is imperative that the similarities or parallels be examined carefully in order to establish their distinctive pertinence and to dismiss those that are merely superficial, imprecise, or even incidental.[16]

Moreover, some writers have concluded that the evangelist has actually borrowed directly from Qumran literature (e.g., Karl G. Kuhn, James H. Charlesworth),[17] and John Ashton even maintains that the evangelist is "more likely to have been an Essene" who was converted.[18] Others, however, have related the Johannine writings to Qumran literature only indirectly (e.g., Raymond E. Brown,[19] Rudolf Schnackenburg[20]). Still others have considered the relation to be "extremely meagre . . . certainly it has not revolutionized the study of John" (so C. K. Barrett;[21] similarly H. M. Teeple[22]). Not long ago, at the Jerusalem Congress on the fiftieth anniversary of the discovery of the Qumran Scrolls in 1997, Richard J. Bauckham, of the University of St. Andrews in Scotland, openly called the "hypothesis of some kind of influence from Qumran on John . . . mistaken."[23] His reason: the use of light/darkness imagery in the Johannine writings and Qumran literature "exhibits far more impressive dissimilarities than has been noticed in the scholarly enthusiasm for drawing conclusions from the comparatively unimpressive similarities."[24] He ended his discussion by conceding only the irony in the publication of the Qumran texts, "which effected a shift in Johannine scholarship towards recognizing the thoroughly Jewish character of Johannine theology," a fact that could have been ascertained "more convincingly by comparison with other Jewish sources."[25] Since I do not share the skepticism of Bauckham, I propose to review the matter with the "sufficient methodological rigor"[26] he advocates, but I shall not restrict my discussion to the "light/darkness imagery," as Bauckham has done, despite the title of his article, for there is more to be considered than merely that aspect of the similarities. My further remarks on the relation of Qumran literature to the Johannine writings will be made under five headings: I. Creation; II. Dualism; III. Spirit of Truth; IV. Love of Community Members; and V. Other Miscellaneous Parallels.

I. Creation

The Old Testament teaching about God as creator is developed in a remarkably similar mode of formulation in Qumran literature and the Johannine gospel. In the *Manual of Discipline* from Qumran Cave 1 we read מאל הדעות כול, הויה ונהייה "From the God of knowledge exists everything that is and will come to be" (1QS 3:15); ובדעתו נהיה כול וכ{ע/ע}ול הויה במחשבתו יכינו ומבלעדיו לוא יעשה, "through his knowledge everything will come to be, and everything that exists he establishes with his design, and nothing is made apart from him" (11:11);

and וכול יעשה לוא רצונכה ובלו, "and apart from your will nothing is made" (11:17). Similar statements can be found in the *Hodayot,* 1QHª 9(old 1):7-8; 18(old 10):2, 9. —"The God of knowledge" is a phrase known from 1 Sam 2:3, אל דעות; it is found again in 1QHª 9(old 1):26.

This formulation can be compared to the prologue of John's gospel, where it is said of ὁ λόγος "the Word": "All things came to be through him, and apart from him not a thing came into being" (1:3). What is striking here is not only the reaffirmation of biblical teaching about creation but the double formulation of it, both in a positive and negative mode, as in the Qumran texts just quoted. One would not expect, of course, to find in the Qumran texts any mention of ὁ λόγος "the Word," in the Christian sense, but the activity that is ascribed there to God's knowledge or will, both positively and negatively, is predicated by the Christian evangelist of "the Word," and the double formulation is not to be missed.

II. Dualism

A noteworthy aspect of Johannine theology is the elaborate dualism one encounters in the gospel and epistles. Here one finds seven pairs of opposites: death and life (John 5:24; 6:49-51, 58; 11:25; 1 John 3:14); flesh and spirit (John 3:6; 6:63; 1 John 4:2-3); light and darkness (John 1:5; 3:19; 8:12; 12:35, 46; 1 John 1:5; 2:8-9, 11); truth and lies/error (John 8:44; 1 John 1:6; 2:21, 27; 4:6); above and below (John 3:31; 8:23); earthly and heavenly (John 3:12-13, 31); Jesus/God/Father and this world (John 3:16-17; 13:1; 16:28; 17:14-16, 25; 1 John 2:16-17; 4:4; 5:4, 19).[27] Bauckham has not adequately described all seven pairs of Johannine dualisms, and when he asserts that "the Qumran texts provide parallels only to the light/darkness opposition, which, of course, is found in other Jewish texts,"[28] he neither analyzes properly the way the light/darkness opposition is presented nor does he inform us which are the "other Jewish texts" that have the same presentation. Although Bauckham has entitled his article "The Qumran Community and the Gospel of John," his discussion is restricted to the similarities and dissimilarities of the light/darkness imagery and its related "spirit of truth," as if that were the only matter of parallelism.

The elaborate Johannine dualistic scheme, briefly set forth above, has no parallel in Qumran literature. What is found, however, is a similarity in the manner in which a certain kind of theological dualism is presented. It is not a comprehensive dualism that sees everything in this world in opposite pairs (such as day and night, sun and moon, male and female), as is found in some other philosophical systems, but rather a theological dualism that envisages human beings and their behavior in the universe as subject to opposing principles of good and evil, which has also been adjusted to Judeo-Christian monotheism. This is a development beyond Old Testament teaching, where one does at times find agents of evil who tempt human beings: the serpent

(Gen 3:2-5), which is cursed eventually by God (Gen 3:14-15), or Satan in God's heavenly court (Job 1:6-12), and evil human beings attacking good ones. C. K. Barrett has admitted: "that John and Qumran both teach a 'modified dualism' is broadly true, but not very significant, since this modified dualism is to be found also in the Old Testament, which is well aware of the way in which good and evil, happiness and pain, life and death, light and darkness, stand over against each other . . . ."[29] Such opposites in the Old Testament may be recalled but, as John Painter has correctly remarked, "We find no developed or systematic expressions of a dualistic position in the Old Testament such as we find at Qumran and in Jn."[30]

In Qumran literature the Old Testament teaching about creation is further developed when it records that God ברא אנוש לממשלת תבל וישם לו שתי רוחות להתהלך בם עד מועד פקודתו הנה רוחות האמת והעול, "created man to rule over the world, and He put in him two spirits so that he might walk according to them until the time of His visitation; these are the spirits of truth and of deceit" (1QS 3:17-19). An extended section in the *Manual of Discipline* (1QS 3:13–4:26), too extended to quote here, develops an elaborate doctrine about these spirits, which contrasts them as light and darkness, righteousness and perversity, under dominion of the Prince of Lights or the Angel of Darkness, and lists all the effects they have on human beings. The latter are called either "sons of light/righteousness" (בני אור/צדק) or "sons of darkness/deceit" (בני חושך/עול, 3:20-21). It is a dualistic system set up by the one God of Israel, which affects human conduct and even has a cosmic dimension. Hence the dualism is monotheistic, ethical, and cosmic.[31] This dualism is not confined to the *Manual of Discipline* but is found also in the *War Scroll,* where "the sons of light" are to engage in an eschatological battle with the "sons of darkness" (1QM 1:1, 9-11), as "the lot of God" taking up arms against "the lot of Belial" (1:5, 14-16; cf. 4QM[f] [4Q496] 3 i 5-7). In the Aramaic text 4QVisAmram[f] (4Q548) 1:7-16 the fate of "the sons of light/righteousness" is contrasted with that of "the sons of darkness/deceit," viz., light, happiness, and rejoicing for the former; darkness, death, and annihilation for the latter. See also 4QCatena A (4Q177) 1-4:8-10; 11QapPs (11Q11) 4 v 7-8.

Not only is such a dualism found in Johannine writings, but it even makes use of some of the same terminology. It is expressed, moreover, as a struggle between light and darkness ("the light shines in the darkness, and the darkness did not overcome it," John 1:5), and also as a conflict between Jesus and the Prince of this World as they seek to influence human beings and their behavior (12:31-32; 14:30).

The similarity of the Qumran and Johannine dualisms is seen, first, in the formulation using light and darkness. Christian believers are urged to become "sons of light": "As long as you have the light, believe in the light, that you may become sons of light" (John 12:36).[32] Now בני אור, "sons of light" is used frequently as a designation of the members of the Qumran community (1QS

1:9; 2:16; 3:13, 24, 25; 1QM 1:1, 3, 9, 11, 13; 4QFlor [4Q174] 1-2 i 8-9; 4QCatena A [4Q177] 10-11:7; 12-13 i 7, 11; 4QD^a [4Q266] 1a-b:1; 4QSongsSage [4Q510] 1:7; and in Aramaic as בני נהורא, 4QVisAmram^f [4Q548] 1:16; partly restored in 4QVisAmram^b [4Q544] 3:1). All other Jews who were not part of their community were בני חושך, "sons of darkness" (1QS 1:10; 1QM 1:1; partly restored in 4QVisAmram^f [4Q548] 1:13).

Now admittedly the simple pair, light and darkness, as symbols of good and evil, is found in the Old Testament itself (Ps 112:4; Prov 4:18-19; Isa 5:20; 45:7).[33] It is noteworthy, however, that neither phrase, "sons of light" or "sons of darkness," is ever found in the Old Testament or in later rabbinic literature, despite the fact that "sons of . . ." is a thoroughly Semitic expression, imitating such phrases as בני חיל, "sons of might" (Judg 18:2; 2 Kgs 2:16), בני מרי, "sons of rebellion" (Num 17:25). What is distinctive, therefore, and what Bauckham and Barrett have failed to notice, is the division of humanity into two groups, using this Semitic phrase, as "sons of light" and "sons of darkness," which is found only in Qumran literature and, at least by implication, in the New Testament. Granted, the second of the two phrases actually is missing in the New Testament, but it is implied in the former. Nevertheless, one does find "the son of destruction" (ὁ υἱὸς τῆς ἀπωλείας), used of Judas in John 17:12, which can be compared with בני הווה, "sons of destruction" (1QH^a 13[old 5]:25; or בני אשמה, "sons of guilt" (1QH^a 13[old 5]:7).[34]

Second, the dualistic spirits bear verbally similar titles. Thus in 1 John 4:6 τὸ πνεῦμα τῆς ἀληθείας, "the spirit of truth," is pitted against τὸ πνεῦμα τῆς πλάνης, "the spirit of error," almost in the same way the two spirits of truth and deceit are cast in 1QS 3:17-19 (quoted above).

Third, the light/darkness imagery, when applied to human conduct, entails a similar walking in light or darkness: Thus "the one who follows me will not walk in darkness but will have the light of life" (John 8:12); "the one who walks in darkness knows not where he goes" (John 12:35); "if we say that we have companionship with him while walking in darkness, we lie and do not practice the truth; but if we walk in the light, as he is in the light, we have companionship . . . " (1 John 1:6-7); "the one who hates his brother is in darkness and walks in darkness . . . " (1 John 2:11). This walking in light or darkness can be compared with Qumran teaching, כול בני צדק בדרכי אור יתהלכו . . . ובדרכי חושך יתהלכו בני עול ובדרכי, "all the sons of righteousness walk on paths of light, but . . . the sons of deceit, and they walk on paths of darkness" (1QS 3:20-21); ללכת בכול דרכי חושך, "to walk on all the paths of darkness" (1QS 4:11); ואני . . . לסוד רמה והולכי חושך, "and I . . . belong to the assembly of worms and to those who walk in darkness" (1QS 11:9-10). Even the "light of life" is found in 1QS 3:7, כיא ברוח עצת אמת אל דרכי איש יכופרו כול עוונתו להביט באור החיים, "for through God's spirit of true counsel are expiated the paths of a human being, all his iniquities, so that he might gaze upon the light of life."[35]

Fourth, walking in light or darkness can also mean "to walk in the truth" (2 John 4; 3 John 3-4). This expression can be compared with כול הולכי בה, "all who walk in it" (i.e., truth, mentioned in the immediately preceding context, 1QS 4:6). This further association of truth and deceit/error with light and darkness means that two of the seven pairs of Johannine opposites are indeed found in Qumran literature.

Fifth, "the one who practises the truth" (John 3:21; also 1 John 1:6 [quoted above]) can be compared with ולעשות אמת וצדקה ומשפט בארץ, "and to practice truth, righteousness, and justice in the land" (1QS 1:5; cf. 8:2); לעשות אמת יחד . . . וענוה, "to practice together truth and humility . . . " (1QS 5:3). In this case both the Johannine writings and Qumran literature could be deriving the expression independently from the Old Testament,[36] but they both have it, and it makes its own contribution to the dualistic whole.

Sixth, bearing witness to the truth: thus "John has borne witness to the truth" (John 5:33); "I have come into the world to bear witness to the truth" (John 18:37); ". . . some of the brethren arrived and bore witness to the truth" (3 John 3). These expressions can be compared with עדי אמת למשפט, "witnesses of truth for justice" (1QS 8:6).[37]

Seventh, Jesus prays to the Father for his disciples, "Sanctify them in the truth" (John 17:17), which can be compared with ואז יברר אל באמתו כול מעשי גבר, "Then God will refine with His truth all human deeds" (1QS 4:20).

Some of the last-mentioned Johannine instances are not explicitly dualistic, because the counter phrase is lacking, but they at least fill out the picture of the way the ideas of truth and deceit, light and darkness function in these two bodies of literature.

The similarities noted concern only two of the seven pairs that comprise Johannine dualism. They are not by any means the principal pairs, and if it seems that they owe some influence to Qumran literature, this would not mean that "Johannine dualism as such derives from Qumran," as Bauckham rightly contests.[38] Moreover, it may be that some Johannine formulations of the light/darkness imagery "have no parallel in the Qumran texts," such as "the true light" (1:9; 1 John 2:8), or "the light of the world" (8:12; 9:5), or "to have the light" (8:12; 12:35-36), or "to come to the light" (3:20-21), etc.[39] But so what? Such omitted formulations are certainly not more significant than those that do have parallels. And who ever said that all the Johannine formulations of light/darkness imagery were or would be found in Qumran literature?

Bauckham has stressed the difference in meaning conveyed by the imagery, because in "the Fourth Gospel the central image of the light shining in darkness has christological and soteriological significance. Christ is the light of the world, come into the world so that people may come out of darkness into the light."[40] That is true, but why should one expect the light/darkness imagery to function in the same way in both bodies of literature? "At Qumran . . . there is no thought of people moving from 'the lot of darkness' into light."[41] True, but it is clearly said that "sons of light" may pass into darkness: "From the Angel of Darkness comes the straying of all the sons of righteousness, and all their sins, their iniquities, their guilt, and their offensive deeds (are) under his dominion" (1QS 3:21-22). In the long run such similarities as exist are more significant than the dissimilarities.

III. The Spirit of Truth

Particularly important, however, is the way in which the cosmic struggle between the spirit of truth and the spirit of deceit that God has put in humans is depicted in the Qumran texts. Thus ביד שר אורים ממשלת כול בני צדק בדרכי אור יתהלכו וביד מלאך חושך כול ממשלת בני עול ובדרכי חושך יתהלכו. ובמלאך חושך תעות כול בני צדק וכול חטאתם ועוונתם ואשמתם ופשעי מעשיהם בממשלתו, "In the hand of the Prince of Lights is dominion over all sons of righteousness; they walk on paths of light. And in the hand of the Angel of Darkness is total dominion over the sons of deceit; they walk on paths of darkness. From the Angel of Darkness (also comes) the straying of all the sons of righteousness, and all their sins, their iniquities, their guilt; their offensive deeds (are) under his dominion" (1QS 3:20-22). Also עד הנה יריבו רוחי אמת ועול בלבב גבר, "up until now the spirits of truth and deceit struggle in the heart of a man" (1QS 4:23). It is important to note that this cosmic figure is quite related to the light/darkness imagery in this section of the *Manual of Discipline*. The "Prince of Lights" is found (partly restored) also in 4QD^b (4Q267) 2:1; 4QD^a (4Q266) 3 ii 5.

Now, the terminology may not be completely the same in the Johannine writings, but the idea of the struggle is present: between Jesus, "the Son of God" (1:34; 5:25; 10:36)[42] and "the Prince of this World," i.e., the devil (12:31).[43] "He has no power over" Jesus (John 14:30), because he "will be cast out" (John 12:31) and "has been judged" already by the coming Paraclete (16:11). This struggle thus resembles that of the Prince of Lights and the Angel of Darkness in the Qumran texts mentioned above.

"Spirit of Truth" is a title not found in the Old Testament, but it occurs several times in Qumran texts as רוח האמת (1QS 3:18-19; 4:21, 23). Along with "the Prince of Lights," it is one of the two good principles dominating the conduct of human beings in this section. One could write simply "spirit of truth" (with lower case s and t), because in some instances the phrase might not connote much more, but the fact that it is paired with "the Prince of Lights" suggests that it too is personified (hence upper case S and T).

Similarly in the Johannine literature, Jesus and the Paraclete who is to come are two good principles, and the latter is even called the "Spirit of Truth" (14:17; 15:26; 16:13), using the very title of one of the Qumran good principles.[44] Moreover, the evangelist not only uses the neuter πνεῦμα of this principle, but deliberately personifies it, calling it by the masculine Παράκλητος.[45] The latter title is also given to Jesus himself implicitly or indirectly in John

14:16, when Jesus prays to the Father, asking that the Father send "another Paraclete" to be with his followers forever; and in 1 John 2:1 Jesus himself is called explicitly Παράκλητος. Furthermore, one must recall that the coming Paraclete is also named πνεῦμα ἅγιον, "holy Spirit" (John 14:26), a translation of Hebrew רוח קדושה, used in 1QS 3:7. In 4:21 רוח קודש, "spirit of holiness," occurs in parallelism with רוח אמת, "spirit of truth" as the means employed by God to purify humankind.[46]

Now Bauckham, who grants that "the Spirit of Truth" is a distinctively Johannine term, maintains that in John it "has no relationship to the light/darkness imagery."[47] That is true, but he fails to recall that "when the Spirit of Truth comes, it will guide you into all the truth" (John 16:13). Although the Spirit of Truth may not be related directly to the light/darkness imagery, it leads Jesus' followers to the truth/error imagery, which is itself connected to the light/darkness imagery.

IV. Love of Community Members

In the Fourth Gospel the evangelist records Jesus' most fundamental command given to his disciples, "A new commandment I give you, that you love one another; even as I have loved you, that you too should love one another. In this shall all people know that you are my disciples, if you have love for one another" (John 13:34-35). The command is reformulated in 15:12; 1 John 3:11, 14; 2 John 5.

In a similar way the *Manual of Discipline* begins by instructing the members of the community not only to "seek God with [all one's heart and] with al[l one's soul] and do what is good and upright before Him, as He commanded through Moses and through all His servants, the prophets," but also "to love all the sons of light, each according to his lot in God's plan" (1QS 1:2-3, 9-10). Similarly the *Damascus Document* ordains that "each one was to love his brother as himself" (לאהוב איש את אחיהו כמהו, CD 6:20; cf. 4QD^d [4Q269] 4 ii 2).[48] This love of another member of the community is further explained by the rule "that one should reprove his fellow-member in truth, in meekness, and compassionate love for each one. Let no one speak to [his brother] in anger or muttering" (1QS 5:25-26; 4QS^d [4Q258] 2:4-5).

This love of "the sons of light" has its counterpart in the detestation of "the sons of darkness": "to hate all the sons of darkness, each one according to his guilt in God's vindication" (1QS 1:10-11), i.e., all Jews not part of the community. This regulation is recorded also by Josephus, who speaks of "the awesome oaths" that the Essenes were made to swear: "to practice piety toward the Deity, observe justice toward human beings, . . . forever hate wrongdoers (τοὺς ἀδίκους) and do battle for the righteous (συναγωνιεῖσθαι τοῖς δικαίοις). . ." (*Bell.* 2.8.7 §139). Such hatred is not found in the teaching of Jesus recorded in the Johannine writings, even though the evangelist does depict Jesus himself purging the Jerusalem Temple of those who were defiling his Father's house (John 2:11-17).

V. Other Miscellaneous Parallels

Under this heading I should like to gather a number of items in Qumran literature that aid in the interpretation of certain Johannine passages. Such miscellaneous parallels are important because they go beyond the light/darkness imagery and may just be equally significant.

First, immediately after the prologue of the gospel, the evangelist records:

> This is the testimony of John, when the Jews sent priests and levites [to him] from Jerusalem to inquire of him, "Who are you?" He admitted and did not deny (it), stating, "I am not the Messiah." Then they asked him, "What then? Are you Elijah?" He said, "I am not." "Are you the prophet?" He answered, "No!" So they said to him, "Who are you? That we may have an answer for those who sent us. What do you say about yourself?" He said, "I am the voice of one crying in the wilderness, Make straight the way of the Lord, as Isaiah the prophet said" (1:19-23).

This well-known passage from the Fourth Gospel thus attests the expectation among first-century Palestinian Jews of three figures: Elijah *redivivus,* who was promised in Mal 3:23; the coming prophet, i.e., the prophet like Moses spoken of in Deut 18:15; and the coming Messiah, an anointed agent of God, such as the one mentioned in Dan 9:25-26, where the word משיח is used for the first time in the Old Testament of an *expected* Anointed One. John the Baptist insisted that he was not any one of them. Instead he identifies himself using Isa 40:3, the well-known words of Deutero-Isaiah, which are quoted in all four gospels to explain why John is out in the desert far from Jerusalem.

From Qumran literature we have learned of the expected figures the community awaited.[49] The *Manual of Discipline* speaks of the original "regulations by which the men of the community began to be instructed, until the coming of a prophet and the messiahs of Aaron and Israel" (עד בוא נביא ומשיחי אהרון וישראל, 1QS 9:10-11). Even though there is no mention of Elijah in this passage,[50] it attests the expected coming of a prophet (like Moses) and two messiahs (priestly and kingly). It thus provides pre-Johannine evidence of a live awareness of expected figures among some Jews in ancient Judea and supplies the background for the questions put to the Baptist by the Jerusalem emissaries in the Johannine gospel.

Second, although חיי עולם, "eternal life" appears in Dan 12:2 as the reward of "the wise,"[51] that concept appears often in Johannine writings as the destiny of believers (John 3:15-16, 36; 4:14; 5:24; 6:27, 40, 47, 54; 10:28; 17:2-3). Similarly, in Qumran literature "eternal life" is promised as "a reward for all who walk in it" (i.e., in the spirit of light or spirit of truth): "healing, abundance of peace in length of days, fruitful seed with all endless blessings, everlasting joy in life eternal, and a crown of glory with majestic raiment in eternal light" פקודת כול הולכי בה למרפא ורוב שלום באורך ימים ופרות זרע עם כול ברכות) עד ושמחת עולמים בחיי נצח וכליל כבוד עם מדת הדר באור עולמים, 1QS 4:6-8). Once again, הנה המחזיקים בו לחיי נצח וכל כבוד אדם להם הוא, "Those who cling steadfastly to it are (destined) for life eternal, and all the glory of Adam is theirs" (CD 3:20).[52]

Third, the idea of "living water" of which Jesus speaks is unique to the Johannine gospel and is never found on his lips in the Synoptic Gospels.[53] In John 4:10-11, in the conversation with the Samaritan woman, Jesus speaks of ὕδωρ ζῶν. Again in 7:38 Jesus invites the one who believes in him to come to him and drink, as Scripture has said, "Out of his innards shall flow rivers of living water," paraphrasing Zech 14:8,[54] and alluding to the coming gift of the Spirit (7:39). Similarly, the author of the *Hodayot* sings symbolically of the favors received from God: ואתה אלי שמתה בפי כיורה שם לכול] [ומבוע מים חיים, "But you, my God, have put in my mouth, as it were, an early rain for all [. . .] and a spring of living water" (1QHa 16[old 8]:16). In 4QDibHama (4Q504) 1-2 v 1 מקור מים חיים, "a source of living water," is found, but the immediate context is missing, so one cannot determine the sense in which it is used; but in line 15 it says כי]א יצקתה את רוח קודשכה עלינו, "[Fo]r you have poured your holy spirit upon us."[55]

Fourth, Bergmeier has called attention to a striking use of τὰ ἔργα τοῦ θεοῦ, "the works of God" (John 6:28-29) and its counterpart, מעשי אל (CD 2:14-15).[56] After depicting Jesus counseling the crowds not to labor for the food that perishes, but for the food that endures unto eternal life, the evangelist records that people asked Jesus, "What must we do to be working the works of God? (ἵνα ἐργαζώμεθα τὰ ἔργα τὰ τοῦ θεοῦ). Jesus' answer: "This is the work of God (τὸ ἔργον τοῦ θεοῦ), that you believe in him whom He has sent." Although commentators have debated the sense of "the works of God," it is now clear that it denotes the deeds that God desires of human beings.[57] This sense is made clear from CD 2:14-15, ועתה בנים שמעו לי ואגלה עיניכם לראות ולהבין במעשי אל ולבחור את אשר רצה ולמאוס באשר שנא להתהלך תמים, "And now, children, listen to me, and I shall open your eyes to see and to understand the works of God, so that you may choose what pleases (Him) and reject what He hates, so as to walk perfectly." The goal of doing what God desires is different in the two writings: faith in John and proper choice in CD, but in both cases "works of God" are seen to be what God demands of human beings.

Lastly, the First Epistle of John ends with the admonition, τεκνία φυλάξετε ἑαυτὰ ἀπὸ τῶν εἰδώλων, "little children, keep yourselves away from idols" (5:21). The author of the *Manual of Discipline* likewise warned the Essenes of Qumran, "Cursed be the one who enters this covenant with the idols that his heart reveres" (ארור בגלולי לבו לעבור הבא בברית הזות, 1QS 2:11-12).[58] Similarly, the *Damascus Document* describes those who enter the community but are slack in the observance of its instructions as having "placed idols in their hearts" (אשר שמו גלולים על לבם, CD 20:9). See also 1QH[a] 12[old 4]:15.

From the above parallels, which differ in their similarity, it is evident that the author(s) of the Fourth Gospel and Johannine epistles did not borrow directly from the Qumran writings. In other words, as Raymond Brown once put it, "the parallels are not close enough to suggest a direct literary dependence of John upon Qumran literature, but they do suggest Johannine familiarity with the type of thought exhibited in the scrolls."[59]

There remains a considerable gap between the christology and soteriology of the Johannine writings and the Qumran literature; the former is a Christian composition in which Jesus of Nazareth plays a central role, and it differs radically from the preoccupation of the latter with the Mosaic law and its observance. The influence of Qumran literature on the Johannine writings thus remains indirect, in some way that it is not possible to specify.

The least one can say is that the Qumran parallels strengthen the theory that the Johannine traditions stem from a Palestinian Jewish background. Moreover, such parallels are important because they are certainly pre-Johannine, which many of the Jewish texts that Bauckham cites as possible influences on the Johannine gospel and epistles are not.[60] Finally, *pace* James H. Charlesworth, the Dead Sea Scrolls have not "revolutionized our understanding of the Gospel of John."[61] The contemporary understanding of the Johannine gospel owes much to many other factors than the Qumran writings, important though the latter be in that understanding.

Postscript (Reply to the questions raised by the Response of Daniel J. Harrington).

The verbal and conceptual parallels in the Johannine writings constitute a real contact, even though it is only indirect, i.e., via some person(s) that one can identify only by speculation. In this category I put the thinking of Raymond Brown about the disciples of John the Baptist, who are mentioned in John 1:35, 37; 3:25, who undoubtedly would have heard the Baptist speaking of Jesus as ὁ ὀπίσω μου ἐρχόμενος "the one who comes after me" (John 1:27), but about whom the Baptist confesses, "I myself did not know him" (John 1:31). Recall too that Brown formulated that speculation in a question; he did not assert it, which indicates his own realization of the speculation. Of another sort would be that of John Ashton, which I did mention, that the evangelist is "more likely to have been an Essene" who was converted. Given the range of such possible speculation, I phrased the matter as I did at the end of my paper, that the influence—or now the contact—"remains indirect, in some way that it is not possible to specify." I continue to think that the Johannine writings manifest a real familiarity with the thought-world of the Essene community of Qumran, and I believe that one cannot dismiss that. Nor do I think that one can ascribe the influence solely to "mainstream first-century Judaism" or to what E. P. Sanders has called "common Judaism."[62] As for Harrington's query about whether the contact might be "merely 'apocalyptic Judaism,'" I should want to know what one means by "apocalyptic" Judaism. That the Essenes were composing apocalyptic writings is clear, but when that adjective is applied to "Judaism" as such, I do not understand what that means. Finally, I am not convinced by Hartmut Stegemann's "union" thesis.

Notes

1. See *CBQ* 17 (1955) 403–19, 559–74. This article was reprinted in an abridged form in Krister Stendahl, ed., *The Scrolls and the New Testament* (New York: Harper & Brothers, 1957) 183–207, 282–91, and in Michael J. Taylor, ed., *A Companion to John: Readings in Johannine Theology* (New York: Alba House, 1977) 69–90. It was translated into German as "Die Schriftrollen von Qumran und das Johannesevangelium und die Johannesbriefe," *Johannes und sein Evangelium*. WdF 82 (Darmstadt: Wissenschaftliche Buchgesellschaft, 1973) 486–528. Brown later shortened and corrected it in the third edition of his *New Testament Essays* (Garden City, NY: Doubleday, 1968; repr. New York: Paulist, 1982) 102–31.

2. In W. D. Davies and David Daube, eds., *The Background of the New Testament and Its Eschatology: In Honour of Charles Harold Dodd* (Cambridge: Cambridge University Press, 1956) 153–71. Long before the discovery of the Dead Sea Scrolls, Albright had published "Some Observations Favoring the Palestinian Origin of the Gospel of John," *HTR* 17 (1924) 189–95.

3. "L'Arrière-fond judaïque du quatrième évangile et la communauté de l'Alliance," *RB* 62 (1955) 5–44.

4. "La literatura de Qumrán y los escritos de San Juan," *Cultura Bíblica* 12 (1955) 250–64.

5. "The Significance of the Qumran Texts for Research into the Beginnings of Christianity," *JBL* 74 (1955) 213–26. See also idem, "Secte de Qumran, Hellénistes des Actes et Quatrième Évangile," *Les manuscrits de la Mer Morte: Colloque de Strasbourg 25–27 mai 1955* (Paris: Presses Universitaires de France, 1957) 61–74, 135–36; "A New Approach to the Interpretation of the Fourth Gospel," *ExpTim* 71 (1959–60) 8–12, 38–43; "Von Jesus zum Stephanuskreis und zum Johannesevangelium," in E. Earle Ellis and Erich Grässer, eds., *Jesus und Paulus: Festschrift für Werner Georg Kümmel . . .* (Göttingen: Vandenhoeck & Ruprecht, 1975) 44–56.

6. "The Dead Sea Scrolls and the Background for the Gospel of John," *BA* 17 (1954) 78–97.

7. Brown also wrote other articles on the same topic: "The Dead Sea Scrolls and the New Testament," *ExpTim* 78 (1966–67) 19–23; reprinted in James H. Charlesworth, ed., *John and Qumran* (London: Chapman, 1972) 1–8, especially 7–8, and in the enlarged version of the same book, *John and the Dead Sea Scrolls* (New York: Crossroad, 1990) 1–8, especially 7–8.

8. See Lawrence H. Schiffman and James C. VanderKam, eds., *Encyclopedia of the Dead Sea Scrolls*. 2 vols. (Oxford and New York: Oxford University Press, 2000) 1:414–17.

9. See Brown, *The Gospel According to John*. AB 29-29A (Garden City, NY: Doubleday, 1966, 1970) lxii–lxvi ("John and Qumran"); idem, *The Epistles of John*. AB 30 (Garden City, NY: Doubleday, 1982) 43–45.

10. See Martin Hengel, *The Johannine Question* (London: SCM; Philadelphia: Trinity Press International, 1989) 111.

11. See R. Alan Culpepper, *The Johannine School: An Evaluation of the Johannine-School Hypothesis Based on an Investigation of the Nature of Ancient Schools*. SBLDS 26 (Missoula: Scholars, 1975) 145–70; Georg Strecker, "Die Anfänge der johanneischen Schule," *NTS* 32 (1986) 31–47; Martin Hengel, *The Johannine Question*, 109–35.

12. See John A. T. Robinson, *Redating the New Testament* (Philadelphia: Westminster, 1976) 311.

13. See C. H. Dodd, *Historical Tradition in the Fourth Gospel* (Cambridge: Cambridge University Press, 1965) 429.

14. E.g., N. Adler, "Die Bedeutung der Qumrân-Texte für die neutestamentliche Wissenschaft," *MTZ* 6 (1955) 286–301, especially 292–93, 299; Günther Baumbach, *Qumrân und das Johannes-Evangelium*. AVTRW 6 (Berlin: Evangelische Verlagsanstalt, 1957); Roland Bergmeier, *Glaube als Gabe nach Johannes: Religions- und theologiegeschichtliche Studien zum prädestinatianischen Dualismus im vierten Evangelium*. BWANT 112 (Stuttgart: Kohlhammer, 1980) 63–116; Otto Betz, "Die Bedeutung der Qumranschriften für die Evangelien des Neuen Testaments," in idem, *Jesus—der Messias Israels: Aufsätze zur biblischen Theologie* (Tübingen: J. C. B. Mohr [Paul Siebeck], 1987) 318–32, especially 320; Otto Böcher, *Der johanneische Dualismus im Zusammenhang des nachbiblischen Judentums* (Gütersloh: Gerd Mohn, 1965); Marie-Emile Boismard, "The First Epistle of John and the Writings of Qumran," *John and Qumran* (n. 7 above) 156–65; Herbert Braun, *Qumran und das Neue Testament*. 2 vols. (Tübingen: J. C. B. Mohr [Paul Siebeck], 1966) 1:96–138, 290–306; 2:118–44; James H. Charlesworth, "A Critical Comparison of the Dualism in 1QS iii, 13-iv, 26 and the 'Dualism' Contained in the Fourth Gospel," *NTS* 15 (1968–69) 389–418; reprinted in *John and Qumran* (n. 7 above), 76–106; idem, "The Dead Sea Scrolls and the Gospel according to John," in R. Alan Culpepper and C. Clifton Black, eds., *Exploring the Gospel of John: In Honor of D. Moody Smith* (Louisville: Westminster John Knox, 1996) 65–97; idem, "Qumran, John, and the Odes of Solomon," *John and the Dead Sea Scrolls* (n. 7 above), 107–36; Joseph Coppens, "Le don de l'Esprit d'après les textes de Qumrân et le Quatrième Evangile," *L'Evangile de Jean: Etudes et problèmes*. RechBib 3 (Louvain: Desclée de Brouwer, 1958) 209–23; Feliks Gryglewicz, "Der Evangelist Johannes und die Sekte von Qumran," *MTZ* 10 (1959) 226–28; C. E. Gyllenhall, "Terminological Connections between the Gospel of John and the Dead Sea Scrolls," *New Philosophy* 90 (1987) 393–414; T. A. Hoffman, "1 John and the Qumran Scrolls," *BTB* 8 (1978) 117–25; Annie Jaubert, "The Calendar of Qumran and the Passion Narrative in John," *John and Qumran* (n. 7 above), 62–75; Karl Georg Kuhn, "Die in Palästina gefundenen hebräischen Texte und das Neue Testament," *ZTK* 47 (1950) 192–211; idem, "Johannesevangelium und Qumrântexte," in W. C. van Unnik, ed., *Neotestamentica et patristica: Eine Freundesgabe Herrn Professor Dr. Oscar Cullmann . . . überreicht*. NovTSup 6 (Leiden: Brill, 1962) 111–22; A. R. C. Leaney, "John and Qumran," in Elizabeth A. Livingstone, ed., *Studia Evangelica 6. Papers Presented to the Third International Congress on New Testament Studies*. TU 112 (Berlin: Akademie-Verlag, 1973) 296–310; idem, "The Johannine Paraclete and the Qumran Scrolls," *John and Qumran* (n. 7 above), 38–61; Leon Morris, *Studies in the Fourth Gospel* (Grand Rapids: Eerdmans, 1969) 321–58; John Painter, "John and Qumran," in idem, *The Quest for the Messiah: The History, Literature and Theology of the Johannine Community* (Edinburgh: T & T Clark, 1991) 29–39; J. L. Price, "Light from Qumran upon Some Aspects of Johannine Theology," *John and Qumran* (n. 7 above), 9–37; Kurt Schubert, "Das Verhältnis der Qumrantexte zum Johannesevangelium und zu den Johannesbriefen," in Johann Maier and Kurt Schubert, eds., *Die Qumran-Essener*. 2 vols. (Basel: Reinhardt, 1982) 131–33.

15. *JBL* 81 (1962) 1–13.

16. For instance, the following are examples of questionable suggestions: Otto Betz, "'To Worship God in Spirit and in Truth': Reflections on John 4,20-26," in Asher Finkel and Lawrence Frizzell, eds., *Standing before God: Studies on Prayer in Scripture and in Tradition with Essays in Honor of John M. Oesterreicher* (New York: Ktav, 1981) 53–72; George J. Brooke, "4Q252 and the 153 Fish of John 21.11," in Bernd Kollmann et al., eds., *Antikes Judentum und frühes Christentum: Festschrift für Hartmut Stegemann . . .* BZNW 97 (Berlin: Walter de Gruyter, 1999) 253–65; A. T. Hanson, "Hodayoth xv and John 17: A Comparison of Content and Form," *Hermathena* 118 (1974) 48–58; A. Shafaat, "*Geber* of the Qumran Scrolls and the Spirit-Paraclete of the Gospel of John," *NTS* 27 (1980–81) 263–69.

17. See n. 14 above.

18. See John Ashton, *Understanding the Fourth Gospel* (Oxford: Clarendon Press, 1991) 205, also 232–37.

19. See nn. 1 and 7 above.

20. *The Gospel according to St John.* 3 vols. (New York: Seabury/Crossroad, 1980–82) 1:126–35.

21. C. K. Barrett, *The Gospel according to St. John: An Introduction with Commentary and Notes on the Greek Text* (2d ed. Philadelphia: Westminster, 1978) 34; see also his *The Gospel of John and Judaism* (London: S.P.C.K., 1975) 56–58.

22. "Qumran and the Origin of the Fourth Gospel," *NovT* 4 (1960) 6–25.

23. See Richard Bauckham, "The Qumran Community and the Gospel of John," in Lawrence H. Schiffman et al., eds., *The Dead Sea Scrolls Fifty Years after Their Discovery: Proceedings of the Jerusalem Congress, July 20–25, 1997* (Jerusalem: Israel Exploration Society/Shrine of the Book, Israel Museum, 2000) 105–15, especially 105.

24. Ibid. 107.

25. Ibid. 114–15.

26. Ibid. 106.

27. See further John Ashton, *Understanding* (n. 18 above), 205–32.

28. "The Qumran Community" (n. 23 above), 106.

29. *The Gospel according to St. John* (n. 21 above), 34.

30. *The Quest for the Messiah* (n. 14 above), 30.

31. See further O. J. F. Seitz, "Two Spirits in Man: An Essay in Biblical Exegesis," *NTS* 6 (1959–60) 82–95.

32. This phrase is also found in Luke 16:8 (opposed to "sons of this world") and in 1 Thess 5:5 (opposed to people "of darkness"); cf. Eph 5:8 ("children of light"), so that it is not distinctively Johannine, but in none of these writings is it associated with the other details that make up and characterize Johannine dualism.

33. As Barrett notes (*Gospel according to St John* [n. 21 above], 34). It is also found, however, in extrabiblical literature, e.g., Plato, *Resp.* 7 §507e-509b, 518a. Indeed, it is almost a natural figure that can be paralleled in many literatures.

Bauckham is right when he says that "the contrast of light and darkness is the most obvious of dualisms observable in the natural world, and has therefore acquired the metaphorical meanings of knowledge and ignorance, truth and error, good and evil, life and death in most and perhaps all cultural traditions" ("The Qumran Community," 107), but it is not just that "both 1QS and the Fourth Gospel make more prominent use of this imagery than most Jewish texts" (ibid.); they use it in a distinctive way not found elsewhere. Even Str-B (2:219) had to admit that "der Ausdruck *běnê ʾôr* 'Kinder des Lichts' . . . ist im Rabbin. überhaupt nicht nachweisbar."

34. Bauckham says, ". . . the use of light and darkness to characterize the alternative eschatological destinies of the two classes of humanity is absent from John, even though this was common in Jewish eschatological imagery (e.g. Tob 14.10; Pss. Sol. 3.12; 14.9; 15.10; *1 Enoch* 1.8; 5.6-7; 46.6; 63.6; 92.3-5; 108.11-15)" (p. 110). Apart from Tob 14:10; *1 Enoch* 63:6; 92:4-5; 108:11-15, however, in all the other instances there is no mention of the pair, but only of either light or darkness. Moreover, in none of the passages listed does one find the distinctive Semitic formulae "sons of light" or "sons of darkness" that make John 12:36 so distinctively similar to the Qumran phrase. It may be a "single coincidence of terminology," as Bauckham calls it (p. 109), but it does not remain that when seen in light of the rest of the light/darkness and truth/error imagery in the Johannine writings.

35. *Pace* H. M. Teeple (n. 22 above), these expressions are a development beyond such OT passages as Isa 2:5; 50:10; Qoh 2:13-14, in none of which does one find "the light of life."

36. The expression ποιεῖν ἀλήθειαν, which occurs in the NT only in the two Johannine passages noted above, is found in the LXX of Gen 32:11; 47:29; Isa 26:10; and in Tob 4:6; 13:6, where the translation reflects the Hebrew of 4QTob^c (4Q200) 2:5, [אמת]ה בעשות.

37. See further Johannes Beutler, *Martyria: Traditionsgeschichtliche Untersuchungen zum Zeugnisthema bei Johannes* (Frankfurt: Knecht, 1972) 130–44.

38. "The Qumran Community" (n. 23 above), 107.

39. Ibid. 110.

40. Ibid. 111.

41. Ibid.

42. The title "Son of God" is found in the Aramaic text 4Q246 2:1 (ברה די אל), but that title for Jesus is not distinctively Johannine and is only noted in passing. On this see Joseph A. Fitzmyer, "The Aramaic 'Son of God' Text from Qumran Cave 4 (4Q246)," in idem, *The Dead Sea Scrolls and Christian Origins* (Grand Rapids: Eerdmans, 2000) 41–61.

43. As Brown has noted, *The Gospel According to John* (n. 9 above) 1:468.

44. It also turns up in Greek in the dualistic writing *TJudah* 20:1-5, which speaks of δύο πνεύματα . . . τὸ τῆς ἀληθείας καὶ τὸ τῆς πλάνης . . . γέγραπται ἐπὶ τὸ στῆθος τοῦ ἀνθρώπου, "two spirits . . . , one of truth and one of error, . . . have been written on the human breast." Here the two spirits are named as in 1 John 4:6.

45. See Raymond E. Brown, "The Paraclete in the Fourth Gospel," *NTS* 13 (1966–67) 113–32; "The 'Paraclete' in the Light of Modern Research," in Frank L. Cross, ed., *Studia Evangelica 4. Papers Presented to the Third International Congress on New Testament Studies,* vol. 1. TU 102 (Berlin: Akademie-Verlag, 1968) 158–65. Cf. Günther Bornkamm, "Der Paraklet im Johannesevangelium," *Festschrift Rudolf Bultmann* (Stuttgart: Kohlhammer, 1949) 12–35; Otto Betz, *Der Paraklet.* AGSU 2 (Leiden: Brill, 1963); George Johnston, *The Spirit-Paraclete in the Gospel of John.* SNTSMS 12 (Cambridge: Cambridge University Press, 1970); Eskil Franck, *Revelation Taught: The Paraclete in the Gospel of John.* ConBNT 14 (Lund: Gleerup, 1985).

46. Cf. 1QS 8:16; 9:3; 1QSb 2:24; CD 2:12; 1QH^a 15[old 7]:6-7; 17[old 9]:32; 20[old 12]:12; 4QŠirŠabb^f (4Q405) 14-15:2, etc. The phrase is derived from the OT (e.g., Ps 51:13; Isa 63:10, 11). Cf. F. F. Bruce, "Holy Spirit in the Qumran Texts," *ALUOS* 6 (1966–68) 49–55.

47. "The Qumran Community" (n. 23 above), 109.

48. And not just "your neighbor as yourself" (Lev 19:18). See further Urban C. von Wahlde, *The Johannine Commandments: 1 John and the Struggle for the Johannine Tradition* (New York and Mahwah, NJ: Paulist, 1990) 243, 269–71.

49. See further Joseph A. Fitzmyer, "Qumran Messianism," *The Dead Sea Scrolls and Christian Origins* (n. 42 above), 73–110.

50. Elijah is mentioned in an Aramaic fragment that is not yet officially published. Years ago Jean Starcky revealed two lines of its text, which he called 4QarP and dated to 50–25 B.C.E. One of the lines reads לכן אשלח לאליה קד[ם, "therefore I shall send Elijah bef[ore . . .]." Starcky translated it "je vous enverrai Elie avant [que ne vienne le jour de Yahweh], cf. Mal., iii, 23" ("Les quatre étapes du messianisme à Qumran," *RB* 70 [1963] 481–505, especially 497–98).

51. See also Sir 37:26, חכם עם ינחל כבוד ושמו עומד בחיי עולם, LXX: ὁ σοφὸς ἐν τῷ λαῷ αὐτοῦ κληρονομήσει τιμήν, καὶ τὸ ὄνομα αὐτοῦ, ζήσεται εἰς τὸν αἰῶνα.

52. See also 4QAgesCreatB (4Q181) 1:4 (לחיי עולם) 6; 4QInstruction^d (4Q418) 69 ii 12-13 (עולם נחלתם}[ם] וב[נ]י שמים אשר חיי[ם] . . . , "and the s[ons of] heaven, whose inheritance is eternal life"); 6QHymn (6Q18) 2:2. Cf. J. C. Coetzee, "Life (Eternal Life) in John's Writings and the Qumran Scrolls," *Neot* 6 (1972) 48–66.

53. It occurs several times in Rev 7:17; 21:6; 22:1, 17.

54. Zechariah writes: והיה ביום ההוא יצאו מים חיים מירושלם, "and it will come to pass on that day that living waters will go forth from Jerusalem."

55. מים חיים also occurs in 11QTemple (11Q19) 45:16, but there it is a question of bathing in "fresh running water," and it has no symbolic meaning.

56. See Roland Bergmeier, "Glaube als Werk? Die 'Werke Gottes' im Damaskusschrift ii, 14-15 und Johannes 6,28-29," *RevQ* 6 (1967–69) 253–60. He rightly points out that the same phrase occurs also in 1QS 4:4, but the use of it there hardly parallels the Johannine usage, as C. K. Barrett rightly notes in his comment on 6:28, while neglecting CD 2:14-15 (*The Gospel according to St. John* [n. 21 above], 287).

57. See Raymond E. Brown, *The Gospel According to John* (n. 9 above) 262.

58. Lines 16-17 add, "May God set him apart for evil, and may he be cut off from all the sons of light because of his straying from following God because of his idols." See also 1QS 4:5.

59. *The Gospel According to John* (n. 9 above) lxiii.

60. Influence on Johannine writings from such late writings as 4 Ezra, Pseudo-Philo, *Liber Antiquitatum Biblicarum, 2 Enoch,* Aristobulus (in Eusebius, *Praep. Evang.*), *Joseph and Asenath,* or even *Syriac Apocalypse of Baruch* is highly questionable.

61. "Reinterpreting John: How the Dead Sea Scrolls Have Revolutionized Our Understanding of the Gospel of John," *BRev* 9/1 (1993) 18–25, 54.

62. On which one should now consult M. J. Martin, "Interpreting the Theodotus Inscription: Some Reflections on a First Century Jerusalem Inscription and E. P. Sanders' 'Common Judaism,'" *ANES* 39 (2002) 160–81.

Response to Joseph A. Fitzmyer, S.J.
"Qumran Literature and the Johannine Writings"

Daniel J. Harrington, S.J.

Weston Jesuit School of Theology

Raymond Brown was one of the first scholars to use the newly discovered texts from Qumran in studying the New Testament. While preparing his doctoral dissertation under William Foxwell Albright on the Semitic concept of "mystery," in which he made abundant and effective use of the Qumran discoveries, he also wrote a two-part essay on "The Qumran Scrolls and the Johannine Gospel and Epistles" for the *Catholic Biblical Quarterly.*

In the fifty years since Brown's first publications on this issue the relevance of the Dead Sea scrolls for interpreting the Johannine writings has remained a topic of controversy. As Father Fitzmyer observes, opinions range from that of James H. Charlesworth that the Qumran texts have "revolutionized our understanding of the Gospel of John" to that of Richard J. Bauckham, who says that the "hypothesis of some kind of influence from Qumran on John . . . is mistaken."

In his essay on "Qumran Literature and the Johannine Writings," Father Joseph A. Fitzmyer, S.J., brings his enormous learning and careful judgment to bear on the topic. After a review of scholarship, he explores what he regards as the most significant verbal and conceptual parallels between the Qumran and the Johannine texts. He first considers their language about creation, especially their double formulation in both positive and negative modes. Second, he discusses various theological dualisms that place humans and their behavior as subject to opposing principles of good and evil. Third, he focuses on the cosmic struggle between the spirit of truth and the spirit of deceit. Fourth, he notes the common emphasis on love among members of the community. And fifth, he deals with "other miscellaneous parallels" pertaining to messianism and to theological expressions such as "eternal life," "living water," "the works of God," and keeping away from idols.

Father Fitzmyer concludes that the author(s) of John's gospel and the Johannine epistles did not borrow directly from the Qumran writings, that whatever influence there may be remains indirect in some way that is not possible to specify, and that at the very least the Qumran parallels strengthen the theory that the Johannine traditions stem from a Palestinian Jewish background.

Father Fitzmyer has done a great service in his comprehensive and careful study of the verbal and conceptual parallels between the Qumran texts and the Johannine writings. Responding to Father Fitzmyer is not easy, because I know (and you know) that he has already thought of everything on the topic and has decided for very good reasons what can and cannot be said. Nevertheless, in my response I am especially interested to see if we can move deeper into the relationship between the Qumran and the Johannine writings.

I will focus on three issues: the significance of the parallels, the Palestinian Jewish roots of the Johannine tradition, and some broader themes that may be important for understanding the Qumran scrolls and the Johannine writings. In an effort to place these parallels in a wider context I will raise three questions: (1) Do the verbal and conceptual parallels constitute a real contact? (2) Was John the Baptist (or his "school," or even a predecessor movement) the historical point of contact? (3) Do the broader thematic parallels help to establish a common worldview for the two groups?

First, the significance of the parallels. What do they mean? Against Richard Bauckham, Father Fitzmyer shows that there are many verbal and conceptual parallels between the Qumran and the Johannine texts. In his introduction, however, he notes Samuel Sandmel's famous caution about "parallelomania." Still, he finds inadequate E. R. Goodenough's reminder that in Euclidean geometry parallel lines never meet. The issue here is: Do the Qumran and Johannine parallels add up to a real contact?

In his conclusion Father Fitzmyer rejects the view that the Johannine writer(s) made direct use of the texts found among the Qumran manuscripts. He states his position in this way: "The influence of Qumran literature on the Johannine writings thus remains indirect, in some way that it is not possible to specify." My question here is: Is there is enough here to qualify as a "contact?" Or are we to be satisfied with Goodenough's concept of "parallels" that never meet? And if there is enough to declare a contact, what are the criteria for doing so and how are we to imagine this contact? Or must we be content with saying that the parallels tell us what was "in the air" or commonplace in first-century Palestinian Judaism?

Second, the Palestinian Jewish roots of the Johannine tradition. Can we be more specific here? In his posthumously published article on "The Gospel and Letters of John" in *The Encyclopedia of the Dead Sea Scrolls* (pp. 414–17), Raymond Brown concluded that the "Qumranian parallels fortify the thesis that the Johannine traditions arose in Palestine." Father Fitzmyer expresses his agreement when he says that "the Johannine traditions stem from a Palestinian Jewish background."

My concern here is whether the parallels allow us to be more concrete about this common background. Is the common background simply mainstream first-century Judaism as E. P. Sanders describes it? Is it merely "apocalyptic Judaism?" Or is it something more concrete, such as the Essene movement or even the broader *Yahad* or "Union" movement proposed by Hartmut Stegemann?

It is possible that some individual who played an important role in producing John's gospel—the Beloved Disciple, or the Evangelist, or even the Redactor—had been an Essene before becoming a Christian. But near the end of his article in *The Encyclopedia of the Dead Scrolls* Brown made what may be a better suggestion in the form of a question. He asked: "Did such Baptist disciples [that is, disciples of John the Baptist] who had been Qumranians filter what they heard from Jesus through the prism of their own dualistic outlook?" (p. 417). This intriguing comment does at least identify a possible conduit or point of contact for the many parallels between the Qumran and the Johannine texts. Almost every essay on Qumran and the New Testament suggests that if there was any direct contact between the two, the most likely candidate for explaining the contact is John the Baptist and the movement he generated (or even some predecessor movement). Moreover, the prominence of John the Baptist and his disciples in John 1:1-51, and especially the indication that the first followers of Jesus had once been followers of John the Baptist has long been a point of great interest among Johannine scholars. Must Brown's suggestion posed as a question at the end of his article remain in the realm of interesting speculation? Or are there ways to develop and confirm the hypothesis that the Qumran parallels to the Johannine writings had their historical point of contact in John the Baptist and his movement?

Third, let me address the broader thematic parallels. Do they contribute to establishing a common worldview for the Qumran and the Johannine communities? Father Fitzmyer has correctly focused on the specific verbal and conceptual parallels. But there is another set of parallels that operate at a broader level and have illuminated both sets of texts with regard to their common worldview and place in Judaism. They concern knowledge of God, community consciousness, and eschatology and ethics.

First, knowledge of God: For both groups the most important object of knowledge is God and God's plan being unfolded in history. And the most effective way toward this knowledge is through divine revelation. For example, in *Hodayot* we read: "I thank you, O Lord, for you have enlightened me through your truth. In your marvelous mysteries . . . you have granted me knowledge" (1QH 15:26-27). In John's gospel Jesus, the Word of God, has been sent by the Father to be both the revealer and the revelation of God. One of the great contributions of the Qumran scrolls to Johannine studies has been to bring the Johannine vocabulary of knowledge back to Palestinian Judaism and its wisdom tradition.

Second, community consciousness: Many commentators refer to the sectarian or "conventicle" consciousness of the two groups. Father Fitzmyer calls attention to the parallels concerning love for fellow community members, and he notes that detestation of those who are not community members is not found in the teaching of Jesus recorded in the Johannine writings. However, there are passages that do refer negatively to "the world" *(kosmos)* and "the Jews" *(hoi Ioudaioi),* and in both cases the principal reason why outsiders are to be "hated" seems to be that the outsiders oppose God's plan and thus show their hatred for God.

Third, eschatology and ethics: Many scholars contrast the realized eschatology of the Johannine writings and the future eschatology of the Qumran texts. In general this perception is correct. However, the Qumran scrolls illustrate nicely that realized and future eschatology can and do stand side by side in early Judaism too. So in John 5:24 Jesus declares that those who hear and believe have entered eternal life and have passed from death to life, while in 5:25-28 he paints a vivid picture of the coming judgment. Likewise, in the *Hodayot* and other Qumran texts there is frequent movement between hope for future vindication and acknowledgment of what God has already done in the community's life and history. Moreover, in the Qumran texts knowledge of the divine mystery *(raz)* or plan is the key to correct action in the present. Likewise in the Johannine writings, even though the word *mysterion* is not used, the revelation revealed by Jesus is fundamental to leading a Christian life in the present.

Part III
Johannine Theology

Chapter Six

The Death of Jesus and the Human Condition

Exploring the Theology of John's Gospel

Craig R. Koester

Luther Theological Seminary

The meaning of Jesus' crucifixion is a question that occupies a central place in Christian theology, and Raymond Brown made invaluable contributions to the discussion of this question through his magisterial commentary on John's gospel and his two-volume study of the Passion narratives.[1] Brown recognized that as a source for theological reflection the Fourth Gospel has few peers. His revised introduction to the gospel observes that if the Christian tradition regularly identified Paul as the Apostle, it hailed John as the Theologian, a title that befits a gospel writer of such depth.[2] Nevertheless, interpreters find that inducing John the Theologian to give a clear answer to a theological question can be a formidable task. We may ask whatever questions we like, but the reply always comes back in the same form: John tells the story of Jesus. The gospel carries no separable theology of Jesus' death; John's understanding of it must be discerned in and through his telling of the story.[3]

Traditionally Christians have woven John's story of the crucifixion together with those of the other gospels to create a single multicolored tapestry. By way of contrast, critical scholarship has more commonly moved in the other direction, seeking to disentangle the four stories so that each can be seen in its own right. Rather than looking for the similarities between the gospels, studies have usually stressed the differences, and John's account does not always fare so well in the process. The reason is that where the Synoptics tell of Jesus' suffering, John tells of Jesus' triumph. In the Synoptic gospels Jesus warns that the Son of Man must undergo great sufferings and be rejected and killed (Mark 8:31; 9:31; 10:33-34 par.). In John, Jesus says that the Son of Man must be "lifted up," an expression that suggests exaltation to glory (John 3:14; 8:28; 12:32), and he speaks of "going away" to the Father, which might imply that his death simply marks the transition between his life in the world below and his resumption of majesty with God above (13:1; 14:2; 16:5, 7).

According to John the soldiers approach Jesus in the garden, but they can arrest him only after falling to the ground when he utters the words, "I Am." On the way to Golgotha, Simon of Cyrene does not bear Jesus' cross; Jesus carries it himself. The scenes of mockery at Golgotha are gone, replaced by a gentle episode in which Jesus entrusts his mother to the Beloved Disciple. There is no pall of darkness, there is no cry of abandonment, but in triumph Jesus declares "It is accomplished," and hands over his spirit. The story seems to be a seamless outworking of the divine will.

Interpreters respond in different ways to John's account of Jesus' death. John Ashton provocatively remarks that the painful and shameful elements are so thoroughly suppressed that in the case of the Fourth Gospel the term "passion"—which means suffering—is really a misnomer, since Jesus controls and orchestrates the whole performance.[4] From this perspective what is disturbing is not the crucifixion, with its horror and shame, but John's treatment of the crucifixion, a treatment that replaces suffering with glory and humiliation with triumph. Others, however, find in John's gospel a deeper sense of paradoxical truth, the truth that divine glory is manifested in human flesh and that life with God is given through a crucified Messiah. They observe that if Jesus being "lifted up" connotes exaltation or glory, it is an exaltation that must be understood in terms of the crucifixion, since Jesus will be lifted up on the cross as Moses lifted up the serpent on the pole (3:14), and the evangelist makes clear that in speaking about being lifted up, Jesus points to the kind of death by which he will die (12:32).[5] These also point out—rightly in my judgment—that the crucifixion plays a defining role in the gospel, from the moment Jesus is introduced as the sacrificial Lamb of God in chapter 1 to the climactic scenes in which the risen Jesus shows his wounds to Thomas in chapter 20. Accordingly, the meaning of Jesus' death must be understood in light of the gospel as a whole.[6]

As we consider John's theology we do well to distinguish between what the gospel presupposes and what the gospel argues. The gospel presupposes that Jesus was a man who died by crucifixion. Throughout the gospel everyone in the story, both friend and foe, assumes that Jesus is a human being. His opponents may question his sanity, but they never doubt his humanity. For the Jewish leaders the issue is not whether Jesus is a human being, but whether he is a human being claiming equality with God. When Jesus declares, "I and the Father are one," they charge that "you, though a man, are making yourself God" (10:33). His humanity is a given; his higher claims are the problem.[7]

In the same way, the gospel assumes that the man Jesus died by crucifixion. The reality of his death is not in question. John's Passion account may help readers see the divine victory in the events surrounding Jesus' death, but the victory remains hidden from the people in the narrative. Readers may see the unfolding of God's purposes, but the participants in the story see only the execution of a man from Nazareth. The Fourth Gospel says that the soldiers arrested Jesus, bound him, and took him to Annas (18:12-13). One of them struck Jesus on the face, and Annas sent Jesus bound to Caiaphas (18:22, 24). Pilate had Jesus scourged; the soldiers hit and mocked him (19:1-3). Pilate handed Jesus over to be crucified, and they crucified him (19:16, 18). If the readers of John's Passion narrative see what follows as a triumph for Jesus, those who perform the execution do not. The gospel says that at the end of the day the soldiers who came to break the legs of the crucified men saw that Jesus "was already dead" (19:33).[8]

The death of the man Jesus is a given for the fourth evangelist. The question is what this death means, and the evangelist recognizes that people see the meaning quite differently depending on their frame of reference. From the perspective of the Jewish leaders in the gospel, the crucifixion is a fitting condemnation of a man who flouts the Law of Moses and threatens social stability (10:33; 11:48-50; 19:7, 12). From the perspective of Pilate, as John depicts him, crucifying a man whom some call king is politically expedient since it shows Pilate's loyalty to the emperor and lets the public know that opposition to Roman rule will not be tolerated (19:12-22). The fourth evangelist wants readers to see the crucifixion differently from the way Pilate or the Jewish leaders see it, and to achieve this he must develop alternative frames of reference. As interpreters we do well to think of multiple frames of reference rather than initially trying to define a single Johannine viewpoint, because the gospel construes the crucifixion in a number of different ways. Here we will consider the crucifixion as an expression of love in human terms, as a sacrifice for sin, as conflict with evil, and as a revelation of divine glory. In the history of theology these perspectives have often followed separate trajectories, but all appear together in John's gospel, opening up multiple dimensions of the singular act of Jesus' crucifixion as well as multiple dimensions of the human condition.[9]

Love in Human Terms

Beginning at the simplest level, John's gospel indicates that Jesus' death conveys love in human terms. During the Last Supper, Jesus said: "Greater love has no one than this, than to lay down one's life for one's friends" (15:13). In a basic sense this saying is a commentary on the crucifixion, indicating that Jesus will go to his death willingly out of love for his friends.[10] The idea is that if people show love by what they give for others, the most complete form of love is revealed through the most complete form of giving, the giving up of one's own life for other people. Readers would not need to belong to the circle of Jesus' followers to understand this. Plato, Aristotle, Seneca, and Paul agreed that true love and friendship might mean that one person would willingly die for another.[11] Drawing on this familiar idea, John's gospel turns it into a lens that brings the meaning of the crucifixion into focus. Jesus defines love by his words so that readers will see that he conveys love by his death.

John's account of Jesus washing the disciples' feet reinforces the point. The passage begins by saying that Jesus, "having loved his own who were in the world, loved them to the end" (13:1). By introducing the scene with an explicit statement about Jesus' love, the gospel enables readers to see the footwashing as a tangible expression of that love—and most early readers would have needed help seeing the footwashing in this way. If Jesus' statement about laying down one's life for one's friends sounds the lofty tones of virtue and heroism, his act of washing feet smacks of scandal and self-abnegation. People normally washed their own feet or had them washed by a slave. Therefore when Jesus the master washes the feet of the disciples he does the work of a slave, and Peter emphatically objects to his behavior, saying "Lord, you will never wash my feet" (13:8). There were, of course, rare instances when a free person would assume the role of a slave and wash another person's feet as an expression of complete devotion, but these were extremes—which is why the action suits Jesus' purposes so well.[12] He washes feet to show extreme love, to convey scandalous devotion, and to foreshadow his consummate act of self-giving on the cross.

The love expressed through the footwashing anticipates the love given through the crucifixion.[13] The gospel links the footwashing to the crucifixion by framing the episode with references to the impending betrayal (13:2, 18-30), and by saying that Jesus "laid down" his garments, echoing what was said earlier about laying down his life (10:17-18; 13:4). The introduction to the footwashing said that Jesus loved his own "to the end," which in Greek is *eis telos* (13:1), and this expression anticipates his final word from the cross: *tetelestai,* "it is accomplished," "the *telos* has been reached." Connecting the footwashing to the crucifixion enables readers to see that the love Jesus shows in a preliminary way by washing feet is the love he gives in a definitive way by laying down his life.

Presenting the crucifixion as love in human terms is theologically important for at least two reasons: First, it shows that if love is to be given to human beings it must be given in forms that can be grasped by human beings. Jesus comes from above, but he cannot reveal the things of God in heavenly speech. Human beings belong to the earth, and in his teaching Jesus refers to the things of the earth—such as bread, light, and water—to convey what comes from above. In the same way, Jesus washes feet like a slave and speaks of laying down one's life for a friend, drawing on patterns of earthly life to communicate with earthly people so that they might grasp the love he gives through his service in life and finally through his death.

Second, love is conveyed in human terms so that it can be lived in human terms. Jesus' death is both the source and the norm for Christian discipleship, according to John. After showing love by washing his disciples' feet Jesus directs them to wash one another's feet, saying, "as I have loved you, you also should love one another" (13:14-15, 34). Again, when explaining that the highest form of love is to lay down one's life for others, he relates this to the new commandment, that the disciples are to love one another as Jesus loved them (15:12-13). Since Jesus' love is the source and norm for Christian discipleship, he gives his love in tangible worldly forms so that his disciples might give their love in tangible worldly forms. Jesus' love is conveyed in human terms so that it may be lived in human terms.[14]

Sacrifice for Sin

Readers find themselves in a different theological context when they consider the death of Jesus through the words of John the Baptist: "Behold the Lamb of God, who takes away the sin of the world" (1:29). Here we move from the realm of love and service to the sphere of sin and sacrifice. Rather than relating the crucifixion to the circle of Jesus' friends, the passage relates it to the world and its sin. This perspective on the death of Christ presupposes a more radical sense of human alienation from God. Although some interpreters have argued that John's Lamb of God imagery is an isolated vestige of early Christian tradition that has little importance for Johannine theology, the final form of the gospel gives the imagery a prominent place.[15] Jesus is called the Lamb of God at the moment he first enters public view in chapter 1, and no one follows Jesus until John the Baptist says again, "Behold the Lamb of God," prompting two of John's own disciples to follow Jesus (1:29, 36). To discern the theological implications we must consider each part of John's statement in turn.

First is the expression "the Lamb of God." Introducing Jesus as the Lamb at the beginning of the gospel anticipates his death at Passover at the end of the gospel. According to John's distinctive chronology Jesus ate his last meal with the disciples on the night before Passover, rather than on Passover evening as in the other gospels (13:1). On the morning before Jesus' execution the Jewish authorities avoided entering the praetorium in order to keep themselves pure for the Passover meal that evening (18:28). Jesus was taken out to be crucified on the day of preparation for the Passover at about noon, when the sacrifice of the Passover lambs began in the Temple (19:14). The slaughter of the lambs was to be completed before sundown, and John relates that the soldiers saw that Jesus was dead before evening fell (19:31). The soldiers broke the legs of the two men who hung beside Jesus, but they did not break Jesus' legs since he was already dead. The gospel relates this to the Scripture passage that says, "His bones shall not be broken" (19:36), citing the Torah's stipulation that the bones of a Passover lamb are not to be broken.[16]

The link between the crucifixion and the Passover sacrifice seems clear, but its meaning is not simple. A Passover lamb was not generally regarded as a sacrifice for sin, but was more closely associated with deliverance from death. According to Exodus 12 the people of Israel observed the first Passover in

Egypt by putting lamb's blood on their doorposts and lintels, not to atone for sin, but to prevent the destroyer from entering their homes and slaying their firstborn. The annual Passover sacrifice of the lambs commemorated this deliverance. To account for the connection between the Lamb of God and sin, some interpreters plausibly suggest that the gospel combines Passover imagery with that of the suffering servant of Isaiah 53, who is compared to a lamb that is led to the slaughter and who is said to bear the sins of many.[17] By drawing on these and other backgrounds the Fourth Gospel develops a new type of imagery in which Jesus the Passover Lamb of God delivers people from death precisely by delivering them from sin.

This brings us to the second element in John the Baptist's testimony: "the sin of the world." Sin, in the Fourth Gospel, is fundamentally a theological notion; it is a problem in one's relationship with God that by extension affects one's relationships with other people. Sin is the alienation from God that is expressed in a refusal to believe in Jesus, the one whom God has sent. The particular sins that people commit manifest this underlying antipathy toward God and Jesus, so that sin encompasses both unbelief and the actions that proceed from it (15:18-25). The sin of the world is fundamentally the world's alienation from God and the one whom God sent.

The third element of John the Baptist's testimony is that the Lamb of God "takes away" sin. The Fourth Gospel regularly uses this verb (*airein* in Greek) to mean taking away or removing something.[18] If sin is the unbelief that separates people from God, then the Lamb of God removes sin by removing unbelief. In Johannine theology sin is taken away when faith is evoked. Sin is the opposite of faith, and both are relational notions. If sin is a deadly alienation from God, then faith is a lifegiving relationship with God, and the death of Christ takes sin away when it moves people from sin into faith. If sin is the hatred that separates people from God, then faith awakens the love that binds people to God, and the death of Christ calls forth human love for God by conveying God's love to humankind.

The dynamics of divine sacrificial love are reflected in John 3, which anticipates that as Moses lifted up the serpent on the pole, so must the Son of Man be lifted up on the cross, so that whoever believes in him may have eternal life (3:14-15). The passage goes on to say that it was because God so loved the world that he gave his only Son—and in light of the previous verses God's giving of the Son includes giving him up to die (3:16). It was because God so loved the world that he gave his only Son up to death, so that whoever believes in him might not perish but have eternal life. If on one level the crucifixion conveys Jesus' love for those who followed him, on another level it conveys God's love for the world that hated him. John's ominous sense of the world's sin is what gives this text its edge. The "world" in John's gospel is not characterized by radiant sunsets and gentle breezes, by the colors of spring flowers or the golden hues of fall—it requires no sacrifice to love a world like that. But in John's gospel God loves the world that hates him; he gives his Son for the world that rejects him; he offers his love to a world estranged from him in order to overcome its hostility and bring the world back into relationship with its Maker. The proper theological term for this is "atonement," for if atonement means reconciling parties that have been separated, then the sacrificial love of God, conveyed through the death of Jesus, brings about atonement in a Johannine sense when it overcomes the hostility of unbelief by bringing about faith.[19]

This way of understanding John's language differs from the views of scholars who assume that if the gospel uses sacrificial language it must construe Jesus' death as a vicarious or substitutionary sacrifice.[20] The notion of vicarious sacrifice revolves around the two poles of justice and mercy or law and grace. The idea is that when someone transgresses a law, justice requires that the person be punished. In cases of severe wrongdoing, justice might require that a person surrender his or her own life. As an act of mercy, however, a transgressor might be allowed to offer something in exchange for his or her life: a vicarious sacrifice. When this paradigm is transferred to the realm of theology, human beings are regarded as sinners who are justly condemned by God. Because God is just, he expects the penalty for sin to be paid, but because God is merciful he allows the penalty for sin to be paid by his own Son Jesus, who dies in the place of sinners. The result is that Jesus' self-sacrifice honors the need for divine justice while making room for divine mercy.

The Fourth Gospel, however, operates with a different theological framework. The gospel does not relate Jesus' death to the need for divine justice but to the need for human faith. When the gospel speaks of the wrath of God it says that the wrath of God threatens those who do not believe (3:31). When Jesus tells his opponents that they will die in their sins he adds that they will die in their sins unless they believe (8:24). When the Advocate, the Spirit, comes to convict the world of sin after Jesus' return to the Father, readers are told that the sin that brings judgment is the world's unbelief (16:8-9). According to the Gospel of John, people fall under divine judgment because of unbelief and they are delivered from divine judgment by being brought to faith (3:17). When the love of God, revealed through the death of Jesus, overcomes the sin of unbelief by evoking faith it delivers people from the judgment of God by bringing them into true relationship with God. This is atonement in the Johannine sense.

Proponents of a substitutionary view sometimes respond that John's gospel might exhibit a vicarious notion of sacrifice in the sayings about the good shepherd laying down his life "for" *(hyper)* the sheep (10:11, 15) and in Caiaphas's remark that one man should die "for" the people (11:50).[21] Nevertheless, there is no suggestion that the good shepherd lays down his life to deliver the flock from divine judgment. Instead, the shepherd shows his devotion by laying down his life for the flock in contrast to the hired hand who cares nothing for the sheep (10:13-14). Later, Caiaphas's comment initially has to do with Jesus dying in order to save the people from the consequences of a popular uprising, rather than from divine judgment. The evangelist interprets the meaning of Caiaphas's comment in terms of Jesus' death unifying his followers (11:51-52). Laying down one's life for *(hyper)* others expresses love, but John's gospel does not develop the idea in terms of vicarious atonement.

The theme of cleansing is another way the gospel relates the death of Jesus to the removal of sin.[22] When Jesus washes the disciples' feet he says, "If I do not wash you, you have no part with me" (13:8). We have already noted that Jesus washes the disciples' feet to show his love for them, and that the love he shows by washing anticipates the love he gives by dying. Therefore when Jesus says he must wash people he indicates that he must cleanse them by the love he conveys through his death. The counterpart to washing is uncleanness, which in John's gospel is associated with opposition to Jesus and the God who sent him. The account of the footwashing specifically identifies Judas as unclean because of the hostility he shows by betraying Jesus (13:11). For people to be made clean, their opposition to Jesus must be removed. They are washed when the love Jesus extends by his death purges away the alienation of sin and brings people into the relationship with Jesus that is faith. To be in such a relationship is to be clean and to have a part with Jesus (13:8; cf. *met' emou*, 17:24).

Presenting Jesus' death as the means of removing sin adds theological depth to the Fourth Gospel in at least two ways. First, it takes seriously the depth of the world's estrangement from God. When we looked at Jesus' death as love in human terms we noted that he spoke of laying down his life for his friends (15:13). Now we see that he lays down his life for a world characterized by sin. Sacrificing one's life for a friend expresses a relationship of love that already exists; sacrificing one's life for a sinful world is done to create a relationship of love where one does not exist. Jesus' death may provide an example of love for people to follow, but a sinful world needs more than an example or it will not follow. The Lamb is sacrificed to create a relationship of faith in the face of the alienation created by sin.

Second, the sacrificial dimension accents the singular quality of what God does through the death of Jesus. Many lambs were slaughtered at Passover, but Jesus is the Lamb of God in the singular. Many human beings have shown their love by laying down their lives for others, but in John's gospel Jesus' death is a unique and definitive action. The Lamb of God is the Lamb *from* God, the Lamb that God provides. It is out of God's love for the world that he gave his one and only Son to be crucified in order to bring an estranged world back into relationship with its Creator.

Conflict and Victory

We enter yet another theological world when we hear Jesus say, "Now is the judgment of this world, now will the ruler of this world be cast out; and I, when I am lifted up from the earth, will draw all people to myself"; the narrator explains that Jesus said this to show by what death he was to die (12:31-33). Rather than speaking of love and friendship or sin and sacrifice, this passage interprets the crucifixion in terms of conflict and victory in a world dominated by a hostile power.[23] Here the basic problem is not so much human sin as it is the oppressive power of evil. People are not only sinful and in need of atonement, they are oppressed by evil and in need of liberation. Jesus' opponent, according to this passage, is the ruler of this world, whom the gospel also calls Satan, the devil, and the evil one (13:2, 27; 17:15). John never fully personifies Satan, but by telling of Jesus' clashes with opponents he alerts readers that evil works through human actions such as hatred and deceit (7:7; 8:44). Therefore, as the battle with evil reaches its climax in the Passion, Jesus must meet hatred with divine love and deceit with divine truth.

Judas is the devil's ally in the Passion story. Judas is initially linked to evil in John 6, but the plot thickens in John 13, where readers learn that the devil himself has determined that Judas will betray Jesus (13:2-3). Jesus' strategy in the conflict with evil is to show unwavering love (13:1). He assumes his battle dress by laying down his garments, girding himself with a towel, and taking up a basin to wash feet. The text makes clear that Jesus does not act out of weakness, but out of the strength of one who has come from God, who is going to God, and who has been given authority by God to manifest his power in an act of devoted love (13:1, 3). God has put all things in Jesus' hands, and Jesus uses his hands to wash the disciples' feet, apparently including the feet of Judas. Therefore if Judas remains unclean, as the text says he does, it is not because Jesus excludes him from his cleansing love, but because Judas is resistant to what Jesus offers (13:11).[24]

The gospel indicates that Jesus possesses superior battlefield intelligence and knows that Judas will hand Jesus over to his enemies. Yet when asked to identify the betrayer, Jesus dips bread into the supper dish and gives it to Judas—a gesture commonly understood to show favor.[25] This gracious act on Jesus' part provokes intense demonic resistance in Judas, for when he receives the bread, Satan enters him (13:27). The action and response disclose the nature of the conflict, for what evil resists is the graciousness that Jesus extends. The gospel says that Jesus chooses Judas, washes Judas, and gives Judas food (6:70-71; 13:1-11, 26), so that Satan's entry into Judas marks opposition to the graciousness Jesus shows. This opposition does not mean that evil is the superior force, however, for Judas does not depart from the table until Jesus gives him leave, saying, "What you are going to do, do quickly" (13:27). Judas leaves the table only at Jesus' bidding, and in scenes to come Jesus will turn the destructive designs of evil toward the accomplishment of God's saving ends.

Jesus tells the disciples who remain with him, "I will no longer talk much with you, for the ruler of this world is coming. He has no power over me, but I do as the Father has commanded me so that the world may know that I love the Father. Rise, let us be on our way" (14:30-31). When Jesus finally leaves the supper and arrives in the garden he is met by Judas and a group of soldiers and police, who serve as agents of the ruler of this world.[26] Jesus seizes the initiative by asking whom they are seeking. When they reply "Jesus of Nazareth," he says "I Am," using words that recall the name of God, and Judas and the soldiers draw back and fall to the ground. The episode bears out that the ruler of this world has no power over Jesus (18:5-6).

Many a scriptwriter would end the scene here, with Judas and the soldiers lying helplessly on the ground and Jesus standing coolly erect after his effortless victory, but John does not do so. At the end of the episode the soldiers arrest Jesus, bind him, and take him away. So why subdue the opposition only to be taken captive? Jesus subdues the opposition long enough to secure the release of his disciples: "If you are looking for me, let these men go" (18:8). John tells the story to show the extent to which Jesus cares for his own. Divine power is used for human deliverance. Jesus subdues the opposition so that others might be set free, but he himself is bound and taken away by his captors because the battle is not yet over and he must infiltrate more deeply into his opponents' territory where judgment will take place.

John's gospel understands that people are judged by their positive or negative responses to Jesus.[27] A saying earlier in the gospel sets the tone: "Those who believe are not condemned; but those who do not believe are condemned already" (3:18). Therefore during the hearings before Pilate and the Jewish authorities the world is judged as it passes judgment on Jesus. Jesus engages in this conflict by rejecting the weaponry of the world and meeting his opponents armed only with truth (18:36-37). In some of the gospel's most ironic scenes, Jesus' accusers make charges that bring Jesus closer to death while bringing the accusers themselves under judgment.[28] The Jewish leaders charge that Jesus opposes Roman rule, yet they are the ones who demand the release of Barabbas the insurrectionist, and they insist that Jesus opposes God by elevating himself to divine status, yet they finally give their highest loyalty to the emperor, one of the men who was regularly elevated to divine status.[29] Pilate the gentile fares no better. He claims to have the power to do whatever he wants with Jesus, and he declares three times that Jesus is innocent, which is true. But if Pilate knows the truth, he proves powerless to do the truth, for in the end he hands over an innocent man to be crucified. In one sense this episode is a defeat, for the claims made against Jesus lead to his death, but in another sense it is a victory for truth since the world's pretensions to power and right are exposed to the readers. In passing judgment on Jesus the world reveals the truth about itself.

"Now is the judgment of this world; now will the ruler of this world be cast out" (12:32). John's gospel describes no mythic fall of Satan, but it intimates that the ruler of this world is cast out as the crucified Jesus is lifted up as the world's true sovereign.[30] Jesus is given his royal robe and crown of thorns during the scourging that prepares him for death; Pilate acclaims him a king before handing him over to his executioners; and Jesus is enthroned by means of crucifixion. If the sign above the cross reads "Jesus of Nazareth, the King of the Jews," it says this in Hebrew, in Latin, and in Greek for all the world to see. On the cross one sees the proper ruler of this world, according to John, the king whose love and truth cast out the power of hatred and deceit. His kingdom is not "from" the world since his power comes from above rather than below (18:36; cf. 6:15), yet Jesus does reign for the world and rightly bears the title "Savior of the world" (4:42).[31]

The theme of conflict and victory enables John's story of the crucifixion to confront readers with two forms of dominion. One is that of the crucified Jesus, whose resolute love, witness to the truth, and obedience to God bring him to his throne on Golgotha. The other is that of the sinister ruler of this world who entwines his allies in a web of hostility and deception as he seeks to bring about the death of the Son of God. From this perspective readers find that there is no place for neutrality. In the cosmic battle between God and evil the question is which claimant to the throne will obtain the readers' loyalty. The fourth evangelist is a participant in the conflict, exposing the pretensions of evil in order to capture the readers for the crucified and risen king.

Love remains central to John's understanding of the crucifixion, but when viewed in the context of conflicting powers it assumes a new vitality. Love is a weapon in a conflict, and it serves along with truth to dethrone the forces that oppose it. Those who follow Jesus are called to love as he loved, and if Jesus wielded love in the face of evil, then his disciples' love may also take militant forms. The expression of love is complex rather than simple. Jesus loved by washing feet and contending with Satan. For those who follow, love means service to others and witness to truth; it entails giving of oneself and opposing evil. For the writer of the Fourth Gospel, authentic love encompasses all of this.

Revelation of Divine Glory

Shifting our perspective one last time, we can consider the crucifixion in terms of glory. Jesus' final prayer before his arrest sounds the theme: "Father, the hour has come; glorify your Son so that the Son may glorify you . . . I glorified you on earth by accomplishing the work you gave me to do. So now, Father, glorify me in your own presence with the glory I had in your presence before the world existed" (17:2, 4-5). The theme of glory takes us into yet another theological world, one that deals with the human need to know God.[32] The word "glory" *(doxa)* sometimes connotes honor (5:41), but in John's gospel glory also has to do with the way God is revealed to human beings. This theological world recognizes that people were created to know God, and the prayer in John 17 therefore states that eternal life means knowing the one true God and Jesus Christ, whom God has sent (17:3). To know God is to be in relationship with God, yet the gospel also recognizes that people have no immediate knowledge of God. "No one has ever seen God," the gospel says (1:18). God's presence is hidden until God chooses to reveal it. The theme of glory has to do with the way revelation takes place.

The prominence of glory in a prayer that concludes the Last Supper and leads into the Passion has, however, generated sharp debate. By looking back to Jesus' ministry as a period of glorifying God on earth and by looking ahead to Jesus resuming his preexistent glory with the Father in heaven the prayer seems to let the cross drop from view. For some interpreters the prayer shows that the Johannine Jesus simply moves from earthly glory to heavenly glory with the crucifixion marking the transition between the two spheres.[33] Others maintain—rightly, I think—that the crucifixion has a more integral role to play in John's understanding of glory.[34] To discern what this might be, we must consider the key parts of Jesus' saying in light of the wider gospel story.

First, Jesus said that he glorified God on earth by accomplishing the work God gave him to do. Jesus' earthly ministry was done to glorify God, and in a basic sense this means he honored God through his faithful obedience to God's commands. During his public ministry Jesus claimed to teach what God wanted him to teach, and to perform the healings and other works God wanted him to perform. Such faithfulness honors God (8:49). In another sense, however, Jesus glorified God by revealing God's power. Biblical writers sometimes use the term *doxa* or "glory" for the way the power of God is brought within the realm of human experience.[35] According to John's gospel, Jesus made divine power visible by the miraculous signs he performed. At the beginning of his ministry Jesus manifested his glory by turning water into wine at Cana (2:11), and at the end of his ministry he revealed the glory of God by calling the dead man Lazarus back to life (11:40). John's account of Jesus' career encompasses these and other miraculous acts, which reveal divine glory by revealing divine power.

A second element in Jesus' prayer concerns the glory he will resume in heaven once his ministry on earth is over. This heavenly glory is something that the Son of God enjoyed before the world existed. To share in such glory is to share in divine honor, divine majesty, and divine power. It was out of love that the Father gave the Son such glory before the foundation of the world, so that sharing in God's glory means sharing in God's love. By means of his Passion, Jesus will return to the Father and enter a heavenly glory his followers on earth cannot fully perceive, but can hope to see in the future. Therefore Jesus concludes his prayer by asking that those God has given him may one day be with him in God's presence to see the fullness of the glory God gave to him in love (17:24).

The prayer traces a movement from glory on earth to glory in heaven, and given only the lines we have considered thus far it would be easy to bypass the cross without comment. Yet other passages do connect glory more directly to the crucifixion itself. When Jesus enters Jerusalem at the end of his ministry he says: "The hour has come for the Son of Man to be glorified," and he compares himself to a seed that must fall into the earth and die (12:23-24). When Judas receives the piece of bread and departs to betray him, Jesus says: "Now the Son of Man has been glorified, and God has been glorified in him" (13:31). The saying does not limit glorification to what happens after the crucifixion, but links glorification to the process of betrayal that culminates in the crucifixion. And this brings us back to the prayer in John 17 where Jesus says that he has glorified God on earth by accomplishing the works God gave him to do. The Greek word for "accomplish" is *teleioun,* the word Jesus will utter at the time of his death when he says *tetelestai,* "it is accomplished." If Jesus glorifies God on earth by accomplishing God's works, he glorifies God by the crucifixion that completes these works. The question is how he does this.

Given the way Jesus manifested divine glory by miraculous acts of power during his ministry, we might expect a battery of miracles to occur during his crucifixion. The patristic writer John Chrysostom evidently had this expectation, but when commenting on how Jesus could be glorified by crucifixion he found no Johannine miracles to suit his needs. To explain how the Fourth Gospel could suggest that the crucifixion manifested divine glory, Chrysostom had to import material from the Synoptics.[36] It was in Matthew, Mark, and Luke that he found the cross most vividly framed with displays of divine power. He understood that the eerie pall of darkness the Synoptics place over the crucifixion was a visible sign of supernatural force, and that the dramatic tearing of the Temple curtain revealed the hand of God. He understood that God's glory was palpable in Matthew's account of the earth quaking and the saints rising on Good Friday.[37] The irony is that these traditional signs of divine power are missing from John's gospel. John gives his readers no portents in heaven or on earth. If readers are to see glory in the crucifixion, they must see it in another way.

Put briefly, if the signs reveal God's glory by displaying divine power, the crucifixion reveals God's glory by disclosing divine love.[38] The crucifixion completes Jesus' work of glorifying God on earth, for by laying down his life he gives himself completely so that the world may know of Jesus' love for God and God's love for the world (3:16; 14:31). By his resurrection and ascension Jesus returns to the heavenly glory God prepared for him in love, and Jesus prays that his followers will one day join him in the Father's presence to share in this glory and love (17:5, 24-26). To the eye of faith, however, the glory of the exalted Lord is already present in the crucified body of Jesus.[39] If glory defines what the crucifixion is, the crucifixion defines what glory is. The crucifixion manifests the scope of divine power by disclosing the depth of divine love.

Concluding Reflections

The meaning of Jesus' crucifixion was the question with which we began, and we have explored the way the Fourth Gospel conveys its meaning from a number of perspectives. We started by considering the human side of Jesus' death and concluded by considering it as divine revelation, but this does not mean that the gospel takes us on a straight-line ascent from the mundane truths of earth to the dizzying heights of heaven only to leave us there. The human and the divine, the sacrificial and the militant dimensions of Jesus' death must all be taken together for readers to gain a sense of the whole. Each dimension also assumes something different about the human condition. In one sense Jesus died for human beings in need of love and friendship; in another sense he died for sinners in need of atonement. In another sense he died for those oppressed by the powers of evil, and in yet another sense he died for those who were created to know God. The human condition has as many dimensions as the crucifixion itself.

Love is the element all these perspectives have in common. One might say very simply that according to John's gospel Jesus died to make God's love known. What keeps this simple statement from becoming simplistic is the way the gospel pulls and stretches its readers by opening up different dimensions of the crucifixion's meaning. Human and divine, giving and resisting—the differing aspects work together like the treble and bass lines in a musical composition, all of which must be played for the music to be heard properly.[40] To say that Jesus died a human death in love for his followers is true, but when taken alone it is inadequate, for it might suggest that Jesus' death was merely one instance among countless others in which a person made a noble self-sacrifice for others. Similarly, saying that his death reveals the glory of divine love is true, but when taken alone, this too is inadequate, for without the human dimension it can turn divine love into a free-floating sentiment that has no tangible expression. The prologue to John's gospel says that from Christ's fullness people receive grace upon grace (1:16), and in telling the story of Jesus, the evangelist weaves together a number of perspectives so that readers may come to know something of the fullness of the crucified Word.

Notes

1. Raymond E. Brown, *The Gospel According to John.* 2 vols. AB 29-29A (Garden City, NY: Doubleday, 1966, 1970); idem, *The Death of the Messiah: A Commentary on the Passion Narratives in the Four Gospels.* 2 vols. ABRL (New York: Doubleday, 1994).

2. Raymond E. Brown, *An Introduction to the Gospel of John,* edited by Francis J. Moloney. ABRL (New York: Doubleday, 2003) 220.

3. Brown, *Death of the Messiah,* 29. Brown plausibly argued that the Fourth Gospel was composed in several stages over a period of years, yet he insisted that one had to deal with the text in its final form, which is the approach taken here (*Introduction to the Gospel of John,* 111). See also Francis J. Moloney, "Raymond Brown's New Introduction to the Gospel of John: A Presenta-

tion—and Some Questions," *CBQ* 65 (2003) 1–21, especially 5, 16. On story and theology see Gail R. O'Day, "The Word Becomes Flesh: Story and Theology in the Gospel of John," in Fernando F. Segovia, ed., *What is John? Volume II: Literary and Social Readings.* SBLSymS 7 (Atlanta: Scholars, 1998) 67–76.

4. *Understanding the Fourth Gospel* (Oxford: Clarendon Press, 1991) 489. Cf. Ernst Käsemann, *The Testament of Jesus: A Study of the Gospel of John in the Light of Chapter 17* (Philadelphia: Fortress, 1968) 4–26; Ulrich B. Müller, "Zur Eigentümlichkeit des Johannesevangeliums: Das Problem des Todes Jesu," *ZNW* 88 (1997) 24–55.

5. See also 8:28, where Jesus refers to being lifted up by his opponents, which will occur when they crucify him. On "lift up" and crucifixion see Francis J. Moloney, *Signs and Shadows: Reading John 5–12* (Minneapolis: Fortress, 1996) 193; Jörg Frey, "Die *'theologia crucifixi'* des Johannesevangeliums," in Andreas Dettweiler and Jean Zumstein, eds., *Kreuzestheologie im Neuen Testament* (Tübingen: J. C. B. Mohr [Paul Siebeck], 2002) 169–238, especially 188.

6. Jean Zumstein, "L'interprétation johannique de la mort du Christ," in Frans van Segbroeck, Christopher M. Tuckett, Gilbert van Belle, and Jozef Verheyden, eds., *The Four Gospels: Festschrift Frans Neirynck.* 3 vols. BETL 100 (Leuven: Leuven University Press/Peeters, 1992) 2119–38; Thomas Knöppler, *Die theologia crucis des Johannesevangeliums: Das Verständnis des Todes Jesu im Rahmen der johanneischen Inkarnations- und Erhöhungschristologie.* WMANT 69 (Neukirchen-Vluyn: Neukirchener Verlag, 1994); Müller, "Zur Eigentümlichkeit," 37.

7. The Johannine epistles argue against those who deny that Jesus Christ came in the flesh (1 John 4:1-3; 2 John 7). Some maintain that aspects of John's gospel are also designed to counter docetic tendencies (Udo Schnelle, *Antidocetic Christology in the Gospel of John: An Investigation of the Place of the Fourth Gospel in the Johannine School* [Minneapolis: Fortress, 1992]). Elements in the gospel can function in an antidocetic way, but in its basic direction the gospel argues neither for nor against the humanity of Jesus, but presupposes it. See Marianne Meye Thompson, *The Humanity of Jesus in the Fourth Gospel* (Philadelphia: Fortress, 1988) 121–22; cf. 87–115 on Jesus' death.

8. On common crucifixion practices and John's Passion narrative see Craig R. Koester, *Symbolism in the Fourth Gospel: Meaning, Mystery, Community* (2nd ed. Minneapolis: Fortress, 2003) 210–16.

9. Gustaf Aulén distinguished theories that considered the death of Jesus to be an example, a sacrifice, and a victory over evil (*Christus Victor: An Historical Study of the Three Main Types of the Idea of the Atonement* [New York: Macmillan, 1969]). Nevertheless, all of these are present in John's gospel. Cf. Barnabas Lindars, "The Passion in the Fourth Gospel," in Jacob Jervell and Wayne A. Meeks, eds., *God's Christ and His People: Studies in Honor of Nils Alstrup Dahl* (Oslo: Universitetsvorlaget, 1977) 71–86. Martinus C. deBoer proposes that some of the gospel's multiple perspectives on Jesus' death developed over time in response to crises within the community (*Johannine Perspectives on the Death of Jesus* [Kampen: Kok Pharos, 1996]).

10. Hartwig Thyen, "'Niemand hat grössere Liebe als die, dass sein Leben seinen Freunden hingibt' (Joh 15:13)," in Carl Andresen and Günther Klein, eds., *Theologia crucis—Signum crucis: Festschrift für Erich Dinkler zum 70. Geburtstag* (Tübingen: J. C. B. Mohr [Paul Siebeck], 1979) 467–81. Cf. Brown, *Gospel According to John,* 664.

11. Plato, *Symposium* 179b; Aristotle, *Nicomachean Ethics* 9.8 1169a; Seneca, *Moral Epistles* 9.10; Diogenes Laertius, *Lives* 10.120; Rom 5:7.

12. On footwashing see Koester, *Symbolism in the Fourth Gospel,* 127–34. For examples of footwashing as a show of devotion see 1 Sam 25:41; *Jos. Asen.* 13:13-15; Catullus, *Poems* 64.158-63.

13. On the relationship between the footwashing and the crucifixion see Brown, *Gospel According to John,* 566; Johannes Beutler, "Die Heilsbedeutung des Todes Jesu im Johannesevangelium nach Joh 13,1-20," in Karl Kertelge, ed., *Der Tod Jesu: Deutungen im Neuen Testament* (Freiburg: Herder, 1976) 188–204; Rudolf Schnackenburg, *The Gospel According to St. John.* 3 vols. (New York: Herder/Seabury/Crossroad, 1968–82) 3:19; Francis J. Moloney, *The Gospel of John.* SP 4 (Collegeville: Liturgical Press, 1998) 373–79.

14. On the love commandment see Raymond F. Collins, *These Things Have Been Written: Studies on the Fourth Gospel* (Louvain: Peeters; Grand Rapids: Eerdmans, 1990) 217–56. On the problems that arise when the Johannine tradition fosters a diminished sense of Jesus' humanity or a truncated view of Christian love see Raymond E. Brown, *The Epistles of John*. AB 30 (Garden City, NY: Doubleday, 1982) 73–86.

15. Those who downplay the sacrificial imagery include Ashton, *Understanding the Fourth Gospel*, 491; Rudolf Bultmann, *Theology of the New Testament*. 2 vols. (New York: Charles Scribner's Sons, 1951, 1955) 2:53; de Boer, *Johannine Perspectives*, 277–81; J. Terence Forestell, *The Word of the Cross: Salvation as Revelation in the Fourth Gospel*. AnBib 57 (Rome: Pontifical Biblical Institute, 1974) 157–66; Müller, "Zur Eigentümlichkeit," 50–51. Those who give greater weight to the sacrificial imagery include Brown, *Gospel According to John*, 918, 951–53; C. K. Barrett, *The Gospel According to St. John* (2nd ed. Philadelphia: Westminster, 1978) 176–77; Lindars, "The Passion in the Fourth Gospel," 72–74; Knöppler, *Die theologia crucis*, 67–101; Frey, "Die *'theologia crucifixi,'*" 200–219; Mary L. Coloe, *God Dwells With Us: Temple Symbolism in the Fourth Gospel* (Collegeville: Liturgical Press, 2001) 190–96; cf. Helge Kjaer Nielsen, "John's Understanding of the Death of Jesus," in Johannes Nissen and Sigfred Pedersen, eds., *New Readings in John: Literary and Theological Perspectives. Essays from the Scandinavian Conference on the Fourth Gospel in Århus 1997*. JSNTSup 182 (Sheffield: Sheffield Academic Press, 1999) 232–54, especially 250–53.

16. Exod 12:46; Num 9:12. Similar words are used for the righteous sufferer of Ps 34:21, whose legs were not broken, but the connection with the Passover lamb is primary (Brown, *Death of the Messiah*, 1185–86). On the complex textual background see M. J. J. Menken, *Old Testament Quotations in the Fourth Gospel: Studies in Textual Form*. CBET 15 (Kampen: Kok Pharos, 1996) 147–66.

17. On the various associations connected with the Lamb of God imagery see Brown, *Gospel According to John*, 60–63; Koester, *Symbolism in the Fourth Gospel*, 219–24.

18. The Fourth Gospel uses the verb *airein* in a physical sense for removing doves from the Temple (2:16), a stone from a tomb door (11:41; 20:1), a branch from a vine (15:2), and a body from its burial place (20:2). In an extended sense it entails taking away life or joy (10:18; 16:22). The verb does not suggest that the Lamb took sin upon himself, but that he took it away (Forestell, *Word of the Cross*, 160–65).

19. On the sacrificial overtones in 3:16 see Brown, *Gospel According to John*, 134, 147. On the role of faith in taking away sin see R. Alan Culpepper, *Anatomy of the Fourth Gospel: A Study in Literary Design* (Philadelphia: Fortress, 1983) 88; Lindars, "The Passion in the Fourth Gospel," 82.

20. A nuanced case for the substitutionary view is that of Andrew T. Lincoln, *Truth on Trial: The Lawsuit Motif in the Fourth Gospel* (Peabody, MA: Hendrickson, 2000) 203. On the role of vicarious sacrifice in atonement theories see Colin Gunton, *The Actuality of Atonement: A Study of Metaphor, Rationality and the Christian Tradition* (Grand Rapids: Eerdmans, 1989) 83–141.

21. For a vicarious interpretation of 10:11-15 and 11:50 see Knöppler, *Die theologia crucis*, 201–16. Those who do not find such a vicarious view operative in John include Beutler, "Die Heilsbedeutung," 190–91, and Frank J. Matera, "'On Behalf of Others,' 'Cleansing,' and 'Return': Johannine Images for Jesus' Death," *LS* 13 (1988) 161–78, at 164–70.

22. See Matera, "'On Behalf of Others,'" 170–72; Gail R. O'Day, "The Gospel of John," *New Interpreters Bible* 9 (Nashville: Abingdon, 1995) 491–865, especially 724.

23. On conflict, victory, and the crucifixion see Judith L. Kovacs, "'Now Shall the Ruler of This World Be Driven Out': Jesus' Death as Cosmic Battle in John 12:20-36," *JBL* 114 (1995) 227–47; Herbert Kohler, *Kreuz und Menschwerdung im Johannesevangelium: ein exegetisch-hermeneutischer Versuch zur johanneischen Kreuzestheologie* (Zürich: Theologischer Verlag, 1987) 237–39. The expression "cast out" *(ekballein)* is used in the other gospels for casting out demons (e.g., Mark 1:34, 39, 43). John, however, reports no exorcisms, but links the casting out of evil to Jesus' Passion. Cf. Eric Plummer, "The Absence of Exorcisms in the Fourth Gospel," *Bib* 78 (1997) 288–94.

24. William Klassen, who deals with Judas sympathetically, is critical of John's portrayal (*Judas: Betrayer or Friend of Jesus* [Minneapolis: Fortress, 1996] 137–59). He does not, however, deal adequately with the gospel's theological dynamics. More helpful is Kim Paffenroth, *Judas: Images of a Lost Disciple* (Louisville: Westminster John Knox, 2001) 33–36. She rightly notes that Judas is not well developed in the gospel. Nevertheless, there are more dimensions to John's portrayal of Judas than are commonly noted (Koester, *Symbolism in the Fourth Gospel,* 73–75).

25. Brown, *Gospel According to John,* 578; Moloney, *Gospel of John,* 384.

26. Cf. Francis J. Moloney, *Glory Not Dishonor: Reading John 13–21* (Minneapolis: Fortress, 1998) 52–53; Coloe, *God Dwells With Us,* 184–85.

27. O'Day, "Gospel of John," 712.

28. On ironic judgment in John 18–19 see Paul D. Duke, *Irony in the Fourth Gospel* (Atlanta: John Knox, 1985) 126–37; Lincoln, *Truth on Trial,* 123–38.

29. Roman emperors were formally deified at their deaths, but the imperial cults sometimes included the living emperors in divine honors. See S. R. F. Price, *Rituals and Power: The Roman Imperial Cult in Asia Minor* (Cambridge: Cambridge University Press, 1984).

30. The saying in 12:31-32 adds that when the ruler of this world is cast out, Jesus will be lifted up and draw people to himself. The lifting up points to his crucifixion, and Brown has plausibly argued that the crucified Jesus demonstrates his power to draw people to himself by drawing Nicodemus and Joseph of Arimathea into asking for the body of Jesus (*Death of the Messiah,* 1265–68).

31. O'Day, "Gospel of John," 830. The title "Savior of the world" was sometimes used for the Roman emperors. See Craig R. Koester, "'The Savior of the World' (John 4:42)" *JBL* 109 (1990) 665–80. Cf. Michael Labahn, "'Heiland der Welt.' Der Gesandte Gottessohn und der römische Kaiser—ein Thema johanneischer Christologie?" in idem and Jürgen Zangenberg, eds., *Zwischen den Reichen: Neues Testament und römische Herrschaft* (Tübingen: Francke, 2002) 147–73.

32. See John Painter, "Inclined to God: The Quest for Eternal Life—Bultmannian Hermeneutics and the Theology of the Fourth Gospel," in R. Alan Culpepper and C. Clifton Black, eds., *Exploring the Gospel of John. In Honor of D. Moody Smith* (Louisville: Westminster John Knox, 1996) 346–68.

33. Käsemann, *Testament of Jesus,* 6–13; Godfrey C. Nicholson, *Death as Departure: The Johannine Descent-Ascent Schema.* SBLDS 63 (Chico: Scholars, 1980) 149–55; Ashton, *Understanding the Fourth Gospel,* 490–96; Müller, "Zur Eigentümlichkeit," 48; Jürgen Becker, *Das Evangelium nach Johannes. Kapitel 11–21.* ÖTK 4/2 (3rd ed. Gütersloh: Gerd Mohn; Würzburg: Echter, 1991) 468–74.

34. D. Moody Smith, *The Theology of the Gospel of John* (Cambridge: Cambridge University Press, 1995) 115–22; Thompson, *Humanity of Jesus,* 87–105; O'Day, "Gospel of John," 790; Donald Senior, *The Passion of Jesus in the Gospel of John* (Collegeville: Liturgical Press, 1991) 15–18; Moloney, *Glory not Dishonor,* 24; Frey, "Die 'theologia crucifixi,'" 186.

35. Brown, *Gospel According to John,* 509.

36. John Chrysostom, *Homilies on St. John* 72.4 (NPNF[1] 14:265).

37. On the way the darkness, the torn curtain, the earthquake, and the rising of the saints show divine power see Brown, *Death of the Messiah,* 1034–43, 1097–1105, 1129–40.

38. C. H. Dodd, *The Interpretation of the Fourth Gospel* (Cambridge: Cambridge University Press, 1953) 207–208.

39. Forestell, *Word of the Cross,* 73–74.

40. Cf. Jan A. du Rand, "Reading the Fourth Gospel Like a Literary Symphony," in Fernando F. Segovia, ed., *What is John? Volume II: Literary and Social Readings.* SBLSymS 7 (Atlanta: Scholars, 1998) 5–18.

The Love of God Incarnate

The Life of Jesus in the Gospel of John

Gail R. O'Day

Candler School of Theology, Emory University

Professor Koester identifies four "frames of reference" through which the Gospel of John "construes the crucifixion": as an expression of love in human terms, as a sacrifice for sin, as conflict with and victory over evil, and as a revelation of divine glory. Professor Koester does a careful job of showing how each of these frames of reference is visible in the story of the Fourth Gospel.

Koester's analysis also shows that these four frames of reference are not really four distinct perspectives, but are inseparably overlapping. The common piece of all four perspectives is the centrality of love. In Koester's discussion the meaning of love comes to the center of each perspective as much as the meaning of the crucifixion does. The centrality of love is explicit in the first category (defining love in human terms), but is also central to the exposition of the other three categories. For the category of sacrifice Koester writes, "[People] are washed when the love Jesus extends by his death purges away the alienation of sin and brings people into a relationship with Jesus that is faith." For the category of conflict and victory Koester writes, "Love is a weapon in a conflict, and it serves along with truth to dethrone the forces that oppose it." For the category of the revelation of God's glory Koester writes of love, "If the signs reveal God's glory by displaying divine power, the crucifixion reveals God's glory by revealing divine love." In his conclusion Koester writes, "One might say very simply that according to John's gospel, Jesus died to make God's love known."

As useful as Koester's paper is in identifying the frames of reference through which one can understand the crucifixion of Jesus in John, the paper rests on a question that is not John's central theological concern. John's shaping theological question is not about the meaning of the death of Jesus; it is about the meaning of the life of Jesus. Koester rightly notes that "the gospel contains no separable theology of Jesus' death," and that John's understanding of the death must be discerned in and through his telling of the story. But he nonetheless treats Jesus' death as a distinct category. In John, Jesus' death is inseparable from his life, which is why love comes to the center in each of Koester's categories. Jesus did not die to make God's love known; Jesus *lived* to make God's love known.

In this response I will explore the inseparability of Jesus' life and death in John from theological and literary perspectives. First I will look at the incarnation, Jesus' life and death, as the definitive theological category for John. Then I will look at how the theological centrality of the incarnation informs the way John tells the story of Jesus' life and death. The gospel integrates the ever-present reality of Jesus' death into the narration of his life.

"And the Word Became Flesh"

For the Gospel of John the defining theological category is and remains the incarnation. This is a commonplace in Johannine studies, but it needs to be re-stated and reasserted in the context of any study of the death of Jesus in John. Three statements in the Prologue warrant special attention for fixing the centrality of the incarnation: the classic statement of 1:14, "And the Word became flesh and dwelt among us and we have beheld his glory, glory as of the only begotten of the Father, full of grace and truth"; 1:16, "From his fullness we have all received grace upon grace"; and 1:18, "No one has ever seen God. It is God the only Son, who is close to the Father's heart, who has made God known."

These verses are the necessary—and to a degree, the only necessary—frame for understanding the revelation of God in Jesus. God is made known in the enfleshed life of the Word in the world, and that life is one of fullness and grace, not sacrifice and emptying. John 1:14 could not be farther removed from the kenotic perspective of Phil 2:6-8, for example. Both Paul and John begin from a pre-incarnational perspective, but they part ways at the moment of the incarnation. For Paul, and this is the perspective that dominates most Protestant conversations about the life and death of Jesus, the incarnation is a moment of emptying, of "giving up" that reaches its nadir in the death on the cross (Phil 2:8). The low point of the death is then balanced by the high point of exaltation (Phil 2:9). But for John the incarnation is not an emptying; it is a moment of fullness.

To say that the Word becomes flesh, *sarx,* leaves little doubt as to the tangible presence of the incarnate Word in the world. The radical theological claim here is often overlooked because (1) many Christians look beyond the incarnation for redemption and salvation in the death of Jesus, and/or (2) we read *sarx* through the lens of Paul and Bultmann and not through John. "Flesh" is never identified with or used as a metaphor for the realm of human sin or even human brokenness in John. *Sarx* is the coinage of human life and mortality. When it is used as a figure of speech, *sarx* is more synecdoche than metaphor in John. It is the part, flesh, standing for the whole, human life. We see this in 1:13 when the gospel contrasts new birth as children of God with birth "of the will of the flesh." The flesh is the realm of ordinary human existence, as it is also in John 3:6, "The one who is born of the flesh is flesh," and 17:2, "you have given him authority over all flesh."

When the Word becomes flesh, flesh is *at that moment* redeemed. Jesus' death is not necessary to redeem humanity; he redeems flesh by becoming flesh. Flesh is now the habitation of the holy. Human flesh is now the embodiment of God in the world. The presence of God dwells in the flesh, not in the *shekinah* of the wilderness tabernacle or of the Holy of Holies. God can be seen and known in a human life and in the fullness of that life. The Word becomes flesh and dwells among us. The intimacy of this theological moment cannot be overemphasized. God is known because the Word, who dwells near the Father's heart, also dwells with human hearts. Indeed, the Word has a human heart. The incarnation places the most positive value on human life.

Koester makes a very helpful distinction in his paper between what John presupposes and what the gospel argues. In announcing the incarnation John presupposes, and does not argue, that the Word-become-flesh will die. One of the marks of the flesh, of a human life, is mortality. By becoming flesh the Word joins humanity in its mortality. It would not be the incarnation if there were no death, which is something that docetics and their opponents readily recognized. It borders on the tautological to say that Jesus is human because he dies and he dies because he is human, but such a tautology has real theological significance. Death is redeemed and redeeming because Jesus dies, because the Word-made-flesh lives a full life.

This affirmation of the life of Jesus, of which his death is a part, as the locus of revelation and redemption runs counter to understandings of soteriology and redemption that place the definitive weight for redemption on Jesus' death on the cross. Koester writes, for example, that "The dynamics of divine sacrificial love are reflected in John 3:16, which says that God so loved the world that he gave his only Son *up to death* so that whoever believes in him might not perish but have eternal life." Koester's sentence is a direct quote of John 3:16, with the significant exception of the addition of the words "up to death" as the interpretation of "give," *didōmi*. While this addition may be warranted by theological interpretations that equate Jesus' decisive gift with his death, I do not think this addition can be supported by the text of the Gospel of John. John 3:16 is about God's act of love in the incarnation, not singly about God giving Jesus up to death.

The importance of the incarnation for this verse is indicated by one of its key words, *monogenēs*. John 3:16 and 18 are the only occurrences of *monogenēs* outside of the Prologue. In the Prologue *monogenēs* is the decisive adjective that gives the incarnation a human face and form. It brings the language of birth and generation into the incarnation. Much of Christian theology moves quickly to the non-literal meaning of this adjective, often translating it as "unique" or "one and only," and dropping the links to the "birth" root meaning. Yet given John's propensity for words conveying a double meaning—especially in this section of chapter 3 *(anōthen, pneuma, hypsoō)*—and for that double meaning to be an essential part of what the word communicates, one wonders if such a double layering is also at play here with the use of *monogenēs*. The word can be read simply in the sense of "unique," but at the same time it communicates the source of the uniqueness, "only begotten." The association of father and son language with *monogenēs* in John 1 and here in John 3 confirms the importance of the birth and generation metaphor field in translating and interpreting *monogenēs*. It belongs to the language of incarnation.

Monogenēs as the language of birth and incarnation also fits with what Jesus has just discussed with Nicodemus in the preceding verses. Nicodemus has difficulty understanding the language of *anōthen,* in part because he cannot hold the physical and the spiritual together. Jesus tries to clarify Nicodemus's misunderstanding by restating the kind of birth he envisions with the phrase "born of water and Spirit." This phrase highlights the new life of which Jesus speaks, because "water" evokes the waters of physical birth and "spirit" points to a new birth from God. The physical birth and the spiritual rebirth go hand in hand, however, because flesh and spirit belong together in the new birth Jesus envisions. One is not reborn to a new life apart from the physical body; one is reborn to a new life within the physical body. In this way what Jesus offers Nicodemus is what Jesus himself models in the incarnation: God-made-present in the flesh.

As the language of incarnation, *monogenēs* helps to interpret the gift of God to which John 3:16 refers and the shape of God's love that is visible in the gift. The fullness that characterizes language about the incarnation in John 1:14-18 ("full of grace and truth," "grace upon grace") is repeated here in the vocabulary of love and gift. One is not required to see a reference to the giving up to death; rather, the Johannine context leads one to see instead the full gift of the incarnation as that which makes eternal life possible.

"My hour has not yet come"

The complete integration of Jesus' life and death in the incarnation shapes the way the gospel story is told. I want to focus on two ways in which this shaping can be seen in the unfolding of the gospel story.

First, the gospel regularly mentions Jesus' death as part of the narration of the events of his life. The two main events narrated in John 2—the miracle at the Cana wedding and the cleansing of the Temple—show this clearly.

The conversation between Jesus and his mother at the Cana wedding is punctuated by Jesus' reference to his "hour": "My hour has not yet come" (2:4). Jesus mentions the non-arrival of his hour in response to his mother's comment that the wine at the wedding is gone. His mother makes no direct request of Jesus, but Jesus responds to what he takes as her implied request, that he do something about the problem. To speak of Jesus' hour in John is to speak of the interrelated moments of Jesus' death, resurrection, and ascension. This constellation of moments will reveal God's glory. Jesus' initial rebuff of his mother in v. 4 seems to suggest that she is asking him to reveal something that can only be revealed in his hour. And yet—and this is the key to this miracle—Jesus acts in advance of his hour. He provides more wine for the wedding, and as the narrator concludes, "Jesus did this, the first of his signs, in Cana of Galilee, and *revealed his glory,* and his disciples believed in him."

Here, in the opening act of his ministry, Jesus does what will also later be said of his hour: he reveals his glory. Nothing in the narration of the miracle story indicates that this is a partial or even proleptic revelation of his glory. To the contrary, this revelation of glory leads his disciples to faith. John 2:1-11 is the first example of what John 1:13 promises: "to all who believed in his name he gave power to become children of God."

This story shows how Jesus' life and death are of a piece. The reference to the hour in v. 4 places the opening act of Jesus' ministry in the context of the closing acts of that ministry, and the narrator's comment in v. 11 suggests that the effects of Jesus' life and death are the same. John 2:4 is the first occurrence of "hour" in John, so the reader is not equipped fully to decipher this reference at this juncture; the significance of the "hour" for the story will become clearer as the story progresses. But the reference to "hour" nonetheless suggests that Jesus' death is not to be isolated to the end of the story. The wonder enacted by this miracle cannot be interpreted apart from the context of Jesus' hour, but equally, Jesus' hour cannot be interpreted apart from the context of his life. The beginning and the ending are both in view in the Cana miracle.

Jesus' death is also imported to the beginning of his ministry in the scene that immediately follows the Cana miracle, the cleansing of the Jerusalem Temple. The conversation between Jesus and the religious authorities in vv. 18-21 hinges around the warrant for Jesus' preceding actions in the Temple ("what sign can you show us?"). As a sign, Jesus challenges the authorities to destroy the temple, which he will then raise up three days later. Jesus' interlocutors respond with details of the construction of the current Temple, and scoff that forty-six years' work could be redone by Jesus in three days. The narrator's comments again, as at 2:11, hold the key to the story. The narrator tells the reader (but Jesus does not tell his interlocutors) that he was "speaking of the temple of his body."

Here again we find a crucial link between the incarnation and the events of Jesus' hour. The temple is the place in cultic Jewish practice where the presence of God is said to dwell. For Jesus to speak of his body as the temple is for him to speak of his body as the place where God dwells, the place where God's presence can be found in the world. Jesus makes a similar claim about himself in 1:51 ("you will see angels ascending and descending on the Son of Man"). In that saying he positions himself as the ladder of Jacob's dream sequence (Gen 28:10-17), the place where the holy becomes available. Both of these affirmations, and the temple affirmation most explicitly, use the language of Jewish religious practice and tradition to express the claim of the incarnation: the Word became flesh and dwelt among us.

The use of *sōma* in 2:21 also warrants our attention. The only other occurrences of *sōma* in John refer to dead bodies (19:31) and most particularly the dead body of Jesus (19:38 [2x], 40; 20:12). In those instances *sōma* functions as a synonym for corpse, a common usage (e.g., Luke 17:37). There is no symbolic use of *sōma* in John; it always evokes the physicality of a human body. There is no conventional eucharistic presentation in which Jesus, holding a piece of bread, says "This is my *sōma*" (Matt 26:26; Mark 14:22; Luke 22:19; 1 Cor 11:24). Jesus' death is a physical, tangible reality that points to the incarnation: the body in which God dwells is a human body that will experience death. God dwells in Jesus' body, and the warrant for Jesus' actions in the Temple will be seen in the death and resurrection *of that body.* But importantly, Jesus acts on those warrants in his lifetime. What will be revealed about God and Jesus in death and resurrection is already enacted by Jesus in the Jerusalem Temple at the beginning of his ministry.

The Temple story illustrates a second major technique the evangelist uses to shift the emphasis in the gospel story from Jesus' death as a single defining moment to Jesus' death as part of the story of the incarnation. In John the Temple story is placed at the beginning of Jesus' ministry, in contrast to its placement as part of the final events of his life in the Synoptics. This has led to many different theories about the chronology of Jesus' ministry and the composition and editing of the Fourth Gospel. Yet the primary lens for these theories is often that of gospel harmonization or the quest for the historical Jesus, and not the Fourth Evangelist's own narrative techniques. I suggest that the placement of the Temple incident at the beginning of Jesus' ministry can most helpfully be understood as an example of something that happens many times in the telling of the Jesus story in John: traditions conventionally associated with the events leading up to the death of Jesus in the other canonical gospels are moved out of the Passion narrative and into the story of Jesus' life and ministry.[1]

Other traditions that are located within the Passion narrative in the Synoptic Gospels and are placed before the account of Jesus' last days in John include the Sanhedrin's decision to put Jesus to death (11:47-53); the anointing at Bethany (12:1-8), which takes place before the triumphal entry; the "agony" in the garden of Gethsemane, which is refracted in 12:27-28; and the eucharistic traditions, to which we will turn below. This handling of some of the "Passion" traditions is consistent with the integration of literary technique and theological interpretation that characterizes this gospel. The evangelist's intent is not to present a chronicle of the life of Jesus, but to interpret the life of Jesus for his community.

I have little doubt that John knew his readers would notice that the cleansing of the Temple was located at the beginning of Jesus' ministry and not with the last events of Jesus' life. We sell John and its readers short when we propose theories that seem to assume that readers would not have noticed the shift of location for this tradition from its placement in other tellings of the Jesus story. Many theories of redaction or displacement inadvertently suggest that the first readers of the gospels were very poor readers. On the contrary, my surmise is that John counted on his readers noticing the shifts he worked with tradition, so that they would then be led to ask about the Temple incident, "why is this story told here?"

There are lots of possible answers to "why is this story told here?" One possibility is that John wanted to create an inaugural event similar to the synagogue inaugural in Luke 4, a tradition Luke moves to the beginning of Jesus' ministry, a shift in the location of this tradition in Mark and Matthew (Mark 6:1-6; Matt 13:53-58). The answer I would like to propose here is that the placement of the Temple story at the beginning of Jesus' ministry is part of an intentional narrative and theological strategy to show how Jesus' life and death are seamless. Placing this tradition in the opening events of Jesus' ministry shows that the decisive and defining moments are not reserved for the story of Jesus' death but are played forward into the story of Jesus' life. This is the realization to which John wants to draw his readers as they ask "why is this story told here?"—not that John did not know the tradition or that the gospel must have had a careless editor, but that the incarnation so infuses the Jesus story with meaning that the last days must be understood as being part of the first days.

John 2:22 ("After he was raised from the dead, his disciples remembered that Jesus had said these things") is one way the gospel explicitly communicates this theological reality to its readers. John 2:22 (and its parallel in 12:12, a narrative comment also associated with a traditional "Passion" event) acknowledges that traditions take on different meanings depending on the contexts in which they are remembered. The reader is simultaneously asked to interpret the Temple incident as part of the opening of Jesus' ministry and to look ahead to its meaning when placed in a post-resurrection perspective. By moving traditions associated with Jesus' death into the beginning and middle of the story of Jesus' life, John asks his readers to incorporate the crucifixion into the larger story of the incarnation.

At the events of Jesus' Last Supper in John 13 there is no conventional narrative of the institution of the eucharistic meal. The supper is marked by the footwashing, not the ritual sharing of bread and wine, and the traditional words of institution appear nowhere in John. Again we misjudge John and his readers if we think John did not assume that his readers would not notice that this key piece of the Jesus story was not present in its traditional form and location in this gospel. The words of institution clearly traveled as a significant piece of oral tradition in early Christianity, as their presence apart from a narrative context in 1 Cor 11:23-26 attests. The absence of a narrative of institution at the last meal would evoke a variety of related questions from early Christian readers, including "Why the foot washing instead of the bread and wine?" and "Where is the story of the institution?"

As with the Temple incident, John has moved the eucharistic traditions out of the traditional chronological frame of the Passion narrative and shifted them forward into the narrative center of the recounting of Jesus' life and ministry. The eucharistic traditions of the gift of Jesus' body and blood are reformed and expanded in the feeding story and discourse of John 6. The extent and significance of eucharistic traditions in this chapter has long been an interpretive crux in Johannine studies and is often a divide between Protestant and Catholic interpreters of John. What John does with the eucharistic traditions does not fit easily with much Protestant eucharistic theology, since most Protestants approach the Eucharist as a meal that commemorates "the night on which he was betrayed." Because John dislodges the eucharistic traditions from the night of betrayal and death, this understanding of the Eucharist and this way of articulating its theological and salvific value for the faith community are not useful interpretive lenses for reading Johannine sacramentalism.

Contained within the rich symbolism of the bread of life in John 6 are associations with the Exodus manna tradition (e.g., John 6:32-34) and the Wisdom tradition of the lifegiving word of God (e.g., John 6:35). All these symbols and resonances shape the narrative and theological context in which John places the traditions about Jesus' flesh and blood (6:51-58). Exodus and Wisdom traditions, paired with "I am" sayings (6:35, 41, 48, 51) that mark Jesus' self-revelation throughout his life, show that the gift of God that Jesus brings is not limited or demarked by the events of the night of betrayal and death. The gospel reader is not asked to choose among these meanings of bread, but to see them as expressions of the multiplicity of ways that Jesus' life makes life available to the believer.

The multiplicity of possibilities can be seen in Jesus' words of 6:51, "I am the living bread that comes down from heaven. Whoever eats of this bread will live forever; and the bread that I will give is my flesh for the life of the world." John 6:51a draws on the Exodus and manna allusions that informed the first part of the discourse; v. 51b can be read as drawing on the Wisdom traditions that shape much of vv. 35-40 ("Whoever comes to me will never be hungry, and whoever believes in me will never be thirsty"). Verse 51c, however, is the decisive theological lens that holds all the multiple images together. The phrase, with its vocabulary of flesh, give, world, and eternal life (live forever), recalls 1:14 ("and the Word became *flesh*) and 3:16 (God so loved the *world* that he *gave* his only Son so that whoever believes in him might not perish but have *eternal life*").

John 6:51c, like 1:14 and 3:16, speaks of the incarnation: the gift of the Word-made-flesh as a sign of God's love for the world. The use of flesh, *sarx*, in 6:51-58 locates this discourse solidly within the rhetoric of the incarnation. Jesus' words do look ahead also to his death, as there are clear resonances of the traditional eucharistic setting in much of John 6. By refracting the eucharistic traditions through the primary lens of the incarnation, however, John reminds his readers that what is revealed in the death has already been revealed in the incarnation. Jesus' life is the life of the Word-made-flesh, already carrying in his flesh God's love for the world.

The institution of the Eucharist is moved forward into the middle of Jesus' ministry so that it can be theologically reconfigured as the feast of the living bread, not the feast of betrayal and death. Jesus' life, not solely his death, is celebrated and experienced in the eucharistic meal. The host of the eucharistic meal provides a superabundance of gifts that surpasses the needs and expectations of those who are present for the feeding. The radical interpretation of the eucharistic traditions that John works in chapter 6 presents the eucharistic meal as a sacrament of the incarnation, a meal of Jesus' living presence for the community.

Conclusion

Professor Koester's approach to the death of Jesus in John and my approach to the life of Jesus in John are not contradictory, yet they are not simply complementary either. It makes a difference for any theological construal of the Fourth Gospel whether one finds redemptive significance in the incarnation as incarnation or whether one places the redemptive weight more on the crucifixion.

I emphasize the need to keep the incarnation in the center of the theological conversation because I am convinced that this is John's distinctive contribution to theological conversations about redemption, atonement, and salvation. John's distinctive theological contribution is often not given its full voice because the weight of centuries of Christian tradition, not to mention other New Testament witnesses, falls more on the crucifixion as the defining locus of redemption. John's distinctive understanding of soteriology and the incarnation is also often muted by popular Christian appropriations of John that reduce John to maxims, and by some of John's own ways of positioning Christian faith in the world.

John's focus on the incarnation nonetheless remains a crucial perspective for contemporary Christian theology and one that needs to be integrated as a full voice in conversations about the meaning of Jesus' life and death. John envisions the possibility of grace and new life that come from fullness, not emptiness and sacrifice, from an image of God that creates new possibilities out of the stuff of human flesh, from love that dwells incarnate.

Notes

1. This view was proposed by Wilhelm Wilkens in the 1950s but has received little attention. See Wilckens, "Das Abendmahlszeugnis im vierten Evangelium," *EvTh* 18 (1958) 354–70, and *Die Entstehungsgeschichte des Vierten Evangeliums* (Zollikon: Evangelischer Verlag, 1958). Wilkens links this move with a redactional theory and carefully delineated antidocetic purpose, but his sense of the ways in which John incorporates the "Passion" into the telling of the life story remains helpful. See also David Rensberger, *Johannine Faith and Liberating Community* (Philadelphia: Westminster, 1988) 71–77.

Chapter Seven

The Resurrection (of the Body) in the Fourth Gospel

A Key to Johannine Spirituality

Sandra M. Schneiders, I.H.M.

Jesuit School of Theology/Graduate Theological Union, Berkeley, CA

I. Introduction

I last saw Raymond Brown a few weeks before he died. By strange coincidence our conversation on that day turned to death, its inevitability, its meaning for us personally and for our work, and what lay beyond that mysterious frontier. Ray told me he had been asked if, following the publication of his massive *Death of the Messiah,* he planned to write a work on the Resurrection. He had replied, "I prefer to research that topic face to face." It was such a quintessentially Raymond Brown remark, deep spirituality buried in a self-effacing *bon mot*. Little could either of us have guessed how soon that research would begin. I venture as fool where his wisdom forbade him to tread. I hope he will accept this essay on the Resurrection as a tribute to his enormous contribution to scholarship, his even greater gift to the church, his wise mentorship, and our friendship.

My purpose in this lecture is to explore the contribution of the Fourth Gospel (henceforth FG, which I will also refer to as John)[1] to our understanding of the meaning of the Resurrection of Jesus, which is the foundation and the distinguishing feature of Christian faith. As such it is, or should be, at the center of Christian spirituality, that is, of the lived experience of the faith. I am going to propose that bodiliness is the linchpin of resurrection faith. The Church professes belief in the resurrection of the body. However, the bodiliness of the Risen Jesus is often discreetly circumvented in both scholarly treatments of and preaching on the subject of resurrection. I suspect that the reason for this reticence is that, for the post-Enlightenment critical mind, bodily resurrection is imaginatively implausible and thus intellectually unassimilable.[2] On this topic faith seeking understanding runs into an imaginative impasse. The Gospel of John might offer the critical mind some resources for negotiating that impasse.

I will proceed in five unequal steps. First, I will lay out some methodological presuppositions for my reading of the text of John 20, the Resurrection Narrative. Second, I will briefly sketch the contours of Johannine anthropology, and third, I will offer a brief synopsis of Johannine eschatology, particularly as it differs from that of the Synoptics. Fourth, I will look at the texts in John that form the context for the interpretation of 20:19-23, the raising of the body of Jesus as the New Temple.[3] Finally, I will interpret John 20:19-23, within the context of the chapter as a whole, as the textual expression of Johannine faith in the personal glorification of the human Jesus, his bodily resurrection, and the spirituality that expresses that faith.

II. Presuppositions

The enormous volume of scholarship on the resurrection in general and John in particular[4] requires me to focus my approach in this lecture clearly. My basic presupposition is that the text itself, i.e., the literary work that is the FG as it now stands, and specifically that text as a narrative, both mediates theological claims and intends to transform its readers through their engagement with it.[5] As the evangelist states explictly in the first conclusion of the gospel, "these things have been written that you may believe that Jesus is the Christ, the Son of God, and that believing you may have life in his name" (John 20:31).[6] In other words, I am using literary criticism to access the theology and spirituality of the gospel rather than historical criticism to establish the facts.[7] I am not asking about the history of the text, either its sources or its redaction, although I will pay attention to historical critical issues when appropriate.[8] Nor am I concerned with the historicity of the events recounted, i.e., "what really happened" after Jesus' death. My research has convinced me that Jesus' dead body was buried and the location of his tomb was known to certain of his disciples, that he actually rose from death to new life, and that he really appeared to his disciples during a certain period of time. In other words, I am assuming that the resurrection account in the gospel is true and has a historical basis even though the meaning of "history" differs in relation to different aspects of "the hour." My concern, however, is with the resurrection account in the Johannine text as we now have it. Consequently, I subscribe to the basic *methodological* presupposition of literary criticism in general, namely, the narrative unity of the final text.[9]

This methodological choice rests on the *theological* presupposition that the mediator of biblical revelation is the text itself rather than the historical events to which the text witnesses. In other words, the locus of revelation is not behind the text but in the text.[10] Of course unless something had happened on the first Easter there would be no story to tell. But finally our only access to the meaning of what happened is the story itself. Engaging an ancient text in such a way that it mediates meaning in the present requires exegesis, i.e., the attempt to understand what the text in its own context says. But finally only interpretation, which goes beyond exegesis, allows the text to exercise its tranformative power on the reader.[11]

Consequently my final presupposition is *hermeneutical.* The purpose of this study is to engage the text as a mediation of meaning. Although I assume that there is continuity between the intention of the real author, i.e., the Fourth Evangelist (henceforth FE), and the meaning of the text as it stands, it is the text that gives us access to new possibilities of Christian being in the world. What is finally important is not what the historical agent we call "John" intended to say but what the text we call John actually does say. The reader's interaction with the text gives rise to meaning that transforms the reader into the believer who has life in Jesus' name.[12]

III. Johannine Anthropology

Much discussion about bodily resurrection is subverted from the start by the fact that modern westerners tend to read the gospel texts through the lens of a basically Greek philosophical anthropology in which the human being is understood very differently from the way it is understood in the Semitic anthropology of the biblical writers, including the evangelists. John's anthropology, although expressed with Greek vocabulary that has clearly influenced his understanding of the person, is thoroughly rooted in the Hebrew language and sensibility.[13] The pertinent Greek terms, ψυχή (usually translated as soul), ζωή (translated as life), θάνατος (death), σάρξ (flesh), αἷμα (blood), πνεῦμα (spirit), and σῶμα (body), constitute a semantic field in which all the terms are interrelated and mutually qualifying. Although in English these terms each denote a *component* of the human being, in biblical usage they each denote the *whole person* from some perspective or under some aspect. Ignoring this difference can result in serious misunderstanding, such as the tendency of many moderns to hear cannibalistic overtones in Jesus' invitation to eat his flesh and drink his blood in John 6:52-58. And mistranslating the terms σάρξ and αἷμα in that passage, i.e., "flesh and blood," as "body and blood," leading to the identification of flesh with body, then leads to an erroneous identification of bodily resurrection with physical resurrection. In other words, it is crucial to understand what these anthropological terms meant in the context of John's first-century Judaism as a basis for understanding how they function in the FG.

John uses the terms for life, ψυχή and ζωή, very consistently. Ψυχή refers to the person as a living human being. In John 10:17-18 Jesus speaks of freely laying down and taking up his ψυχή, meaning his natural human life.[14] Ζωή, which also means life, is virtually always explicitly or implicitly qualified in John with the adjective αἰώνιος (eternal), not in the sense of indefinite temporal extension of natural life but as a qualitatively different kind of life. "Eternal life" is a technical theological term in John meaning God's own life lived by Jesus as the λόγος incarnate, and participated in, before as well as after death, by those who, born of God through the Spirit, are now τέκνα θεοῦ, children of God (cf. John 1:12-13; 3:5-6). Jesus sums up the purpose of the incarnation: "I have come that they may have ζωή, and have it abundantly" (10:10). The term refers not to some quality or even power possessed by the human being, but to the whole person as divinely alive.

Θάνατος, the opposite of life in both its natural and its divine sense, is a richly ambiguous term in John. It means the human person without life. But, as Jesus' lapidary self-revelation to Martha in 11:25 makes clear, there is death and death. Those who die, as all humans must, may, like Jesus' opponents in 8:24, "die in their sins," i.e., be finally dead, denizens of Sheol where they are cut off from all meaningful personal and communal existence and especially from communion with the living God (cf. Ps 6:6). Or, conversely, even though they die, they may, like Jesus, live with eternal life in the glory of God. In John 11 Lazarus is a symbolic instrument on which are rung all the changes and interrelations of which the concept of θάνατος as opposition to both ordinary human life and eternal life is susceptible.[15] In John, Jesus' death was simultaneously real human death and his glorification as Son of Man (cf. 12:23 and elsewhere).[16] But once again, death is not simply an event; it is a condition of the whole human subject.

Σάρξ and αἷμα, usually translated as "flesh" and "blood" respectively, are closely related terms. For moderns these terms denote substances that are separable components of a human being. Flesh, in John's anthropology, is not a part of the human but the human being as natural and mortal.[17] To say that in Jesus the Word of God (λόγος) became flesh (σάρξ) is to say that he became fully human, i.e., subject to death.[18] In the Psalms especially we see "flesh" used to speak of humanity in its weakness and mortality: "God remembered that they were flesh, a passing breath that returns not" (Ps 145:21, see also 56:5; 65:3, and elsewhere). In John 6:51 Jesus says that he *is* the living bread come down from heaven, and that the bread he will *give* for the life of the world "is [his] flesh." Jesus is not talking about a physical part of himself. He is saying that in giving himself totally in death, which is only possible because he is flesh, i.e., mortal, he gives life to the world.

If flesh denotes the human as mortal, "blood" used in combination with flesh focuses on the mortal as living. Blood is not simply a part of the human being but the "livingness" of one vulnerable to death. In Gen 9:4 God says to Noah that all living creatures are given to humanity as food but "flesh with its lifeblood still in it you shall not eat." Blood, then, can stand for life itself and "flesh and blood" means the living human being. When Jesus, in John 6, says that believers must consume his flesh and blood he is not talking about eating and drinking physical substances but about receiving as food his living human self in the community's eucharistic meal.

The rich ambiguity of the word θάνατος which can refer to physical or eternal death, is reflected in the ambiguity of the word πνεῦμα. Spirit can mean the breath of life, i.e., God's creating gift to every mortal that returns to God when the creature dies, or the Spirit of God who came to rest permanently on Jesus (cf. John 1:31-33), who gives this Spirit without measure (cf. 3:34) to those who believe in him, making them children of God whose divine life death cannot touch. Jesus says in 6:63 that "the flesh" is futile, i.e., doomed to death, but that "the spirit" gives life (πνμεῦμά ἐστιν τὸ ζωοποιοῦν). When he then goes on to say that his words are "S/spirit and life" (πνεῦμά . . . καὶ ζωή) he plays on the ambiguity of spirit as both human life and divine life.

The most important term in this anthropological semantic field in relation to the Resurrection of Jesus, and the one John uses in a subtle way that marries Semitic and Hellenistic understandings of the human, is σῶμα, "body."[19] Because moderns tend to think of the body as a distinct substance in the human composite, the physical component as distinguished from the spiritual, they tend to equate it with flesh, itself misunderstood as the soft, solid component in distinction from blood and bones. In other words, body is understood as a physical substance that is integral to but only a part of the person.[20]

For John, body is the person in symbolic self-presentation. The person may be living or dead,[21] but it is the whole self, the bodyself, who is living or dead. In Semitic thought once the dead body begins to decay, to fall apart, the person is no longer a person. Whatever trace of the individual may survive in Sheol, it is not a human being because it does not enjoy subjectivity, community, or union with God.[22] The body is quintessentially the person as self-symbolizing, i.e., as numerically distinct, self-consistent, and continuous, a subject who can interact with other subjects, and who is present and active in the world.[23] A corpse, in John's vocabulary, is also called a body (John 19:31, 38, 40) precisely because it symbolizes the whole person, the bodyself, in its transition from being to non-being or from presence to absence. It is the symbolic (i.e., perceptively real) person in the process of becoming absent, and when the person is finally and fully absent, when the corpse has decomposed (which does not happen in the case of Jesus), it is no longer considered a body. In short, if Jesus as flesh, that is, as earthly human being, is the symbolic presence of God's glory in this world, Jesus as body is his own symbolic presence to his contemporaries. Prior to his death the two, flesh and body, i.e., the human person, are coterminous, as they are in all humans in this life. The issue of "body" as distinct in some sense from flesh only arises when Jesus dies and the two are no longer strictly coterminous.[24]

The issue of Jesus' real presence in and after his passage through death dominates the Last Supper in John (chs. 13–17) as well as the Resurrection Narrative (ch. 20). Where is the Lord? Has he gone where his disciples cannot follow? Are they orphans, deprived of the glory of God that had been present in the flesh of Jesus? Are future believers condemned to a faith based on hearsay about events in which they did not and do not participate? Unless

Jesus is bodily risen, i.e., unless he is alive in the full integrity of his humanity symbolized in his body, he is not present, either as the presence of humanity in God or as God's divinely human presence to us.

The crucial anthropological-theological issue for the topic of resurrection is, then, the relation of flesh to body, i.e., of the pre-Easter person of Jesus as mortal human being to the post-Easter person of Jesus as glorified Son of Man. By way of anticipatory summary I will propose that the relation of flesh to body is precisely what is altered by Jesus' glorification. In his pre-Easter existence as flesh the body of Jesus, i.e., his personal symbolic presence, was conditioned by his mortality. He was subject to death and to the limitations of space, time, and causality that natural human life entails. In his glorification Jesus goes to the Father as a human bodyself and in his resurrection he returns to his own in the full integrity of his humanity. His body is real, both continuous and discontinuous with his earthly body. He is numerically distinct, a personal subject who can be intersubjectively present and active,[25] but he is no longer subject to death or determined by the spatial, temporal, or causal coordinates of historical existence. And he will be present as this same bodyself throughout post-Easter time in the range of symbols through which his personal presence will be manifest.

IV. Johannine Eschatology

A final preliminary subject that is crucial for a consideration of bodily resurrection in John is eschatology. It has long been recognized that John's treatment of the end of Jesus' earthly life is quite unlike that of the Synoptics. Jesus' Passion and death in the FG are not presented as a *kenosis* that requires divine vindication through resurrection. Indeed, Bultmann suggested in the middle of the last century that

> If Jesus' death on the cross is already his exaltation and glorification, *his resurrection* cannot be an event of special significance. No resurrection is needed to destroy the triumph which death might be supposed to have gained in the crucifixion.[26]

The Resurrection Narrative in the FG, in such a view, is merely a concession to the tradition which, by the time John was written, considered the resurrection intrinsic to the kerygma. I would suggest that, while it is true that the resurrection of Jesus is not understood in the same way and does not play the same role in John that it does in the Synoptics, it is nevertheless essential to John's theological purpose. Integral to understanding John's presentation of the resurrection is a grasp of his eschatological presuppositions especially as they differ from those operative in the synoptic tradition.

As is well known, early Israelite eschatology was a collectivist, national, and this-worldly expectation of Israel's ongoing prosperity if it remained faithful to the covenant (see, e.g., the classic formulation in Deut 30:15-20). However, the conundrum of the suffering just person and the prosperous sinner (e.g., Psalm 73; Job) gradually led toward a more universalistic hope for individual vindication beyond death. In the figure of the Suffering Servant of Deutero-Isaiah (Isa 42:1-4; 49:1-6; 50:4-9; 52:13–53:12) Israel achieved a central insight into the redemptive potential of the suffering of the just person within and for the guilty community. This insight was developed in both the intertestamental literature (ca. 200 B.C.E. to 100 B.C.E.),[27] and within the latest books of the Jewish Bible, notably Daniel, 2 Maccabees, and Wisdom of Solomon, where we find traces of two strands of eschatological speculation, each of which supplied categories for the Christian interpretation of Jesus' death and resurrection.[28]

The Synoptic Gospels operate primarily within the earlier of these two strands, which for convenience I will label "resurrection eschatology," developed in the context of the Syrian persecutions and the Hasidean-Hasmonean controversies in Palestine in the second to first centuries B.C.E. Faithful Jews were being persecuted and even martyred for their fidelity to Torah, but they were strengthened by the hope that they would be vindicated by God after death. The clearest OT expression of this eschatology is found in Dan 12:1-3 and 2 Maccabees 7, both of which are influenced by the Suffering Servant image in which the martyrs are assured that they will be restored even in their bodies, that Israel will be reconstituted, and that the unjust will be finally punished.

The eschatology that functions in the Synoptic treatment of resurrection, like that of Daniel and 2 Maccabees, is fundamentally futuristic and apocalyptic. It envisions an "end of the world" at which all the dead will be bodily raised to appear before the glorified Christ, the divine judge, who will assign them to eternal reward or punishment on the basis of their comportment in this life (cf. Matt 25:31-46). This final event is conceived in apocalyptic terms as an unexpected cosmic cataclysm (see Matt 14:15-44; Mark 13:1-37; Luke 17:22-37). Those who die before the final event are judged at death and go to an interim reward or punishment, like Lazarus and Dives in Luke 16:19-31, or perhaps even to purgative suffering (see, e.g., Matt 18:23-35), while awaiting the universal judgment at the end of time when individual fates will become definitive. This is essentially the Pharisaic eschatology of Jesus' own time. The role of bodily, even physical resurrection in this eschatology is essentially functional. It renders the just and the unjust present for final vindication.

John operates within the other strand of late pre-Christian Jewish eschatology, which I will label "exaltation eschatology."[29] It developed in the Hellenistic context of Diaspora Judaism, probably in the late second to first centuries B.C.E. Jews who had remained faithful to Torah even far from Palestine were being persecuted not only by non-Jewish authorities but by their assimilated and worldly coreligionists. Once again there is appeal to a post-death solution to the problem of the intrahistorical victory of the unjust. The clearest (deutero) canonical expression of this eschatology occurs in Wisdom 1–6, probably written in Greek by an Alexandrian Jew. In these chapters a Torah-loving "wisdom hero"[30] is persecuted by the foolish who mock his fidelity to the Law, repudiate his claim to be God's son, and are infuriated by his accusation that they are unfaithful to their training and tradition (cf. Wis 2:10-20). Unlike the traditional wisdom hero, e.g., Joseph or Susanna, who is rescued before death, the Jews for whom Wisdom of Solomon is written were being killed. Thus it became necessary to introduce the possibility of post-death salvation. The influence of the LXX version of the fourth Suffering Servant Song from Isa 52:13–53:12 and of the Daniel 7 figure of the Son of Man on the hero in Wisdom of Solomon is virtually certain.[31] The theme of exaltation-for-judgment is combined with the theme of entering into an intimate relationship with God in a nonterrestrial realm. The text tells us that even though the hero is killed, "the souls of the just are in the hand of God. . . . They seemed, in the view of the foolish, to be dead . . . but they are in peace. . . . God took them to himself" (Wis 3:1-6).

Bodily resurrrection does not figure explictly in this sapiential understanding of the destiny of the just and unjust because the judgment of the ungodly takes place in their very choice of evil by which they "summon death" (cf. Wis 1:16), and the just are exalted by and/or assumed to God in their seeming death. However, the assumption or exaltation of the just is not simply immortality of the soul in the Greek philosophical sense, that is, the natural indestructibility of a spiritual substance. It is life in the Jewish sense, i.e., a gift from God, who alone possesses it by nature[32] and who freely bestows it on those who are loyal to the covenant. And life, even after death, in which the body did not participate in some way would have been inconceivable to the Jewish imagination. So while nothing is said of bodily resurrection in sapiential eschatology, it is fundamentally susceptible to it.[33]

The predominantly realized, non-apocalyptic eschatology of John's Gospel as well as John's presentation of the resurrection of Jesus reflect this exaltation eschatology. In the FG a person's fundamental option to believe or not believe in Jesus (cf. John 5:29) situates her or him, even in this world, in eternal life or eternal death (cf. John 3:15-19; 5:24 in relation to Wis 1:16).[34] People are thus divided into two groups, the children of God and the children of the devil (John 8:41-47). Death is not a moment of judgment but one of definitive establishment in that state of life or death in which the person has been living before death (cf. 8:2 in relation to 11:25). Judgment is neither a universal nor a future phenomenon, for those who believe are never judged (5:24) and those who do not believe are already judged, not by Jesus but by their very choice of unbelief (3:18-19).

Two conclusions can be drawn about sapiential exaltation eschatology in relation to the Gospel of John:

1. Bodily resurrection is compatible with, perhaps even implicit in, but not explictly affirmed in sapiential eschatology. However, it *could* easily become

explicit if the right pressures were brought to bear upon it, e.g., by the Easter experience of the first followers of Jesus.

2. If bodily resurrection *did* become explicit within a sapiential eschatology it would not have the same meaning it has in a future, apocalyptic eschatology. It would not be seen as vindication of the persecuted, since this vindication takes place in the very death/exaltation of the just one, nor as a victory over death, because death never has any real power over the one who is a child of God. It would be essentially a manifestation of the meaning for the whole person of life in God now lived in all its fullness. And in the case of Jesus it would be a condition of possibility for his post-Easter personal presence to his disciples and his continuing action in the world.

I would suggest that the bodily resurrection of Jesus in John is presented in terms of the sapiential anthropology and eschatology of the Wisdom of Solomon. The Resurrection Narrative in John 20 is, therefore, not a concession to the constraints of early Christian tradition but a narrative-theological exploration of the Easter experience of the first disciples and its implications for the spirituality of the Johannine community. This entails making a distinction between the glorification or exaltation of Jesus on the cross (i.e., the passage of Jesus to God) and his resurrection (i.e., his return to his own), which, though related, are not strictly identical in John.

V. The Textual Framework for John's Resurrection Narrative

Bearing in mind the gospel's narrative unity and against the background of John's sapiential anthropology and eschatology, we turn now to the text of the FG with our original question: what is John's contribution to our understanding of the bodily resurrection of Jesus? Pertinent texts occur in virtually every chapter of the gospel, but since I intend to concentrate on John 20:19-23, Jesus' appearance on Easter night to his disciples, I will briefly situate that passage in relation to the texts most important for understanding it and make reference in passing to other texts.

A. The Prologue[35]

John 1:1-18, the Prologue, differs notably in form, content, and function from the rest of the gospel, which is concerned with the career of the Word incarnate. The Prologue begins in eternity, in the bosom of God, from whom the Word came forth to tent or tabernacle among us (ἐσκήνωσεν ἐν ἡμῖν) by becoming flesh (σὰρξ ἐγένετο), i.e., human, in Jesus Christ. The term λόγος designating the pre-incarnate Word, never appears again in the gospel even though the activity and speech of Σοφία, the Word personalized as divine Wisdom, are ubiquitous in the earthly career of Jesus. Jesus, the human being, has become the symbolic presence of God in history that the Word is in eternity.

An analogous linguistic strategy occurs in the other direction at the end of the gospel when the earthly Jesus becomes the Risen Lord. Jesus says, "I came forth from the Father and have come into the world; again I leave the world and go to the Father" (John 16:28). As the Word through incarnation became flesh, i.e., assumed the existential mode of humanity in time, so the human Jesus through his glorification assumes a new mode of being in God that transcends history and that, without repudiating his humanity, transforms it. John 20 is a narrative exploration of this new mode of presence and its significance for Jesus' followers.

B. The Textual Framework for the Symbolic Use of Body

Two nested prophecy-fulfillment schemas with parallel structures culminate in the central event of the Resurrection Narrative, the raising of the New Temple of Jesus' glorified body in the midst of his community. The major schema is constituted by the logion of Jesus in the Temple during his first Passover in Jerusalem, John 2:19-22, and its fulfillment in the appearance to his disciples on Easter evening, John 20:19-23. Nested within that overarching schema is another with the same structure: the logion of Jesus in the Temple at the Feast of Tabernacles in 7:37-39, and its fulfillment in the piercing of Jesus' side in 19:34

1. The first prophecy-fulfillment schema: Jesus as Temple

Jesus' first public act in John, which has the programmatic significance of his appearance in the Synagogue of Nazareth in Luke 4, is his prophetic gesture in the Temple. Mary Coloe, correctly in my opinion, sees this not as a cleansing of the Temple in which valid worship was still possible, but rather as a termination of the Temple and its cult, which Jesus would replace.[36] "The Jews"[37] demand an authenticating sign. Jesus replies, "'Destroy this temple (ναός) and in three days I will raise it" (2:19). "The Jews" take him literally, a clear Johannine indication that Jesus was not speaking of the physical Temple in which they were standing. The evangelist clarifies, "He [Jesus] was speaking of the temple of his body" (σῶμα), which his disciples would understand only after his resurrection (cf. 2:20-22). This is the first time the word, σῶμα, "body," is used in John, and it is explictly identified with ναός Temple.[38] Σῶμα will not be used again until Jesus has been glorified on the cross (19:31, 38, 40). Like the use of λόγος in the Prologue, which looks back to eternity and is not used of the historical Jesus who is the Word made σάρξ "flesh", σῶμα is used here in prediction and will not be used again until Jesus is glorified. In other words, what flesh is to λόγος its symbolic locus in the pre-paschal dispensation, σῶμα is to the glorified Jesus, his symbolic locus in the post-paschal dispensation.

This prophetic logion, which occurs in Jesus' first public appearance, is balanced by a narrative at the end of the gospel that fulfills it. In John 20:19 we are told that the glorified Jesus "stood into the midst" or "rose up in the midst" of his disciples, who were behind closed doors.[39] This image of Jesus arising in the midst of the community evokes the raising of the New Temple, the new presence of God in their midst, which Jesus had promised in ch. 2.

2. The second prophecy-fulfillment schema: Body as Temple

Between these two scenes is another prophecy-fulfillment schema, this time constituted by the logion of Jesus in the Temple at the feast of Tabernacles in John 7:37-39 balanced by the narrative that fulfills it, the scene at the cross as Jesus dies in John 19:25-34.

The context is again the Temple in Jerusalem, this time at the joyful feast of Tabernacles celebrating the Sinai covenant. It is the last and the "great day" of the feast, the eighth day evoking both creation and eschatological fulfillment, just as the sabbath that follows Jesus' death is a "great day," namely, Passover (cf. John 19:31).[40] The symbols used in the feast of Tabernacles are water from the pool of Siloam and light from innumerable torches shining in the darkness,[41] both Johannine symbols for Jesus.[42] Jesus now identifies himself as temple. He cries out to all who thirst to come to him and drink, again, as in ch. 2, citing Scripture.

The translation as well as the source of the Scripture text Jesus evokes in this scene are much debated.[43] Two translations are grammatically possible. Following the argumentation of Germain Bienaimé, and without denying that the ambiguity in the text may have been intentional on the part of the FE, I prefer, for the theological reasons given below, the translation that would make Jesus, rather than those who believe in him, the originating source of the living water.

> If anyone thirst, let [that one] come to me
> And let the one who believes in me drink
> As the Scripture said, "Out of his interior (κοιλία) [or from within him]
> Will flow rivers of living water (7:37-38).

The evangelist, as in ch. 2, clarifies Jesus' saying: he was speaking of the Spirit that "was not yet [given]" because Jesus was not yet glorified. Once again Jesus' word can only be understood after "the hour" of the Paschal mystery.

The search for the OT source of Jesus' citation, which would clarify the meaning of the "rivers of living water," has led scholars to Exod 17:6, where God tells Moses to strike the rock in the desert and water will flow (and Pss 78:14-16 and 105:41, which celebrate that event); Zech 14:8, which predicts that in the eschatological day living waters will flow from Jerusalem (and Ps 46:5-6, which celebrates the streams that gladden the holy city); Isa 55:1-3, which invites all who are thirsty to come to the water.[44] Given John's symphonically allusive use of the OT, I would not reject any of these texts as part of the background for the logion in John 7:38, but I think the most important text, which controls the use of the others, is Ezekiel 47, where the prophet is shown the abundant streams of lifegiving waters that flow from the side of the Temple, beginning as a trickle (47:2) and growing to a mighty river giving life, health, and freshness to all living things. This is certainly a description of the Spirit promised in John 7:37-38, which is unleashed in the world as a trickle of water from the pierced side of the glorified Jesus, specifically identified now as "body" (19:31).

The translation of κοιλία has also exercised exegetes. It means literally the inner cavity of the human body, whether the breast, the womb, or the belly, and consequently, symbolically, the interiority of the bodyself. Rivers of living water, the Spirit, will come from within the body of Jesus glorified as the water sprang out of the cleft rock in the desert to give life to the historical people and will flow from within the eschatological temple to give life to the world.

The text that fulfills the prophetic logion in John 7 is 19:34, which recounts that a soldier opened the side of the glorified Jesus with a lance and blood and water flowed out. Throughout the Fourth Gospel water is symbolic of or closely associated with the Spirit, as it is in John 7. Blood, as we saw earlier, is the locus or bearer of the life of the person as mortal. Just before the dead body of Jesus is pierced he has "handed over the Spirit" (v. 30), an expression used nowhere in Scripture or secular Greek to refer to death. Consequently most commentators agree that John used it to convey the coincidence of Jesus' physical death, i.e., his glorification, and the outpouring of the Holy Spirit.[45] Blood (symbolizing his human life, given for the life of the world [cf. 6: 51]) and water (symbolizing the Spirit) flow from the New Temple to give life to the New Israel, the community gathered at the foot of the cross. The evangelist in 19:37 cites Zech 12:10, "they shall look on him whom they have pierced," which evokes the Suffering Servant but also Zechariah 13 and 14, which describe the messianic gift of purifying and flowing waters of which Jesus had spoken in John 7:38. Jesus' body on the cross is both the New Paschal Lamb slain to give life[46] and the New Temple from which that life pours forth.

In summary, the schemas we have examined weave a symbolic tapestry within which the glorified Jesus can be discerned as the New Temple raised up in the midst of the New Covenant people. From him flows the Spirit who will be, in them, the promised presence of Jesus throughout all time.[47]

VI. The Glorified Body of the Risen Jesus in John 20

A. *The Significance of the Resurrection of the Body for Christian Faith*

We turn finally to the Resurrection Narrative in John 20 to explore the role of the body of Jesus in the post-paschal dispensation. I have suggested that just as the term "flesh" functioned, throughout the lifetime of the historical Jesus, to denote his real presence in his mortal humanity, "body" functions after the glorification to speak of his real, divinely human presence as Risen Lord in and among his disciples. If Jesus ceased, at his death, to be a living human being then Christian faith as Christian has no real object. Bodiliness, the condition of possibility and symbolic realization of human self-identity and continuity, intersubjective presence, and action in the world, is integral to the meaning of real, living humanity. But if bodiliness can only be understood in terms of the physical materiality that characterized the earthly Jesus, it is imaginatively implausible and consequently incredible for many if not most people today, as it was for Paul's listeners in Athens (cf. Acts 17:32) and some of his converts at Corinth (1 Cor 15:12-19).

In what follows I am proposing that the Resurrection Narrative in John functions not primarily to proclaim or explain what happened to *Jesus* after his death (since, in John, he was glorified on the cross and has no need of vindicatory restoration) but to explore what his glorification meant and means for his *followers*. In other words, the glorification in John is Jesus' passage to God and the resurrection is Jesus' return to his own. This twofold destiny of Jesus is not a chronological succession of separate events but two dimensions of his post-paschal life. As Jesus promised on the eve of his death, "I go away (ὑπάγω) and I come to you (ἔρχομαι πρὸς ὑμᾶς) [14:28], both verbs in the present. The bodily resurrection is the condition of possibility for the fulfillment of that promise.

B. Structure and Content of John 20

Proposed structures—historical, chronological, literary, theological, and spiritual—for John 20 are legion.[48] Any well-crafted literary work is susceptible to diverse structurations depending on how it is read. So, without disagreeing with most of those that have been proposed, I will offer a layered literary-theological-spiritual structure that I think can help us address the question of the body of the Risen Lord.[49]

1. Literary structure

On the surface level the chapter is *narratively* divided into two parts: 1-18 and 19-29, each unified by place and time (Figure 1). In Part I, which takes place on Easter morning in the garden of the tomb, we read of Mary Magdalene's discovery of the open tomb (vv.1-2), the Beloved Disciple coming to believe on the basis of what he and Simon Peter saw in the tomb (vv. 3-10), and Jesus' appearance to and commissioning of Mary Magdalene (vv. 11-18). In Part II, which takes place in Jerusalem where the disciples were gathered on Easter evening and again the following Sunday, we read of Jesus' appearance to and commissioning of his assembled disciples (vv. 19-23) and his

Figure 1
NARRATIVE STRUCTURE OF JOHN 20

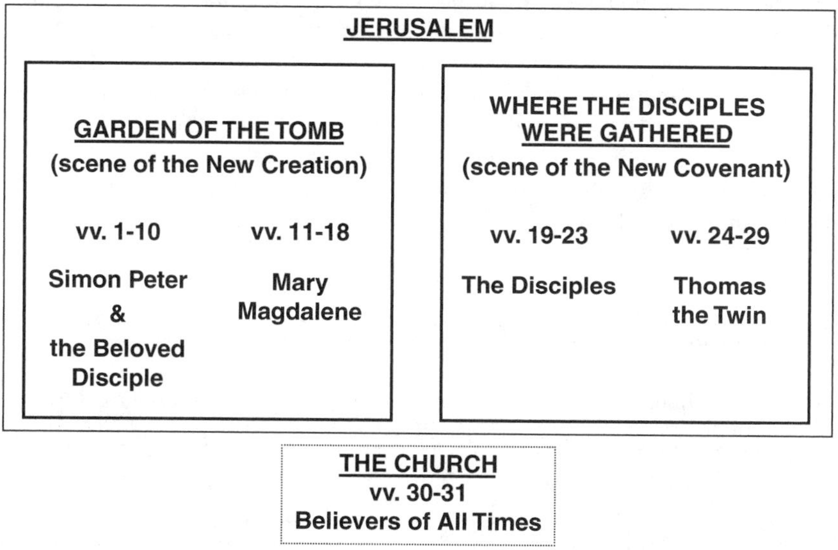

JERUSALEM

GARDEN OF THE TOMB (scene of the New Creation)		WHERE THE DISCIPLES WERE GATHERED (scene of the New Covenant)	
vv. 1-10	vv. 11-18	vv. 19-23	vv. 24-29
Simon Peter & the Beloved Disciple	Mary Magdalene	The Disciples	Thomas the Twin

THE CHURCH
vv. 30-31
Believers of All Times

appearance a week later to Thomas (vv. 24-29). In vv. 30-31 the evangelist concludes both ch. 20 and the gospel as a whole by telling his readers that henceforth the gospel text will function for them as the signs of Jesus had for his first disciples, i.e., as mediation of revelation leading to salvific faith.[50]

Figure 2
DRAMATIC STRUCTURE OF JOHN 20

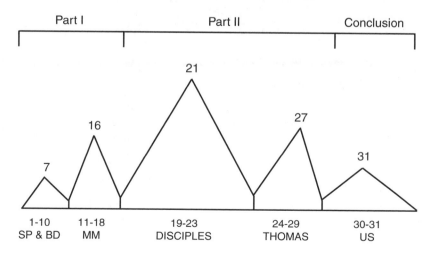

At a deeper level (Figure 2) the five scenes form a *dramatic* literary whole in which the first two scenes rise from the situation of the earthly disciples to the culminating appearance of Jesus to the community and the last two descend from that appearance toward the post-Easter audience. Each scene has its own revelatory crisis and subsequent resolution that prepares for the succeeding scene. In the first scene this crisis is v. 7, the BD seeing the face cloth; in the second, v. 16, Jesus calling Mary by name; in the third, v. 21, Jesus identifying his disciples with himself in mission; in the fourth, v. 27, Jesus inviting Thomas to believe; and in the fifth, v. 31, the evangelist identifying the "the things which are written" as the signs for later believers.

Figure 3
THEOLOGICAL-SPIRITUAL STRUCTURE OF JOHN 20

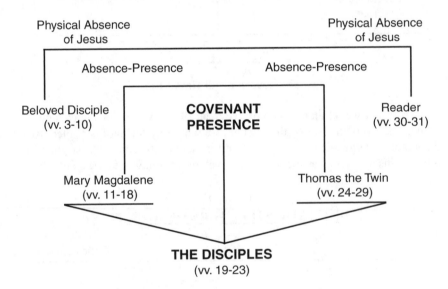

2. Theological and spiritual structure

Most important for our purposes, however, is the *theological* structure of ch. 20, which is a careful answer to the question, "Where is the Lord?" and the resulting response to the *spiritual* question, "How can he be encountered today?"[51] Our primary interest is in the central scene, the appearance to the disciples, but what precedes is crucial preparation and what follows focuses the Easter event on post-Easter disciples.

The first scene opens with Mary Magdalene coming to the tomb early on Easter morning and seeing the *stone* taken away. She concludes instantly, "They have taken the *Lord* out of the tomb and we do not know *where* they have put him" (20:2). She voices the position of one who has not grasped the meaning of "the hour," Jesus' transition from the dispensation of the flesh to the dispensation of glory. She is seeking "the Lord" whom she equates with his corpse. The equation of person with body and body with flesh, therefore of person with flesh, is precisely what Easter faith must transcend. Mary Magdelene personifies the theological problem of how the earthly Jesus (the Word made flesh) is related to the glorified and risen Lord. And at the end of the chapter, the Thomas scene will suggest that this is precisely the problem for Jesus' disciples of all time.

At Mary's report Simon Peter and the Beloved Disciple run to the tomb and examine its contents. Both see in the tomb the abandoned burial cloths and the veil (σουδάριον) that had been on Jesus' face, not lying with the cloths but carefully and definitively wrapped up and placed aside. We are told that the BD (not Peter) "saw and believed" (20:8). In John, to see and believe is to respond in faith to a revelatory sign (σημεῖον). But the question is, "What did he believe?" since the next verse tells us that "as yet they did not know the scripture that he must rise from the dead" (20:9).

Johannine symbolism as well as the literary structure of the episode suggests to me that the sign that led the Beloved Disciple to believe was neither the open tomb nor the linen cloths but the face veil, linguistically related to the face veil that Moses wore to protect the Israelites from the glorification of his face by his encounter with God on Sinai (cf. Exod 34:27-35).[52] Jesus, the New Moses, had definitively left behind the veil of his earthly flesh as he returned to the glory he had as Son with God before the world was made (cf. 17:24).[53] The first installment of the answer to the question, "Where is the Lord?" has been supplied: Jesus is with God, i.e., he has been glorified. Neither the fact nor the meaning of the Resurrection as Jesus' return to his own is yet available.

The next scene, redolent of allusions to both the garden of the first creation (cf. Gen 2:8-15 and 3:8-10) and the Song of Songs (especially Cant 3:1-4),[54] brings the lover, Mary Magdalene, to the garden of the tomb searching for her Beloved and refusing comfort or enlightenment from anyone, even angels, who cannot tell her where he is. No one doubts that the center of this episode is the recognition scene in which Jesus, whom Mary takes for the gardener, directly addresses her, "Mary." He is indeed the divine gardener inaugurating the New Creation, the Good Shepherd calling his own by name, and the Spouse of the New Covenant rewarding the search of the anguished lover. Mary recognizes him as her Teacher.[55] But she is still struggling out of the darkness of her pre-paschal literalism into the light of Easter. Jesus forestalls her attempt to touch him, to encounter him in the flesh as his disciples could and did prior to his glorification. Jean Zumstein helpfully provides a paraphrastic translation of v. 17a, the famous "Do not touch me" verse, as *"For you* I am not yet ascended to the Father."[56] Jesus, glorified on the cross, has indeed gone to the Father, but in Mary's perception he has not yet ascended, for she has not yet integrated into her realization that Jesus is risen the fact that he has also been glorified. Jesus redirects her to the community of his brothers and sisters, which is, in a mysterious way, his glorified body. Mary understands that the "brothers and sisters" means "the disciples" and she arrives as the first apostle of the resurrection, announcing: "I have seen the Lord" (20:18).

Furnished with the essential knowledge that Jesus is both glorified (from the first scene) and risen (from the second scene), that is, with the theological answer to the question *"Where is the Lord?"* the reader is prepared for the chapter's central scene, which will answer the question *"How are postpaschal disciples to encounter the Risen Lord?"* The negative answer from the first two scenes is that it is not through physical sight or touch of his earthly body, that is, not in the flesh, but somehow in his disciples. Scene three narratively explores this cryptic answer.

The central scene is the shortest and least circumstantial in the chapter. Its depth derives largely from the fact that it is suffused with the Last Discourse(s) material, which itself is suffused with the themes and even the language of the New Covenant from Isaiah 51–56 and 65–66, Jeremiah 31, and Ezekiel 36–37.[57] These themes include the sealing of the New Covenant itself and its gifts of peace, joy, seeing the Lord, knowledge of the Lord, purification from sin, a New Spirit, and a new heart. The New Covenant will unite YHWH with his purified and faithful spouse, the New Israel, and the sign of their mutual belonging will be the New Tabernacle, God's own presence, raised up in their midst.

When the scene is displayed structurally (Figure 4) it is clearly perfectly balanced, with one all-important exception. The scene falls into two parts, evoking the two dimensions of the Sinai covenant, the theophany followed by the gift of Torah (cf. Exod 19:16–20:17). Each part of John 20:19-23, the christophany and the giving of the Spirit who is the New Law placed in their hearts, opens with a solemn declaration, "Peace be to you," the fulfillment of Jesus' promise that he would see them again and give them a peace that the world cannot give or take away (cf. 14:27).

Part I, the christophany, is the revelation of the Risen Jesus to the community of his disciples. The Jesus standing in their midst is no shade from Sheol. He is Jesus, the one who had been crucified and pierced, who had died, and whose body had been buried. His body, marked with the signs of his glorification through death and its lifegiving fruit of the Spirit, establishes both his identity in himself and his capacity to reestablish his presence to and relationship with them. But the Jesus standing in their midst is not simply resuscitated. He is alive with a new life that is bodily but no longer subject to death or to the laws of historical space, time, and causality. He is the same person, Jesus, but in a new mode of being and presence.

Part II of the scene is the giving of the New Law, i.e., the Spirit, promised in Isa 55:7, Jer 31:33, and Ezek 36:26-27 and 37:1-10, 14, 24. This Spirit both unites them to Jesus and empowers them for a new life in which, sent as Jesus

Figure 4
STRUCTURE OF JOHN 20:19-23

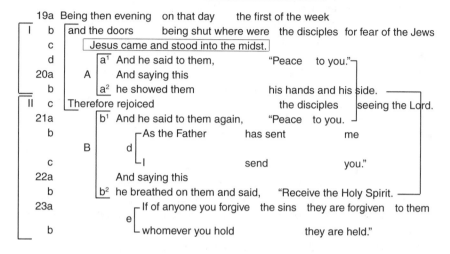

was sent by the Father, they will continue his mission as the Lamb of God who takes away the sin of the world (cf. 1:29 with 20:21-23). Jesus bestows the Spirit of the New Covenant by breathing on his disciples, as God had breathed the first human into life and new life into the dry bones in Ezekiel's vision, a clear indication that this *New People,* the community with whom this *New Covenant* is made, is indeed a *New Creation.*[58]

This brings us back to the one notable exception to the perfectly balanced structure of the passage. Except for v. 19c, "Jesus came and stood (or rose up) in(to) the(ir) midst," every member in the passage has a corresponding member. We have just been told that the doors where the disciples were gathered had been closed (κεκλεισμένων) for fear of "the Jews." Suddenly Jesus arises among them.[59] (He does not, as some have naïvely pictured it, come through the doors or walls!) The preposition εἰς with the accusative suggests motion to the interior. But the interior in this text is not a physical place. It is "where the disciples were gathered together" (20:19).[60] Jesus arises in the midst of the community. The verb "to stand" or "to arise" evokes Jesus' promise in ch. 2 to raise up the New Temple, his body that his enemies will have destroyed. In the OT the sign of the New Covenant was to be that YHWH would establish his tabernacle in the midst of the renewed people:

> I will make with them a covenant of peace; it shall be an everlasting covenant with them, and I will multiply them, and put my sanctuary among them forever. My dwelling shall be with them; I will be their God and they shall be my people. Thus the nations shall know that it is I, the Lord, who make Israel holy, when my sanctuary shall be set up among them forever (Ezek 37:26-28).

This New People will worship not in a physical place, whether temple or mountain, but in Spirit and in Truth (cf. John 4:21-24). Jesus the Truth now pours out on them his Spirit.

What is structurally exceptional about this line, "Jesus came and stood in(to) the(i)r midst," is that there is no corresponding member at the end of the scene. Literarily there should be a notice that, having finished that for which he came, Jesus left, or that he vanished from their sight (cf. 20:2 in relation to v. 1, and 20:10 in relation to v. 3). But even though Jesus will come again, he never leaves, suggesting the new mode of Jesus' presence to his disciples.

Two further points, which cannot be explored in depth here, must be made before leaving this central scene. First, the *group* to which the Risen Jesus comes in John 20 is not the Twelve, the seventy-two, the apostles, the trio of Peter, James, and John, or any other select group.[61] He comes to "the disciples," which in John is an inclusive group of men and women, itinerants and householders, Jews, Samaritans, and Gentiles.[62] Believers, the Church as community and not as hierarchical institution, is the foundational symbolic expression of the Risen Jesus. The Church is his body.[63]

Second, the *commission* in John is to continue the work of Jesus who came to take away the sin (singular) of the world, i.e., the fundamental sin of unbelief. The disciples will carry on this mission by forgiving sins (plural), the expressions of unbelief that are renounced by those who come to believe in Jesus. Sometime after the third century a linguistic anomaly in which "retention of sins" was gratuitously paired with "forgiveness of sins" found its way into the translation of v. 23 and was eventually enshrined dogmatically in the decrees of the Council of Trent.[64] The exegetical basis for this move was interpreting John 20:23 as a parallel of Matt 16:19 and 18:18 on binding and loosing through interpretation of the law, thus reading John 20:23 as an eliptical antithetical parallelism. The apologetic basis was the establishment of the Catholic discipline of confession as a sacrament against its rejection by the Reformers.[65]

Whatever might be said about the apologetic motive, it is highly questionable to read John in terms of Matthew, especially when the respective contexts differ completely. In any case the text of John 20:23 does not say anything about "retaining sins." Translated literally it says: "Of whomever you forgive the sins, they are forgiven to them; whomever you hold are held fast."[66] In the second member there is no direct object, "sins," nor indirect object, "to them." The verb "to hold," κρατέω does not mean, in secular or biblical Greek, "retain." It means "hold fast," "grasp," even "embrace" (cf. Matt 28:9 where κρατέω is correctly translated "held" or "embraced"). And it normally takes an objective genitive, as it does in this case, τινων, "whomever." In other words, the text as it stands is a synthetic or progressive parallel. The community that forgives sins must holds fast those whom it has brought into the community of eternal life. This may be a reference to baptism, but hardly to penance.[67] But whether or not there is an explicit sacramental reference, translating this text as it stands rather than by supplying supposedly missing words to create a parallel to Matthew accords well, in both form and content, with Jesus' own descriptions of his mission from the Father, which he is here committing to his disciples.

> "All that the Father *gives* me will come to me and the one who comes to me I *will not cast out.*" (6:37)
>
> ". . . it is the will of the One who sent me "that I should *lose nothing* of all that he has *given* me." (6:39)
>
> "I *give them eternal life* and they shall *never perish,* and *no one shall snatch them out of my Father's hand.* My father, who has *given* them to me, is greater than all, and *no one is able to snatch them out of the Father's hand.* I and the Father are one. (10:27-29)
>
> While I was with them, I *kept* in your name those whom you have *given* me, and I guarded them, and *not one of them is lost.* (17:12)
>
> This was to fulfill the word which he had spoken, "Of those whom you have *given* me I have *not lost* any. (18:9)[68]

The importance of this point lies in how John understands the community of the New Covenant. The community is the ongoing bodily presence of Jesus in the world. As the Father had sent him, so he sends his disciples (v. 21). They are to live by his Spirit, which he breathes upon them (v. 22), and to carry on his mission of receiving those whom the Father gives them and holding them fast in the community (v. 23) as Jesus received his disciples from the Father and held them fast amid the evils and dangers of the world. Jesus (in the flesh) is no longer in the world, but they (his body) are in the world (cf. 17:11). They are to do his works, and even greater works than he had done in his earthly career (cf. 14:12). The community is not, according to John, an agent of a departed Jesus exercising judgment, which Jesus explicitly said he was not sent to do and does not do (12:47). The community in all its members is Jesus at work in the world and his work is to take away sins by giving life in all its fullness.

There is no indication in the text, as this church founding scene ends, that the reader should expect anything further. So the next scene opens unexpectedly with the news that one of the Twelve, Thomas, was not with the community when Jesus came. Significantly, Thomas is called "the twin." He has a double identity: he is both a disciple of the earthly Jesus and he shares the experience of later disciples who were not present on Easter.[69] Narratively the evangelist establishes the identity of pre-Easter and post-Easter disciples, for whom the structure of faith is essentially the same.

The glorified Jesus, not bound by earthly conditions of physicality, is again sensibly, i.e., bodily, present even though the doors are closed, and he knows of Thomas's refusal to believe on the basis of the disciples' witness, "We have

seen the Lord." Jesus invites Thomas to touch him even as he challenges him
to renounce the unbelieving demand to do so and become believing (v. 27).[70]
Thomas rises to the challenge. He confesses what he cannot see with his bodily eyes, that the Jesus who addresses him is "My Lord and my God" (v. 28).

Jesus' response is all-important. He accepts Thomas' confession of what he
cannot see based on what he has seen, both in his pre-paschal experience of
Jesus and in this Easter experience. But Jesus equates Thomas' "seeing" to the
"not seeing" of all disciples down through the centuries who will not have seen
Jesus in the flesh or in Easter appearance (20:29).[71] Their believing will be
based on "seeing" him in sacramental signs, "hearing" him in the community's
witness, and especially in the "things written" in the gospel. Following Jesus'
turn in blessing to his future disciples in v. 29, the evangelist addresses the
readers directly by equating the signs of the earthly Jesus with the gospel text
itself. Just as his first disciples had to discern in his ambiguous historical signs
the revelation of God in Jesus, and the Easter community had to discern their
Lord and God in the mysterious person risen in their midst whom they are not
to touch physically, so all later disciples must discern the new bodily presence
of Jesus in the ecclesial community, Eucharist, and Gospel. In all these cases
Jesus, as the locus and revelation of God's glory, is perceptible only to the eyes
and ears of faith responding to the symbolic modes of his presence.

John 20 as a whole, and especially the contrast between the Mary Magdalene
and Thomas scenes in light of the central scene of the raising of the Temple of
Jesus' body in the midst of the New Covenant people, tells us something crucial
about the body of the glorified and risen Jesus. It is human and material but not
physical.[72] In other words, mortal flesh has become glorified body. In the Mary
Magdalene scene Jesus restrains Mary from trying to touch him physically not
because he is a ghost or because he disdains her love and desire. It is because
she does not completely grasp that he has not been resuscitated like Lazarus to
life in the flesh. Jesus redirects Mary's attempt to relate to him by pointing her to
his presence in the community where she will touch him, encounter him, in a
new way corresponding to his new mode of being and presence.

In the Thomas scene Jesus invites Thomas to touch him. The glorified Jesus
can self-symbolize quasi-physically if that is necessary, but this is not how he
ordinarily chooses to be present, to Thomas or to us. Thomas becomes "not unbelieving but believing" when he, like Mary, moves from the dispensation of the
flesh to the dispensation of glory. He recognizes Jesus as the person he knew in
the flesh but who, while remaining himself, is no longer in the context of history.

These two seemingly contradictory facts, that Jesus is himself in the full integrity of his humanity and that he is no longer subject to the historical coordinates of space, time, and causality, are mediated by the concept of body as
symbol. In the context of history the human person self-symbolizes in and as
her or his mortal (i.e., fleshly) bodyself. Person as subject, body as symbolic
self-expression, and flesh as physical, i.e., mortal, locus of the person as body-

self are coterminous, which leads us to spontaneously identify them without distinction. John's Resurrection Narrative suggests (as does Paul in 1 Corinthians 15 and Luke in the Damascus road event in Acts 9:5) that the glorified person, Jesus himself in his divine humanity, continues to self-symbolize, that is, to be bodily present and active, but no longer in mortal flesh. He can be present when, where, and how he wills: in the community itself and in its actions of preaching the Word, celebrating Eucharist, and ministering to the needy. He can be present to the individual believer in prayer or even in vision, although John, like spiritual writers down through the centuries, warns that this is an exceptional and always ambiguous occurrence that is not to be sought or privileged. Materiality as the condition of symbolic self-expression is what bodiliness connotes. It is that which marks the person Jesus as distinct from other persons and self-continuous, as a subject who can relate to other subjects, and as one who can act effectively in the world even though not conditioned by it. Materiality, which is the condition of possibility of sensibility, is no longer equated with physicality. The glorified body is a body, Jesus as body, but it is no longer a fleshly, that is, a mortal or historical body.

VII. Conclusion

In summary and conclusion: The bodiliness of Jesus' resurrection is crucial to Christian faith, theology, and spirituality for a number of reasons. First, only if Jesus is alive in the full integrity of his humanity, which entails bodiliness, *can he be in God the first fruits of humanity's incorporation into divinity.* Humanity is not a transitory mode of the Word that he abandoned in death.

Second, because body is the symbolic mode of presence, both self-presence as subject and intersubjective presence to others, *the real and personal existence of Jesus as human after his death and his continuing presence to his followers* requires bodily resurrection.

Third, symbols are the perceptibility of what is otherwise not able to be encountered and because body as material (not as physical) is the condition of possibility of perceptibility, *Jesus can only self-symbolize in various ways* if his post-resurrection humanity is bodily.

Fourth, body is not exhausted in the notion of "flesh," i.e., humanity as mortal. Jesus as the Word-made-flesh experienced the condition of mortality but by his glorification he transcended that condition and *became capable, in his humanity, of a range of self-symbolization that is not limited by space, time, or causality.*

Fifth, the *Church's faith in the real presence of Jesus* in his ecclesial body, in his Eucharistic body, in the textual body of Scripture, is also expressed in the spirituality tradition of those mystics whose direct experience of Jesus as friend, lover, and spouse has been nurtured especially by the Canticle of Canticles and the Fourth Gospel. We see this Jesus mysticism in writers such as

Origen, Gertrude of Helfta, Bernard of Clairvaux, Catherine of Siena, Francis of Assisi, Teresa of Avila, John of the Cross, and later writers.

In short, John's Gospel is a primary source and resource for the experience in the church of the glorified human Jesus, personally alive, present, and active throughout all time. The church's spirituality is an ongoing exploration of the existential meaning of Jesus' promise:

> I will not leave you orphans: I am coming to you. Yet a little while and the world sees me no longer, but you see me, for because I live you also will live. In that day you will know that I am in the Father, and you in me, and I in you. (John 14:18-20)

Notes

1. For convenience I will refer to the Fourth Gospel and to the evangelist as "John" without thereby implying any particular position on the identity or gender of this individual. I basically accept the reigning consensus of scholars that the Fourth Gospel was written, sometime between 80 and 110 (probably around 90) C.E., by an anonymous second-generation Christian who was part of a "school" within the Johannine cluster of communities. See Maarten J. J. Menken, "Envoys of God's Envoy: On the Johannine Communities," *Proceedings of the Irish Biblical Association* 23 (2000) 45–60 for a good summary of the results of scholarship concerning the matrix out of which this gospel emerged.

2. I have dealt with this issue at some length in an earlier article, "The Resurrection of Jesus and Christian Spirituality," in Maureen Junker-Kenny, ed., *Christian Resources of Hope* (Dublin: Columba Press, 1995) 81–114.

3. Throughout this paper I am indebted to the excellent work of Mary Coloe, *God Dwells with Us: Temple Symbolism in the Fourth Gospel* (Collegeville: Liturgical Press, 2001). Her treatment of Jesus' action in the Temple in John 2 is the best interpretation I have read, largely because it places this mysterious episode within the theological context of the gospel as a whole rather than reading it as a Johannine version of the Synoptic accounts, which have somewhat different functions within their respective Passion Narratives.

4. Giovanni Ghiberti published two exhaustive bibliographies on the Resurrection covering material up to 1974: "Bibliografia sull'esegesi dei racconti pasquali e sul problema della risurrezione di Gesù (1957–1968)," *La Scuola Cattolica* 97 (1969 [Supplemento bibliografica 2]) 68–84, and "Bibliografia sulla Risurrezione di Gesù (1920–1973), *Resurrexit* (Vatican City: Vaticana, 1974) 643–764. A Portuguese bibliography on the resurrection including more than 500 items was published in 1989: Isidro Alves, "Ressurreição e Fé Pascal," *Didaskalia* 19 (1989) 277–541. Three recent international symposia on resurrection that supply bibliography are the following: Stephen T. David, Daniel Kendall, and Gerald O'Collins, eds., *The Resurrection: An Interdisciplinary Symposium on the Resurrection of Jesus* (Oxford: Oxford University Press, 1996); Stanley E. Porter, Michael A. Hayes, and David Tombs, eds., *Resurrection*. Papers from the Conference on Resurrection on 21 February 1998 in Roehampton, England. JSNTSup 186 [Roehampton Institute London Papers 5] (Sheffield: Sheffield Academic Press, 1999); Friedrich Avemarie and Hermann Lichtenberger, eds., *Auferstehung—Resurrection*. Fourth Durham-Tübingen Research Symposium on Resurrection, Transfiguration and Exaltation in Old Testament, Ancient Judaism and Early Christianity, Tübingen, September 1999 (Tübingen: J. C. B. Mohr, 2001). Recent bibliography on the resurrrection in John can be found in John Paul Heil, *Blood and Water: The Death and Resurrection of Jesus in John 18–21*. CBQMS 27 (Washington, DC: Catholic Biblical Association of America, 1995) 172–80.

5. See Gail R.O'Day, *Revelation in the Fourth Gospel: Narrative Mode and Theological Claim* (Philadephia: Fortress, 1986) for an excellent treatment of this subject.

6. Translations of texts from the Gospel of John are either my own or that of the NRSV unless otherwise noted. Translations of other parts of the Bible are from the NRSV.

7. See the very helpful "Excursus: Narrative Approaches to the Fourth Gospel," by the editor in Raymond E. Brown, *An Introduction to the Gospel of John,* edited, updated, introduced, and concluded by Francis J. Moloney. ABRL (New York: Doubleday, 2003) 31–39. Moloney supplies excellent bibliography on literary approaches and their necessary relation to historical approaches to the biblical text.

8. A renewed interest in the historical and literary processes that produced the Fourth Gospel as well as the sources the evangelist might have used is reflected in the collection edited by Robert T. Fortna and Tom Thatcher, *Jesus in Johannine Tradition* (Louisville: Westminster John Knox, 2001).

9. Jean Zumstein, "Lecture narratologique du cycle pascal du quatrième évangile," *ETR* 76 (2001) 1–15, gives a very good explanation of how the "incoherencies" that historical critical work discovers are often products of the method itself and that, if the text is dealt with as a narrative, many of these apparent "seams," "aporias," "doublets," and inconsistencies cease to be such.

10. O'Day, *Revelation in the Fourth Gospel,* makes this point with full argumentation. She concludes, *"Revelation lies in the Gospel narrative and the world created by the words of that narrative"* (p. 94, emphasis in the text). I would nuance this somewhat by saying that revelation occurs in *interaction with the text* in order to avoid the possible implication that revelation is somehow quasi-propositional.

11. See the conclusion, on "Reading for Transformation," of Dorothy Lee, *Flesh and Glory: Symbol, Gender, and Theology in the Gospel of John* (New York: Crossroad, 2002) 233–37.

12. See Paul Ricoeur, *Interpetation Theory: Discourse and the Surplus of Meaning* (Fort Worth: Texas Christian University Press, 1976), especially 91–95 on "appropriation."

13. A good introduction to Semitic anthropology is Hans Walter Wolff, *Anthropology of the Old Testament* (Mifflintown, PA: Sigler, 1996) (originally published by SCM in 1974). The Gospel of John, as we will see in dealing with his eschatology, is not devoid of hellenistic influences coming probably through OT sapiential materials, especially Wisdom of Solomon. However, this influence is controlled by Hebrew understandings of God, the human, and the end of human life. A thorough study of Johannine anthropology, which is completely beyond the scope of this paper, would proceed by tracing the path from concrete and stereometric (to use Wolff's term) Hebrew usage through the changes rung on the terms in the Greek of the LXX into the FG. I suspect that the most original development is precisely John's exploitation of the distinction, not possible in Hebrew but possible in Greek, between σάρξ and σῶμα.

14. Andrew T. Lincoln, "'I am the Resurrection and the Life': The Resurrection Message of the Fourth Gospel," in Richard N. Longenecker, ed., *Life in the Face of Death: The Resurrection Message of the New Testament* (Grand Rapids and Cambridge: Eerdmans, 1998) 129, makes the important point that Jesus could not have been speaking of laying down his divine life. However, he immediately slips into the mistaken identification of ψυχή with σάρξ, leading to an understanding of bodily resurrection as fleshly or physical resurrection.

15. I have dealt with this topic in greater detail in "The Community of Eternal Life (John 11:1-53)," in my *Written That You May Believe: Encountering Jesus in the Fourth Gospel* (2nd revised and expanded ed. New York: Crossroad, 2003) 171–83.

16. I am grateful to Francis Moloney for sharing with me his fine paper, as yet unpublished, "The Johannine Son of Man Revisited." His understanding of the Johannine use of "Son of Man" for the revelation of God in the human event of Jesus Christ, especially in his being "lifted up" on the cross, is very helpful for understanding resurrection in John.

17. Flesh is a good translation of *sarx,* a more differentiated term than the Hebrew *bāśār,* which denotes the human in his/her infirmity or weakness (Wolff, *Anthropology,* 26–31). But the

Hebrew term covers the territory of "body" virtually completely whereas Greek distinguishes *sarx* from *sōma,* a crucial distinction for John's theology of resurrection.

18. For a very rich treatment of the meaning of flesh in John see Lee, *Flesh and Glory,* 29–64.

19. Here I disagree with Lee, *Flesh and Glory,* 45–46, who suggests that there is no significant difference between σάρξ and σῶμα. I will argue that there is a critically important difference. Jesus does not rise as "flesh," but as "body."

20. It is interesting that psychosomatic medicine is discovering in various ways how completely the whole human is "body," not in the reductive sense of being nothing but material, but in the sense of being, as a whole, a "body person." This understanding is closer to the biblical understanding than the reductionistic anthropology spawned by the scientific revolution and the Enlightenment. Nevertheless, contemporary understandings of the human are still quite dichotomous, as is evidenced by the mechanistic approaches to medical procedures.

21. The Hellenistic influence on John's thought as well as the exploitation of the possibilities of the Greek language are clear here. *Bāśār* is not used to speak of a corpse (although *nepeš* occasionally is) but only of living creatures, whereas John does not use *sarx* (which the LXX uses for *bāśār*) but *sōma* to speak of the corpses on the cross (19:31) and specifically of the dead body of Jesus (19: 38, 40) and of his risen body (2:21-22).

22. John L. McKenzie, "Sheol," *Dictionary of the Bible* (Milwaukee: Bruce, 1965) 800, says that Sheol "is less a positive conception of survival than a picturesque denial of all that is meant by life and activity."

23. I have dealt at length with the concept of symbol, especially as it functions in John's Gospel, in *Written That You May Believe,* 63–77. See also Lee, *Flesh and Glory,* 9–28. A still very important work on symbol in theology and especially on the body as the primary symbol by which a person is present to him/herself as well as to others is Karl Rahner, "The Theology of the Symbol," *Theological Investigations 4, More Recent Writings,* trans. Kevin Smyth (Baltimore: Helicon, 1966) 221–52, especially 245–52 on the body. It is especially interesting that the term "body" does not seem to play a distinct enough role in Semitic thought to merit a term of its own in distinction from "flesh." The only bodies known to human experience were fleshly ones, either the potential human, the "earth creature" *(hā ādām)* of Gen 2:7, or the living person, *nepeš* or *bāśār.*

24. I find very suggestive the point made by Mary Coloe in "Like Father, Like Son: The Role of Abraham in Tabernacles—John 8:31-59," *Pacifica* 12 (February 1999) 1–11: "In speaking of Jesus as both Temple and Tabernacle there is no dichotomy as the two are intrinsically related as the flesh (1:14) is related to the body (2:21). The Tabernacle and the Temple serve the same symbolic function even though they recall different historical eras" (p. 4, n. 6). I think that in fact flesh and body denote different and subsequent modes (analogous to historical eras) of the presence of Jesus to his disciples. Flesh indicates his career as a mortal and body, his glorified life. But the two terms denote the same person and the same presence of the glory of God among humans in that person.

25. Just after finishing work on this paper, and too late to incorporate it substantively into this text, I came upon a fascinating article on the body of Jesus in its displacements, transformations, and resignifications that brings a confirming postmodern light to bear on this topic. See Graham Ward, "Bodies: The Displaced Body of Jesus Christ," in John Milbank, Catherine Pickstock, and Graham Ward, eds., *Radical Orthodoxy: A New Theology* (London and New York: Routledge, 1999) 163–81, especially 168 on the point here. See also his article, "Transcorporeality: The Ontological Scandal," *BJRL* 80 (August 1998) 235–52.

26. Rudolf Bultmann, *Theology of the New Testament,* vol. 2, trans. Kendrick Grobel (New York: Charles Scribner's Sons, 1955) 56.

27. Although the dating of the "intertestamental" period as well as the category itself is debated I am using it here to suggest the overlapping of late pre-Christian Jewish thought and the development of the canonical New Testament. My thanks to my colleagues, John Endres, Barbara

Green, Gina Hens-Piazza, as well as to GTU research librarian Kristine Veldheer for help with this and other sections in the paper.

28. I have explored the historical development of eschatological thought in Israel in the post-exilic and intertestamental periods at some length in my doctoral dissertation, *The Johannine Resurrection Narrative: An Exegetical and Theological Study of John 20 as a Synthesis of Johannine Spirituality* (Ann Arbor: University Microfilms International, 1983) 2:76–89. The treatment offered here is a very brief and oversimplified synopsis whose purpose is simply to contrast apocalytic and sapiential eschatology in order to account for the distinctive Johannine treatment of the death and resurrection of Jesus. For a succinct treatment of NT eschatology see Adela Yarbro Collins, "Eschatology and Apocalypticism," in Raymond Brown, Donald Senior, John R. Donahue, and Adela Yarbro Collins, "Aspects of New Testament Thought," *NJBC* 81:25–56.

29. For an excellent, and provocatively suggestive, treatment of the Wisdom of Solomon, its eschatology in relation to its *Sitz-im-Leben,* and its possible relation to the NT see Barbara Green, "The Wisdom of Solomon and the Solomon of Wisdom: Tradition's Transpositions and Human Transformation," *Horizons* 30 (Spring 2003) 41–66.

30. For the development of the extrabiblical literary genre of "wisdom tale" within which we meet wisdom heroes in noncanonical dress who resemble Joseph, Daniel, and Susanna whose "wisdom," however, is fidelity to Torah, see G. W. Nicholsburg, *Resurrection, Immortality, and Eternal Life in Intertestamental Judaism.* HTS 26 (Cambridge, MA: Harvard University Press, 1972) 49–55.

31. See Schneiders, *The Johannine Resurrection Narrative,* 2:98–101 for the textual evidence supporting this position.

32. This was explained well by Joseph Moignt, "Immortalité de l'âme et/ou résurrection,"*LumVie* 21 (1972) 65–78, who takes essentially the same position as Oscar Cullmann in his classic text, "Immortality of the Soul or Resurrection of the Dead: The Witness of the New Testament." The Ingersoll Lecture, 1955. *Harvard Divinity School Bulletin* 21 (1955–1956) 5–36.

33. It is important, however, but beyond the scope of this essay, to note that Jewish anthropology was influenced by Hellenistic philosophy in the immediate pre-Christian period. This is evident in the use of terms such as "incorruption" (ἀφθαρσία) in Wis 2:23 and "immortality" (ἀθανασία) in Wis 3:4. On the other hand, the biblical influence appears in the notion that death is not intended by God but entered the world through the envy of the devil (cf. Wis 2:23-24) in contrast to the notion of death as natural passage into nonexistence that the enemies of the wisdom hero enunciate in Wis 2:1-22.

34. This "moral dualism" of the FG is not absolute, and 1 John 2:19; 3:4-10 in relation to 5:16-17 suggests that the historical Johannine community had trouble with it. However, it seems to stem from the "two-way theology" that appears pervasively in the OT (e.g., in Hos 14:9; Amos 5:14-15; Mic 4:2, 5; Jer 5:4; Ps 1:1, 6; Prov 2:12-15, and elsewhere), but which comes to very explicit articulation in the Wisdom of Solomon (e.g., 1:4-8, 14; 2:24; 3:7-19; 5:6-7). Interestingly, Nickelsberg, *Resurrection, Immortality, and Eternal Life,* 165–66, says that the "two way theology," which is perfectly compatible with an eschatology of immediate assumption at death, was combined with a notion of bodily resurrection only after 70 C.E., e.g., in *4 Ezra* and *Epistle of Barnabas.*

35. See Coloe, *God Dwells With Us,* 15–29, for a very good treatment of the structure and content of the Prologue, particularly in relation to the issue of the presence of God in Jesus that is our concern here. Coloe also summarizes other influential theories concerning the structure and dynamics of the text.

36. Mary Coloe's interpretation of Jesus as replacement of the Temple, the place of divine glory, with Jesus as the locus of the glory of YHWH is strongly reinforced by the article of Carey C. Newman, "Resurrection as Glory: Divine Presence and Christian Origins," *The Resurrection,* 59–89. Newman convincingly argues that the real cause of the break between the early Christian

community and Judaism was "that the resurrection of Jesus, as depicted in early Christian creeds, confessions, and hymns, was interpreted as his investiture with, and inauguration of, eschatological divine presence—that is, the Glory of Yahweh" (p. 87).

37. I will use the convention of placing "the Jews" in quotation marks when the expression denotes the so-called "Johannine Jews," that is, the collective representative figure in the Fourth Gospel that signifies rejection of the light, in order to warn the reader not to equate this literary stereotype with actual Jews, either those of Jesus' time or those of later periods.

38. Lincoln in "'I am the Resurrection and the Life,' 126, says of the Temple episode, "it is made clear that not only will the incarnate Logos die, but also that he will rise and the *bodily* form of his resurrection will continue to be an essential feature of his identity" (emphasis added). However, on pp. 128 and 141 Lincoln seems to equate risen *bodiliness* with *physicality,* which may reflect a lack in his philosophical repertoire of a notion of materiality that is not physical rather than a conscious position on the nature of glorified bodiliness. His evident concern is to affirm the bodiliness of the Risen Jesus.

39. I am indebted to my colleague David Johnson, who pointed out to me that the Greek "ἔστη" was rendered in the Peshitta (Syriac version from 5th century C.E. but related to the much earlier Old Syriac) by the term *qâm,* from the root *qom,* which means either "stand" or "arise as from sleep or from death" as well as "to stand up" or "to be present." See R. Payne Smith, *A Compendious Syriac Dictionary, founded upon the Thesaurus syriacus of R. Payne Smith*, edited by J. Payne Smith (Oxford: Clarendon, 1903). John's construction, Jesus "stood into " (ἔστη εἰς), suggests that the more dynamic translation is to be understood since simply appearing or standing would not suggest motion. I am inclined to think that "stand into" is best translated as "arose among," especially in light of John 2:19 and 21-22 where Jesus predicts that he will "raise up" (ἐγερῶ) the new temple and the evangelist clarifies that Jesus was referring to the temple of his body, which the disciples would understand after he "was raised from the dead" (ἠγέρθη ἐκ νεκρῶν).

40. P. Van Dieman, in his 1972 Rome dissertation, *La semaine inaugurale et la semaine terminale de l'évangile de Jean: Message et structures,* proposed a modification of Marie-Émile Boismard's thesis of the "weeks" of Jesus' life as a structure of the FG. Van Dieman argued that in John the first and last weeks of Jesus' life are actually composed of six days and an eighth day while the seventh day, the Jewish Sabbath, is passed over in silence. The eighth day is both the first day of creation and the eschatological day of the New Creation. Consequently this "last and great day of the the feast" of Tabernacles is a day symbolic of both the New Creation and the Resurrection while the day after Jesus' death is Passover, the silent end of the old dispensation, and the resurrection, inaugurating the new, occurs on the eighth day.

41. See Coloe, *God Dwells With Us,* 119–22, for description of the rituals of Tabernacles in relation to John 7–8.

42. The evangelist will identifiy Jesus, the Sent One, with the waters of Siloam in John 9:7, and Jesus will identify himself as "the light of the world" in 8:12 and 9:5. This is not the only time the FE "recalls" something that has not yet happened.

43. Germain Bienaimé, "L'annonce des fleuves d'eau vive en Jean 7,37-39," *RTL* 21 (1990) 281–310, 417–54, summarizes and evaluates virtually every recent study of this passage in re: punctuation, the provenance of the citation, and the relation of v. 39 to vv. 37-38. He includes an exhaustive bibliography.

44. Bienaimé, "L'annonce des fleuves d'eau vive," 422–31, discusses the positions of C. C. Torrey and André Feuillet among others on these suggestions. He himself regards Exod 17:6 as the "texte fondamental de la citation" (431–32), which is enriched by Pss 78 and 105 and Ezekiel 47. He concludes, however, that the primary point of the evocation of Ezekiel 47 is to recall that the water flowing from the Temple is the water of the new paradise and thus that the text in John 7 is more about the New Creation than about Jesus as the New Temple (454). I would place the emphasis the other way around.

45. James Swetnam, "Bestowal of the Spirit in the Fourth Gospel," *Bib* 74 (1999) 556–76, cites Edwyn Hoskyns (*The Fourth Gospel* [London: Faber, 1947] 532) on the peculiar language for the death of Jesus, παραδιδόναι τὸ πνεῦμα. In Mark Jesus "gave up the ghost" or expired [ἐξέπνευσεν] . . . in Matthew he "yielded up his spirit" [ἀφῆκεν τὸ πνεῦμα]; in Luke he "gave up the ghost" or breathed his last [ἐξέπνευσεν]. Swetnam says John's expression is "unparalleled in the Greek language as a description of death" (564). Hence his conclusion, following Hoskyns, is that the primary meaning of the account is the "bestowing of the Spirit" rather than simply Jesus letting go of his human life. However, it also obviously means that Jesus died.

46. See Maarten J. J. Menken, "The Old Testament Quotation in John 19,36: Sources, Redaction, Background," in Frans van Segbroeck, Christopher M. Tuckett, Gilbert van Belle, and Jozef Verheyden, eds., *The Four Gospels 1992. Festschrift Frans Neirynck.* 3 vols. BETL 100 (Leuven: Leuven University Press, 1992) 3:2101–18 for an investigation of the sources for the citation. Menken concludes that the citation identifies Jesus as both the Suffering Servant and the Paschal Lamb.

47. Brown, in *The Gospel According to John.* 2 vols. AB 29-29a (Garden City, NY: Doubleday, 1966–70] 1139 says, "It is our contention that John presents the Paraclete as the Holy Spirit in a special role, namely, as the personal presence of Jesus in the Christian while Jesus is with the Father." It is unusual for Brown to label a position as his personal opinion rather than presenting it as a convincing conclusion from the data he has provided. I think he understood the originality of his "contention." He may be suggesting that Spirit is the mode of bodiliness of the glorified Jesus, which is my position. But because the dichotomous western mind tends to equate "spirit" with "disembodied" as in "pure spirit" it is difficult for this term to function clearly in discussing bodily presence. The fact that Brown entitled one of his books *The Virginal Conception and Bodily Resurrection of Jesus* (London and Dublin: Geoffrey Chapman, 1973) suggests that he considered Jesus/the presence of the glorified and risen Jesus as bodily. Hence the importance of the statement above.

48. Robert Crotty, "The Two Magdalene Reports on the Risen Jesus in John 20," *Pacifica* 12 (June 1999) 156–68, lists some of the more interesting recent proposals: Raymond E. Brown, *The Gospel According to John,* 965; Francis J. Moloney, *The Gospel of John.* SP 4 (Collegeville: Liturgical Press,1988) 516; Brendan J. Byrne, "The Faith of the Beloved Disciple and the Community in John 20," *JSNT* 23 (1985) 83–97; Dorothy A. Lee, "Partnership in Easter Faith: The Role of Mary Magdalene and Thomas in John 20," *JSNT* 53 (1995) 37–49; Liliane Dupont, Christopher Lash, and Georges Levesque, "Recherche sur la structure de Jean 20," *Bib* 54 (1973) 482–98; Donatien Mollat, "La foi pascale selon le chapître 20 de l'évangile de saint Jean," in Edouard Dhanis, ed., *Resurrexit. Actes du Symposium International sur la Résurrection de Jésus (Rome 1970)* (Vatican City : Libreria Editrice Vaticana, 1974) 316–34; Ignace de la Potterie, "Génèse de la foi pascale d'après Jn 20," *NTS* 30 (1984) 26–49. More recently, Raymond Brown again addressed the subject in "The Resurrection in John 20—A Series of Diverse Reactions," *Worship* 64 (May 1990) 194–206. A fascinating study of the use of numerical proportions among the verbs in ch. 20 to structure the narrative is Joost Smit Sibinga, "Towards Understanding the Composition of John 20," *The Four Gospels 1992,* 2139–52. He concludes that 20:16 emerges as the center of gravity of the chapter (p. 2149).

John Paul Heil in *Blood and Water: The Death and Resurrection of Jesus in John 18–21.* CBQMS 27 (Washington, DC: Catholic Biblical Association of America, 1995) 6, structures ch. 20 as six scenes arranged in four "sandwiches" that move the action forward and draw the reader forward by an intercalation: A¹, B¹, A², B², A³, B³, C, coresponding respectively to the following scenes: A¹ 20:1-2; B¹ 20:3-10; A² 20:11-18; B² 20:19-23; A³ 20:24-25; B³ 20:26-29; C 20:30-31. Jean Zumstein, "Lecture narratologique," (n. 9 above) has already been mentioned as an excellent example of narratological structuring.

49. I developed the structural theory I am proposing here (with slight revisions) in my 1976 doctoral dissertation, *The Johannine Resurrection Narrative,* 189–216.

50. The debate continues about whether the verb in v. 31 is a present subjunctive (πιστευήτε) suggesting that the intended audience is the Christian community itself, or an aorist subjective (πιστεύσητε), which would suggest that the gospel is directed to possible converts. Gordon D. Fee, "On the Text and Meaning of John 20,30-31," *The Four Gospels 1992,* 2193–2204, argues convincingly, against D. A. Carson, "The Purpose of the Fourth Gospel: John 20:31 Reconsidered," *JBL* 106 (1987) 639–51, that both from a text-critical standpoint and in terms of meaning the present tense reading is preferable. I agree with this position and assume it in what follows.

51. A leitmotif of the Christian mystical tradition is the question of how to find, how to encounter, the seemingly absent Lord. John of the Cross begins his classic poem on the mystical life, *Cántico Espiritual,* with the anguished address of the bride-soul to Jesus, "Where have you hidden, Beloved, and left me groaning?" (see *The Collected Works of Saint John of the Cross,* rev. ed., trans. Kieran Kavanaugh and Otilio Rodriguez [Washington, DC: Institute of Carmelite Studies, 1991], citation from p. 44). But the question predates John of the Cross by centuries, e.g., Augustine's famous "interrogation of the creatures," and continues up to the present. The path runs from the Canticle of Canticles in the OT through the Gospel of John in the NT into the Jesus mysticism (sometimes called "bridal mysticism") of the subsequent tradition.

52. Σουδάριον is the Greek transliteration of a Latin loanword, *sudarium.* The root suggests that it was a "towel" or a "handkerchief". Most significantly, it appears in the Aramaic of Targums Ps.-Jonathan and Yerushalmi (Codex Neofiti I) as *soudârâ,* סוּדָרָא or סוּדָר, to translate מַסְוֶה, a unique word for the face-veil of Moses in Exod 34:33-35. It has the same sense in Syriac. In other words, σουδάριον in the FG is probably equivalent to the LXX's κάλυμμα in Exodus 34, meaning "veil," and if John's community was originally Aramaic-speaking and read or heard the OT in Aramaic they would have heard σουδάριον as equivalent to the LXX's κάλυμμα in reference to the face-veil of Moses. Σουδάριον, however, would be preferable to the very common word κάλυμμα if the intention was to call attention to the unique character of Jesus' face-veil, as Moses' face-veil was designated by a unique word. That Jesus' face-veil was not simply a normal burial cloth seems to be suggested by the notation that it was not lying with the burial clothes but wrapped up into a place by itself. Paul's use of the face-veil of Moses (2 Cor 3:6-18) to speak of the passing away of the Old Covenant and the establishment of the New suggests that this symbolism was not unfamiliar in early Christian circles. Jesus, in John, is the mediator of the New Covenant. The relation of מַסְוֶה to סוּדָרָא was pointed out decades ago by F.-M. Braun, *Le Linceul de Turin et l'évangile de S. Jean: Étude de critique et d'exégése* (Tournai and Paris: Casterman, 1939) 34–35.

53. Brendan Byrne, in "The Faith of the Beloved Disciple and the Community in John 20," *JSNT* 23 (1985) 83–97, also proposes that the σουδάριον is the sign, but he explictly disagrees with me about its meaning. He locates the meaning in the contrast of Jesus' face-veil with Lazarus's: Lazarus had to have the veil removed by others, whereas Jesus removed his own. I would not reject that interpretation, but I think there is considerably more involved, namely the evocation of the Mosaic-covenantal motif. However, Byrne's thesis concerning the relation of the "seeing and believing" in the 3-10 episode to that in 24-29 is a real contribution. In a sense the whole of ch. 20 is an exploration of the "absence" (I would say the absence/presence) of Jesus and the role of signs, historical signs and ecclesial ones, in the handling of that experience. I am in substantial agreement with his conclusion: "The Gospel of John seems to me to be composed very largely to give subsequent believers access to the central events of Jesus' life, death, resurrection and return to the Father and to assure them that in this access they can have an encounter with Jesus every bit as valid and indeed more fruitful than that of those who actually saw him" (p. 93). I am, however, not persuaded that there is a hierarchical comparison, explicit or implicit, in 20:29.

54. The influence of the Song of Songs on John 20 was suggested by André Feuillet, "La Recherche du Christ dans la Nouvelle Alliance d'après la Christophanie de Jo. 20,11-18: Comparaison avec Cant. 3, 1-4 et l'épisode des pélerins d'Emmaüs," in Jacques Guillet, et al., *L'Homme devant Dieu: Mélanges offerts au père Henri de Lubac.* Théologie 56 (Paris: Aubier, 1963–64) 93–112.

John, in ch. 20, uses κῆπος for "garden." In the LXX the garden of creation is παράδεισος, while the garden in the Song of Songs is κῆπος, suggesting that the stronger allusion is to the Canticle. However, there is a progression in the OT from the paradise in which humanity was created in union with God and from which it was expelled because of sin, through the alternating possession and loss of the land (a garden or a desert) because of Israel's fidelity or infidelity to the covenant, to the garden of union in the Song of Songs. So the allusion in ch. 20 is probably to both paradise regained, i.e., the New Creation, and the New Covenant. For a different interpretation of the use by John of κῆπος see John N. Suggit, "Jesus the Gardener. The Atonement in the Fourth Gospel as Re-Creation," *Neot* 33 (1999) 161–68, at 166.

55. "Teacher" is the quintessential identity of the historical Jesus in John, as the primary relationship to him is that of "disciple." This address by Mary, with her attempt to touch him physically, suggests that she is still short of full Easter faith which, somehow, she seems to possess by the time she reaches the disciples to whom she announces, not that she has seen the Teacher or even Jesus, but that she has seen the Lord.

56. Zumstein, "Lecture narratologique," 7.

57. I was impressed by the paper delivered by Rekha Chennattu, "'If You Keep My Commandments': Exploring Covenant Motifs in John 13–17," at the August 2003 convention of the The Catholic Biblical Association of America, in which she used the account of the covenant renewal in Joshua 24 to highlight the covenant themes she proposes that John used to structure his presentation of discipleship as a covenant relationship. If John presents discipleship as a covenantal relationship there is all the more reason to think that his undestanding of the post-Paschal community's relationship with God in Jesus is the realization of the New Covenant.

58. Ἐνεφύσησεν (ἐμφυσάω) in v. 22 is a NT *hapax legomenon*. There are only three uses of the term in the OT, all directly connected with creation: Gen 2:7, the enlivening of the "earth creature" with God's breath; Wis 15:11, which refers to that event; Ezek 37:9, in which the prophet is told to breathe upon the bones of the house of Israel that it might be recreated. The use of the word in the LXX of 1 Kgs 17:21 is either a mistranslation or a reinterpretation of the verb יִתְמֹדֵד (stretched or measured) in the Hebrew text.

59. See n. 39 on the possible meaning "arise" for "came and stood."

60. Charles H. Cosgrove, "The Place Where Jesus Is: Allusions to Baptism and the Eucharist in the Fourth Gospel," *NTS* 35 (1989) 522–39, presents a fascinating argument for the community as the "flesh" of Jesus and the "hard saying" in John 6 as directed at the crypto-Christians in the Johannine community who want a faith that does not express itself in public community participation. Because "the life of the Spirit is present nowhere else but in the concrete fleshly existence of the community" (p. 535) it is only by participating in the Eucharist (and thus identifying oneself publicly with Jesus) that one can have life. I think this is a very thoughtful suggestion. The community in its historical existence would be the flesh of the glorified Jesus who is, in himself, glorified body.

61. James Swetnam, "Bestowal of the Spirit in the Fourth Gospel," represents well the position, with which I am here disagreeing, that the Spirit was given in 20:22 to "a restricted group of disciples, possibly only to the 'Twelve'" as "an agent of empowerment to help [the restricted group] to act with regard to the forgiveness of sins" (p. 572). I agree with Raymond Brown, *The Gospel According to John,* 1044: ". . . we doubt that there is sufficient evidence to confine the power of forgiving and withholding of sin, granted in John xx 23, to a specific exercise of power in the Christian community, whether that be admission to Baptism or forgiveness in Penance. These are but partial manifestations of a much larger power . . . given to Jesus in his mission by the Father and given in turn by Jesus through the Spirit to those whom he commissions. . . . John does not tell us how or by whom this power was exerecised . . . [but] that it was exercised."

62. The gospel, especially ch. 4 which includes the story of the conversion of the Samaritans at Sychar and of the (probably Gentile) royal official and "his whole household," suggests that at least after the resurrection the community included not only Jews but Samaritans and Gentiles.

63. John's use of body is quite different from Paul's, which is an image for the unity and mutuality of the "members" within the church of which Christ is the head. In John the church is a mode of Jesus' presence, his bodyself, present and active in the world.

64. The pertinent decrees were made in the 14th session of the Council of Trent (1551). See Heinrich Denzinger and Adolf Schönmetzer, *Enchiridion Symbolorum: Definitionum et Declarationum de Rebus Fidei et Morum* (34th ed. Freiburg: Herder, 1965) 1703, defining John 20:23 as the institution of the sacrament of Penance, and 1710, concerning the requirement of an ordained minister for the sacrament.

65. Raymond Brown takes a judicious position on the Tridentine declarations that John 20:23 is the establishment of the Roman Catholic penitential discipline as a sacrament that can only be administered by the ordained. He distinguishes between what the text (or the text's author) intends, which could hardly be what Trent defined, and the legitimate and diverse disciplines developed by various Christian communities. See *The Gospel According to John*, 1044–45.

66. Raymond Brown, "The Resurrection in John 20," accurately translates this text: "If you forgive people's sins, their sins are forgiven; if you hold them they are held fast." He takes it for granted that "them" refers to sins, which is not really what the text suggests since there is a real textual parallel between ἄν τινων in 23a, which he reads as "people," and ἄν τινων in 23b, which he reads as "sins" (implied). He says, however, that whatever positions Patristic or Tridentine writers took, "there is no requirement to think that the evangelist had them in mind" (p 204, n. 16). I suspect that this is one of the cases in which Brown tries to walk a tightrope between the results of his scholarship and official church teaching based on pre-*Divino Afflante Spiritu* approaches to Scripture.

67. T. Worden, "The Remission of Sins," *Scripture* 9 (1957) 65–79, 115–27, is a study of virtually all Patristic references to the possibility of forgiveness of sins committed after baptism. In the first three centuries, when this was a hotly debated issue, there is no reference to John 20:23 as warrant for such a practice, even by those Fathers who held adamently to this possibility. This argues strongly that John 20:23 was not understood by those closest to its composition as having anything to do with the sacrament of Penance, which in all likelihood did not exist in any form in the Johannine communities.

68. It is interesting to note that there is only one passage in the OT where ἀφίημι and κράτεω occur together in reference to an object. It is Cant 3:4, a passage whose influence on John 20 has already been noted. The words constitute a negative and a positive expression of the union between the spouse and the Beloved (Israel and YHWH). "I held (ἐκράτησα) him and would not let him go (ἀφῆκα)."

69. When, two decades ago, I suggested this symbolic significance to the identification of Thomas the Twin in *The Johannine Resurrection Narrative*, 579–85, it seemed "too symbolic" for some readers. Recently, however, perhaps as literary approaches have made scholars more amenable to symbolic material in the gospel, John N. Suggit, in "Jesus the Gardener" (n. 54 above), proposed that Thomas is the twin "to remind disciples that Thomas is *their* (emphasis in original) twin. Thomas, the twin, the representative of every disciple, was prepared to accompany Jesus to share in his death"—referring to 11:16 (p. 162). Interestingly, Suggit feels he still has to justify (p. 167) this type of interpretation!

70. Brown, "The Resurrection in John 20," 205, says that Jesus turns the tables on Thomas. Thomas demanded to probe Jesus physically and Jesus now probes him spiritually by inviting him to do what he demanded.

71. There is no basis in the text for reading a hierarchy of "blessedness" in Jesus' macarism. Thomas is blessed for his believing based on seeing; later disciples are blessed for their their believing although they have not seen.

72. Ward, "Bodies" (n. 25 above) 176, says: "The body of Jesus Christ [after the resurrection and ascension], the body of God, is permeable, transcorporeal, transpositional." I find this an intriguing way of expressing the mode of being of the glorified Jesus.

The Resurrection (of the Body) in the Fourth Gospel as a Key to Johannine Spirituality

A Response to Sandra M. Schneiders, I.H.M.

Donald Senior, C.P.

Chicago Theological Union

More than a focus on Johannine literature makes the scholarship of Sandra Schneiders reminiscent of the extraordinary biblical scholar whose memory we honor in this conference. Like Raymond Brown, Sandra Schneiders writes with great clarity and with wonderful control of the literature. Also like him, she is not afraid to tackle challenging issues of interpretation that often have profound consequences for Christian life. All of those virtues are on display in Sandra's paper on bodily resurrection in the Gospel of John.

First and foremost I want to congratulate Sandra for taking on this topic in such a direct and imaginative and forceful way. As she notes at the outset of her study, for most post-Enlightenment scholarship the notion of bodily resurrection is—citing a phrase of Newman—"imaginatively implausible and thus intellectually unassimilable." Thus there is relatively little said about it even in major works on the resurrection. For example, I checked N. T. Wright's recent massive eight-hundred-page study,[1] thinking that I might find there a dialogue partner with Sandra's work. While, as one might expect, his book is a superb review of the New Testament evidence, Wright does not really delve into what bodily resurrection might mean other than affirming his conviction that Jesus did rise body and spirit and that the tomb was empty. I remember some years ago reading a small book by Gerald O'Collins in which he, too, decried the lack of imagination and perhaps courage on the part of Christian theologians when it came to bodily resurrection—often settling either for uncritical affirmation of the doctrine in terms that approached resuscitation or else simply dismissing it and reaching for some kind of psychological or cultural explanation such as altered states of consciousness or a memorial type of explanation for what is meant by resurrection. Science, he noted, was delving with imagination and passion into the mystery of matter as if into a new universe while theology was content with uncomplicated and unimaginative categories to probe one of the central affirmations of Christian faith.[2] Some time later I happened to sit next to a nuclear physicist at a conference for the U. S. bishops and asked him about O'Collins' assertion. He said that science was finding that the structure of matter was so much more complex than at first realized that what the scientific world most needed were people with imagination who could leap ahead of the mass of data and frame a new way of understanding it.

I do not want to repeat what Sandra has clearly presented in her paper. But I do want to test a bit my understanding of her central thesis and then offer a few comments. At the heart of Sandra's study is her tracing of Johannine anthropology, where key terms describe not individual components of the human being but in holistic fashion delineate the overall human being seen from some particular vantage point or perspective. Two of the most important terms for understanding Sandra's thesis are the words "flesh" and "body." Thus "flesh" *(sarx),* for example, is "not a part of the human but the human being as natural and mortal." Likewise "body" *(sōma)* is not to be equated with "flesh" in the common notion of that word as a physical substance but, rather, body is the whole person "in symbolic self-presentation." "The body is quintessentially the person as self-symbolizing, i.e., as numerically distinct, self-consistent, and continuous, a subject who can interact with other subjects, who is present and active in the world" (p. 172). The human person may be living or dead, and as long as their body—or their corpse—is reasonably intact, the "body" continues to symbolize the whole person—the person either as living or, in the case of an intact corpse, as in transition from being to nonbeing or from presence to absence.

Sandra applies this to the body of Jesus. During his earthly life his "body" and his "flesh" were coterminous, but after his death they are no longer so. In his pre-Easter experience as "flesh" the body of Jesus, i. e., his personal symbolic presence, was conditioned by his mortality—as all flesh is. Now after his resurrection the "body" of Jesus is no longer coterminous with his flesh. Now the "body" of the Risen Christ is no longer subject to the limitations of mortality. Not only does the glorified Jesus go to his Father, he can also, in the full integrity of his human bodyself, return to his own and be present to them without the limits of mortality.

This anthropological analysis, as I understand it, is at the heart of Sandra's thesis, is derived from the analysis of the Johannine texts, and determines the focus of her theological reflection. This analysis also explains the significance of the empty tomb narrative and the resurrection appearance stories in the Fourth Gospel. Although what Sandra calls John's "glorification eschatology" puts the spotlight on the death of Jesus as the moment of the triumph of the crucified Christ over the power of death and his exaltation back to the Father, the resurrection stories are not anticlimactic but deal with the crucial and still unfinished business of the nature of the risen Christ's relationship to the community. The bodily resurrection of Jesus—understood in the terms Sandra has defined it—determines the presence of the risen Christ to his followers, now no longer confined to the limits of space and time.

This interpretive framework gives cogency to the meaning of the encounters with the risen Christ narrated in the Fourth Gospel, including Mary Magdalene's poignant meeting with Jesus in the garden. For Mary—who is still thinking of Jesus in terms of the "flesh" rather than his risen "body"—Christ has not yet ascended to his Father (even though the reader knows this has taken place at the moment of his death). She is directed to the community, where the risen Christ will be present in a new way.

Likewise the encounter with doubting Thomas and Jesus' gift of the Spirit to the community of the disciples in the final scenes of chapter 20 cohere with this interpretation of flesh and body. These scenes answer the key question of where Jesus is and how post-Easter disciples are to encounter the risen Lord. He is no longer to be found in the "flesh" of his earthly existence, but in the community of the disciples where his body is uniquely present. Thus the resurrection appearance stories, understood in the mode of Johannine anthropology and exaltation eschatology, are the foundation for John's bold ecclesiology. Through the potency of his risen body Jesus takes on a new mode of existence and salvific presence within the Christian community. Here, as Sandra concludes, believers can encounter him in sacramental signs and hear him in the community's witness, including the words of the gospel themselves.

Some Reflections

I found Sandra's analysis of what the bodily resurrection means within the perspective of Johannine theology very compelling and fruitful. Allow me to add just a few reflections of my own that might invite further exploration into this profound and complex subject.

1. First of all, while Sandra's definitions of the key terms "flesh" and "body" seem to accurately reflect Johannine usage, I wonder if the Fourth Evangelist is absolutely consistent in this. My conundrum is chapter 6, particularly the use of the term "flesh" that is repeatedly employed there. Sandra does not dwell on this text but does refer to it in a tantalizing footnote referring to the article of Charles Cosgrove on allusions to baptism and Eucharist in John.[3] When John refers to "flesh" in 6:51—"the bread that I will give is my flesh for the life of the world"—is this referring solely to Jesus' death and therefore to his bodyself as mortal (and therefore consistent with Sandra's view)? Or does the use of "flesh" here also have a future use—as in the exchange that follows in 6:52-59, which seems to refer also to those who will encounter the post-Easter Jesus in faith and probably in sacrament, a use more consistent with the term "body" as Sandra has defined it? Such possible

inconsistency would not be a mortal blow to Sandra's overall interpretation but might have to be wrestled with.

2. Second, I wonder if there are some other consequences of Sandra's interpretation that need to be reckoned with—some unintended "collateral damage," as it were! While the *distinction* between "flesh" and "body" makes sense to me, I am less clear about whether Sandra's interpretation allows any intrinsic *relationship* between the two. In other words, is there any real continuity between "flesh" and "body"? Does "flesh"—which after all, as the Prologue of John's Gospel also affirms, is created by God through or in the pattern of the Logos and in which the Logos is incarnate and through which one can see the glory of God—have any inherent value beyond its mortality? Rudolf Bultmann wrestled with this eloquently in his famed commentary on John 1:14. Does the mortal flesh of Jesus disappear without a trace in the finality of death once the risen body of Christ comes on the scene? Or is there a transformation of the matter that is flesh into the body that is risen? Or is there any level of genuine continuity between the two that offers the possibility of a theology of creation in John? In other words, in John's theology does the Incarnation create or reveal a new reality for the "flesh" that now transcends its sole designation as destined for mortality?

Otherwise, does not this interpretation of the "flesh" as solely mortal, when all is said and done, bear the potential of also being thoroughly world-denying even as it affirms the doctrine of bodily resurrection? The body, as defined here, might be confused with a ghost or be hauntingly similar to the *kah* of Muslim tradition, a body that looks like the flesh and blood we knew but really in the final equation isn't at all. Perhaps more needs to be said about a non-biblical term that Sandra slips in toward the end of her paper but, perhaps for that reason, does not define as thoroughly as other key terms. I am referring to the term "material." She notes that the glorified body of Jesus is "human and material but not physical" (p. 188). Later she seems to equate "material" with "sensible," or able to be perceived by the human eye. She notes, for example, that Mary Magdalene fails to understand that while Jesus' appearance is "sensible, that is, material, it is not physical" (ibid.).

Could "materiality" be the link between the mortal "flesh" and the immortal "body"? Does "material" simply mean "perceptible" by human senses—a kind of sacred hologram? Or is the risen body of Christ a result of the ultimately radical transformation of human flesh? Should we, too, like the scientist I mentioned earlier, be careful not to underestimate the complexity of matter in its most radical structure and its capacity for God-induced transformation?

3. This previous point also leads into my third. Sandra's enticing reflection on bodily resurrection focuses mainly on the resurrection of Jesus and its implications not only for the risen Christ himself but especially for Christ's presence to the community. Through that presence, as she notes, the Christian community becomes the presence of the risen Christ to the world. This is a

beautiful and fruitful ecclesiology. But I am also wondering about the implications for the destiny of the individual Christian who dies in the flesh. Should Christians expect the same destiny as that of Jesus? Will they, too, have a new mode of existence and a new unlimited bodyself? And is that hoped-for destiny also a source of commitment and guidance for Christian spirituality while in this mortal created world? Here especially, when dealing with the destiny of the individual human, we engage the unimaginable and therefore implausible nature of the Christian doctrine of bodily resurrection. Perhaps it might be more digestible for the post-Enlightenment mind to accept a unique affirmation concerning the destiny of the risen Christ but much less so for the destiny of the mass of human beings who believe in Christ and yet experience death.

Sandra's thoughtful and imaginative analysis of Johannine anthropology points the way toward an engagement with the meaning of the human flesh and the human body that may indeed entice the minds and hearts of the post-Enlightenment child of God. For all of us, the question put to Paul by the Corinthians still hangs in the air: "How will the dead be raised—and with what kind of a body will they come?" (1 Cor 15:35).

Notes

1. *The Resurrection of the Son of God* (Minneapolis: Fortress, 2003).
2. See Gerald O'Collins, s.j., *What Are They Saying About the Resurrection?* (New York: Paulist, 1978) 68–86.
3. See her n. 60: Charles H. Cosgrove, "The Place Where Jesus Is: Allusions to Baptism and the Eucharist in the Fourth Gospel," *NTS* 35 (1989) 522–39.

Part IV
Interpreting the Work of Raymond Brown

Chapter Eight

Raymond Brown and Paul Ricoeur on the Surplus of Meaning

Robert F. Leavitt, s.s.

St. Mary's Seminary and University

Introduction

The hermeneutical question I intend to discuss in this paper concerns "surplus meaning" in the Bible.[1] This question deals with how biblical texts were originally written to say something intended by their authors and yet were later seen to carry more significance or implication than either their authors or original audiences would or could have foreseen. The literal sense of a passage is what the words meant at the time the text was written and what its author presumably intended to say (to the degree this can be accurately ascertained). The "surplus meaning" of a text is what others (contemporaries or not) have taken the words to imply even if that implication could not have been in the author's mind.

The pitfalls along the path of surplus meaning, however, are many. Fanciful, arbitrary, forced, or fabricated readings of texts violate the literal sense of a passage and the built-in constraints of the text. They may serve purposes tangential or even opposed to the text's meaning and reference. In such cases the text is little more than a pretext.

At the same time, it is also true that the Christian faith only developed by successive reinterpretations of the Bible and later commentary by subsequent readers. Changed historical circumstances cast new light on old texts and posed fresh questions to Scriptures never written to address or answer them. We have no choice but to set out on this path of reinterpretation, but the theory that describes it and the constraints that control it are critical.

Raymond Brown began his scholarly career with a dissertation on this very issue of "surplus meaning," then called the *sensus plenior* or "fuller meaning."[2] But throughout his career he devoted his formidable exegetical skills almost entirely to identifying and specifying the literal sense of major texts he

207

studied—the Gospel of John, the Infancy Narratives, and the Passion Narratives. For him surplus meaning belonged to biblical trajectories, to doctrine, and to homiletic application. He aimed to pin down the literal sense to provide the "exegetical coordinates" for any extension or amplification of meaning. Well-intentioned pieties of the theological right, left, and center aside, the text first of all says what it says. If we break the ties to the literal sense, in Brown's view, we are adrift in a sea of exegetical intuition without a compass. His great contribution was to identify the narrow path of the literal sense through which richer or fuller reinterpretations had to pass.

To his credit, Brown recognized the hermeneutical deficiencies of the *sensus plenior* theory and called for a language-centered hermeneutics to replace it.[3] He was never able to incorporate this into his own work, but his students have into theirs, and many of them have turned to the philosophical and biblical hermeneutics of Paul Ricoeur to justify newer approaches to the issue of "surplus meaning." In this paper I will summarize Brown's treatment of this topic and then indicate how Ricoeur provides the language-centered hermeneutics that respects the literal sense while demonstrating how language and texts, by a kind of semantic dynamism, nourish the process of reinterpretation beyond the horizon of any author.

Authors, in many cases, are also teachers. I studied New Testament with Raymond Brown at St. Mary's in the 1960s and belong to that generation for whom the literal sense itself was a discovery of fuller meaning in its own way. From him I learned a great respect for the skills and obedience required to track down all the textual and historical clues in order to identify the Bible's literal sense.

I also had the good fortune to study with Paul Ricoeur in the 1970s as he was just beginning to elaborate the linguistic foundations of his hermeneutics after writing a decade earlier about symbolism. Studies in metaphor, texts, narrative, literary and historical criticism gave Ricoeur's hermeneutics a natural affinity for the issue of surplus meaning and biblical interpretation.

At one time in the 1980s I entertained the idea of bringing both of these scholars together at St. Mary's Seminary for a discussion of the hermeneutics of literal and surplus meaning, but it never came to pass. This paper will have to substitute for what would have been a memorable exchange and serve as a small homage to two master teachers in the exegesis of the literal sense and the hermeneutics of surplus meaning.

Accordingly, the purpose of this paper is to analyze the concept of surplus meaning in the works of Raymond Brown and Paul Ricoeur and to show how Ricoeur's thought provides the language-centered hermeneutics Brown considered a prerequisite for explaining the relationship between the author, the literal sense, and the fuller or wider senses of the Bible.

I will first summarize Raymond Brown's understanding of the relationship between the literal sense and the *sensus plenior* and how his viewpoint shifted in his later works and was complemented by his studies of biblical trajectories and doctrinal development. Then I will present an overview of Paul Ricoeur's hermeneutical theory as it applies to the issue of surplus meaning.

Raymond Brown

1. The Literal Sense and Sensus Plenior

Raymond Brown began his biblical career with a dissertation on the *sensus plenior* before going on to devote his entire exegetical efforts to practicing and refining the methods aimed almost exclusively at establishing the literal sense. He considered the literal sense the permanent semantic platform for the responsible discovery and articulation of biblical or doctrinal surplus meaning. Like Moses in Deuteronomy 34, toward the very end of his long career Raymond Brown caught a glimpse of what he was striving for—a language-centered hermeneutics of surplus meaning in the Bible—but he died too soon to incorporate or apply it in his own exegesis.

The hermeneutical theory of the *sensus plenior* of Scripture was first developed by Andres Fernandez in 1927 as a way to explain how doctrines, including recently defined Marian doctrine, might find textual anchors in Scripture.[4] A number of Catholic biblical scholars attacked it for undermining the authority of the historical-literal sense and paving the way for exegetical fabrications. In the mid 1950s Brown wrote: ". . . around the theory of the *sensus plenior* has raged one of the sharpest and most complicated disputes of present-day Scripture and theology."[5]

Storms pass, and by 1970 interest in the *sensus plenior* had virtually disappeared. An article by James Robinson in 1965 convinced Brown that some of the aims of the *sensus plenior* theory might be realized in the "New Hermeneutic" then in vogue in Germany.[6] Subsequently Brown insisted that the development of a language-centered hermeneutics alone could recover the insight the *sensus plenior* had attempted, but failed to explain.[7] Constructed on the basis of the scholastic idea of causality and authorial intention, the theory was ill-suited to the requirements of textual and literary composition needed for a complete hermeneutics.

Originally Raymond Brown defined the *sensus plenior* as "that additional, deeper meaning, intended by God but not clearly intended by the human author, which is seen to exist in the words of a biblical text (or group of texts, or even a whole book) when they are studied in the light of further revelation or development in the understanding of revelation."[8] He returned to this concept in his major articles on hermeneutics and in occasional essays from 1963 through his final work in 1996.[9] And he insisted that the theory pointed to an essential issue in biblical interpretation, namely, how texts meant one thing when they were written and came to mean something more later. Brown's main concern was spelling out the right criteria for determining an authentic development of meaning from misreadings and misinterpretations. His main criterion for development from the literal sense to a *sensus plenior* was homogeneity. He wrote that the *sensus plenior* is "not simply a new sense, but the homogeneous *approfondissement* of the literal sense."[10]

The theological root of this problem of the fuller sense of passages, in Brown's opinion, lay in part with the aporias associated with certain theories of divine inspiration.[11] The hermeneutical root of the problem rested on how to recast the issue of authorial intention and textual autonomy. To this end, in the *New Jerome Biblical Commentary,* Brown included a section in his article on hermeneutics written by Sandra Schneiders about recent literary theories of interpretation better suited to the issues of authorship, texts, and reader response.[12]

2. Raymond Brown's Later Hermeneutics of Wider Meaning

In Raymond Brown's last major work, *An Introduction to the New Testament* (1996), he offered his final sketch of biblical hermeneutics. At this stage of his thought he defines hermeneutics as the study of interpretation or the quest for meaning on three different levels: (1) the very use of language to convey meaning, (2) translation from one language to another, and (3) commentary on or explanation of what someone has said or written.[13] Language itself, translation, and commentary, then, represent the three expressions of hermeneutics. He further holds for a diversity of exegetical methods, saying that "different approaches to the text must be combined so that no 'criticism' becomes the exclusive manner of interpretation," and that "interpreters who employ the various forms of criticism in a complementary way will arrive at a much fuller meaning of the biblical text."[14] Finally, in this final study of hermeneutics Brown invokes Ricoeur's notion of the "world behind the text," the "world of the text," and the "world before the text" to describe the "total range of biblical meaning." All subsequent readings and commentary are grouped under the hermeneutical rubric of the "world before the text."[15]

Buried within the issue of fuller meaning, of course, are the questions about inspiration and revelation that concern the divine authorship of Scripture. An act of God lies at the root of the biblical word. But Brown also insisted that another act of God was implied in its authentic interpretation. God's role as author of Scripture does not remove the limitations of the human authors who could not foresee later questions or issues in the church.[16] On the side of subsequent commentary on Scripture, it is the Spirit that guides ongoing authoritative interpretation of Scripture in the church.[17] The divine authorship of Scripture on the one hand is complemented on the other hand by the divine assistance in interpretation linked to the doctrine of the Holy Spirit.

Brown's hermeneutics rests on the priority of the literal sense. He calls it "what the biblical authors intended and conveyed to their audiences by what they wrote."[18] Authorial intention, of course, is not something an interpreter knows directly. It is, rather, inferred from an exegesis of the words and their historically conditioned senses at the time they were used. The literal sense for Brown, for the Pontifical Biblical Commission, and for many others must remain the semantic foundation and exegetical starting point for any further extensions of biblical meaning.[19] Yet that sense may be seen to have a dynamism that in certain instances carries a potential for surplus meaning. A dynamic notion of the literal sense recently invoked by the Pontifical Biblical Commission has clear advantages in clarifying the multiple senses of Scripture.[20] It avoids the idea that other fuller or deeper meanings can simply be layered over, invented, or arbitrarily asserted as textual meanings without being related to the literal sense of the text.

For Brown the hermeneutical role of the literal sense regarding wider biblical meaning is to provide a "conscience and a control" on the quest for a larger sense.[21] Doctrines develop by "symbiosis" from the literal sense.[22] Searching for terms to express the complex relationship between the literal sense and wider senses, Brown speaks of a "tension" and "selectivity" between what the Bible meant and what it means to the church doctrinally.[23] In his view clear criteria are needed for all more-than-literal readings to protect them from becoming merely arbitrary. Such criteria should include (a) wide agreement on the proposed interpretation, (b) some basis in already existing scriptural patterns, and, in the case of the *sensus plenior,* (c) being homogeneous with the literal sense. The judgment about semantic homogeneity, of course, is not a simple one.[24]

Brown identifies three reasons for the claim that the Bible has a "wider meaning" beyond its literal meaning.[25] The first is theological, namely, the belief in God as the divine author of the Bible. The *sensus plenior* or "fuller sense" flows from this conviction since it is understood as "the deeper meaning intended by God (but not clearly intended by the human author) seen to exist in the words of Scripture when they are studied in the light of further revelation or of development in the understanding of revelation."[26] The crucial metaphor of God as the "author" of the Bible, of course, requires some interpretation itself. Its hermeneutical import is in asserting the authority of the Bible and its mysterious potential for revealing God and deciphering God's saving activity.

In addition to divine authorship, Brown identifies two other hermeneutical sources for wider biblical meaning that overlap the *sensus plenior.* The first is the placement of a biblical text within the canon of Scripture. The decision to include these and only these books in the Bible has created a significant and unavoidable hermeneutical situation by that very act. The Bible is essentially a collection of writings characterized by profound affinities, filiations of meaning, historical and religious discontinuities all at once. The canon has changed the hermeneutical location and potential of all the books. On the other hand, attempting to deconstruct the biblical canon into the smallest units of meaning and then to separate them from each other is both abstract and hermeneutically naïve, however much it may yield valid and useful information.

The second source for the discovery of wider biblical meaning Brown calls "subsequent reading," which essentially embraces everything from technical exegetical commentary to more popular or homiletic application. Without putting all these rereadings at the same level, Brown simply seeks to indicate how texts detach themselves from their authors and create their own readers. He says, "once written, a text is no longer under the author's control and can never be interpreted twice from the same situation."[27] At this stage of his thinking Brown has appropriated the hermeneutics of the text we shall explore in the second part of this paper, yet his exegetical concerns remain over "the criteria for determining an authentic development from a distortion."[28]

3. Biblical Trajectories and Surplus Meaning

Two other aspects of the issue of literal sense and surplus meaning should be mentioned briefly. The first is Brown's interest in biblical "trajectories."[29] These are texts in which images, figures, or ideas seem to blaze a trail of meaning beyond each individual passage. A direction of thought is indicated but also somehow left in suspense within the New Testament, like semantic ellipsis points inviting further development. Brown's approach to trajectories interpretation is to look for indications in the New Testament of disputed theological questions—for example, regarding the Petrine office, Mary, sacraments, or the church—and exegetically to show the semantic map in the New Testament that suggests subsequent commentary aimed at different doctrinal conclusions. His participation in the ecumenical studies on Peter and Mary and his own research into early apostolic communities in the New Testament demonstrated the value of the trajectory concept as a way of showing how texts aim beyond themselves and imply, without necessarily requiring, different future developments.[30] Trajectories interpretation, in this sense, is another example of surplus biblical meaning passing toward theology and doctrine.

4. The Literal Sense and the Question of Doctrine

The second related issue of surplus meaning is the relationship between the literal sense and the development of doctrine.[31] Brown asserted the right of the church to move beyond the Bible in formulating doctrine, but argued as Vatican II does that the magisterium itself is "answerable in some way to the Scriptures."[32] Moreover, in an ecumenical situation Brown believed strongly that the literal sense should function as a common point of departure in theological reasoning and controversy.

In reviewing certain doctrines he had studied, Brown identified cases in which biblical texts were later subsumed as the bases for fuller readings of dogma, classifying some as doctrines with an incipient but abundant basis in Scripture, others as doctrines with a slender biblical basis, and finally still others as doctrines about which the Scriptures are virtually silent.[33] This typology of weighted biblical anchors on later doctrines is no basis for a hierarchy of truths, since something as central as the bodily resurrection falls into the category of doctrines with a slender biblical basis.

Brown's hermeneutics of the Bible has been described as "Chalcedonian"[34] because of his insistence on divine authorship but also on the real humanity and human limitations of the writers of Scripture, just as the Council of Chalcedon speaks of the real divinity and real humanity of Christ. This approach accents the limitations of biblical authors who cannot foresee later doctrinal questions. Contemporary hermeneutics would draw a further implication. The limitation of the author's full awareness of the semantic consequences of his text is inevitable, but the very fact of inscription makes possible new readings the author could not have foreseen.

Thus we can summarize that on the question of surplus biblical meaning Raymond Brown consistently supported the intention and insight (even as he gradually abandoned the mechanics) of the *sensus plenior.* He recognized that biblical studies needed a language-centered hermeneutic to replace it, and he demonstrated how surplus meaning is generated from the literal sense in biblical trajectories and later doctrinal teaching. For Brown the priority of the literal sense is a necessary control against the tides of traditional accommodation or complete textual autonomy. He insisted on "criteria" for a more-than-literal reading in order to avoid arbitrary interpretation. For him such criteria included wide agreement on the proposed interpretation, some basis in already existing scriptural patterns, and, in the case of the *sensus plenior,* homogeneity with the literal sense.

Toward the end of his career Raymond Brown attempted to find a place within his hermeneutics for the kind of interpretation theory developed by Paul Ricoeur. Other scholars, including Sandra Schneiders on the revelatory text, and Craig Koester and Dorothy Lee on the range of symbolism in the Gospel of John, have applied Ricoeurean concepts of text and symbol hermeneutics to the Gospel of John that Brown himself acknowledged as a valuable contribution to Johannine studies.[35] Finally, we should mention Francis Moloney's recent editing of Raymond Brown's revised *Introduction to the Gospel of John* (2003), which incorporates in his own "Editor's Conclusion" some hermeneutical points consistent with Brown's more recent development and directly related to Ricoeur's overall approach.[36]

This brings me to the second part of this paper, an exposition of Paul Ricoeur's philosophical and biblical hermeneutics as an example of the language-centered hermeneutic Brown was looking for to replace the *sensus plenior* and advance the case for surplus biblical meaning.

Paul Ricoeur

I will now attempt to survey some key hermeneutical concepts in Paul Ricoeur's thought and their applications for biblical interpretation in general and the question of surplus meaning in particular. I will begin with his view of the importance of the literal sense in symbolism and text-interpretation.

Ricoeur and Brown represent a kind of inverse parallelism in hermeneutics. Brown is best known for his emphasis on the historical-critical or literal sense of Scripture, while Ricoeur's writings have largely dealt with the hermeneutics of multiple meaning. I propose initially to link them together at the point of the literal sense itself and on the unlikely example of symbolism.

Paul Ricoeur initially defined hermeneutics in relation to symbolic meaning,[37] but he insisted that the symbol "gives" its symbolic meaning only in and through its literal meaning. The symbol is a metaphor bound to the body, time, and the cosmos. It is neither a pretext for arbitrary readings nor an allegory veiling a hidden sense.[38] The literal sense of the symbol is the semantic impulse for its fuller significance. Without the literal sense, fuller symbolic meaning floats in air. This Ricoeurean point relates directly to Brown's demand that the literal sense be the starting point in hermeneutics and that the *sensus plenior* be "homogeneous" with it.

Ricoeur has also recently remarked on the importance of the historical-critical meaning of the biblical text. He says: "the meaning of a text is in each instance born at the intersection between, on the one hand, those constraints that the text bears within itself and that have to do in large part with its *Sitz im Leben* and, on the other hand, the different expectations of a series of communities of reading and interpretation that the presumed authors of the text under consideration could not have anticipated."[39] In other words, the literal sense furnishes the "constraints" that demarcate the range of interpretative possibilities for a text. Texts should not be pretexts.

Let me recall as well Raymond Brown's constant stress on the literal sense and the kinds of "textual constraints" it provides for a hermeneutics of surplus meaning. These go beyond the individual passage. They include homogeneity with the literal sense, midrashic and biblical interpretative patterns, chains of texts, and major biblical teachings. These textual and canonical constraints could be supplemented by further re-readings in the tradition that develop the literal and fuller meanings.

I will also offer a comment on the dynamic dimension of the literal sense as such. The literal sense of a biblical text is not a permanently fixed point of meaning. New discoveries constantly enrich its denotative and connotative dimensions. Much more than a mere index of authorial intention, the literal sense enjoys its own particular surplus value. As historical criticism has often revealed, the "world behind the text" is a fuller, more multi-layered, and more complex world than the sense of the words alone would ever suggest.

I would say that the "world behind the text" actually reveals and holds in suspense historical meanings and references that are indefinitely capable of reinterpretation and fuller actualization. History is not some finished past. It is constructed of "traces," e.g., old and recently discovered documents and artifacts, that may reconfigure the earlier picture we had of the past. These traces and the larger patterns they suggest provide analogies for the world we inhabit.[40] Historical criticism and the literal sense already offer an analogy of "fuller meaning" by filling out the wealth of detail of a forgotten and quite foreign biblical world. That historical-critical "sympathetic re-enactment in imagination"[41] of a past world, therefore, is fuller with meaning and implication than we imagine. The "world behind the text" need not be regarded as a finished, one-dimensional, or religiously uninspiring world. Certainly in the treatment Raymond Brown gave it, it never was.

Before proceeding to explain Ricoeur's language-centered hermeneutics I will briefly comment on his philosophical method, which makes his approach particularly useful for biblical hermeneutics. Unlike many philosophers, Ricoeur has developed his own system largely in dialogue with and interpretative retrieval of other philosophical and non-philosophical texts. One of his early books (1950) was a translation and exegetical commentary on a major work by Edmund Husserl (*Ideen* I) about phenomenology.[42] Later monographs and essays incorporate the results of biblical exegesis, linguistics, psychoanalysis, hermeneutical theory, Frankfurt social criticism, literary criticism, narrative, and the theory of history into Ricoeur's phenomenological method.[43] He taught the history of philosophy in Strasbourg in the 1950s, so interpretative commentary on great philosophic works and the appropriation of concepts from different systems is integral to his method. He was a practiced interpreter of philosophic texts first before learning to appropriate the results of biblical criticism.

Paul Ricoeur's announced project of a philosophy of the will took its first major hermeneutical detour in 1960 with his exegetical and phenomenological investigation of the biblical symbolism of evil.[44] At this stage of his thought he defined hermeneutics as the interpretation of symbols. While this work included theoretical elements, *The Symbolism of Evil* (1960) was far from an abstract study of method. To the contrary, the major advantage of this book was Ricoeur's masterful application of the exegesis of biblical texts and narratives, which he joined to a linguistic phenomenology of symbols. He did this by what he calls a "re-enactment in sympathetic imagination"[45] of the intentional aims of symbolism. Those aims point toward surplus meaning and the implied philosophical correlates of the symbolism under investigation.

Ricoeur justified this sudden detour into hermeneutics as part of a larger project in the study of philosophical method. The point was clarified in Ricoeur's programmatic essay, "The Hermeneutics of Symbols and Philosophical Reflection" (1961), which responded to a question posed to him by the editorial board of the *International Philosophical Quarterly,* where it was first published in English.[46] In that essay Ricoeur indicated how he would graft philosophical thinking onto the hermeneutics of symbols without sacrificing the conceptual rigor or methodological autonomy of philosophic reflection. This, in effect, paved the way for showing how symbolic language lends itself to later philosophical retrieval and articulation, and it established a paradigm for the progression from symbol to concept that marks all interpretation.

A striking example of the maturity and fruitfulness of this approach appeared in Ricoeur's essay "Original Sin: A Study of Meaning" (1960).[47] There he lengthened his study of the symbolism of evil to include a critical exegesis of Rom 5:12-21, an analysis of Augustine's early Manichean phase and later anti-Pelagian writings, a summary of Kant on radical evil and Hegel on speculative negation. In the process Ricoeur offered a detailed example of how the symbolism of evil established a trajectory of meaning tending in the direction of the polemical but conceptually "inconsistent" notion of original sin.[48]

The essay on original sin shows the importance of the hermeneutical shifts that occur in the translation of meaning from symbolic language to theological expression to doctrinal formulation to philosophical speculation—a cascading tradition of different interpretations fed by a primary symbolic and narrative source. The essay indicated how Ricoeur would concretely apply his hermeneutical theory to a particularly difficult question in biblical studies, patristic theology, church doctrine, and the philosophy of evil.

Almost forty years later (1998), in collaboration with the Old Testament scholar Andre LaCocque, Paul Ricoeur published *Thinking Biblically: Exegetical and Hermeneutical Studies.*[49] In it he again attempted to demonstrate how a philosophical hermeneutics might build upon historical-critical and literary exegesis of major Old Testament texts. In his most recent essays he accomplishes this by elaborating a chain of re-readings from the biblical text through other scriptural texts and commentary toward appropriate and relevant philosophical reflection. This chain expresses the complex logic of subsequent readings and the process of the discovery of surplus meaning in the Bible as a canonical and post-canonical progression from the literal sense. In the intervening years between 1960 and his more recent exegetical studies Paul Ricoeur has arguably developed the most comprehensive philosophical and biblical hermeneutics of our time. It is impossible here to track the complex and interwoven series of studies that comprise his overall work.[50] My following remarks will concentrate on only three points: (1) Ricoeur's theory of language as use, (2) his views on polysemy, metaphor, and symbolism, and (3) his notions of the text and literary work.

Paul Ricoeur's Hermeneutics

1. Toward a Language-Centered Hermeneutics

Raymond Brown's study of the *sensus plenior* theory and the New Hermeneutics led him to the conclusion that only a language-centered hermeneutics was capable of addressing the issues raised by the multiple senses of Scripture and the fuller sense above all.[51] Ricoeur's thought, in my opinion, provides such a foundation for biblical hermeneutics. I wish to show this by first explaining his theory of "language as use."[52] Ricoeur is unusual among continental philosophers in that he draws upon British ordinary language philosophy as a factor in his interpretation theory, while also incorporating more basic notions derived from structural linguistics.

At the level of discourse or speech, language can be understood semantically and pragmatically by the uses to which we put it. There may be a single dictionary but there are at least three different ways language is employed. These are communication, argumentation, and invention.

First, the ordinary use of language aims at communication. It refers to the world of common sense and the surrounding environment shared by two interlocutors. All its traits facilitate communication and negotiation within an everyday, shared world.

The scientific use of language, on the other hand, aims primarily at argumentation. Its words need precise meanings and those meanings need to be maintained throughout the argument. Precision is gained by the use of technical vocabulary, conceptual control is achieved by abstraction, and the advance of knowledge is attained by argument. Finally, the poetic use of language aims at linguistic inventions and creativity in such things as wordplays, poetry, and narrative fiction. Here the goal is not so much communication and argument, though these may be included, but the application and deployment of the metaphoric resources of language as such. This is most evident, of course, in poetry, fiction, and religious language with their evident preference for metaphor, symbol, and narrative plot. The critical question in the creative use of language, and even more so in its religious use, remains that of "reference" and "truth," which I will address in two stages.

On the issue of reference, ordinary discourse is the easiest to understand. It refers to the world around us and is confirmed by its ability to effectively point things out and get things done. Ricoeur calls this "ostensive reference."[53] Scientific discourse uses abstractions to understand and control different domains of knowledge. It is validated through axiomatic formulae, empirical verification, or technical application.

But how do we explain the issue of reference for poetic, fictional, or religious uses of language? What do the metaphors in poems, stories, or religious language tell us? How are they understood, justified, or even verified? Do we naïvely understand them as versions of ordinary or scientific language describing reality as those other languages do? Or do religious metaphors and symbols refer back to the feelings of those who invented them? Are they merely the linguistic traces of emotion?

These are crucial questions for religious language, for biblical texts, and *a fortiori* for any theology and doctrine built upon them. Ricoeur attempts to sketch out an answer, not entirely satisfactory perhaps, to these questions by initially developing a theory of truth-as-manifestation. He invokes the category of non-ostensive reference to explain the referential and cognitive claims of poetic and religious discourse. Poetic types of language, he says, invite us to rethink the world and our existence within it, starting from the metaphoric re-description of the world they provide in symbol and narrative. The re-described world of metaphor is the referential equivalent of the "world in front of the text."[54]

2. Polysemy, Metaphor, and Symbol

The second level of Ricoeur's language-centered hermeneutics is built on his studies of linguistic polysemy, the semantics of metaphor, and symbolism.[55] These three words embrace the potentials for multiple significations contained in human language, and they are built one upon the other. Polysemy is that trait of words, or lexical units as they are called in linguistics, by which they may carry multiple potential meanings at once. Without polysemy, human language would require an infinite number of words to carry each discrete meaning. Instead, polysemy allows words to have multiple meanings that the context filters for the appropriate one at any given time.

Ricoeur calls metaphor "a work in miniature"[56] because its interpretation presents many of the problems associated with larger texts. Metaphor is the smallest unit of speech to pose most sharply the question of odd meaning and non-ostensive reference. In Ricoeur's approach, metaphor is at once the explanation for lexical polysemy and linguistic creation. New meanings in language (including new meanings for words) are created by the use of metaphors in which the literal meaning no longer makes sense. The interpreter of the metaphor has to figure out a sense compatible with common sense and with the claims of the metaphoric expression. In time, original metaphors die as semantic novelties but are quietly reborn as part of the literal sense. The dictionary, Ricoeur says, is a graveyard of dead metaphors.[57]

Metaphors, we know, strain interpretation far more than ordinary discourse does. We may use them for a variety of reasons: ornamental, rhetorical, emotional, or semantic. The first three are important, but the last one interests Ricoeur above all. Certain metaphors are created precisely to say what language cannot yet say, maybe cannot say ever, and certainly cannot say easily by other means.

Metaphors create their meaning through an act of interpretation that makes sense of them. This is, of course, especially the case with all religious language, which is fundamentally metaphoric and symbolic.

Ultimately, as with all poetic language, the most crucial and difficult issue about metaphor is reference. Some say it refers simply to a more imaginative, emotionally appealing, and visually compelling version of what we already know or believe from common sense. This is the case with many metaphors, but not with the most creative or most enduring ones. Startling, powerful, and classical metaphors ask us to reconsider the data of common sense, loosen the grip of the ordinary upon us, and reveal dimensions of experience and reality denied us otherwise. The "tension" in the metaphorical utterance opens up another interpretation that resolves the absurdity of taking the utterance literally.[58] Ricoeur says that such metaphors have "non-ostensive reference." They do not act as linguistic coordinates of or descriptors for an ordinary world around us. They reveal another way of seeing and acting in the world. Poetry, fiction, songs, movies, and religious texts, among others, employ this metaphoric world of reference. They open up other ways of being and seeing denied us by common sense, scientific abstractions, or technological control.

Finally, symbolism is constructed upon the linguistic foundation of polysemy and the semantic foundation of metaphor. A symbol is a specific type of metaphor that has an extraordinary power of permanence and endurance by virtue of its rootedness in the cosmos, nature, or the social world.[59] Symbols draw their force and permanence from a pre-linguistic level of experience. They say more because more always remains unsaid in them. Symbols, for Ricoeur, are opaque and irreducible.[60] That irreducible element derives from the fact that they are forged out of the material of the universe and establish correspondences of meaning between one level of experience and another.[61] The vault (nave) of a chapel mimics the hull of a ship (Latin *navis*) as well as the human ribcage. The church building symbolically and simultaneously is both an ark and a body. For that reason symbols are the preferred language of religion. Surplus meaning, at the level of words at least, is made possible by the very structure of linguistic polysemy, by the peculiar predication of metaphor, and by the inexhaustible rootedness of symbols.

3. The Hermeneutics of the Text and the Literary Work

Ricoeur's language-centered hermeneutics has incorporated a very comprehensive analysis of the nature of written language or texts, their configuration as literary works, and the changes that take place in meaning and reference as a result of inscription and literary configuration.[62] This is central to biblical hermeneutics, which deals with Scripture and with the seventy-two canonical books, all configured by authors into literary works.

The textual elements implied in a general hermeneutics, according to Ricoeur, include the following and their implications for interpretation: the inscription of meaning in a text, the notion of a literary work, the world of the text, distanciation, and the appropriation of meaning. For him these five elements also apply to biblical hermeneutics, but the Bible, due to its unique character as a religious text, inverts this general hermeneutics into its own instrument.[63]

a. The Importance of Inscription in Language

The most significant contribution Ricoeur has made to hermeneutics is his comprehensive theory of the written text and the complex effects that inscription creates for the interpretation of meaning.[64] That theory explains why hermeneutics is necessary and correspondingly complex. With inscription the direct mediation of meaning in oral speech is replaced by the indirect mediation of the written text. This requires special technical strategies for deciphering it. In the case of the text, the interlocutors disappear and the problems of textual interpretation replace face-to-face exchange and understanding. If this is a loss in immediacy, it is an enormously important gain in complexity and consequence. The text creates its readers, is the reference point for subsequent translation and interpretation, and inspires the commentary and application that change thinking, lives, and institutions. Authorial intention is an inference from the literal sense of the text, but now the text survives its author, his or her situation, and begins a career all its own.

The most fundamental word in our faith after the personal name of Jesus Christ, after all, is the word "Scripture," which means writing. These are the inscribed meanings that testify to Christ, that first interpret him in narrative and symbol, and that have formed the textual basis for later theological and doctrinal interpretations in the tradition of the Christian faith.

Its inscription as a text significantly alters every feature of oral communication. That is why hermeneutics cannot model itself on interpersonal communication, but has to adopt a more indirect strategy of determining meaning and appropriating it.

b. Literary Work and Narrative

The second factor in Ricoeur's general hermeneutics is the significance of literary forms or genres, what Ricoeur calls "literary works."[65] Language is never simply spoken or written in general; it is always produced as a specific type of language game or written work. Written language, above all, is structured as some literary form or literary genre—a letter, a resumé, an invitation, a polite refusal.

The Bible is a small library of books, all of which are structured and restructured as works by authors and editors. The literary form of a biblical text, however, is not just a way to classify a text. Ricoeur emphasizes literary form as a mode of producing meaning and shaping distinctive types of meaning. This is the foundation for his conviction that different literary forms in the Bible produce meaning in distinctive ways and to different effect. The Bible's five major biblical literary forms—narrative, prophecy, law, proverb, and psalm—may all deal with the same subjects or use similar language, but these diverse forms will affect the meaning and bring out different dimensions of the same event or experience.[66]

Ricoeur calls this effect on meaning by different literary forms the "polyphonic" dimension of biblical meaning. His approach is very different from earlier methods in biblical theology that sifted expressions in the Bible for biblical themes. Instead, Ricoeur respects the distinctiveness and semantic potentials of ideas expressed in different literary genres and the way these impact, qualify, and complement the same images or motifs in other forms.

Of all the biblical forms, narrative is the most dominant and important. It largely structures the Pentateuch and the gospels. The Bible tries to tell a story by linking and interweaving mythical, ancestral, historical, and kerygmatic narratives together. The gospels above all are structured as narratives, but they are not biographies or strictly historical chronicles or accounts of the life of Jesus.

In Ricoeur's hermeneutics the narrative form is intimately connected with the reconfiguration of human temporality and identity. Human time is structured in and by the story. Narratives constitute the identity of the community that tells and retells the story. The plot refigures the existence of the reader and interpreter whose imagination is inspired by it.[67]

c. The World of the Text

In linguistic theory all language has both sense and reference. Sense is its immanent meaning, while reference is what this meaning intends to speak about. The question of reference is obviously crucial for religious language, and here we rejoin our earlier comments on the poetic and religious uses of language. Ricoeur says: "the unique referential dimension of the work of fiction or poetry raises, in my view, the most fundamental hermeneutical problem. If we can no longer define hermeneutics in terms of the search for the psychological intentions of another person which are concealed behind the text, and if we do not want to reduce interpretation to the dismantling of structures, then what remains to be interpreted? I shall say: to interpret is to explicate the type of being-in-the-world unfolded in front of the text."[68]

The concept of the "world of the text" is one of Ricoeur's major contributions to hermeneutics. As language has reference, literary texts create a world. That world emerges from the configuration of the text as such. Ricoeur says: ". . . [as] the world of the text is real only insofar as it is imaginary, so too it must be said that the subjectivity of the reader comes to itself only insofar as it is placed in suspense, unrealized, potentialized. . . . As a reader I find myself only by losing myself. Reading introduces me into the imaginative variations of the ego."[69]

The world of the text is Ricoeur's category for the text's referential aim when that aim goes beyond ostensive reference and speaks about absent or fictive or religious dimensions of life. All texts create a "world" filled in by commentary and appropriation in front of or flowing from them; biblical texts invest these worlds with ultimate hope and authority. Great individual and social consequence rests on them. They elicit faith and call for changes in life. Unlike the purely private aesthetic enjoyments of an epic poem or a novel, religious metaphors, symbols, and texts and the truth claims they make have significant personal and historical consequences.

e. Productive Distanciation

In linguistic communication, of course, we want to understand the other person. This goal of oral communication has often been superimposed on the hermeneutics of texts, but Ricoeur believes it is profoundly mistaken and leads to problems and dead ends in interpretation. Communing with the author of a text, re-experiencing the meaning the author had in mind is a kind of psychologism that misses the referential and textual potentials of writing. Written texts and the time and space separating them from readers/interpreters create what Ricoeur calls "distanciation" in hermeneutics. With this term Ricoeur seeks to argue against an intersubjective image of hermeneutics in which the interpreter or reader is attempting to get inside the mind of the biblical author.

In Ricoeur's view the written text sets the stage for a "productive notion of distanciation" that permits a new kind of communication, "communication in and through distance."[70] Unless a biblical hermeneutics has a theory that makes the text and the lapse of time from its moment of composition to the present moment a productive but inevitably complex enterprise, it will always be tempted back toward a fundamentalist identification with the author's experience, feelings, and mentality.

f. The Appropriation of Meaning

If textual "distanciation" in all its forms creates the necessity for exegetical methods, indirect strategies, and the gradual hermeneutical recovery of meaning and reference, the ultimate object of hermeneutics is the way a text finally influences a human being seeking to understand it. Hermeneutics understood this way is the appropriation of new meaning and an understanding of oneself in light of the referential potential of a text or the reconfigured world projected in front of the text. Appropriation of an ancient or strange text's meaning replaces the answer in the oral dialogical situation.

I have reviewed the major elements in Ricoeur's language-centered hermeneutics beginning with language as use, polysemy, metaphor, and symbol, and finally the very nature and consequence of inscription of language as a written text. These concepts define the situation, the challenges, and the aims of interpretation. They also redefine the way we should regard the issue of the literal sense and wider surplus meaning in biblical hermeneutics. The issue of authorial intention is significantly changed by writing and reading and by the literary configuration of a text with its metaphors and symbols.

The Hermeneutical Constitution of Christianity

In the following section of the paper I will treat Ricoeur's views of biblical hermeneutics with particular attention to what he calls the "hermeneutical constitution" of the Christian faith in Scripture. This paves the way for his understanding of the internal biblical movement from the literal sense to multiple meaning and implication.

In an early essay on Rudolf Bultmann, Ricoeur tried to identify what he called the "hermeneutical constitution" of the Christian faith.[71] This constitution occurs on three levels.

(1) The first level is the fact that Christianity came into being as a rereading of the Hebrew Scriptures, which rereading is actually called in Christian theology the "Old Testament." The first Christian hermeneutics, Ricoeur says, is "a mutation of meaning inside the ancient Scripture,"[72] a point underscored as well by the recent document of the Pontifical Biblical Commission on the Hebrew Scriptures.[73] Christianity is initially shaped theologically as a first-century rereading of the Hebrew Scriptures by converts who seek to interpret the story of Jesus by quoting passages that, in their reinterpretation, applied to him. They saw the Scriptures as containing meanings held in suspense until they were focused, revealed, and fulfilled by the figure of Jesus and his death and resurrection.

(2) The second dimension of Christianity's inherently hermeneutical situation anticipates the later multiple senses of Scripture. Paul is the first to interpret human experience in light of the paschal event of Christ's death and resurrection. Before becoming a theological axiom, this paschal interpretation of life was itself a hermeneutical invention of Paul and early Christian preaching. In the Pauline rereading the paschal event becomes the hermeneutical clue for deciphering human existence as such. Christ's unique personal fate is transformed into an existential theme.[74] The Passion Narratives and Resurrection Narratives are hermeneutically "passing over," we might say, into existential surplus meaning.

The Christian believer is now invited to see himself or herself in light of Jesus' death and resurrection. This existential interpretation of the cross and resurrection is the Pauline source of the fourfold sense of Scripture. According to Ricoeur the multiple senses of Scripture mean that Christian symbolism "is coextensive with the entire economy of Christian existence. Scripture appears here as an inexhaustible treasury which stimulates thought about everything, which conceals a total interpretation of the world."[75] "Hermeneutics," he remarks further, "is the very deciphering of life in the mirror of the text," saying "*liber et speculum* is basic to hermeneutics."[76]

(3) The third, and only recently appreciated, dimension of Christianity's hermeneutical situation is far more radical. It holds for a distance, however minimal, between the historical person of Jesus and his interpretation and

reinterpretation in the New Testament. One Christ is expressed in four canonical gospels—three parallel Synoptic narratives and one distinctively Johannine account. Ricoeur summarizes the important hermeneutical point here: "the fact is that the literal meaning is itself a text to be understood, a letter to be interpreted."[77] The Word of God in Christ, a Johannine theme *par excellence,* transcends the Scriptural word testifying to Christ with conflicting and tensional metaphors and narratives. The Scriptural text, in short, is not revelation as such, but a foundational witness to it that scripturally opens up the Christian mystery. That revealed mystery transcends the text as both its divine origin and horizon. This original distance from the event of Christ to the writing called the New Testament has only become striking and problematic by virtue of the historical and cultural distance between the world of the New Testament and the modern world. It has created the problematic question about the authority of the literal sense itself.

By virtue of its scriptural inscription the Christian faith is one that began with the rereading of an earlier Scripture and that itself passes over into subsequent rereadings—homiletic, theological, doctrinal—in the community of faith. That process occurs already within the New Testament itself. This hermeneutical constitution of Christianity requires us to rethink what we mean by inspiration, revelation, and theology. Because biblical revelation is given in a canon of books whose composition, authors, topics, and points of view are so various it provides what Ricoeur calls a polyphonic and polysemous notion of revelation. It is polyphonic due to its rich mixture of literary forms, and polysemous in terms of its complex metaphors and symbolic meanings. More is given in the biblical corpus than any theology can conceptually summarize or reduce to abstractions. Nevertheless, the work of theological articulation is necessary in order to elaborate the mediating notions that serve to conceptually maintain the Bible's polysemous complexity and tension at a higher level of discourse. Theologies should be judged by how adequately they rearticulate the full range of polysemy and polyphony of the Bible.[78]

Ricoeur often speaks with a kind of caution and qualification about theology. He likes to point out that theological language is a "mixed discourse"—part biblical metaphor, part doctrinal language, and part philosophical theory fused together. For him the distinction between the primary symbols and genres of faith and the concepts and arguments of theology is critical for all interpretation.

I began with Paul Ricoeur's language-centered hermeneutics as one model of the more-than-literal interpretation Raymond Brown considered a prerequisite for any theory of surplus meaning in the Bible. In our summary we reviewed his hermeneutics of metaphoric, symbolic, textual, and narrative expressions. The potential for surplus meaning is woven into the Bible with metaphor and symbol and into the canon through the polyphony of biblical genres. And we saw that Christianity is hermeneutical to its very core by virtue of its constitution as the reinterpretation of the potentiality of surplus meaning in the Hebrew Scriptures. Finally, the Ricoeurean concept of the autonomy of written texts and the world in front of the text laid the foundations for subsequent interpretation that goes beyond the world of the biblical author.

The written work, in short, and Scripture above all, provides a semantic gravitational field around the entire work of interpretation it has set in motion. A poet is perhaps better able to capture in a single metaphor the tension between the constraints imposed by the literal sense and the potential for surplus meaning made possible by inscription, symbol, and narrative. Josephine Jacobsen, former poet laureate of the United States, captured this admirably in a short piece aptly named "The Poem Itself" in the collection *The Shade-Seller.*[79] Of the poem as a work she says:

> The man responsible
> died, eventually.
> When the dust of his brain left the bones
> the bond snapped. It escaped to itself.
> It no longer answered.
> On the shelf, by the clock's tick, in the black
> stacks of midnight: it is. A moon
> to all its tides.

Conclusion

In conclusion let me offer a suggested linkage between the hermeneutical idea of surplus meaning and the doctrine of grace as a "surplus gift." Paul Ricoeur has occasionally suggested in his writings elements of what might be called a Pauline, Synoptic, and Johannine hermeneutics of grace. He draws its Pauline strain from Romans 5:12-21 and the repeated key Greek expression in that passage *pollọ mãllon,* "how much more"—"how much more has grace superabounded over sin." The excess of grace over sin in the rhetorical repetition of Romans 5 is the first form of this theological hermeneutics.[80]

The Synoptic equivalent of this Pauline "superabundance" appears in the "surplus" logic of the parables of the Kingdom. Ricoeur points out how parabolic hyperbole and extravagance implies, in another genre and form of discourse, the surplus logic of grace beyond the normal human logic of equivalence and justice.[81]

Finally, in John 1:16 we read "and of his fullness we have all received, grace upon grace." That fullness is expressed in various ways throughout Johannine symbolism, narratives, and discourses. In a special way it is expressed in the symbolism of the vine and the branches in John 15:1-17. For Ricoeur this image adds a mystical dimension of grace (as "grafting") to the juridical symbols of justification or acquittal.[82] All together these rhetorical, parabolic, and poetic expressions of grace point toward something more, something other, and something deeper than we otherwise know in the encounter with God. And, we might add, the "new life" of the resurrection parallels these rhetorical expressions of grace. For it is a mysterious "beyond" to our historical lives, something fulfilled and completed in God's eternal kingdom. The resurrection expresses the hope that our earthly existence would be fulfilled both in other lives and in "another life" we can only believe we shall be given.[83]

The hermeneutical idea of surplus meaning, then, correlates with a fundamental thematic of the Christian message in terms of grace, eternal life, and the resurrection itself. If Ricoeur notes these biblical symbols and others like them in his writings, he is careful and patient in spelling out the various philosophical and ethical approximations to them. The hermeneutics of surplus meaning in Scripture has to articulate an intermediate trajectory of analogies, homogeneous images, and historical approximations linking the literal sense to its wider potential meaning.

Ricoeur often invokes the saying from the gospels, "For those who would save their life will lose it, and whoever loses life for my sake will find it" (Matt 16:25) This paschal irony, in the form of a proverb, seems to summarize his whole philosophical itinerary as well as his hermeneutics. That itinerary is characterized by letting go of a self-sufficient self to discover a new self formed by the Bible and the traditions flowing from it. Ricoeur favors a long and complex pedagogy of interpretation and attempted actualizations over the immediacy of direct religious experience and absolute knowledge. For him one discovers one's identity not in immediate self-consciousness, but by encountering and passing through the worlds of others. This long pedagogy of faith would imply the exegetical necessity of the first "otherness" of the "world behind the text," the literal sense Raymond Brown labored so carefully to uncover. It would also include the trajectories within the Bible and canonical reinterpretation as the fuller "world of the text." Finally, it embraces all intervening commentary between those worlds and ours—subsequent readings within the community of faith.

Ultimately the fuller meaning in Scripture not only concerns an act of hermeneutic reinterpretation but, prior to that, an act of faith that allows the Bible, in all its narrative and symbolic meaning, to fulfill itself in our existence. For Raymond Brown and Paul Ricoeur the hermeneutical circle is rounded completely when the surplus meaning of a text finds its personal, social, and religious fulfillments in new justifiable readings and in the actual existence of believers.

Notes

1. The expression "surplus meaning" is borrowed from Paul Ricoeur, *Interpretation Theory: Discourse and the Surplus of Meaning* (Fort Worth: Texas Christian University Press, 1976). Ricoeur had treated the topic of the surplus or excess signification of signs in his earlier works *The Symbolism of Evil* (New York: Harper & Row, 1960) and *Freud and Philosophy: An Essay on Interpretation* (New Haven: Yale University Press, 1970). His major theoretical study of the lin-

guistics of surplus meaning is *The Rule of Metaphor: Multi-disciplinary studies of the creation of meaning in language* (Toronto: University of Toronto Press, 1977).

2. Raymond E. Brown, *The Sensus Plenior of Scripture* (Baltimore: St. Mary's Seminary and University, 1955). This was Brown's doctoral thesis at St. Mary's Seminary (directed by Edward Cerney, s.s.). Earlier Brown published "The History and Development of the Theory of a Sensus Plenior," *CBQ* 15 (1953) 141–62, and later he surveyed the literature on the topic in "The Sensus Plenior in the Last Ten Years," *CBQ* 25 (1963) 262–85. He finally summarized the mounting difficulties with this theory in "The Problems of the Sensus Plenior," *ETL* 43 (1967) 460–69.

3. In 1967 Brown wrote, " Perhaps we must shift our approach and deal with the possibility of a SP more from the analysis of language than from the analysis of the mind of the author. In modern literary approach much is made of the thesis that the words of an author can have a life of their own and take on a richer signification than their author intended." ("The Problems of the Sensus Plenior," *ETL* 43 [1967] 467).

4. Andrea Fernandez, "Hermeneutica," *Institutiones Biblicae* (2nd ed. Rome: Pontifical Biblical Institute, 1927) 306–307.

5. Brown, *The Sensus Plenior of Scripture,* xiii.

6. James M. Robinson, "Scripture and Theological Method," *CBQ* 27 (1965) 6–27.

7. Raymond E. Brown, "Hermeneutics," in Raymond E. Brown, Joseph A. Fitzmyer, and Roland E. Murphy, eds., *The Jerome Biblical Commentary* (Englewood Cliffs, NJ: Prentice-Hall, 1968) 614–18.

8. Brown, *The Sensus Plenior of Scripture,* 92.

9. In addition to works already cited see Raymond E. Brown, "Hermeneutics," in Raymond E. Brown, Joseph A. Fitzmyer, and Roland E. Murphy, eds., *The New Jerome Biblical Commentary* (New York: Doubleday, 1990) 1146–65, §§71-92; idem, *An Introduction to the New Testament* (New York: Doubleday, 1997) 20–47. In this latter work, on pp. 41–42, Brown connects more recent hermeneutical theories to the *sensus plenior* ("fuller sense") and includes them under the heading "wider meanings beyond the literal."

10. Brown, "The Problems of the Sensus Plenior," *ETL* 43 (1967) 460.

11. Ibid. 461.

12. Brown, "Hermeneutics," in *The New Jerome Biblical Commentary*, 1146–65, §§71-92; the section on literary criticism, §§55-61, was written by Sandra Schneiders.

13. Brown, *An Introduction to the New Testament,* 20, n. 1.

14. Ibid. 28.

15. Ibid.

16. Brown consistently argued that the fact of the divine authorship of Scripture did not remove the normal historical limitations imposed on the biblical writers by their social and linguistic conditions. See Raymond E. Brown, *Biblical Exegesis and Church Doctrine* (New York: Paulist, 1985), especially Chapter 1.

17. Ibid. Chapter 2. Also see Raymond E. Brown, *The Critical Meaning of the Bible* (New York: Paulist, 1981) Chapters 1 and 2.

18. *Introduction to the New Testament,* 35.

19. Pontifical Biblical Commission, *The Interpretation of the Bible in the Church* (Boston: St. Paul Books & Media, 1993) 78, provides a brief summary of Ricoeur's notion of "distanciation" as well as a discussion of the literal sense and *sensus plenior.* The commission refers to the "dynamic aspect of many texts" and points out that the exegetical task, in addition to establishing its historical-critical meaning, is "to determine the direction of thought expressed by the text" (p. 83).

20. Pontifical Biblical Commission, *The Jewish People and Their Sacred Scriptures in the Christian Bible* (Boston: Pauline Books & Media, 2002) 53–62 and 216–19.

21. Brown, *The Critical Meaning of the Bible,* 33.

22. Ibid. 41.

23. Ibid. 41–42.

24. Brown, *An Introduction to the New Testament,* 41.

25. Ibid. 41–46.

26. Ibid. 42.

27. Ibid. 45.

28. Ibid.

29. See Raymond E. Brown, Karl P. Donfried, and John Reumann, eds., *Peter in the New Testament: A Collaborative Assessment by Protestant and Roman Catholic Scholars* (New York: Paulist, 1973), and Raymond E. Brown, Karl P. Donfried, Joseph A. Fitzmyer, and John Reumann, eds., *Mary in the New Testament: A Collaborative Assessment by Protestant and Roman Catholic Scholars* (New York: Paulist, 1978).

30. Raymond E. Brown, *The Churches the Apostles Left Behind* (New York: Paulist, 1984).

31. Raymond E. Brown, *Biblical Exegesis and Church Doctrine* (New York: Paulist, 1985).

32. Ibid. 29.

33. Ibid. 31–45.

34. See K. Duffy, "The Ecclesial Hermeneutic of Raymond E. Brown," *HeyJ* 39 (1998) 50.

35. See Sandra Schneiders, *The Revelatory Text: Interpreting the New Testament as Sacred Scripture* (San Francisco: HarperSan Francisco, 1991); Craig Koester, *Symbolism in the Fourth Gospel: Meaning, Mystery, and Community* (2nd ed. Minneapolis: Fortress, 2003); Dorothy Lee, *Flesh and Glory: Symbolism, Gender, and Theology in the Gospel of John* (New York: Crossroad, 2002).

36. Raymond E. Brown, *Introduction to the Gospel of John,* edited and updated by Francis J. Moloney. ABRL (New York: Doubleday, 2003) 325.

37. Paul Ricoeur, *The Symbolism of Evil* (New York: Harper & Row, 1967) 14–16. He asserts that "symbols precede hermeneutics; allegories are already hermeneutic" (p. 16).

38. Ibid.

39. See André LaCocque and Paul Ricoeur, *Thinking Biblically: Exegetical and Hermeneutical Studies* (Chicago: University of Chicago Press, 1998) xi.

40. See Paul Ricoeur, *The Reality of the Historical Past* (Milwaukee: Marquette University Press, 1984) for his treatment of some basic issues in the epistemology of history. A comprehensive study by Ricoeur of the relationships among language, narrative, fiction, and history is found in Paul Ricoeur, *Time and Narrative.* Vols. 1–3 (Chicago: University of Chicago Press, 1984).

41. Ricoeur uses this expression often to identify part of the phenomenological method of analysis. See Ricoeur, *The Symbolism of Evil,* 3.

42. Paul Ricoeur, *Husserl. An Analysis of his Phenomenology* (Evanston, IL: Northwestern University Press, 1967).

43. For a comprehensive multilanguage bibliography of Ricoeur's publications 1935–1994 see Lewis Edwin Hahn, ed., *The Philosophy of Paul Ricoeur.* Library of Living Philosophers 22 (Chicago: Open Court, 1990), Part Three: "Bibliography of Paul Ricoeur: A Primary and Secondary Systematic Bibliography," compiled by Frans D. Vansina and Paul Ricoeur, 609–815.

44. Ricoeur's philosophy of the will was contained in, first, a phenomenological study of voluntary and involuntary action that appeared as *Freedom and Nature: The Voluntary and the Involuntary* (Evanston, IL: Northwestern University Press, 1966). The second part included two different studies, one devoted to fallibility and the other to guilt. They appeared as *Fallible Man* (Chicago: Henry Regnery, 1967) and *The Symbolism of Evil* (New York: Harper & Row, 1967).

45. Ricoeur, *The Symbolism of Evil,* 19.

46. Paul Ricoeur, "The Hermeneutics of Symbols and Philosophical Reflection," *International Philosophical Quarterly* 2 (1962) 191–218. The same essay also appears in Paul Ricoeur, *The Conflict of Interpretations: Essays in Hermeneutics* (Evanston, IL: Northwestern University Press, 1974) 287–314.

47. Paul Ricoeur, "'Original Sin': A Study of Meaning," in *The Conflict of Interpretations: Essays in Hermeneutics,* 269–86. The original article appeared in *EgT* 23 (1960) 11–30.

48. Ibid. 270–71.

49. See n. 39 above.

50. The major relevant hermeneutical studies by Paul Ricoeur, in chronological order, include: *The Conflict of Interpretations* (Evanston, IL: Northwestern University Press, 1974), a collection of twenty-two previously published articles from the 1960s and early 1970s; *Interpretation Theory: Discourse and the Surplus of Meaning* (Forth Worth: Texas Christian University Press, 1976) where Ricoeur spelled out the hermeneutics of the written text; *The Rule of Metaphor. Multi-Disciplinary Studies of the Creation of Meaning in Language* (Toronto: Toronto University Press, 1978) comprising eight studies dealing with the rhetorical, semiotic, semantic, and hermeneutical aspects of metaphor; *Essays in Biblical Interpretation*, ed. Lewis S. Mudge (Philadelphia: Fortress, 1980), which includes important essays on Bultmann, revelation, and testimony; *Hermeneutics and the Human Sciences. Essays on Language, Action, and Interpretation* (Cambridge: Cambridge University Press, 1980) containing eleven already-published essays indicating the application of Ricoeur's language-centered hermeneutics to the social sciences; *From Text to Action. Essays in Hermeneutics, II*, (Evanston, IL: Northwestern University Press, 1991), including several important previously unpublished texts in English including one on philosophical and biblical hermeneutics; *Figuring the Sacred: Religion, Narrative, and Imagination* (Minneapolis: Fortress, 1995), composed of twenty-one more recent essays dealing with religion, biblical time and narrative, narrative and selfhood, and ethics. The essay "The Summoned Subject in the School of the Narratives of the Prophetic Vocation," 262–75, and its complementary study, "The Self in the Mirror of the Scriptures," 201–20, in *The Whole and Divided Self*, ed. David E. Aune and John McCarthy (New York: Crossroad, 1997), were the last two of Ricoeur's Gifford Lectures at the University of Edinburgh (1986), but by virtue of their religious subject matter were intentionally excluded from the published form of these lectures entitled *Oneself as Another* (Chicago: University of Chicago Press, 1992); and *Thinking Biblically: Exegetical and Hermeneutical Studies*, by Andre LaCocque and Paul Ricoeur (Chicago: University of Chicago Press, 1998), in which Ricoeur co-authored the Preface (with LaCocque) and contributed six hermeneutical studies of major Old Testament texts complementing LaCocque's historical-critical interpretation.

51. Brown, "Hermeneutics," *NJBC*, 1157.

52. Paul Ricoeur, "Creativity in Language: Word, Polysemy, Metaphor," *Philosophy Today* 17 (1973) 97–111.

53. Ricoeur, *Interpretation Theory*, 34–37.

54. Ibid. 46–53. See also "The Hermeneutical Function of Distanciation," in *From Text to Action: Essays in Hermeneutics, II*, 84–88.

55. See Ricoeur, *Interpretation Theory*, Chapters 1 and 3.

56. Ricoeur, "Metaphor and the Central Problem of Hermeneutics, in *Hermeneutics and the Human Sciences*, 167.

57. Ricoeur, *Interpretation Theory*, 52.

58. Ibid. 50.

59. Ibid. 53–63, where Ricoeur speaks of the semantic and non-semantic moments of symbolism.

60. Ibid. 57 and 61.

61. Ibid. 62–63.

62. Ricoeur, *From Text to Action: Essays in Hermeneutics, II*, especially the essay "Philosophical Hermeneutics and Biblical Hermeneutics," 89–101.

63. Ibid. 89–90.

64. See Paul Ricoeur, "What is a Text?" in *From Text to Action: Essays in Hermeneutics, II*, 105–24. Ricoeur sought to demonstrate the theoretical value of the model of "text interpretation" for the social sciences in general, and especially for history, in "The Model of the Text: Meaningful Action Considered as a Text," ibid. 144–67. This essay arguing the case for the application of text-interpretation principles to the interpretation of social signs was originally published in *Social Research* 38 (1971) 529–62.

65. Paul Ricoeur, "Toward a Hermeneutic of the Idea of Revelation," *HTR* 70 (1977) 1–37; reprinted in *Essays in Biblical Interpretation* (1980). This essay represents Ricoeur's programmatic philosophical redefinition of the idea of revelation, starting from a theory of religious language and biblical literary form and intending to replace a speculative-psychological model of revelation resulting in what Ricoeur characterizes as a divine "insufflation" of meaning.

66. Ibid. 3–17.

67. Ricoeur, *Figuring the Sacred* (1995). See especially "Interpretive Narrative," 181–99. The philosophical underpinnings for Ricoeur's biblical applications of narrativity may be found in *Time and Narrative*, vols. 1–3, and in *Oneself as Another* (Chicago: University of Chicago Press, 1992), especially "Personal Identity and Narrative Identity," 113–39, and "The Self and Narrative Identity," 140–68.

68. Ricoeur, "The Hermeneutical Function of Distanciation, " in *Hermeneutics and the Human Sciences*, 141.

69. Ibid. 144.

70. Ibid. 131–32.

71. Ricoeur, "Preface to Bultmann," in *The Conflict of Interpretations: Essays in Hermeneutics*, 381–88.

72. Ibid. 383.

73. Pontifical Biblical Commission, *The Jewish People and their Sacred Scriptures in the Christian Bible*.

74. Ricoeur, "Preface to Bultmann," 384.

75. Ibid. 385.

76. Ibid. 386.

77. Ibid. 387.

78. See Ricoeur, "Toward a Hermeneutic of the Idea of Revelation" (n. 65 above).

79. Josephine Jacobsen, *The Shade-Seller: New and Selected Poems* (New York: Doubleday, 1974) 103.

80. Ricoeur, "The Hermeneutics of Symbols and Philosophical Reflection," in *The Conflict of Interpretations: Essays in Hermeneutics*, 311 and 314; also idem, *The Symbolism of Evil*, 271–72, where the author explores the Adamic symbolism in Genesis and Paul as the background for the Pauline "how much more" *(pollǭ mãllon)* from Romans 5 on grace.

81. Ricoeur, "The Logic of Jesus, the Logic of God," in *Figuring the Sacred: Religion, Narrative, and Imagination*, 279–83.

82. Ricoeur, *The Symbolism of Evil*, 275–78.

83. On the idea of the resurrection see Paul Ricoeur, "Sentinel of Imminence," in *Thinking Biblically: Exegetical and Hermeneutical Studies*, 180–83. For a more personal account of Ricoeur's views of resurrection and afterlife see Paul Ricoeur, *Critique and Conviction: Conversations with François Azouvi and Marc de Launay*, trans. Kathleen Blamey (New York: Columbia University Press, 1998) 155–59.

The Challenge of Brown's Hermeneutics:
Fidelity to Both Historicial Criticism and the Church's Tradition
A Response to Robert Leavitt

Francis Schüssler Fiorenza

Divinity School, Harvard University

Raymond Brown had been both my teacher and my spiritual advisor/confessor. For me this dual role sums up his life and his work: he was both an academic scholar and a Roman Catholic priest. He lived out this dual vocation by striving to unite two very distinct goals: he sought as biblical scholar to have his research live up to the most exacting demands of scholarship and he sought as a Sulpician priest to serve in fidelity to the Roman Catholic Church. The demands of scholarship required the practice of historical criticism that included philological analysis, literary analysis, source criticism, form criticism, and redaction criticism. Scholarship was for Raymond Brown a matter of an unrelentless search for and adherence to truth. I will never forget when I had gone to him for my weekly confession and I mentioned among my other sins that I had lied that week. Instead of dismissing me with a light penance he gave me a stern lecture. Knowing that I wanted to become a scholar and teacher, he exhorted me not to view lies as peccadilloes because becoming a scholar meant that nothing is more important than the truth. If I wanted to be a scholar I had to be totally dedicated not only to searching for the truth, but also to telling the truth. A scholar had to acknowledge and to speak the truth even when it was unsettling. Father Brown's exhortation expressed clearly the dedication of his life as a priest and a scholar.

Brown's vocation of fidelity to the Roman Catholic Church led him not only to be faithful to the doctrines of the church but also to be concerned about reconciling the results of historical criticism with the tenets of the Roman Catholic faith. The distinctive and specifically Roman Catholic view toward the Scriptures is that they should be interpreted according to the long-standing traditions of the church and in accordance with its rule of faith. The standard was the rule of faith of the most ancient apostolic dioceses, as Augustine underscored in *On*

Christian Doctrine.[1] The methods of historical criticism, however, appear to advocate criteria of truth independent of the Catholic principles of tradition and the rule of faith. It should not be forgotten that Brown's career began at a time when historical scholarship was still in dispute within the Catholic Church. Although Pius XII had written *Divino Afflante Spiritu,* the battles leading up to *Verbum Dei* had not yet been fought out and won. Many Roman Catholic exegetes were under attack in the immediate years before the Council, for example, Stanislas Lyonnet and André Feuillet (a fellow Sulpician).[2] Raymond Brown sought to show that ultimately any conflicts that exist between historical scholarship and Roman Catholic scholarship could be reconciled or overcome. In my view his attempt to reconcile these differences is what led him to work on the notion of *sensus plenior,* according to which a text may have one meaning within historical criticism but yet a fuller meaning in the life of the church, its Scriptures, traditions, and conciliar decisions.

Father Robert Leavitt makes several important points in his excellent paper, He brings together Raymond Brown's early interest in the *sensus plenior* and Paul Ricoeur's hermeneutical theory, which from his early analysis of symbol to his later analyses of metaphor and narrative underscores the surplus meaning of the text. Leavitt argues that Ricoeur's interpretation of the surplus meaning of the text articulates in a philosophical and foundational way some of the points that Brown sought to articulate throughout his career. In fact, his argument has a subtext that, if I perceive it correctly, suggests that if Raymond Brown had engaged more explicitly and thoroughly with Ricoeur's theory of interpretation he would have found an important philosophical resource for the way in which he sought to develop the further significance and meaning of biblical texts. In addition Leavitt provides helpful suggestions that show the value for theology of Ricoeur's theories for understanding Scripture and the notion of revelation. His concluding reflections show how Brown's recently published revised introduction to John's gospel indicates a further appreciation for the work of those interested in canonical criticism and appropriating contemporary hermeneutical theory.

I basically agree with Father Leavitt's paper. Raymond Brown's interpretation of *sensus plenior* concurs with Pierre Benoit against John O'Rourke in that the human author must not have some vague consciousness of the *sensus plenior.* Such a view does indeed cohere with an emphasis on the autonomy of the text. Moreover, insofar as Brown disagrees with Pierre Benoit's limitation of the *sensus plenior* to the relation between the Old Testament and the New Testament, and therefore positively evaluates the possibility that a fuller sense can be found in the Qumran texts (even though they are not inspired), it appears that the fuller sense served a much more generic interpretive function for Brown.[3] These points support Father Leavitt's proposal that Paul Ricoeur's general hermeneutical theory about the surplus meaning of the text can provide a helpful tool that could amplify Raymond Brown's work.

My response will complement Father Leavitt's argument by suggesting that an examination of Paul Ricoeur's modifications of Hans-Georg Gadamer's hermeneutical theory would lend further support to his views. This complementarity comes to the fore especially in the extent to which Ricoeur's theory of interpretation combines both explanation and understanding in contrast to Wilhelm Dilthey's legacy of the contrast between the natural sciences and the cultural sciences (the humanities). However, differences between Ricoeur and Brown emerge when one examines their *de facto* practice of interpretation. Finally, I suggest that a reception hermeneutics provides a hermeneutical theory that approximates elements of Raymond Brown's interpretation of texts.

Hermeneutic Theory as Critique of Historicism

Robert Leavitt's paper noted that Raymond Brown was aware of the significance and importance of Hans-George Gadamer's hermeneutical theory. He proposes that Paul Ricoeur's hermeneutics would have provided Brown with an ample resource for his exegesis and understanding of interpretation. Hermeneutical theory from Gadamer to Ricoeur can be seen as reacting against two interpretive tendencies, the Romantic hermeneutics of Friedrich Schleiermacher and the historicism of the German historical school (Dryson, York, and von Ranke).[4] For Gadamer the Romantic hermeneutic falsely identified meaning with authorial intention and inadequately presupposed that, despite all individuality, a common human nature makes interpretation possible. Against the Romantic hermeneutic both Gadamer and Ricoeur argue that a text has a plurality of meanings. Similarly, Gadamer sees the historical school also as a continuation of Enlightenment hermeneutics that sought to specify the exact meaning of a text so that it has only one meaning or one "sense" in contrast to the multiple senses of traditional Christian interpretation. To counteract these tendencies Gadamer relies on the example of a classic as a great work that is both in history and outside of history to ground both the authority of a text and its multiple meanings, in that a classic is meaningful to successive generations. Moreover, using the analogy of law, he argues that just as the meaning of a law is understood when it is applied to a new case here and now, so too a classic is understood when its claim upon us in the present is acknowledged.

Although James Robinson acknowledges Gadamer's significance, he asks whether the appeal to Gadamer and to *sensus plenior* results in downplaying historical criticism.[5] Jürgen Habermas had made a parallel criticism of Gadamer's hermeneutical theory with reference to the importance of the critique of ideology.[6] Paul Ricoeur intervenes in the debate between Gadamer and Habermas by outlining a mediating position that seeks to take into account both the hermeneutical retrieval of a tradition and the critical analysis of a tradition.[7] Such a mediating position provides a resource that Raymond Brown could have appropriated for his own position as he sought to mediate between the traditions of the church's interpretation of Scriptures and the methods of historical critical exegesis.

Ricoeur's Combination of Explanation and Understanding

Paul Ricoeur develops his mediating approach by emphasizing four elements.[8] First, the distanciation that is produced by fixation in writing is a condition of the autonomy of the text with relation to the intention of the author, the cultural situation of the text, and the original addressee. Consequently, the meaning of what the text signifies can be reduced to what the author intended or to psycho-sociological conditions of production. Second, interpretation has to overcome the contrast and distinction between explanation and understanding by incorporating both of them into interpretation. Third, the referential world of the text is changed in the course of time and thereby offers new possibilities. Finally, the appropriation of a text involves an enlargement of the self by the world of the text. These elements show the validity of Leavitt's argument that Ricoeur's theories of interpretation could have buttressed Raymond Brown's endeavors.

In combining both explanation and understanding Ricoeur argues that the interpretation of the text should not spring over explanatory methods, but in and through its use of explanatory methods display the meaning of a text and show how it opens new possibilities of meaning and a new way of envisioning the world and the self. If, as the common *bon mot* claims, Gadamer's book *Truth and Method*[9] should have been more properly entitled *Truth or Method*, then Ricoeur's approach could be described as seeking to include both truth and method—understanding that goes through explanation rather than without it. This aspect of Ricoeur's hermeneutics would lend support to Brown's attempt to combine respect for scientific historical-critical method with respect for the meaning of a text as it comes down through the historical tradition of Christian interpretation.

Differences in the Practice of Exegesis and Reception Hermeneutics

Nevertheless, there are differences between Raymond Brown and Paul Ricoeur in their *de facto* practice of interpretation. These need to be considered, for they relate to the explanatory method used in interpretation and to the relation between interpretation and normativity.

Explanatory Method in Exegesis: Although the explanatory methods include the full range of historical criticism (historical-critical methods, social analysis, psychological methods, etc.), whenever Paul Ricoeur engages in interpretation (and it is also a strong part of his understanding of the nature of the text), he engages structural and semiotic analysis. He is appropriating a form of scholarly analysis that had been very prevalent in French literary circles, especially in the heyday of French Structuralism. One sees this in several French scholars, for example in Albert Vanhoye's interpretation of Hebrews. However, when one examines Brown's interpretation of John's gospel one finds that he tends to emphasize source and traditions history to a much stronger degree. His exegesis of the gospel is very much influenced by his colleague at Union Theological Seminary, J. Louis Martyn, who reconstructs the various stages of the history of the gospel and the opponents of those various stages. Leavitt is quite correct in pointing out that, in his most recent *Introduction to the New Testament,* Brown points to the importance of the meaning of the final text.[10] However, it seems to me that despite that assertion Brown in fact places greater emphasis on the history of traditions, their diverse contexts, and the distinct layers of editorship. This concern is even evident in the *Introduction.* The type of semiotic and structural analysis that Ricoeur exercises on the objectified text is less present in Brown's exegesis.

My own view is that Hans Robert Jauss's development of Gadamer's hermeneutical theory into reception hermeneutic (referred to sometimes as the Konstanz School of hermeneutics) would be closer to Raymond E. Brown's interpretive strategies. Jauss's specific reception hermeneutics emphasizes much more strongly both the original audience (synchronic) and the diverse receptions of a text through history (diachronic).[11] Such a hermeneutic would allow Raymond Brown to take into account the surplus of meaning of the text, the critique of Romantic hermeneutics, and yet would also allow some reflection on the distance between the author's audience and the audience today. One would then in reference to the reception of Isaiah point to the audience of the text when it was first written and received, then to the reception in later Jewish communities, and then to its reception in the early and later Christian communities. Though he was open to historical criticism in terms of the history of religions, in practice Brown focused much more on the interpretation of the New Testament writings as receptions of the Hebrew Scripture (and concerned with the official church's reception of the meaning of New Testament texts) than he was concerned with the comparative religious approach that Ricoeur does in his writings on evil or that New Testament scholars such as Helmut Koester, Hans-Dieter Betz, or Hans-Joseph Klauck do. In proposing that reception hermeneutics might have provided a more appropriate resource for Brown's interpretive theory I am not so much disagreeing with Leavitt's point in regard to *sensus plenior* as I am suggesting that Brown's *de facto* practice of exegesis dealt much more with historical contextualization along the lines of a reception hermeneutical modification of Gadamer than along the lines of Ricoeur's practice of relying on structuralism.

Interpretation and Normative Significance: In his explicit considerations on the relation between the interpretation and the normative significance of texts Raymond Brown appropriated the distinction between what a text meant and what it means today. He borrows this distinction from Krister Stendahl.[12]

This distinction allows Brown to distinguish between the historical task of exegesis and the theological task of the meaning of the text for us today. It is this distinction that the hermeneutical theories of both Hans-Georg Gadamer and Paul Ricoeur seek to lessen, if not to overcome. For Gadamer understanding takes place precisely in the application of text to the present situation and entails a fusion of horizons. For Ricoeur the textuality that makes possible the objectification and distanciation of text allows the possibility of new reference and opens a new world that should be appropriated in the very act of understanding. Therefore Elisabeth Schüssler Fiorenza draws on hermeneutical theory in criticizing this distinction as part of her argument for an ethics of interpretation and public discourse in biblical studies.[13] These considerations suggest that if Brown had engaged more seriously with Ricoeur's hermeneutics he might have been able to articulate a more complex understanding of the relation between the interpretation and appropriation of a biblical text in a way that would take into account the ethics of interpretation. Nevertheless, it should be noted that Brown's popular summaries of his scholarly works show that he in fact tried in those books to demonstrate that the world of the text and what it meant has also enlarged our understanding of ourselves. In short, despite advocacy of the distinction in practice, he exercised a type of Ricoeurian hermeneutic that Father Leavitt advocated and that Father Witherup will so eloquently elaborate in his presentation.

Notes

1. Augustine's *On Christian Doctrine* spells out this rule very clearly in regard to the rule of faith and the most ancient apostolic churches.

2. See the brief essay by the French Sulpician Scripture scholar Henri Cazelles, "Anwendung und Erfahrungen mit der Historisch-Kritischen Methode in der Katholischen Exegese," in Helmut Redlinger, ed., *Die Historisch-Kritische Methode und die Heutige Suche Nach Einem Lebendigen Verständnis der Bibel* (Freiburg: Katholische Akademie/Schnell und Steiner, 1985).

3. Raymond E. Brown, "The *Sensus Plenior* in the Last Ten Years," *CBQ* 25 (1963) 262–85.

4. Hans Georg Gadamer, *Truth and Method* (2nd rev. ed. New York: Crossroad, 1989), 173–92.

5. James Robinson, "Scripture and Theological Method," *CBQ* 27 (1965) 6–27.

6. Jürgen Habermas, "A Review of Gadamer's Truth and Method," and "The Hermeneutical Claim to Universality," and Hans-Georg Gadamer, "Reply to my Critics," in Gayle L. Ormiston and Alan D. Schrift, eds., *The Hermeneutic Tradition. From Ast to Ricoeur* (New York: SUNY Press, 1990) 213–99. Paul Ricoeur, "Gadamer and the Critique of Ideology" in idem, *Hermeneutics and the Human Sciences,* ed. John B. Thompson (Cambridge: Cambridge University Press, 1980).

7. For the difference between Gadamer's hermeneutics as one of belonging and Ricoeur's as one of objectification see Francis Schüssler Fiorenza, "Hermeneutics and History," in James Livingston and Francis Schüssler Fiorenza, *Modern Christian Thought: The Twentieth Century.* Vol. 2 (Upper Saddle River, NJ: Prentice-Hall, 2000) 341–85.

8. See Paul Ricoeur, *From Text to Action: Essays in Hermeneutics, II* (Evanston, IL: Northwestern University Press, 1991).

9. Hans Georg Gadamer, *Truth and Method* (2nd rev. ed. New York: Crossroad, 1989).

10. Raymond E. Brown, *An Introduction to the Gospel of John,* edited and updated by Francis J. Moloney. ABRL (New York: Doubleday, 2003).

11. Hans Robert Jauss, *Toward an Aesthetic of Reception* (Minneapolis: University of Minnesota Press, 1982), and idem, *Wege Des Verstehens* (Munich: Fink, 1994), and with Rainer Warning, *Probleme Des Verstehens: Ausgewähtle Aufsätze* (Stuttgart: Reclam, 1999).

12. See Krister Stendahl, "Biblical Theology, Contemporary," in *The Interpreter's Dictionary of the Bible* (Nashville: Abingdon, 1962) 1:418–32, and his "Method in the Study of Biblical Theology," in J. P. Hyatt, ed., *The Bible in Modern Scholarship* (Nashville: Abingdon, 1965) 196–209.

13. Raymond E. Brown, *The Critical Meaning of the Bible* (New York: Paulist, 1981). For the criticism of this distinction see Elisabeth Schussler Fiorenza, *But She Said: Feminist Practices of Biblical Interpretation* (Boston: Beacon, 1992), and eadem, *Rhetoric and Ethic: The Politics of Biblical Studies* (Minneapolis: Fortress, 1999).

Chapter Nine

The Incarnate Word Revealed
The Pastoral Writings of Raymond E. Brown[1]

Ronald D. Witherup, s.s.

Sulpician Provincial Residence, Baltimore

"In the beginning was the Word . . . and the Word became flesh and made his dwelling among us" (John 1:1, 14). In his magisterial two-volume commentary on John's gospel, Raymond Brown makes the following observation on these lines: "The Prologue [of John's Gospel] does not say that the Word entered into flesh or abided in flesh but that the Word *became* flesh. Therefore, instead of supplying the liberation from the material world that the Greek mind yearned for, the Word of God was now inextricably bound to human history."[2]

I take this comment to be of utmost importance for evaluating Raymond Brown's contribution to biblical studies in his pastoral writings.[3] In effect it provides an underlying hermeneutical principle that appears throughout his writings. Brown took the Incarnation seriously. The world is infused with the Word of God. The original Word, Jesus Christ—the splendor of the Father—reveals the will of God through Sacred Scripture. When Brown interpreted biblical texts he believed he was promoting the encounter not only with the inspired words of these sacred texts but with Jesus Christ himself, *the* Word. This perspective offers a lens through which we can explore the legacy of Brown's pastoral writings. They are an invitation to encounter the incarnate Word revealed not in some remote, ethereal way but in the everyday world around us, where the Word has come to dwell in our midst.

This essay contains five sections. The first will briefly address the extent of the pastoral writings. The second will delineate their characteristics. The third will discuss their impact on the life of the church. The final two sections offer, respectively, a modest critique and a conclusion.

238

I. Extent of the Pastoral Writings

Delineating the extent of Brown's pastoral writings could be a matter of some debate. He had a fairly regular practice of working on smaller projects at the same time that he had a larger, scholarly project underway. Some of them, in fact, took shape during extended vacations in the Caribbean (of which he was very fond in Januarys) or even, in one case, while waiting for planes at airports! Once he adopted a laptop computer as the primary means for writing, there was no venue too remote or mundane for him to continue working on such pastoral projects. One could justifiably say that all of Brown's writings were pastoral. Even his larger, imposing works attained a popularity among the masses, appealing far beyond the scope of scholars. He had the rare gift of being a scholar's scholar who could nonetheless communicate rather complex, esoteric topics in ways easily digested by the majority of people who had no professional exegetical training. For purposes of this essay, however, I will restrict my discussion to book-length treatments of topics intended for the broadest possible audiences.[4]

II. Characteristics of the Pastoral Writings

Scholars would be mistaken to think that Brown's smaller works have little to say to them just because they were written for broader audiences. They are replete with choice observations about multiple topics, most of which remain of great interest to scholars today. When one takes the time to reread Brown's pastoral writings as a distinct body of writings, there are at least six characteristics that surface.

(1) The first striking observation is the sheer number of topics they address. Without intending to be exhaustive, we can list the following:

- the nature and importance of the historical-critical method of biblical interpretation;
- the nature of the Bible as the Word of God in human words;
- the role of theologians in the Roman Catholic Church and their relationship to the magisterium, especially in the wake of the Second Vatican Council (1962–65);
- the biblical foundations of many church doctrines, including christological and Marian dogmas (e.g., the extent of Jesus' knowledge, the historicity of the virginal conception and bodily resurrection of Jesus, and the role of Mary in the church);
- the application of the Bible for ordinary Christians, especially the Gospel and Epistles of John;
- the development of church doctrine;
- the nature of inspiration and the role of the Holy Spirit in the church and in the world;

- many ecclesiological themes, such as the biblical foundations of the church, the priesthood and the episcopacy;
- the preaching of the revised lectionary;
- the role of catechetics in the church;
- the results and importance of modern biblical archaeology, including the Dead Sea Scrolls;
- the ecumenical dimensions of biblical studies in a post-Vatican II world (with topics such as the Petrine ministry, the role of Mary, and justification by faith);
- controversial topics, such as the ordination of women, the role of the papacy, divisions within the Catholic Church (especially between "liberals" and "conservatives"), the pace of change in the church, and even the Shroud of Turin.

If one were to include the topics of Brown's public lectures, some of which appeared in formats other than as collected essays, the list would be even broader.[5] One might say that Brown was willing to address almost any topic of timely interest that had a biblical perspective to it.

(2) A second observation is that virtually all of Brown's writings (including the scholarly ones beyond the scope of this paper) reflect the unique period in history during which he was privileged to have lived.[6] Brown accomplished his professional biblical studies in the years just prior to the Second Vatican Council, at a time when modern Catholic biblical studies were just beginning to emerge from a very shadowy existence, primarily from behind the walls of monasteries. Biblical studies in general, and as conducted by Roman Catholics in particular, were still much in dispute. Brown often pointed to the significance of Pius XII's groundbreaking encyclical *Divino Afflante Spiritu* (1943), which gave impetus to the nascent biblical movement among Roman Catholic scholars. With his graduate studies at Johns Hopkins University and the Catholic University of America and service on the Pontifical Biblical Commission, Brown was on the ground level of the biblical movement that was to thrust the Bible once more into the very heart of the church's life. Decades of Catholic neglect of the Bible were suddenly ended by this rebirth. Brown benefited greatly from this historical reality. No longer would biblical studies be considered the exclusive domain of Protestant scholars. Essentially, Brown's pastoral writings quenched a deep thirst among Catholics to get to know the Bible more intimately even while they appealed to broader ecumenical audiences as well.

(3) Related to this point is a third characteristic—the fervent desire to see that the results of modern biblical studies were disseminated widely to the general public. He had this orientation from his earliest days as a scholar, as is seen in a comment from the 1970s: "I go on with my New Testament research, always with an eye on implications for the Church and for ecumenism."[7] He

also states explicitly in his only book dedicated exclusively to the contribution of biblical archaeology to biblical studies: "I think it an essential religious duty to make respectable and reliable biblical knowledge available to the non-specialist. It is one way of protecting ordinary Jews and Christians from the malady of biblical fundamentalism."[8] Brown was no "ivory-tower" theologian. He did not believe that the results of biblical scholarship should languish in thick, arcane studies on the dusty bookshelves of scholarly libraries. Nor did he believe that scientific Scripture study inevitably led to a sterile and anti-spiritual reading of Scripture. To the contrary, he believed in the ultimate applicability of the Scriptures to modern life, albeit in a fashion that was non-fundamentalist. And he had a rare gift for clarity of thought and speech, with a wonderful command of language, that made his writings and lectures broadly appealing.

(4) A fourth characteristic is the single-minded focus on the historical-critical method of biblical studies. It is no exaggeration to assert that a primary purpose of Brown's pastoral writings was to disseminate and defend the use of the historical-critical method. He accepted the applicability of this method not only for the Bible but for magisterial documents as well. Historical criticism acknowledges that all human documents, even those inspired by God, have historical contexts that are crucial to the understanding of their meaning. This method, with its roots in the seventeenth, eighteenth and nineteenth centuries, is actually a conglomeration of methods, many of which began in the universities of Europe and emigrated to North America over time.[9] At the basis of the historical-critical approach to the Bible is the emphasis on the Bible as God's Word in human words. Contrary to prior ways of viewing the Scriptures as divine texts to be accepted at face value, even in terms of science or history, historical criticism raised questions about the historical reliability of some parts of the Bible. Much of Brown's focus in his pastoral writings is to defend the historical-critical approach as basically trustworthy and not necessarily opposed to a faith perspective on the Bible,[10] but in this regard his writings caused considerable controversy, a topic to which we will return below.

(5) Coupled with the above point is the fifth observation, namely, that Brown's writings contain a characteristic faith stance. Contrary to the impressions sometimes given by his sharpest critics, Brown's involvement in biblical studies was not exercised from a strictly academic perspective, but also from commitment to his faith. While it may be a small point, it is worth noting that Brown always lectured wearing his Roman collar, regardless of the setting. He was quite conscious that he was a priest of the Roman Catholic Church. Even as a biblical scholar he saw no opposition to the faith in this role. Indeed, almost all his writings reveal that biblical scholarship contributed greatly to his faith.

Contrary to those who saw modern biblical sciences, especially historical criticism, as undermining the faith, Brown saw them as a means of bolstering the faith and placing it on firmer ground. He also believed that it was impor-

242 of scholars with a faith perspective to be in conversation with their coun-

tant for scholars with a faith perspective to be in conversation with their counterparts in secular settings. To leave the scholarly conversation only to academia risks losing sight of the origin of the biblical writings in the communities of faith that produced them. He felt no need to apologize for this viewpoint. But he also believed that biblical studies properly encouraged people to think. Using one's mind to the fullest extent, and always asking questions of the sacred texts, does not undermine the authority of Scripture but is the natural outgrowth of God-given human knowledge.[11] This was part of what I would term his "incarnational" tendency—grace at work *through* human nature. The huge impact of his writings among scholars of all stripes indicates that this faith perspective was not a liability. This is true as well for the generations of preachers who have benefited from his writings.[12] Brown was at home in both worlds, scientific and religious, and he was masterful at bridging the two.

(6) A sixth characteristic is the balance with which Brown addressed issues. He pointed out on numerous occasions that the Catholic Church in the last third of the twentieth century found itself splintered, with multiple factions vying for dominance in their interpretation of the impact of the Second Vatican Council.[13] It is probably characteristic of other periods of history that factionalism tends to occur in the church in the wake of major councils. Brown believed that the contemporary divisive situation was harming the church and that biblical studies could point the way to moderation in the debate. His emphasis was on the truth rather than ideological positions, and the truth, in his judgment, was most often to be found in the middle. Thus in his book *Biblical Exegesis and Church Doctrine* he criticizes forcefully the positions of both liberals and conservatives in the church with regard to the relationship between biblical criticism and dogma.[14] In his latter years Brown's approach made him as critical of the liberal conclusions of the Jesus Seminar as of the naïve positions of literalists and biblical fundamentalists. He believed both distorted the truth. Responsible scholarship required that he point out these limitations and provide a more centrist and accurate reading of Scripture.[15]

I would also note, however, that Brown's analysis of this situation was not merely formulaic. He recognized variations in such diametrically opposed positions. One example is a chapter in his book *Crises Facing the Church* in which he points out multiple positions of interpreters regarding twentieth-century teaching on christology. His analysis pointed to a broad continuum of positions, ranging from "non-scholarly liberalism" on the one hand to "non-scholarly conservatism" on the other, with three scholarly positions in between.[16]

The emphasis on balance, however, could also be said to apply even more broadly to his *method* in biblical studies. Not only did he criticize what he felt were untenable positions from the right and the left; he was also willing to address even the most extreme positions in a judicious manner, to the point, some would say, of including irresponsible or reactionary positions that scarcely needed to be mentioned. Examples include the treatment in *Biblical*

Exegesis and Church Doctrine of the controversy over the Shroud of Turin and the extreme positions of René Laurentin regarding the historicity of the infancy narratives of the gospels.[17] Even Brown's more scholarly works included lengthy discussions of positions that many scholars would discount as exaggerated or irrelevant.[18] This may be due as much to Brown's thoroughness as a scholar as to his desire for balance and objectivity.

III. The Impact of the Pastoral Writings on the Life of the Church

If the above characteristics reflect accurately Brown's approach to the Bible in his pastoral writings, we can move to another level of inquiry. What is of lasting value for us and for the church, and what impact, if any, will Brown's approach have as we move further into the third Christian millennium? I point to three distinct aspects of Brown's pastoral writings that continue to influence the life of the church.

(1) Of utmost importance, in my judgment, is Brown's contribution to discussions about the relationship between faith and scientific study. He was convinced that the historical-critical method had lasting value for both biblical studies and church doctrine. Three of his pastoral writings, in particular, can be singled out for setting directions in this discussion.

The first is *Biblical Reflections on Crises Facing the Church,* published in 1975. The range of issues addressed shows how Brown perceived the broad implications of the scientific study of the Bible for Catholic doctrine. The book addresses such controversial issues as the ordination of women, the papacy, and the role of Mary. He prefaced it with a short overview of how the Catholic perspective had changed in the course of the twentieth century. His essays demonstrate the shift in the church from being fearful and condemnatory of scientific biblical study to the application of such method following Pius XII's encyclical (mentioned above) and later, in a post-Vatican II context, the increased openness to such study. He also felt it essential to make clear to his readers what the church's official stance was with regard to biblical studies. To that end he included in the appendix to that book excerpts of official magisterial documents outlining the growth of this more open perspective, a practice he continued in other books. Essentially, Brown capitalized on Vatican II's teaching that the church itself is ruled by and responsible to Sacred Scripture.[19]

The second book, *The Critical Meaning of the Bible,* published six years later, outlined even more explicitly how modern scientific biblical studies do not oppose authentic faith but support and nuance it. One of the essays addressed specifically what he called "myths" about the relationship between theologians and the magisterium of the church. He further applied his principles to delicate topics like the nature of the priesthood and the episcopacy.[20] He demonstrated that ultraconservative Catholics wrongly set up false dichotomies between the theological enterprise and the goal of the church to promote authentic faith. In explaining the importance of his approach to the president of Union Theological Seminary, where he had already taught for many years, Brown wrote:

> I am bringing together a whole series of these lectures for publication . . . under the title *The Critical Meaning of the Bible.* They all concern in one way or another the theme that biblical criticism is constructive, and when properly used is capable of moving the Church and Christians. In my own Roman Catholic Church, by remaining firmly in the mainstream of the Church's life, biblical scholars have been able to influence constructively a reform movement.[21]

Four years later, in *Biblical Exegesis and Church Doctrine*, he addressed similar themes in more explicit ways. The second essay of the book in particular provides an exquisite statement on the implications of critical biblical exegesis for the development of doctrine.[22] Other essays address the false approaches of both "liberals" and "conservatives" when it comes to controversial church discussions. In the midst of these discussions his own centrist approach stands out.

Some of Brown's harshest critics did not seem to recognize his scholarly moderation and his fidelity to the church and the magisterium. Despite the scholarly assessment that Brown was clearly "centrist" in his approach, ultraconservative critics accused him of heretical teachings. Particularly galling for them were his two books, *The Virginal Conception and Bodily Resurrection of Jesus* and *Priest and Bishop*. They wrongly charged Brown with denying church teachings about these matters, a charge that any careful reading of Brown's work would dispel. Brown's close colleague and good friend, Joseph Fitzmyer, has chronicled some of these outrageous attacks on Brown, so we need not rehearse them here.[23] The main point is that Brown took the implications of his professional study of the Bible to their logical conclusion and saw that they did not pose a threat, but were a great resource for the church and the faith. He was fond of quoting Pope John XXIII's statement that opened the Second Vatican Council: "The substance of the ancient doctrine of the deposit of faith is one thing, and the way in which it is presented is another."[24]

One factor that Brown's critics failed to take seriously was the confidence church authorities had in his scholarship. When he was named in 1972 one of twenty scholarly members of the reconstituted Pontifical Biblical Commission, Pope Paul VI noted that these were scholars "outstanding for their learning, prudence, and Catholic regard for the magisterium of the Church." One does not get appointed to such a commission (twice, the second time by Pope John Paul II in 1996), or become an advisor to the Vatican Secretariat for Christian Unity, or represent the official church in ecumenical dialogues, or receive imprimaturs for his books, or have books highly recommended by the U. S. bishops,[25] without being a loyal, devoted Catholic of outstanding faith and morals. For Brown his scholarship was at the *service* of the Church, not something that threatened it. He never succumbed to the idea of a "shadow magisterium," but always believed that his scholarship could ultimately be at the service of the church's official teachings. Even Cardinal Joseph Ratzinger, head of the Congregation for the Doctrine of the Faith, commended Brown's type of scholarship in the context of a conference that explored the dangers of some of the excesses of the historical-critical method.[26]

While we should not exaggerate this issue, we should note that even five years after Brown's death his ultraconservative detractors were still vilifying him as promoting dissension in the church and being unfaithful to magisterial teaching. One such attack appeared in an official diocesan newspaper, reporting on a conference held in June 2003 in Scranton, Pennsylvania.[27] Apparently even after his death his sharpest critics fear the wide-ranging influence of Brown's scholarship, and their attacks on him and on historical criticism in general continue.[28]

(2) A second lasting contribution of Brown's approach is his unswerving dedication to the application of the Sacred Scriptures to the contemporary situation. In fact, the most likely reason for his broad appeal to average Christians in the pew is that he showed them that the Bible matters. It has pastoral applicability to their lives. An advantage of Brown's approach was his emphasis on beginning the process of interpretation with the literal meaning of the text before seeking deeper meanings. This approach, coupled with his insistence on reading the final form of the text as it exists in our Bible today (a stance that became characteristic of his later works), helped to keep the Bible accessible to the average person. Most of his pastoral writings provide testimony to this general approach, but I highlight two books.

Brown himself viewed his book *The Churches the Apostles Left Behind* as a companion to two earlier, more technical studies, *The Community of the Beloved Disciple* and *Antioch and Rome* (the latter co-authored with John P. Meier). Both of these works were more intricate attempts to unearth the history of some early Christian communities, and their methodology required extensive exegetical detective work and scientific deduction, the results of which were never expected to be completely accepted. With *The Churches the Apostles Left Behind,* however, his pastoral sensitivity was evident. It was a masterful display of how the New Testament books offer a diverse set of ecclesiological images that have applicability to how we view the church today. Brown showed that the biblical data provided no univocal understanding of the church. Rather, various New Testament writings had strengths and weaknesses that ought to be acknowledged (Matthean, Markan, Lukan, Johannine, Pauline, etc.). Each biblical image contributes something to the life of the church in every age, but in a way that also makes clear the need for ongoing reformation in the church in every era.[29]

A second example is his book *Reading the Gospels with the Church*. It was composed of revised essays that had been done for a more popular format

(*Catholic Update,* published by St. Anthony Messenger Press). The book analyzes the biblical readings in the liturgical cycle between Christmas and
Easter. In each instance Brown shows that the readings (i.e., the infancy narratives, the Passion narratives, the resurrection narratives, etc.) tell us something
about how we view Jesus, the church, ethics, and the Bible itself. For instance,
in commenting on the diverse stories of the resurrection of Jesus, Brown says:

> We come back to the important pastoral question with which we began: What
> can we learn from the fact that the Gospel accounts of the Resurrection differ
> from each other? The answer is centered on the risen Jesus as God's ultimate
> revelation directed to all times and places. The evangelists shaped the Resurrec-
> tion narratives to be meaningful to audiences of differing life-styles and back-
> grounds in the first century. . . . The Church of our century cannot present a
> different Christ. But by the way it preserves the varied Gospel messages, it lets
> Jesus speak to the differing needs of the audiences of our time.[30]

All of Brown's pastoral writings exhibit this sensitivity. He had the knack for
making the biblical data attractive and applicable to people, not in a simplistic
way, but in an informative and interesting format. While he clearly rejected a
fundamentalist approach that asserted a narrow, one-to-one correspondence between the biblical data and the contemporary world, he nonetheless always believed that what the Bible said (or did not say) matters in the modern world.[31]

(3) The third lasting contribution is Brown's participation in ecumenical
dialogue. Throughout his pastoral writings Brown displays great sensitivity to
the ecumenical and interfaith prospects that arose after the Second Vatican
Council. Not only was he involved in major formal dialogues; his twenty-year
experience as a faculty member at Union Theological Seminary in New York
greatly impacted his work. He was well connected in ecumenical and interfaith circles, counting many Protestants and Jews among his friends (and students). He also could approach his teaching situation—as a Catholic teaching
at a Protestant institution—with characteristic humor.

In a book that had its origins in a series of lectures at another Protestant
seminary (the "other Union" in Richmond, Virginia), Brown wrote the following anecdote. The catalogue of Union Theological Seminary (New York City)
at the time claimed that the faculty represented "the wide range of theological
and church outlook which is characteristic of Protestantism at its best." Brown
goes on to say that this was brought to the attention of the President, who in
turn asked him whether he was offended. Brown replied, tongue in cheek (he
says): "No, for I think that a balanced Roman Catholic represents the *best* in
Protestant outlooks."[32] Again, however, with characteristic balance, Brown
noted that his ecumenical approach was informed by his own consciousness
of his faith as a Roman Catholic. He wrote:

> Loyalty to one's own church and an indebtedness to a wider scholarship are a
> combination that has enriched my appreciation of what New Testament diver-

sity can mean to various churches—a combination that I would defend against all criticism.[33]

It is little wonder, then, that he could see the value of ongoing reform and self-reflection in both Roman Catholic and Protestant settings, as is seen in his essay, "Moving all the Churches to Reform."[34] In the contemporary situation, when cooperative ecumenical ventures seem less frequent and lower in priority than in the heyday of the Council, Brown offers a wonderful model to emulate. Ecumenical and interfaith discussions on both the scholarly and popular level are important to the lives of all our churches and other faiths. Indeed, the world is sorely in need of cooperative religious ventures to help dispel the fears and misunderstandings that continue to creep into and deteriorate human relations.

IV. A Modest Critique

Thus far I have focused on Brown's pastoral contributions, and it is probably evident that I am an unabashed admirer of his incredible legacy. However, as with all human beings, he had his limitations. From a scholarly standpoint I call attention to two.

(1) The first limitation is that he at times engaged in polemics in a way that detracted from the overall efficacy of his arguments. Unlike his critics, he never reduced his arguments to *ad hominem* diatribes; he always tried to keep the focus on the content. However, he did allow the criticism to affect him emotionally. He was most upset by the ongoing opposition he experienced from certain ultraconservatives in the Roman Catholic Church. His lectures at times invited protests by a small group of boycotters. I could understand his annoyance at being attacked in writing, for instance, in an irresponsible publication like *The Wanderer,* but there are those who believe he should have ignored his opponents rather than trying to respond to them. It is one thing to address scholarly opposition, something he did with flair, but he sometimes drifted into debates with lesser minds that showed the depth of his frustration and anger.[35] He probably should have allowed this harsh criticism to roll off him as so much detritus of uninformed, frightened opinion. However, it was his pastoral sensitivity that goaded him to respond to these critics. The very people who could easily be swayed by the unbalanced arguments of a vocal few were the average persons in the pew—the audience that Brown thought deserved access to the best of biblical scholarship.

(2) A second limitation is Brown's hesitance to allow other biblical methods besides historical criticism to influence his scholarship. He was deeply suspicious of some newer exegetical and hermeneutical methods, not without some justification. Certain methods, such as semiotics, invented complex and arcane systems of interpretation while producing precious little advance in our

knowledge of the text. Other approaches, such as those from feminists and liberation theology, could at times have inbuilt biases that allowed eisegetical readings and outside agenda to take precedence over objectivity (something that, to be sure, is also true of historical criticism, but that is sometimes overlooked). Even granted the serious limitations of newer methods, Brown was slow to adapt his own approach to some useful methodologies, although his later major scholarly works began to show some influence from methods such as narrative, literary, and social-scientific criticism.[36] I personally think part of his reluctance was his age. In private conversations with me he opined that it was difficult to keep abreast of so many methodological advances. He honestly felt he was too old for taking on new approaches to biblical studies.

Nonetheless, I suspect that had he lived to complete the revision of his commentary on the Gospel of John it would most likely have contained many newer insights based on methods beyond the limits of historical criticism.[37] In addition, his treatment of the Gospel of John in his marvelous *A Retreat with John the Evangelist* demonstrated that he could be quite literarily creative and even whimsical in his approach to biblical studies.

V. Conclusion

To bring this essay to a close, let us return to the image of the incarnate Word revealed. Brown expressed profound gratitude that he had been able to devote the lion's share of his scholarly life to the Gospel of John. In his last year of teaching (1990) he commented:

> The autumn saw my last course on the Gospel of John, a course that I have enjoyed giving many times at Union. I think I remain as enthusiastic about that Gospel as when I first began studying it back in the 1950s.[38]

The Johannine tradition was his constant inspiration and preoccupation. I maintain that one of the great contributions of that venerable tradition and one that imbued Brown's writings is, in fact, the Incarnation. It is that unwavering focus on the Word-made-flesh, the God who chose to come to earth, the revelation that happens in *the* Word, that made Brown's writings, scholarly and pastoral, so profound. He took the Incarnation seriously.

I believe the legacy of his writings will continue to inspire new generations of the faithful who seek to make that Word of God an intimate part of their own lives. In his book *A Retreat with John the Evangelist* there is a passage that demonstrates the ease with which he applied the Johannine tradition to the contemporary scene. Speaking of the Paraclete, the Johannine tradition's unique contribution to pneumatology, he writes:

> Without the vitality of the Spirit, Christians and a church can become authoritarian and fossilized, so worried about new and dangerous ideas that they prefer

no ideas at all. Without authoritative guidance, on the other hand, Christians and a church can become faddist and a babble of contradictory voices, ultimately destined to be torn apart.

A real test for both individual Christians and the church is to respect the tension between being led by the Spirit and being guided by authoritative teachers and teaching. . . . Holding in tension authoritative teaching and new insights from the Spirit can keep Christians and the church both faithful to Christ and responsive to the needs of the times.[39]

It is with that characteristic balance and wisdom that Raymond Brown bequeaths us both a challenge and a hope. Incarnational theology always breeds tension, but Brown showed us that tension can also produce life. It promotes growth, it leads to reform, it results in conversion. And it is under just such conditions that one encounters authentically the incarnate Word revealed.

Notes

1. I thank Professor John R. Donahue, s.j., the first Raymond E. Brown Distinguished Professor of New Testament Studies at St. Mary's Seminary and University, for the invitation to write this paper.

2. *The Gospel According to John (i–xii).* AB 29 (New York: Doubleday, 1966) 31 (emphasis in the original).

3. Note that the word "pastoral" is used intentionally, as distinct from "popular." In my judgment many of Brown's works listed in the next note are not merely samples of *haute vulgarisation* but sophisticated expositions written out of genuine pastoral concern for the applicability of the Scriptures to daily life.

4. These include: *Priest and Bishop: Biblical Reflections* (New York: Paulist, 1970; repr. Eugene, OR: Wipf and Stock, 1998); *The Virginal Conception and Bodily Resurrection of Jesus* (New York: Paulist, 1973); *Biblical Reflections on Crises Facing the Church* (New York: Paulist, 1975); *The Critical Meaning of the Bible* (New York: Paulist, 1981); *Recent Discoveries and the Biblical World* (Wilmington: Michael Glazier, 1983; repr. Eugene, OR: Wipf and Stock, 2003); *The Churches the Apostles Left Behind* (New York: Paulist, 1984); *Biblical Exegesis and Church Doctrine* (New York: Paulist, 1985; repr Eugene, OR: Wipf and Stock, 2001); *An Adult Christ at Christmas: Essays on the Three Biblical Christmas Stories* (Collegeville: Liturgical Press, 1978); *A Crucified Christ in Holy Week: Essays on the Four Gospel Passion Narratives* (Collegeville: Liturgical Press, 1986); *A Coming Christ in Advent: Essays on the Gospel Narratives Preparing for the Birth of Jesus (Matthew 1 and Luke 1)* (Collegeville: Liturgical Press, 1988); *A Risen Christ in Eastertime: Essays on the Gospel Narratives of the Resurrection* (Collegeville: Liturgical Press, 1991); *The Jerome Bible Handbook* (with Joseph A. Fitzmyer and Roland E. Murphy; Collegeville: Liturgical Press, 1992); *A Once-and-Coming Spirit at Pentecost: Essays on the Liturgical Readings between Easter and Pentecost, Taken from The Acts of the Apostles and from the Gospel According to John* (Collegeville: Liturgical Press, 1994); *Christ in the Gospels of the Ordinary Sundays: Essays on the Gospel Readings of the Ordinary Sundays in the Three-Year Liturgical Cycle* (Collegeville: Liturgical Press, 1998); *Responses to 101 Questions about the Bible* (New York: Paulist, 1990); *Reading the Gospels with the Church: From Christmas Through Easter* (Cincinnati: St. Anthony Messenger, 1996); and *A Retreat with John the Evangelist* (Cincinnati: St. Anthony Messenger, 1998). Two modest-sized books might be considered more scholarly than pastoral, although they were widely read, viz., *The Community of the Beloved Disciple* (New York: Paulist, 1979) and *Antioch and Rome* (with John P. Meier; New York: Paulist, 1983).

5. Audiotapes of many of his public lectures are available through Welcome Recordings, Deeside, Wales, listed in the comprehensive bibliography of Brown's publications that concludes this volume.

6. He notes explicitly, "In my intellectual career I was fortunate enough to miss the first third of the [twentieth] century when the Roman Catholic Church stood in opposition to biblical criticism. By the time I came on the scene of biblical study, my Church was already accepting the methodology of biblical criticism. Perhaps that is why it has come naturally to me to have a positive attitude toward the Church's authority, which I have found friendly and not repressive in my biblical growth." *Crises Facing the Church*, viii.

7. Annual report to the President and Board of Union Theological Seminary (1976–1977), in the Sulpician Archives, Baltimore, MD.

8. *Recent Discoveries,* 12.

9. For an overview see John S. Kselman and Ronald D. Witherup, "Modern New Testament Criticism," in Raymond E. Brown, Joseph A. Fitzmyer, and Roland E. Murphy, eds., *The New Jerome Biblical Commentary* (Englewood Cliffs, NJ: Prentice-Hall, 1990) 1130–45.

10. Over time Brown grew more conscious of the limitations of historical criticism. For example, in *The Death of the Messiah: From Gethsemane to the Grave.* 2 vols. ABRL (New York: Doubleday, 1994) he commented frequently on the inability to know with certainty some aspects of the historical situations behind the Passion narratives. Also, the inclusion of an appendix by a former student, Marion L. Soards, on the form of a possible pre-Marcan Passion narrative, shows how frustrating and inconclusive multiple scholarly theories can be when preoccupied with historical and source questions. (Vol. 2, "Appendix IX: The Question of a PreMarcan Passion Narrative," 1492–1524).

11. Note the title of a chapter, "Moving All Christians to Think," in *Critical Meaning*, 82–95. He went on in the same book to apply the concept to "rethinking" the priesthood and episcopacy.

12. This observation is especially true of the six volumes on the lectionary cycle published by Liturgical Press (see n. 4 above), but applies to his major commentaries as well. Brown's spiritual insights have helped preachers effectively apply the Word of God to the modern world from a rich faith perspective.

13. For example, *Crises Facing the Church,* viii–ix; *Biblical Exegesis and Church Doctrine,* 10–13.

14. Chapters Three and Four, 54–85.

15. That Brown saw himself as a centrist does not mean that he was naïve about how others saw him. In an early interview he once commented: "Like everybody else, I always think I am in the center. I probably [am], but in the Biblical spectrum along those lines I probably would be classified as center or slightly right of center. Yet in my own church spectrum, since we were extremely right of center, in the Biblical field I would be looked [on] as one of the most advanced in some ways. A lot depends on where you start. . . . I would place myself somewhere to the right of center." Interview with Professor Malcolm L. Warford (March 11, 1977),\ 3, in the Sulpician Archives, Baltimore, MD.

16. Namely scholarly liberalism, Bultmannian existentialism, and moderate conservatism (p. 22). Complexity and balance were also characteristic of many of his scholarly writings, such as "Not Jewish Christianity and Gentile Christianity but Types of Jewish/Gentile Christianity," *CBQ* 45 (1983) 74–79.

17. Pp. 147–61.

18. Examples could include passages interspersed throughout *Gospel of John*, *Death of the Messiah*, and *The Birth of the Messiah: A Commentary on the Infancy Narratives in the Gospels of Matthew and Luke.* ABRL (new updated ed. New York: Doubleday, 1993).

19. See *Dei Verbum* ("Dogmatic Constitution on Divine Revelation") §21.

20. His early book *Priest and Bishop* remains a classic statement on the New Testament foundations of these ordained ministries. It is still used as a textbook for courses on the priesthood. I

note also that one of the best recent treatments by a systematic theologian of the topic of the origins of the episcopacy uses Brown's book extensively as the major resource for the biblical period, strong testimony to its enduring value. See Francis A. Sullivan, *From Apostles to Bishops: The Development of the Episcopacy in the Early Church* (New York: Newman, 2001).

21. Annual report to the President and Board of Union Theological Seminary (May 23, 1981), in the Sulpician Archives, Baltimore, MD.

22. "Critical Biblical Exegesis and the Development of Church Doctrine," 26–53.

23. "Raymond E. Brown, S.S.: In Memoriam," *USQR* 52 (1998) 12–18. Not all of Brown's critics were "crackpots." One unfortunate situation arose in the mid-1970s when Cardinal Lawrence Shehan, the archbishop of Baltimore and a good acquaintance of Brown's, became frightened by the implications of Brown's book, *Priest and Bishop*. He was fearful of the prospect that the historical underpinnings of the episcopacy might not be able to be traced back—literally and historically—in an unbroken line to the apostles. The cardinal, who was not a trained biblical theologian, took it upon himself (against the counsel of his advisors) to attempt a refutation of Brown in a public lecture at St. Mary's Seminary and University, with disastrous results. To his credit Shehan did try to engage some biblical scholarship with limited tools and information. Although this incident strained the relationship between the two, to Brown's credit he did not try to respond to Shehan in public.

24. *Crises Facing the Church*, 10.

25. His controversial book, *The Virginal Conception and Bodily Resurrection of Jesus*, was listed by the (then) National Conference of Catholic Bishops as a recommended resource for their pastoral letter on Mary (November 1973).

26. See Richard J. Neuhaus, *Biblical Interpretation in Crisis: The Ratzinger Conference on Bible and Church*. Encounter Series 9 (Grand Rapids: Eerdmans, 1989) 1–23. Ratzinger's lecture offered criticisms of some excesses in biblical scholarship, but he was personally complimentary of Brown and his scholarship in public interviews. He said, "I would be very happy if we had many exegetes like Father Brown." Quoted in *Origins* 17/35 (February 11, 1988) 595.

27. See articles by Maria Gapinski and Sal Ciresi in *The Arlington Catholic Herald* (June 26 and July 7, 2003). Gapinski's article, entitled "Scranton Conference Focuses on Biblical Questions," reports on the first annual conference of an apparently new organization called the "International Catholic Council on Biblical Inerrancy (ICCBI)." Panelists who appeared at the conference were listed as Father Brian W. Harrison, o.s. (professor at the Pontifical University of Ponce, Puerto Rico), Robert Sungenis (president of Catholic Apologetics International), Sal Ciresi (columnist for *The Arlington Catholic Herald* and a faculty member at Notre Dame Graduate School of Christendom College), and Gerry Matatics (president of Biblical Foundations International). I first became aware of Father Harrison's role in attacking the legacy of Raymond Brown around 2001 when I received in the mail an unsolicited audiotape titled "Demythologizing the Golden Legend," in which he attacked Brown and others for allegedly distorting the church's teaching on Scripture through the use of the historical-critical method. The tape was a "gift" from an organization called "romancatholicpriest.com," apparently distributed gratis to bishops and priests in the U.S. I found the *ad hominem* form of argument on the tape both offensive and distorted.

28. In a more responsible vein, some mainline biblical scholars have also raised strong objections to the excesses of historical-critical method as detracting from some people's faith. See Luke Timothy Johnson and William S. Kurz, *The Future of Catholic Biblical Scholarship: A Constructive Conversation* (Grand Rapids: Eerdmans, 2002). While their position also has some serious limitations, their views are not reduced to attacks on individuals in the manner of some less professional critics. See my review of this book in *CBQ* 65 (2003) 640–42.

29. Note the chapter titled "Moving All the Churches to Reform" in *Critical Meaning*, 107–23. It reflects Brown's conviction that biblical studies could properly contribute to the healthy reform of all churches, including the Roman Catholic Church. If some would object to the very notion that the church should be reformed, we should remember that Vatican II itself taught

the need for continual renewal in the church. (Cf. the expression, "under the action of the Holy Spirit, never ceases to renew itself" *[seipsam renovare non desinat], Lumen Gentium* §9; cf. §8 and §40; also *Unitatis Redintegratio* §6).

30. *Reading the Gospels with the Church,* 75.

31. One of Brown's interests on the pastoral level was combating biblical fundamentalism. He frequently addressed this topic. See, for example, *101 Questions,* 43–48, 137–42, and *Reading the Gospels,* 77–86. For more on a Catholic perspective on this question see Ronald D. Witherup, *Biblical Fundamentalism: What Every Catholic Should Know* (Collegeville: Liturgical Press, 2001).

32. *Churches the Apostles Left Behind,* 8. The essays assembled in that book for publication were the Sprunt Lectures, delivered at Union Theological Seminary in Richmond, Virginia, January 28–30, 1980.

33. Ibid. 9.

34. *Critical Meaning,* 107–23.

35. One glimpses this in an explicit passage, "If there is impatience in this book, it is not with Catholics who need time to make a personal adjustment to the Church's change of attitude toward biblical criticism; my impatience is with those who want to move us back to the first third of the [twentieth] century by repressing the freedom that the Church has gradually granted to biblical criticism." *Crises Facing the Church,* viii.

36. It is noteworthy that the Pontifical Biblical Commission issued an important document in 1993 highlighting the many methods current in biblical studies and noting that each has advantages and disadvantages. No method is dismissed outright by Catholics, although fundamentalism is rejected as a viable option. See *The Interpretation of the Bible in the Church* (Boston: St. Paul Books & Media, 1993).

37. This can already be seen in Brown's final book, *An Introduction to the Gospel of John,* edited and revised by Francis J. Moloney. ABRL (New York: Doubleday, 2003). Hints are also evident in Brown's *Death of the Messiah* and *An Introduction to the New Testament* (New York: Doubleday, 1997).

38. Annual report to the President and Board of Union Theological Seminary (March 29, 1990), in the Sulpician Archives, Baltimore, MD.

39. *A Retreat with John the Evangelist,* 97–98.

Appendix One

Biography and Bibliography of the Publications of Raymond E. Brown, S.S.

Prepared by Ronald D. Witherup, S.S., and Michael L. Barré, S.S.

Biography of Raymond E. Brown, s.s.

Ronald D. Witherup, s.s.

The sudden death of renowned biblical scholar Raymond E. Brown at the age of seventy on August 8, 1998, deprived the church and the world of an eminent churchman and a premier exegete. The singular achievements of this remarkable person are unparalleled by any Catholic biblical scholar in the twentieth century. As a prelude to the comprehensive bibliography of his publications, a brief biographical sketch is in order.

Raymond Edward Brown was born on May 22, 1928 in the Bronx, New York City. He was the son of Reuben H. and Loretta (Sullivan) Brown, who also had one other son, Robert. Brown began his education in the Bronx, but in 1944 his family relocated to Miami Shores, Florida, where he completed high school. In 1945 he entered St. Charles College in Catonsville, Maryland, a college seminary program run by the Society of St. Sulpice, which is where he first encountered that community of priests he later joined (thus the initials after his name). The Sulpicians, as they are commonly called, are a community of diocesan priests founded in Paris in 1641, with the special ministry of initial and ongoing formation of Roman Catholic priests.

Already a prodigious academic talent, Brown entered an accelerated program of studies and transferred to The Catholic University of America in 1946, where he became a Basselin Scholar and obtained both a B.A. (1948) and M.A. (1949) in Philosophy. He then began advanced seminary studies at the Gregorian University in Rome (1949–50), but at the request of his bishop he returned to the United States the following year to complete studies for the priesthood at St. Mary's Seminary and University in Baltimore, Maryland. St. Mary's is the oldest Roman Catholic seminary in the United States, founded by the Sulpicians in 1791 at the invitation of John Carroll, the first bishop of the United States. There Brown completed his theological training for priesthood, obtaining S.T.B. (1951) and S.T.L. (1953) degrees. He was ordained a priest on May 23, 1953 for the Diocese of St. Augustine (Florida) by Archbishop Joseph Hurley, but he was immediately released to the Society of St. Sulpice since he was attracted to biblical studies and the formation of future priests and had become a candidate for the Sulpicians in 1951. He entered the Society formally in 1955 after completing the requirements for full membership.

Many people have wondered how Brown became attracted to biblical studies, and fortunately he left a testimony of that process. While he was in Rome as a seminarian the Korean War broke out, and his bishop recalled him to the United States to enroll him in second theology at St. Mary's. Given the rigidity of curricula in those days and the differences between the Roman and the American systems of education, transferring was difficult. He was out of sequence and had missed some of the introductory Bible courses. A professor told him to study Old Testament on his own and he would then test him by an examination. Brown's own words describe what happened next:

> Well, he didn't tell me how much to study, so I started reading the Old Testament and studying. I was fortunate enough to be able to read French and Italian and some German, so that actually I was reading better books than were available in English. And when I took the exam, he was highly complimentary. He virtually told me, "I didn't mean you had to know that much." He asked me whether I was interested in the Bible. I said it was the most interesting thing I had ever done in my life; it was fascinating. (I had always wanted to teach. . . .) The professor said, "We do need teachers in Bible."[1]

When Brown's bishop released him to the Sulpicians in 1953 he was assigned to teach at St. Charles Seminary in Catonsville, Maryland. This position also allowed him to complete a doctoral degree in theology at St. Mary's Seminary (S.T.D., 1955) and to begin doctoral studies in Semitic languages at Johns Hopkins University. There he became a student of the world-renowned scholar William Foxwell Albright, known as "the dean of biblical archaeologists." Brown finished his dissertation (Ph.D.) in 1958, a work that was to demonstrate his longstanding interest in combining Near Eastern and Old Testament studies with the study of the New Testament. As he once commented: "I always rejoice, by the way, that I taught Old Testament for six years. To me, it is wonderful to have taught the whole Bible."[2] Later, Brown also completed a Licentiate in Sacred Scripture from the Pontifical Biblical Institute in Rome (S.S.L., 1963), to round out his biblical education where he had obtained an earlier Baccalaureate in Sacred Scripture (S.S.B., 1959).

At the end of his doctoral studies at Johns Hopkins, Brown was fortunate in 1958–59 to be invited to work on the Dead Sea Scrolls in Jerusalem and Jordan, where he and fellow doctoral student and close friend Joseph A. Fitzmyer toiled diligently to create a preliminary concordance of those remarkable archaeological documents. Upon his return from Jerusalem the Sulpicians assigned Brown to teach at his alma mater, St. Mary's Seminary and University in Baltimore.

During those years, until 1971, he taught at St. Mary's and continued to engage in scholarly research. He also worked on the commentary that was to thrust him into the limelight of modern biblical scholarship, the two-volume Anchor Bible commentary on the Gospel of John (A10 and A16 below).

In 1971 Brown moved to New York, where he accepted a joint professorship at the Jesuit Woodstock College and Union Theological Seminary (1971–74). When Woodstock closed he accepted a full-time position at Union, where he taught for twenty years until his early retirement in 1990 as Auburn Distinguished Professor of Biblical Studies. Upon his "retirement," which was actually a cessation of teaching duties in order to be fully invested in research and publication, Brown took up residence at the Sulpician-run St. Patrick's Seminary in Menlo Park, California, at the invitation of then-Archbishop John R. Quinn. It was there that he died on August 8, 1998 of cardiac arrest, after experiencing difficulty breathing. His funeral liturgy was celebrated on August 17, 1998 at the same chapel in Catonsville, Maryland where he had begun his teaching career forty years earlier, and he was laid to rest at the Sulpician cemetery on the grounds of the former seminary that now serves as Charlestown Retirement Community.

A brief summary of major achievements provides an overview of his extensive career. From the publication of his dissertation in 1968 (finished in 1958; digested as *The Semitic Background of the Term "Mystery" in the New Testament*, A4 and A12 below) to the last book, which appeared five years after his death, he published dozens of books, large and small, and hundreds of articles and major book reviews, which are assembled in the accompanying bibliography.

Brown also received many honors in his career, including more than thirty honorary doctorates. Among the more notable are honorary degrees from American and European universities like Edinburgh (1972), Uppsala (1974), DePaul (1974), Villanova (1975), Louvain (1976), Boston College (1977), Glasgow (1978), Fordham (1977), Hofstra (1985), Catholic University of America (1989), San Francisco (1994), Northwestern (1995), and Catholic Theological Union (1998). Among many other distinctions in the course of his career, a few are worth highlighting. He served as a *peritus* (advisor) to his bishop, Archbishop Hurley, during the first session of Vatican Council II (1962) and became the first Roman Catholic to address the Faith and Order Conference of the World Council of Churches in Montreal, Canada (1963). He was also the first person to serve as president of the three most prestigious societies for New Testament study, the Catholic Biblical Association (1971–72), the Society of Biblical Literature (1976–77), and the Society for the Study of the New Testament (1986–87).

Brown was active in many church affairs and in several ecumenical ventures of importance. Pope Paul VI appointed him a consultant to the Vatican Secretariat for Christian Unity (1968–73), and he served as the only American

Catholic member of the Faith and Order Commission (1968–93). He also participated in the national dialogue between Roman Catholics and Lutherans (1965–74) and was a member of the special commission established by the World Council of Churches and the Roman Catholic Church to research the topic of "Apostolicity and Catholicity" (1967–68).

In an oft-quoted article, *Time* magazine named Brown "probably the premier Catholic Scripture scholar in the U.S.," and the Catholic Theological Society of America named him "the outstanding American Catholic theologian of the year' (1971). Pope Paul VI named Brown the only American member of the Pontifical Biblical Commission (1972–78), and he was honored again with membership in that prestigious body when Pope John Paul II appointed him in 1996, serving until his death. He was also inducted into Phi Beta Kappa, the American Academy of Arts and Sciences, and the prestigious British Academy. Many of his publications won book awards, including the National Catholic Book Award for *The Jerome Biblical Commentary* (1969), Volume 2 of *The Gospel According to John* (1971), and *The Virginal Conception and Bodily Resurrection of Jesus* (1973); the National Religious Book Award for *The Birth of the Messiah* (1977), and *Mary in the New Testament* (1978); the Catholic Press Association Book Award for *Antioch and Rome* (1984), and *An Introduction to New Testament Christology* (1994); and the Biblical Archaeological Society Award for *The Churches the Apostles Left Behind* (1986), and *The Death of the Messiah* (1995).

Although Brown spent the lion's share of his scholarly career in only two institutions, St. Mary's Seminary and Union Theological Seminary, he held many visiting professorships, including positions at the Pontifical Biblical Institute (1973, 1988), the Albright School of Archaeology in Jerusalem (1978), and the North American College in Rome (1983, 1988). He also delivered dozens of lectures in prestigious series such as Thomas More (Yale, 1966, 1987), Boylan (Dublin, 1971), W. H. Hoover (Chicago, 1975), Shaffer (Yale, 1978), Cole (Vanderbilt, 1980), Bellarmine (St. Louis, 1980), Sprunt (Union Theological in Richmond, 1980), Martin D'Arcy (Campion Hall, Oxford, 1996), and T. W. Manson Memorial (Manchester, U.K., 1996).

To his death Brown remained in demand as a popular lecturer. Some of those lectures are now available in audio cassettes, listed in the bibliography. Although a full assessment of his scholarly career remains to be done, Brown's work has already been the topic of numerous dissertations and studies. Examples include: D. W. Wuerl, *The Priesthood: The Doctrine of the Third Synod of Bishops and Recent Theological Conclusions* (S.T.D. diss.; Rome: Angelicum, 1974); R. L. Hatchett, *Towards a Post-critical Christological Hermeneutic: An Analysis of the Hermeneutics of Raymond E. Brown* (Ph.D. diss.; Fort Worth, TX: Southwestern Baptist Theological Seminary, 1989); K. Duffy, *The Centrism of Raymond Brown: Historical Criticism in Catholic Christianity* (Ph.D. diss.; University of London [Heythrop], 1990);

and V. Costa, *História e Fé na Comunidade Joanina segundo Raymond E. Brown* (S.T.D. diss.; Rome: Gregorian, 1991).

Although his scholarship was wide ranging, Brown's most significant lasting contribution to biblical scholarship is doubtless in the area of Johannine studies. He devoted his entire career to the Johannine literature, beginning with the publication of his magisterial two-volume commentary on the Gospel of John (1966, 1970) and the subsequent publication of *The Community of the Beloved Disciple* (1979) and *The Epistles of John* (1983). His last publication, *An Introduction to the Gospel of John* (2003), had been intended to be the introduction to a major revision of his famous Anchor Bible commentary, but he did not live to see the project fulfilled. Nonetheless, it remains a valuable contribution to the field and provides a final statement of Brown's position on the Fourth Gospel and how his thought had grown over the years.

Among Brown's other major works were two encyclopedic commentaries on the Infancy Narratives of the Gospels (*The Birth of the Messiah*, 1977, rev. ed. 1993) and on the Passion Narratives (*The Death of the Messiah*, 2 vols., 1994), and a widely respected *Introduction to the New Testament* (1997).

The bibliography that follows is divided into four sections: A, Books and Monographs; B, Articles; C, Reviews; and D, Audio Tapes. Since many of the articles have been gathered into books, the bibliography is completely cross-indexed by section and entry number. Many of Brown's books, large and small, have been translated into multiple languages, most recently Chinese, Russian, and Czech. Since more translations will be appearing in the years ahead, this bibliography should be considered a "work in progress."

Notes

1. Transcript of oral interview for "Oral History of the Catholic Biblical Association," conducted by John Endres (December 3, 1996) 1; Sulpician Archives, Baltimore, MD.

2. Transcript of "Oral History of the Catholic Biblical Association," 15.

A Bibliography of the Publications
of Raymond E. Brown, s.s.*

Prepared by Michael L. Barré, s.s.

A. Books and Monographs

1949

(1) "A Scholastic Investigation of the Space-Time Continuum of Relativity" (M.A. [Philosophy] Diss.; The Catholic University of America, 1949), ii + 69 pp.

1953

(2) "The *Sensus Plenior* of Sacred Scripture" (S.T.L. Diss.; St. Mary's Seminary and & University, 1953), ii + 90 pp.

1955

(3) *The Sensus Plenior of Sacred Scripture* (S.T.D. Diss.; St. Mary's Seminary and & University, 1955 [printed by Furst]), xiv + 161. Reprinted by photo-offset (Ann Arbor, MI: Edwards, ca. 1960).

1958

(4) "The Semitic Background of the Pauline *Mystērion*"" (Ph.D. Diss.; The Johns Hopkins University, 1958), iii + 243 pp. Digested in ##A12, B11, 12.

1960

(5) *The Gospel of John and the Johannine Epistles.* New Testament Reading Guide 13 (Collegeville: Liturgical Press, 1960), 128 pp. Revised 2d ed., 1965. Further revised 3d ed., 1982. Replaced in 1988 by #A33. *Translations:* Spanish: *Evangelio y Epistolas de S. Juan* (Santander: Sal Terrae, 1966).

---

* Abbreviations for journals, series, and major reference works follow those listed in Patrick H. Alexander et al., eds., *The SBL Handbook of Style: For Ancient Near Eastern, Biblical, and Early Christian Studies* (Peabody, MA: Hendrickson, 1999) 89–121. These abbreviations are used in *The Catholic Biblical Quarterly* and *The Journal of Biblical Literature.*

1962

(6) *The Book of Daniel.* Pamphlet Bible Series 34 (New York: Paulist, 1962), 80 pp.

1963

(7) *The Parables of the Gospels.* Doctrinal Pamphlet Series (New York: Paulist, 1963), 31 pp.

1965

(8) *New Testament Essays* (Milwaukee: Bruce, 1965), xvi + 280 pp. British ed. (London: Chapman, 1966). Reprinted with new pagination and some revision (Garden City, NY: Doubleday, 1968). Reprinted by photo-offset from the Bruce edition with minor revisions (New York: Paulist, 1982).

(9) *The Book of Deuteronomy.* Old Testament Reading Guide 10 (Collegeville: Liturgical Press, 1965), 126 pp.

1966

(10) *The Gospel According to John (i-xii).* AB 29 (Garden City, NY: Doubleday, 1966), cxlvi + 538 pp. For vol. 2, see #A16. Section of the Introduction reprinted in H. K. McArthur, ed., *In Search of the Historical Jesus* (New York: Scribners, 1969) 103–107. British ed. 2 vols. (London: Chapman, 1971). *Translations:* Italian: *Giovanni: Commento al Vangelo spirituale.* 2 vols. (Assisi: Cittadella, 1979); Spanish: *El Evangelio según Juan.* 2 vols. (Madrid: Cristiandad, 1979; 2d ed. 2000).

1967

(11) *Jesus God and Man: Modern Biblical Reflections* (Milwaukee: Bruce, 1967), xiv +109 pp. Reproduces ##B46 and 61 (enlarged). Reprinted in paperback (New York: Macmillan, 1972). British ed. (London: Chapman, 1967). *Translations:* Dutch: *Jesus God en Mens*, with foreword by Piet Schoonenberg (Antwerp: Patmos, 1970); Italian: *Gesù Dio e Uomo* (Assisi: Cittadella, 1970); Spanish: *Jesus, Dios y Hombre* (Santander: Sal Terrae, 1973).

1968

(12) *The Semitic Background of the Term "Mystery" in the New Testament.* FBBS 21 (Philadelphia: Fortress, 1968), vii + 72 pp. Reprints ##B12 and 11, which are abridgements of #A4.

(13) *The Jerome Biblical Commentary (JBC),* ed. Raymond E. Brown, Joseph A. Fitzmyer, and Roland E. Murphy. 2 vols. in one (Englewood Cliffs, NJ: Prentice-Hall, 1968), xxxvi + 637 + 835 pp. Brown edited the General Articles (nos. 40, 41, 46, 47, and 66 through 80). See #A35. British ed. (London: Chapman, 1969). *Translations:* Spanish: *Comentario Bíblico "San Jeronimo."* 5 vols. (Madrid: Cristiandad, 1971–72); Italian: *Grande Commentario Biblico Queriniana* (Brescia: Queriniana, 1973).

(14) *Exégèse et Théologie: Les Saintes Écritures et leur interprétation théologique: Donum natalicium Iosepho Coppens septuagesimum annum complenti D.D.D. collegae et amici,* ed. Gustave Thils and Raymond E. Brown. BETL 26 (Gembloux: Duculot, 1968), x + 327 pp. From the 17th Journées Bibliques of Louvain, September 1966. Pp. 72–81 reprint #B64.

1969

(15) *Biblical Tendencies Today: An Introduction to the Post-Bultmannians,* with P. J. Cahill (Washington: Corpus, 1969), vii + 72 pp. Pp. 1–39 reprint (with editing) #B36.

1970

(16) *The Gospel According to John (xiii-xxi).* AB 29A (Garden City, NY: Doubleday, 1970), xvi + 539–1208. For British ed. and translations, see #A10.

(17) *Priest and Bishop: Biblical Reflections* (New York: Paulist, 1970), 86 pp. The first section was reprinted in various papers and popular magazines for priests. Reprint, Eugene, OR: Wipf & Stock, 1998. *Translations:* Italian: *Il Prete e il Vescovo: Riflessioni bibliche* (Fossano: Esperienze, 1971); Portuguese: *Sacerdote e Bispo: Reflexões Bíblicas* (São Paulo: Loyola, 1987).

1973

(18) *The Virginal Conception and Bodily Resurrection of Jesus* (New York: Paulist, 1973), viii + 136 pp. Reprints #B82. British ed. (London: Chapman, 1973). *Translations:* Dutch: *Jezus de Christus: Geboren uit een vrouw, Opgestaan uit de dood* (Boxtel: Katholieke Bijbelstichting, 1975); Italian: *La concezione verginale et la risurrezione corporea di Gesù.* Giornale di Teologia 99 (Brescia: Queriniana, 1977; 2d ed. [reprint], 1992); Portuguese: *A Concepção Virginal e A Ressurreição Corporal de Jesus* (São Paulo: Loyola, 1987).

(19) *Peter in the New Testament: A Collaborative Assessment by Protestant and Roman Catholic Scholars,* ed. Raymond E. Brown, Karl P. Donfried, and John Reumann (New York: Paulist, 1973), x + 181 pp. British ed. (London: Chapman, 1974). *Translations:* French: *Saint Pierre dans le Nouveau Testament.* LD 79 (Paris: Cerf, 1974); German: *Der Petrus der Bibel: Eine ökumenische Untersuchung* (Stuttgart: Calwer Verlag and/Katholisches Bibelwerk, 1976); Spanish: *Pedro en el Nuevo Testamento.* Palabra Inspirada 15 (Santander: Sal Terrae, 1976); Dutch: *Petrus in het Geloof van de jonge Kerk* (Boxtel: Katholieke Bijbelstichting, 1976); Japanese (Seibunsha, 1977); Italian: *Pietro nel Nuovo Testamento* (Rome: Borla, 1988).

1975

(20) *Biblical Reflections on Crises Facing the Church* (New York: Paulist, 1975), x + 118 pp. British ed. (London: Darton, Longman & Todd, 1976). *Translations:* Dutch: *Kerk waarheen nu? Bijbelse kanttekeningen bij hedendaagse crises en de Kerk* (Boxtel: Kathlieke Bijbelstichting, 1976); Portuguese: *Crises na Igreja? Reflexões Bíblicas* (São Paulo: Loyola, 1987).

1977

(21) *The Birth of the Messiah* (Garden City, NY: Doubleday, 1977), 594 pp. See #A39. British ed. (London: Chapman, 1978). *Translations:* Italian: *La nascità del Messia secondo Matteo e Luca* (Assisi: Cittadella, 1981); Spanish: *El nacimiento del Mesías* (Madrid: Cristiandad, 1982).

1978

(22) *Mary in the New Testament: A Collaborative Assessment by Protestant and Roman Catholic Scholars,* ed. Raymond E. Brown, Karl P. Donfried, Joseph A. Fitzmyer, and John Reumann (New York: Paulist, 1978), xii + 323 pp. British ed. (London: Chapman, 1979). *Translations:* German: *Maria im Neuen Testament: Eine ökumenische Untersuchung* (Stuttgart: Katholisches Bibelwerk, 1981); Spanish: *María en el Nuevo Testamento* (Salamanca: Sigueme, 1982); Italian: *Maria nel Nuovo Testamento* (Assisi: Cittadella, 1985).

(23) *An Adult Christ at Christmas: Essays on the Three Biblical Christmas Stories— Matt 2 and Luke 2* (Collegeville: Liturgical Press, 1978), viii + 50 pp. Unifies ##B99, 105, 106, 108. *Translations:* Spanish: in article form in *Biblia y Vida* (Yucatan) 44 (December 1980) 25–31; 45 (January 1981) 10–14; 46 (February 1981) 7–14; 56 (December 1981) 21–28; unofficial publication: Universidad Iberoamericana, 1990; official publication: *Un Cristo adulto en Navidad* (Buenos Aires: San Pablo, 1994); Italian: *Racconti biblici natalizi.* Meditazioni 79 (Brescia: Queriniana, 1988; 2d ed. [reprint], 1992); Portuguese: *Um Cristo Adulto no Natal* (São Paulo: Loyola, 1990); Chinese (Hong Kong: Catholic Truth Society, 1994); Catalan: *Un Crist adult per Nadal* (Barcelona: Claret, 1994); Korean (Seoul: St. Paul's, 1995); Japanese (Tokyo: Joshi-Pauro-Kai [Paoline], 1996); German: *Der Messias in der Krippe: Versuche über die drei biblischen Weihnachtsgeschichten* (Würzburg: Echter Verlag, 1997).

1979

(24) *The Community of the Beloved Disciple* (New York: Paulist, 1979), 204 pp. British ed. (London: Chapman, 1979). Philippine ed. (Manila: St Paul's, 1996). *Translations:* German (abridged): *Ringen um die Gemeinde* (Salzburg: Müller, 1982); Italian: *La comunità del discepolo prediletto* (Assisi: Cittadella, 1982); Spanish: *La comunidad del discípulo amado* (Salamanca: Sigueme, 1983; 2d ed., 1987; 3d ed., 1991; 4th ed., 1996); French: *La communauté du disciple bien-aimé.* LD 115; (Paris: Cerf, 1983; reprint 2002); Portuguese: *A comunidade do Discípulo Amado.* Nova Coleção Bíblica 17 (São Paulo: Paulus, 1984; 2d ed. 1992; 4th ed. 1999).

1981

(25) *The Critical Meaning of the Bible* (New York: Paulist, 1981), x + 150 pp. Adapts and reuses ##B103, 111, 116, 119, 123, 124, 125. British ed. (London: Chapman, 1982). *Translations:* Portuguese: *O Significado Crítico da Bíblia* (São Paulo: Loyola, 1987); Korean of Chapter Six ("An Example: Rethinking the Priesthood Biblically for All," pp. 96–106): *Mee Joo Catholic Digest* 11-12 (November/December 1991) (reprinted in *Lumen Gentium* [1993], 57–71); French: *Croire en la Bible à l'Heure de l'Exégèse* (Paris: Cerf, 2002).

1982

(26) *The Epistles of John.* AB 30 (Garden City, NY: Doubleday, 1982), xxvii + 812 pp. British ed. (London: Chapman, 1983). *Translations:* Italian: *Le Lettere di Giovanni* (Assisi: Cittadella, 1986).

1983

(27) *Antioch and Rome: New Testament Cradles of Catholic Christianity,* with John P. Meier (New York: Paulist, 1983), xii + 242 pp. British ed. (London: Chapman, 1983). *Translations:* Italian: *Antiochia e Roma* (Assisi: Cittadella, 1987); French: *Antioche et Rome: Berceaux du christianisme.* LD 131 (Paris: Cerf, 1988).

(28) *Recent Discoveries and the Biblical World* (Wilmington: Michael Glazier, 1983). Reprint, Eugene, OR: Wipf & Stock, 2003), 101 pp. Revision of #B129. 2d (corrected) printing, 1985. Philippine ed. (Manila: St. Paul's, 1994). *Translations:* Portuguese: *As recentes descobertas e o mundo bíblico* (São Paulo: Loyola, 1986).

1984

(29) *The Churches the Apostles Left Behind* (New York: Paulist, 1984), 156 pp. The Sprunt Lectures of January 1980 (Union Theological Seminary, Richmond). Chapter 8 abridged in *God's Word Today* 7 (January 1985): 40–45. British ed. (London: Chapman, 1984). Philippine ed. (Manila: St. Paul's, 1994). *Translations:* Portuguese: *As Igrejas dos Apóstolos* (São Paulo: Paulinas, 1986); French: *L'Église héritée des apôtres.* Lire la Bible 76 (Paris: Cerf, 1987); Italian: *Le Chiese degli Apostoli: Indagine esegetica sulle origini dell'ecclesiologia* (Casale Monferrato: Piemme, 1992); Dutch: *Kerkvormen in het spoor van de apostelen* ('s-Hertogenbosch: Katholieke Bijbelstichting, 1993); Indonesian (Jakarta: Penerbit Kanisius, 1997); Japanese (Yotsuya Tokyo: Don Bosco [Salesian], 1998).

1985

(30) *Biblical Exegesis and Church Doctrine* (New York: Paulist, 1985), 171 pp. Adapts and reuses ##B126, 128, 130, 131, 132, 140, 143, 145, 146. British ed. (London: Chapman, 1985). Reprint Eugene, OR: Wipf & Stock, 2002.

1986

(31) *A Crucified Christ in Holy Week: Essays on the Four Gospel Passion Narratives* (Collegeville: Liturgical Press, 1986), 71 pp. Reuses ##B96, 137, 138, 142, 148. *Translations:* Italian: *La Passione nei Vangeli.* Meditazioni 72 (Brescia: Queriniana, 1988); Spanish: *Cristo Crucificado* (Mexico City: Universidad Iberoamericana, 1989); Chinese (Hong Kong: Catholic Truth Society, 1992); Catalan: *Un Crist crucificat en la Setmana Santa* (Barcelona: Claret, 1994); *Un Cristo Crucificado en Semana Santa* (Buenos Aires: San Pablo, 1995); Portuguese: *Um Cristo crucificado na Semana Santa* (São Paulo: Ave Maria, 1996); Japanese (Tokyo: Joshi-Pauro-Kai [Paoline], 1997).

(32) *A Wise and Discerning Heart: Studies Presented to Joseph A. Fitzmyer, s.j. in Celebration of His 65th Birthday,* ed. Raymond E. Brown and Alexander A. Di Lella (Washington: Catholic Biblical Association, 1986) = *CBQ* 48/3 (July 1986).

1988

(33) *The Gospel and Epistles of John: A Concise Commentary* (Collegeville: Liturgical Press, 1988), 136 pp. A major rewriting of #A5, using the Revised NAB as basic text. Indian ed. (Bombay: St. Paul, 1993). Philippine ed. (Manila: St. Paul's, 1994). *Translations:* Italian: *Il Vangelo e le Lettere di Giovanni.* Biblioteca Biblica 14 (Brescia: Queriniana, 1994).

(34) *A Coming Christ in Advent: Essays on the Gospel Narratives Preparing for the Birth of Jesus—Matt 1 and Luke 1* (Collegeville: Liturgical Press, 1988), 71 pp. Unifies ##B151, 152, 155, 158, 159. *Translations:* Italian: *Avvento: il Cristo che viene.* Meditazioni 83 (Brescia: Queriniana, 1989); Chinese (Hong Kong: Catholic Truth Society, 1994); Spanish: *Cristo llega en Adviento* (Buenos Aires: San Pablo, 1994); Catalan: *Un Crist que ve (arriba) en l'Advent* (Barcelona: Claret, 1994); Japanese (Tokyo: Joshi-Pauro-Kai [Paoline], 1996); German: *Der kommende Christus: Eine Auslegung der Evangelien im Advent* (Würzburg: Echter Verlag, 1997); Slovak: *Kristus v Advent* (Trnava: Dobrá kniha, 2000).

1989

(35) *The New Jerome Biblical Commentary* (*NJBC*), ed. Raymond E. Brown, Joseph A. Fitzmyer, and Roland E. Murphy (Englewood Cliffs, NJ: Prentice-Hall, 1990), xlviii + 1475. Brown edited the General Articles (40, 45, 65-83). For the *JBC* (1968) see #A13. British ed. (London: Chapman, 1990). Indian ed. (Bangalore: Theological Publications, 1990). Student (paperback) ed. (London: Chapman, 1993). *Translations:* Italian: *Nuovo Grande Commentario Biblico* (Brescia: Queriniana, 1997).

1990

(36) *Responses to 101 Questions on the Bible* (New York: Paulist, 1990), 147 pp. British ed. (London: Chapman, 1990). Indian ed. (Bombay: St. Paul, 1991; 2d ed. 1993). Philippine ed. (Quezon City: Claretian, 1993). *Translations:* Italian: *Risposte a 101 domande sulla Bibbia* (Brescia: Queriniana, 1991); French: *101 Questions sur la Bible.* Lire la Bible 98 (Paris: Cerf, 1993); Chinese (Hong Kong: Catholic Truth Society, 1993; 2d ed., 2001); Portuguese: *101 perguntas sobre a Bíblia* (Lisbon: Circulo de Leitores, 1994); Malayalam (Kerala) (Ernakulam: St. Paul's, 1994); Japanese (Tokyo: Joshi-Pauro-Kai, 1995); Spanish: *101 preguntas y respuestas sobre la Biblia.* Nueva alianza 138 (Salamanca: Sigueme, 1996; 2d printing, 1997); Slovak: *Biblia 101 otázok a odpovedí* (Trnava: Dobrá kniha, 1999).

1991

(37) *A Risen Christ in Eastertime: Essays on the Gospel Narratives of the Resurrection* (Collegeville: Liturgical Press, 1991), 95 pp. Unifies ##B176, 179, 181. *Translations:* Italian: *I racconti evangelici della Risurrezione.* Meditazioni 100 (Brescia: Queriniana, 1992); Catalan: *Un Crist ressuscitat en temps de Pasqua* (Barcelona: Claret, 1994); Chinese (Hong Kong: Catholic Truth Society, 1994); Spanish: *Un Cristo Resucitado en Tiempo Pascual* (Buenos Aires: San Pablo, 1995); Korean (Seoul: St Paul's, 1996); Portuguese: *Um Cristo Ressuscitado na Páscoa* (São Paulo, Brazil: Ave Maria, 1996); Japanese (Tokyo: Joshi-Pauro-Kai [Paoline], 1997).

1992

(38) *The New Jerome Bible Handbook*, ed. Raymond E. Brown, Joseph A. Fitzmyer, and Roland E. Murphy (London: Chapman, 1992), 456 pp. American ed. (Collegeville: Liturgical Press, 1992).

1993

(39) *The Birth of the Messiah: New Updated Edition*. ABRL (New York: Doubleday, 1993), 752 pp. See #A21. British ed. (London: Chapman, 1993). *Translations:* Italian: *La nascità del Messia secondo Matteo e Luca* (Assisi: Cittadella, 2002).

1994

(40) *The Death of the Messiah: From Gethsemane to the Grave: A Commentary on the Passion Narratives of the Four Gospels*. 2 vols. ABRL (New York: Doubleday, 1994), xxvii + 1608 pp. British ed. (London: Chapman, 1994). *Translations:* Italian: *La Morte del Messia: dal Getsemani al sepolcro, un commentario ai raconti della passione nei quattro vangeli*. BTC 108 (Brescia: Queriniana, 1999).

(41) *A Once-and-Coming Spirit at Pentecost: Essays on the Liturgical Readings between Easter and Pentecost, Taken from the Acts of the Apostles and from the Gospel according to John* (Collegeville: Liturgical Press, 1994), iii + 98 pp. *Translations:* Catalan: *Un esperit que ha vingut i que ve en la Pentecosta* (Barcelona: Claret, 1994); Italian: *Azione e promessa dello Spirito a Pentecoste*. Meditazioni 114 (Brescia: Queriniana, 1995); Spanish: *El Espíritu que viene en Pentecostés* (Buenos Aires: San Pablo, 1995); Japanese (Tokyo: Joshi-Pauro-Kai [Paoline], 1997); Slovak: *Duch Svätý Na Turíce* (Trnava: Dobrá kniha, 2001).

(42) *An Introduction to New Testament Christology* (New York: Paulist, 1994), xii + 226 pp. Philippine ed. (Manila: St. Paul's, 1996). *Translations:* Italian: *Introduzione alla cristologia del Nuovo Testamento* (Brescia: Queriniana, 1995); French: *Jésus dans les quatre évangiles: Introduction à la christologie du Nouveau Testament.* (Lire la Bible 111; (Paris: Cerf, 1996); Catalan: *Jésus en el Nou Testament* (Barcelona: Claret, 1997); Czech: *Ješíš v Pohledu Nového Zákona úvod do Christologie* (Prague: Vyšehrad, 1998); Korean (Weagwan, Korea: Benedict Press, 1999).

1996

(43) *Reading the Gospels with the Church: From Christmas Through Easter* (Cincinnati: St. Anthony Messenger, 1996), 90 pp. Collected and reshaped from issues of *Catholic Update* plus added material. Indian ed. (Bandra: St. Paul, 1998). *Translations:* Italian: *Leggere i vangeli con la chiesa: Da Natale a Pasqua* (Brescia: Queriniana, 1997); Russian (Moscow: Bibleysko-Bogoslovskiy Institut, 2002); French: *Lire les Évangiles avec L'Église de Noël à Pâques* (Paris: Cerf, 2004).

1997

(44) *An Introduction to the New Testament* (New York: Doubleday, 1997), xlvi + 878 pp. *Translations:* French: *Que sait-on du Nouveau Testament?* ed. Pierre Debergé; (Paris: Bayard, 2000) (with additional bibliographies of commentaries and studies in

French); Italian: *Introduzione al Nuovo Testamento* (Brescia: Queriniana, 2001); Spanish: *Introducción al Nuevo Testamento.* (2 vols.; Biblioteca de Ciencias Biblical y Orientales; (Madrid: Trotta, 2002).

1998

(45) *A Retreat with John the Evangelist: That You May Have Life* (Cincinnati: St. Anthony Messenger, 1998), 102 pp. Indian ed. (Malleswaram, Bangelore: Claretian Publications, 2001). *Translations:* Spanish: *Para que tengáis vida: A solas con Juan Evangelista* (Santander: Sal Terrae, 2002); French: *Une retraite avec Saint Jean: "Pour que vous ayez la vie"* (Paris: Cerf, 2004).

(46) *Christ in the Gospels of the Ordinary Sundays: Essays on the Gospel Readings of the Ordinary Sundays in the Three-Year Liturgical Cycle* (Collegeville: Liturgical Press, 1998), viii + 110 pp. *Translations:* Italian: *Cristo nei Vangeli Domenicali del Tempo Ordinario* (Brescia: Queriniana, 2000).

2003

(47) *An Introduction to the Gospel of John,* edited and revised by Francis J. Moloney. ABRL (New York: Doubleday, 2003), xxvi + 356 pp. Moloney's edition and revision, with updated bibliography, of Brown's new introduction to the Gospel of John, which was to be part of a complete revision of his John commentary. Foreword by Ronald D. Witherup, s.s.

B. Articles

1953

(1) "The Spirit and the Letter," *The Voice of St. Mary's Seminary* 30 (February 1953) 14–15, 27–30.

(2) "The History and Development of the Theory of a *Sensus Plenior,*" *CBQ* 15 (1953) 141–62.

1955

(3) "Ancient Treasures [the Dead Sea Scrolls]," lecture digested by J. A. Horn, *The Voice of St. Mary's Seminary* 32 (March 1955) 14–15, 26.

(4) "St. John the Baptist," *The Voice of St. Mary's Seminary* 33 (November 1955) 8–9, 25–26.

(5) "Communications to the Editor: Père Lagrange and the *Sensus Plenior,*" *CBQ* 17 (1955) 451–55.

(6) "The Qumran Scrolls and the Johannine Gospels and Epistles," *CBQ* 17 (1955) 403–19, 559–74. Reprinted in shortened form in Krister Stendahl, ed., *The Scrolls and the New Testament* (New York: Harper, 1957) 183–207, 282–91; also in M. J. Taylor,

ed., *A Companion to John: Readings in Johannine Theology (John's Gospel and Epistles* (New York: Alba House, 1977) 69–90; and in #A8 (Bruce ed. pp. 102–31). *Translations:* German: in K. H. Rengstorf, ed., *Johannes und sein Evangelium.* WdF 82 (Darmstadt: Wissenschaftliche Buchgesellschaft, 1973) 486–528.

1956

(7) "Communications to the Editor: Counterreply," *CBQ* 18 (1956) 47–53. A reply to J. P. Weisengoff, "Communications to the Editor: Père Lagrange and the *Sensus Plenior,*" ibid. 47–49.

(8) "Priest and King: The Qumran Concept of Messiah," *The Voice of St. Mary's Seminary* 34 (December 1956) 8–9, 22.

1957

(9) "The Messianism of Qumran," *CBQ* 19 (1957) 53–82.

1958

(10) "A Valuable Gift—The Father Edward Arbez Scripture Library," *The Voice of St. Mary's Seminary* 35 (February 1958) 8–9, 30.

(11) "The Pre-Christian Semitic Concept of 'Mystery,'" *CBQ* 20 (1958) 417–43. Reprinted in #A12.

(12) "The Semitic Background of the New Testament *Mystērion,*" *Bib* 39 (1958) 426–48; 40 (1959) 70–87. Reprinted in #A12.

1959

(13) "Discoveries in the Judaean Desert," *The Voice of St. Mary's Seminary* 36 (February 1959) 7–9, 29–30.

1960

(14) "The Date of the Last Supper," *The Voice of St. Mary's Seminary* 37 (February 1960) 6–7, 24–25. Reprinted in #A12 (U.S. ed. pp. 160–67). See #B38. *Translations:* Italian: "L'ultima Cena avvenne di martedi?" *BeO* 2 (1960) 48–53.

(15) "Three Quotations from John the Baptist in the Gospel of John," *CBQ* 22 (1960) 292–98. Reprinted in #A8 (U.S. ed., pp. 132–40).

(16) "The Bible and Unity," *The Harvester* 23 (Autumn 1960) [Kenmore, Wash.: St. Thomas Seminary] 8–10, 21.

1961

(17) "The Beatitudes according to St. Luke," *The Voice of St. Mary's Seminary* 38 (February 1961) 8–9, 25–27. Reprinted in *TBT* 18 (1965) 1176–80; also in *The Bible Today Reader: Selected Articles from the First Ten Years of The Bible Today* (Collegeville: Liturgical Press, 1973) 302–306, and in #A8 (U.S. ed. pp. 265–71). *Translations:* Italian: "Le 'beatitudini' secondo San Luca," *BeO* 7 (1965) 3–8.

(18) "Incidents that are Units in the Synoptic Gospels but Dispersed in St. John," *CBQ* 23 (1961) 143–60. Reprinted in #A8 (U.S. ed. pp. 192–213).

(19) "The Pater Noster as an Eschatological Prayer," *TS* 22 (1961) 175–208. Reprinted in #A8 (U.S. ed., pp. 217–53). Abridged in *TD* 10 (Winter 1962) 3–10. *Translations:* Spanish (abridged): "Sentido escatológico del Padrenuestro," *Selecciones de teología* 1 (July/September 1962) 54–62.

(20) "What Do the Scrolls Tell Us?" *America* 106 (October 7, 1961) 10–13. *Translations:* Spanish (abridged): "La voz de los documentos de Qumrán," *Selecciones de teología* 1 (February 1962) 37–39.

1962

(21) "The Problem of Historicity in John," *CBQ* 24 (1962) 1–14. Reprinted in #A8 (U.S. ed., pp. 143–60).

(22) "Parable and Allegory Reconsidered," *NovT* 5 (1962) 36–45. Reprinted in #A8 (U.S. ed., pp. 254–64).

(23) "The Johannine Sacramentary Reconsidered," *TS* 23 (1962) 183–206. Reprinted in #A8 (U.S. ed., pp. 51–76).

(24) "The Eucharist and Baptism in St. John," *Proceedings of the Catholic College Teachers of Sacred Doctrine* 8 (1962) 14–23. Reprinted in #A8 (U.S. ed., pp. 77–95).

(25) "The Gospel Miracles," in John L. McKenzie, ed., *The Bible in Current Catholic Thought: Published in Honor of Michael J. Gruenthaner* (New York: Herder & Herder, 1962) 184–201. Reprinted as a pamphlet at the Second Trinity College Biblical Institute (Burlington, VT, 1967). Also in #A8 (U.S. ed., pp. 168–91).

(26) "Our New Approach to the Bible," *Guide* 171 (October 1962) 3–10. Also in *Proceedings of the First Annual Midwestern Institute of Pastoral Theology* (Detroit: Sacred Heart Seminary, 1962) 13–24. Reprinted in #A8 (U.S. ed., pp. 3–16). *Translations:* Italian: "Come ci accostiamo oggi alla Bibbia," *BeO* 5 (1963) 161–69.

(27) "The Challenge in Using the Bible in Our Teaching," *Proceedings of the Catholic College Teachers of Sacred Doctrine* 8 (1962) 25–36.

(28) "The Message in Christmas," *Miami Herald* (December 16, 1962) front page.

(29) Reply to editorial, "A notable record," *ChrCent* 79 (January 24, 1962) 99–100; (April 11, 1962) 462–63.

1963

(30) "The Gospel of Thomas and St. John's Gospel," *NTS* 9 (1962–63) 155–77.

(31) "The *Sensus Plenior* in the Last Ten Years," *CBQ* 25 (1963) 262–85.

(32) "The Old Testament Covenant and Its New Testament Ramifications," *Franciscan Around the Province* (May 1963). Summarized lecture given at St. Joseph Seminary, Teutopolis, IL.

(33) "The Unity and Diversity in New Testament Ecclesiology," *NovT* 6 (1963) 298–308. A paper given at the World Council of Churches Faith and Order Plenary

Meeting in Montreal, 1963. Reprinted in #A8 (U.S. ed., pp. 36–47). Abridged in *TD* 13 (Autumn 1965) 231–33. *Translations:* German: "Einheit und Verschiedenheit in der neutestamentlichen Ekklesiologie," *Ökumenische Rundschau* 13 (1964) 63–73; Danish: "Enhet og mangfold i det NTes ekklesiologie," *Lumen* 7 (1964) 73–82.

(34) "The Theology of the Incarnation in John," *TBT* 9 (1963) 586–89. Reprinted in M. Rosalie Ryan, ed., *Contemporary New Testament Studies* (Collegeville: Liturgical Press, 1965) 292–95. Also in #A8 (U.S. ed., pp. 96–101).

(35) "Père Lagrange and the Fourth Gospel," unrevised and unsupervised printing from an audio tape in R. T. A. Murphy, ed., *Lagrange Lectures 1963* (Dubuque, IA: Aquinas Institute, 1963) 42–69.

1964

(36) "After Bultmann, What? An Introduction to the Post-Bultmannians," *CBQ* 26 (1964) 1–30. Reprinted in #A15. Abridged as "Bultmann and the Post-Bultmannians," *TBT* 14 (1964) 905–10.

(37) "Our New Translations of the Bible," *America* 111 (November 14, 1964) 601–604. Interview by the National Catholic News Service on the new epistle and gospel translations for the liturgy (November 1964).

(38) "The Date of the Last Supper," *TBT* 11 (1964) 727–33; English form of the Italian in #B14. Reprinted in *The Bible Today Reader: Selected Articles from the First Ten Years of The Bible Today* (Collegeville: Liturgical Press, 1973) 322–28. Also in #A8 (U.S. ed., pp. 160–67).

(39) "Ecumenism and New Testament Research," *JES* 1 (1964) 299–314. Reprinted in #A8 (U.S. ed., pp. 17–35).

1965

(40) "Rudolf Bultmann and His Biblical Studies," *The Catholic Mind* 63 (February 1965) 42–47.

(41) "The Fourth Gospel in Modern Research," *TBT* 20 (1965) 1302–10.

(42) "Daniel, Book of," in *The Catholic Encyclopedia for School and Home*. 12 vols. (New York: McGraw-Hill, 1965) 3:387–90.

(43) "John, St., Epistles of," ibid. 6:13–15.

(44) "John, St., Gospel of," ibid. 6:15–19.

(45) "Mystery," ibid. 7:399–400.

(46) "Does the New Testament Call Jesus God?" *TS* 26 (1965) 545–73. Reprinted in #A11.

1966

(47) "J. Starcky's Theory of Qumran Messianic Development," *CBQ* 28 (1966) 51–57.

(48) "Third International Congress on New Testament Studies (1965)," *CBQ* 28 (1966) 58–60.

(49) "Recent Roman Catholic Translations of the Bible," *McCQ* 19 (May 1966) 1–10.

(50) "We Profess One Baptism for the Forgiveness of Sins," *Worship* 40 (May 1966) 260–71. Reprinted in P. C. Empie and W. W. Baum, eds., *Lutherans and Catholics in Dialogue, II: One Baptism for the Remission of Sins* (New York: U.S.A. National Committee; Lutheran World Federation, 1966) 9–21. Also available in P. C. Empie and T. Austin Murphy, eds., *Lutherans and Catholics in Dialogue, I≠III* (Minneapolis: Augsburg, 1974) 9–21.

(51) "The Emmaus Story," *Witness* 2 (April 3, 1966) 6–7.

(52) "The Dead Sea Scrolls and the New Testament" [Second Thoughts series, no. 10], *ExpTim* 78 (1966–67) 19–23. Reprinted in James H. Charlesworth, ed., *John and Qumran* (London: Chapman, 1972) 1–8 (reprinted as *John and the Dead Sea Scrolls. Christian Origins Library* [New York: Crossroad, 1990]).

1967

(53) "Allegory in the Bible," in *The New Catholic Encyclopedia.* (New York: McGraw-Hill, 1967–96) 1:321.

(54) "Essenes," ibid. 5:552–53.

(55) "John, Apostle, St.," ibid. 7:1005–1006.

(56) "John, Epistles of St.," ibid. 7:1078–80. See #B162.

(57) "John, Gospel According to St.," ibid. 7:1080–88. See #B162.

(58) "Mystery (in the Bible)," ibid. 10:148–51.

(59) "Parables of Jesus," ibid. 10. 984–88.

(60) "The Paraclete in the Fourth Gospel," *NTS* 13 (1966–67) 113–32. Abridged by J. Mary Hurley, *TBT* 36 (April 1968) 2485–88. Abridged in *TD* 16 (1968) 244–50. *Translations:* Spanish (abridged): "El 'Paráclito' en el cuarto Evangélio," *Selecciones de Teología* 24 (October/December 1967) 299–307.

(61) "How Much Did Jesus Know? A Survey of the Biblical Evidence," *CBQ* 29 (1967) 315–45. Enlarged in #A11. Abridged in *TD* 17 (1969) 44–50. *Translations:* Italian (abridged): "L'ambito della conoscenza di Gesù: Indagine sul dato biblico," *Rassegna di Teologia* 11 (1970) 269–81.

(62) "The Kerygma of the Gospel According to John: The Johannine View of Jesus in Modern Studies," *Int* 21 (1967) 387–400. Reprinted in R. A. Batey, ed., *New Testament Issues.* Harper Forum Books (New York: Harper & Row, 1970) 210–25.

(63) "The Resurrection and Biblical Criticism," *Commonweal* 87 (November 24, 1967) 232–36. *Translations:* Hungarian: "A feltamadás és bibliokritika," *Mérleg* 4 (1968) 138–50.

(64) "The Problems of the *Sensus Plenior*," *ETL* 43 (1967) 460–69. Reprinted in #B14, pp. 72–81. *Translations:* Spanish (*Lumen* 17 [1968] 82–90).

1968

(65) "The Paraclete in the Light of Modern Research," in F. L. Cross, ed., *Studia Evangelica IV: Papers Presented to the Third International Congress on New Testament Studies, Oxford, 1965.* 2 vols. TUGAL 102 (Berlin: Akademie Verlag, 1968) 1:158–65.

(66) "The Literary Forms of Scripture," *The Catechist* 1 (May 1968) 8–10.

(67) "The Bible and Authority in Contemporary Roman Catholicism" (typed, unpublished address delivered at Perkins School of Theology, Southern Methodist University, Dallas [October 9, 1968]).

(68) "Apocrypha; Dead Sea Scrolls; Other Literature," *JBC*, article 68, 2:535–60.

(69) "Miracles, Parables, Resurrection, Twelve and Apostles," *JBC*, last part of article 78 ("Aspects of New Testament Thought") 2:784–99.

(70) "Biblical Geography," with Robert North, *JBC*, article 73, 2:633–52.

(71) "Canonicity," with James Turro, *JBC*, article 67, 2:513–34.

(72) "Church Pronouncements," with Thomas A. Collins, *JBC*, article 72, 2.:624–32.

(73) "Hermeneutics," *JBC*, article 71, 2:605–23.

(74) "Texts and Versions," with Patrick W. Skehan and George W. MacRae, *JBC*, article 69, 2:580–89.

1969

(75) "Rome and the Freedom of Catholic Biblical Studies," in J. M. Myers et al., eds., *Search the Scriptures: New Testament Studies in Honor of Raymond T. Stamm.* Gettysburg Theological Studies 3 (Leiden: Brill, 1969) 129–50.

(76) "The Teacher of Righteousness and the Messiah(s)," in Matthew Black, ed., *The Scrolls and Christianity.* SPCK Theological Collections 11 (London: S.P.C.K., 1969) 37–44, 109–12.

1970

(77) "Introduction" and footnotes to the Gospel and Epistles of John in *The New American Bible* (Paterson, NJ: St. Anthony's Guild, 1970). Brown did the basic translation of these NT works from Greek but withdrew his name from the list of contributors because of problems with the editing of his translation.

(78) "Biblical Reflections on the Christian Message," *The Catholic Mind* 68 (December 1970) 19–23. A paper given at the International Concilium Congress at Brussels, September 12–17, 1970. *Translations:* French: "Le Message chrétien: Réflexions bibliques," *Concilium*, Supplement to 60 (December 1970) 71–75; Dutch: "De christelijke boodschap (bijbelse overdenkingen)," ibid. 63–70.

1971

(79) "Jesus and Elisha," *Perspective* 12 (Spring 1971) 85–104.

(80) "The Myth of *The Gospels without Myth* [L. Evely]," review article, *St. Anthony Messenger* 78 (May 1971) 45–48.

(81) "How Things Are in Glocca Morra," *UTS Journal* 1 [New York; Union Theological Seminary] (October 1971) 3–5.

1972

(82) "The Problem of the Virginal Conception of Jesus," *TS* 33 (1972) 3–34. Republished in #A18. Abridged in *USQR* 27 (Spring 1972) 131–35.

(83) "Hans Küng Makes a Proposal [Why Priests?]," *America* 126 (May 20, 1972) 531–32.

(84) "Jesus with Mary at Christmas," *NC News Service Supplement* (December 1972).

1973

(85) "'This is the Jesus that God Has Raised Up,'" *NC News Service Easter Supplement* (March 1973).

(86) "A Heritage from Israel," *America* 128 (March 10, 1973) 221.

(87) "Catechetics in an Age of Theological Change," *Origins* 2 (April 19, 1973) 677–80, 689–92. NCEA Keynote Address, New Orleans, April 24, 1983. Reprinted in *The Catholic Mind* 71 (September 1973) 25–37; *The Month* 235 (April 1974) 531–36, and in Miriam Ward, ed., *Biblical Studies in Contemporary Thought* (Burlington, VT: Trinity College, 1975) 55–67, and in #A20 *(Biblical Reflections,* 3–19). Abridged in *Focus on Adults* 1 (August/September 1973) 4–10. *Translations:* Spanish: "La catequesis en una época de cambio teológico," *Criterio* [Buenos Aires] 48 (May 22, 1975) 264–70.

1974

(88) "John 21 and the First Appearance of the Risen Jesus to Peter," in Edouard Dhanis, ed., *Resurrexit: Actes du Symposium international sur la résurrection de Jésus, Rome 1970* (Rome: Vatican, 1974) 246–60.

(89) "Jesus of History and Christ of Faith," in Sean Freyne, ed., *Jesus Christ Our Lord*. Papers of the Maynooth Union Summer School (1971) (Dublin: Talbot, 1974) 17–27. Related to #B91.

(90) "The Resurrection of Jesus," ibid. 28–38.

(91) "'Who Do Men Say That I Am?' Modern Scholarship on Gospel Christology," *Hor* 1 (1974) 35–50. Reprinted in *The Catholic Mind* 74 (June 1975) 21–33; adapted in *PRSt* 2 (1975) 107–24. Also reprinted in #A20 *(Biblical Reflections,* 20–37).

(92) "Luke's Description of the Virginal Conception," *TS* 35 (1974) 360–62.

(93) "The Relation of the 'Secret Gospel of Mark' to the Fourth Gospel," *CBQ* 36 (1974) 466–85.

1975

(94) "Priestly Character and Sacramental Ordination," *The Priest* 31 (February 1975) 13–15.

(95) "'Change—the Kingdom of God is at Hand,'" *Roman Echoes* 7 (1975) [North American College, Rome].

(96) "The Passion According to John: Chapters 18 and 19," *Worship* 49 (March 1975) 126–34. Adapted lecture reprinted at Southwestern Baptist Theological Seminary (April 15, 1981). Reused in #A31.

(97) "Luke's Method in the Annunciation Narratives of Chapter One," in J. W. Flanagan and A. W. Robinson, eds., *No Famine in the Land: Studies in Honor of John L. McKenzie* (Missoula: Scholars Press, 1975) 179–94. Reprinted in Charles H. Talbert, ed., *Perspectives on Luke-Acts.* Special Studies 5 (Danville, VA: Assocation of Baptist Professors of Religion, 1978) 126–38.

(98) "Roles of Women in the Fourth Gospel," *TS* 36 (1975) 688–99. Reprinted in Walter J. Burghardt, ed., *Woman: New Dimensions* (New York: Paulist, 1977) 112–23; also in #A24 (*Community, 183–98*). *Translations:* German: "Die Rolle der Frau im Vierten Evangelium," in Elisabeth Moltmann-Wendel, ed., *Frauenbefreiung: biblische und theologische Argumente.* Gesellschaft und Theologie, systematische Beiträge 12 (Munich: Kaiser, 1978) 133–47.

(99) "The Meaning of the Magi, the Significance of the Star," *Worship* 49 (December 1975) 574–82. Reprinted in #A23.

1976

(100) "Genealogy (Christ)," *IDBSup* (Nashville: Abingdon, 1976) 354.

(101) "Peter," ibid. 654–57.

(102) "Virgin Birth," ibid. 940–41.

(103) "Difficulties in Using the New Testament in American Catholic Discussions," *LS* 6 (1976) 144–58. Honorary doctorate lecture, Louvain University, June 30, 1976. Reprinted in *The Catholic Mind* 75 (June 1977) 10–23; also in #A25 (*Critical Meaning, 64–81*).

(104) "'On Being a Christian' [H. Küng] and Scripture," *America* 136 (November 20, 1976) 343–45. Review article.

(105) "The Meaning of the Manger, the Significance of the Shepherds," *Worship* 50 (November 1976) 528–38. Reprinted in #A23.

1977

(106) "The Presentation of Jesus (Luke 2:22-40)," *Worship* 51 (January 1977) 2–11. Reprinted in #A23.

(107) "The 'Mother of Jesus' in the Fourth Gospel," in Marinus de Jonge et al., eds., *L'Évangile de Jean: sources, rédaction, théologie.* BETL 44; Papers from the 26th session of the Journées Bibliques of Louvain, August 20-22, 1975 (Gembloux: Duculot, 1977) 307–10.

(108) "The Finding of the Boy Jesus in the Temple: A Third Christmas Story," *Worship* 51 (November 1977) 474–85. Reprinted in #A23.

(109) "Johannine Ecclesiology—The Community's Origins," *Int* 31 (1977) 379–93. Reprinted in James Luther Mays, ed., *Interpreting the Gospels* (Philadelphia: Fortress, 1981) 291–306. See #A24.

1978

(110) "'Other Sheep Not of This Fold': The Johannine Perspective on Christian Diversity in the Late First Century," *JBL* 97 (1978) 5–22. Presidential address to the Society of Biblical Literature, San Francisco, December 29, 1977. See #A24.

(111) "Bishops and Theologians: 'Dispute' Surrounded by Fiction," *Origins* 7 (April 13, 1978) 673, 675–82. NCEA Keynote Address, St. Louis, March 29, 1978. Reprinted in *The Catholic Mind* 76 (September 1978) 13–29; *Chicago Studies* 17 (1978) 290–307; Charles E. Curran and Richard A. McCormick, eds., *Readings in Moral Theology 3: The Magisterium and Morality* (Ramsey, NJ: Paulist, 1982). Also in #A25 (*Critical Meaning*, 45–63). Abridged in *A.D. Correspondence* [Notre Dame] 16 (April 22, 1978).

(112) "Documentation and Reflection: The Venice Statement," *AThR* 60 (1978) 306–32. Comments on the Venice Anglican-Roman Catholic Statement in a discussion article by J. Robert Wright.

(113) "Five Facts about the Bible," *Sunday Visitor National Magazine* (September 10, 1978).

(114) "Assessment of the World Council Faith and Order Meeting at Bangalore (August 16-30, 1978)," *Religious News Service Release* (September 5, 1978), Section 1.

1979

(115) "The Relationship to the Fourth Gospel Shared by the Author of I John and by His Opponents," in Ernest Best and R. McLean Wilson, eds., *Text and Interpretation: Studies in the New Testament Presented to Matthew Black* (Cambridge: Cambridge University Press, 1979) 57–68.

(116) "The Challenge of the Three Biblical Priesthoods," *St. Mary's Seminary and University Bulletin* 10 (Autumn/December 1979) 23–27. Homily on the Golden Jubilee of the Roland Park Building of St. Mary's Seminary, Baltimore, October 1, 1979. Also in #A25 (*Critical Meaning*, 96–106). Reprinted in *The Catholic Mind* 74 (March 1980) 11–20; *Emmanuel* 86 (1980) 314–22; *The Serran* (June 1980) 4–10; *Catholic Free Press* [Worcester, MA] (June 11, 1982) 3–5.

1980

(117) "The Christians Who Lost Out," *New York Times Book Review* (January 20, 1980) 3, 33. Review article of Elaine Pagels, *The Gnostic Gospels*.

(118) "Reflections on a Review: A Reply," *Ampleforth Review* 84/2 (1980) 57–60. A reply to J. McHugh, "On Exegesis and Dogma in Church Dogmatics," ibid. 55–57.

(119) "*Episkopē* and *Episkopos:* The New Testament Evidence," *TS* 41 (1980) 322–38. Reprinted in *Episkopē and Episcopate in Ecumenical Perspective*. Faith and Order Paper 102 (Geneva: World Council of Churches, 1980) 15–29. Also in #A25

(Critical Meaning, 124–46). *Translations:* Spanish (abridged): *Selecciones de Teología* 21 (October/December 1982) 244–56.

(120) "The Role of History in the Understanding of the Gospels," *The SCRC Vision* [Southern California Renewal Communities] 7 (July 1980) 6–7.

(121) "New Testament Commentary," *Emmanuel* 86 (1980) 528–32. Review article of Rudolf Schnackenburg, *The Gospel According to St. John: Volume Two: Commentary on Chapters 5–12* (New York: Seabury, 1980).

(122) "The Virgin Shall be with Child," *The SCRC Vision* 7 (December 1980) 4–5.

(123) "The Meaning of the Bible," *TD* 28 (Winter 1980) 305–20. A sequel to #B124. Reprinted in #A25 *(Critical Meaning,* 23–44); also in Miriam Ward, ed., *A Companion to the Bible* (New York: Alba House, 1985) 49–74.

1981

(124) "'And the Lord Said': Biblical Reflections on Scripture as the Word of God," *TS* 42 (1981) 3–19. Reprinted in #A25 *(Critical Meaning,* 1–22).

(125) "The Importance of How Doctrine is Understood," *Origins* 10 (May 7, 1981) 737–43: NCEA Keynote Address, New York, April 22, 1981. Reprinted in *The Catholic Mind* 79 (June 1981) 8–18; also in #A25 *(Critical Meaning,* 82–95).

(126) "New Testament Background for the Concept of Local Church," *Proceedings of the Catholic Theological Society of America* 36 (1981) 1–14. Reused in Chapter 7 of #A30.

1982

(127) "Rachab in Mt 1, 5 Probably Is Rahab of Jericho," *Bib* 63 (1982) 79–80.

(128) "Mary in the New Testament and in Catholic Life," *America* 146 (May 15, 1982) 374–79. Also in *Menlo Papers: Mary* (St. Patrick's Seminary Symposium; Menlo Park, Calif. [privately printed], 1982) 23–37. Reused in Chapter 5 of #A30.

(129) "Recent Contributions to Our Knowledge of the Bible," in Mortimer J. Adler, ed., *The Great Ideas Today—1982* (Chicago: Encyclopaedia Britannica, 1982) 104–57. Reprinted in #A28.

1983

(130) "Not Jewish Christianity and Gentile Christianity but Types of Jewish/Gentile Christianity," *CBQ* 45 (1983) 74–79. Reused in Chapter 7 of #A30.

(131) "Diverse Views of the Spirit in the New Testament," *Worship* 57 (May 1983) 225–36. Also in *Menlo Papers: The Holy Spirit* (St. Patrick's Seminary Symposium; Menlo Park, Calif. [privately printed], March 1983) 30–39. Reused as Chapter 6 of #A30.

(132) "Preaching in the Acts of the Apostles," in J. Burke, ed., *A New Look at Preaching.* GNS 7; (Wilmington: Michael Glazier, 1983) 59–73. Reused as Chapter 8 of #A30.

(133) "John, Epistles of," *The Encyclopedia Americana: International Edition*. 30 vols. (Danbury, CT: Grolier, 1983) 16:115.

(134) "John, Gospel According to Saint," ibid. 16:115–17.

(135) "John, Saint," ibid. 16:103.

(136) "Virginal Conception of Jesus," in Anthony Richardson and John Bowden, eds., *The Westminster Dictionary of Christian Theology* (Philadelphia: Westminster, 1983) 597–98.

1984

(137) "How to Read the Passion Narratives of Jesus," *Catholic Update* (April 1984). Also published as "Why the Accounts of Jesus' Death Differ," *St. Anthony Messenger* 91 (April 1984) 37–40. Reused in #A31, 43. Australian ed.: "How To Read the Passion Narratives," *INFORM: Current Thinking on Catholic Issues* 47 (February 1996). Considerably revised version of #B137.

(138) "The Passion According to Matthew," *Worship* 58 (March 1984) 98–107. Reused in #A31.

(139) "Faith in the Late New Testament Works in Relation to the Contents of the Early Creeds," in Hans-Georg Link, ed., *The Roots of Our Common Faith: Faith in the Scriptures and in the Early Church*. Faith and Order Paper 119 (Geneva: World Council of Churches, 1984) 73–77.

(140) "Brief Observations on the Shroud of Turin," *BTB* 14 (October 1984) 145–48. Reused as Chapter 9 of #A30.

1985

(141) "Danger Also from the Left," with Joseph. A. Fitzmyer, *TBT* 23 (March 1985) 105–10. Reprinted in the *Canadian Catholic Biblical Association Bulletin* 39 (July/August 1985) 4–5.

(142) "The Passion According to Mark," *Worship* 59 (March 1985) 116–26. Reused in #A31.

(143) "More Polemical than Instructive: R. Laurentin on the Infancy Narratives," *Marianum* 47 (1985) 188–207. The T. V. Moore Lecture given at the Catholic University of America, September 29, 1984. Reused in Chapters 4 and 10 of #A30.

(144) "Did Jesus Know He Was God?" *BTB* 15 (April 1985) 74–79.

(145) "Historical Critical Exegesis and Attempts at Revisionism," *TBT* 23 (May 1985) 157–65. Contains an additional part of the T. V. Moore Lecture (see #B143). Reused in Chapter 1 of #A30.

(146) "Liberals, Ultraconservatives, and the Misinterpretation of Catholic Biblical Exegesis," *Cross Currents* 34 (Fall 1984) 311–28. Appeared in June 1985. Reused in Chapters 3 and 4 of #A30.

(147) "All Gaul is Divided: A Review Essay," *USQR* 40 (1985) 99–103. A review of René Laurentin's views on the Matthean and Lukan infancy narratives and Mariology.

1986

(148) "The Passion According to Luke," *Worship* 60 (January 1986) 2–9. Reused in #A31.

(149) "Gospel Infancy Narrative Research from 1976 to 1986: Part I (Matthew)," *CBQ* 48 (1986) 468–83.

(150) "Gospel Infancy Narrative Research from 1976 to 1986: Part II (Luke)," *CBQ* 48 (1986) 660–80.

(151) "Why the Infancy Narratives Were Written," *Catholic Update* (November 1986) and *St. Anthony Messenger* 94 (November 1986) 34–38. Reused as Chapter 1 of #A34 and in #A43. See also #A190. Australian ed.: "The Story of Christmas: What Do The Gospels Say?" *INFORM: Current Thinking on Catholic Issues* 31 (November 1992). *Translations:* Japanese in *Seinan Journal of Cultures* 10 (1996) 135–40.

(152) "Matthew's Genealogy of Jesus Christ: A Challenging Advent Homily," *Worship* 60 (November 1986) 482–90. Reused as Chapter 2 of #A34. Reprinted as "The Savior is Born of Scandal and Scorn," *U.S. Catholic* 55 (November 1990) 34–36.

1987

(153) "The *Gospel of Peter* and Canonical Gospel Priority," *NTS* 33 (1987) 321–43.

(154) "Scripture and Dogma Today," *America* 157 (October 31, 1987) 286–89.

(155) "The Annunciation to Joseph (Matthew 1:18-25)," *Worship* 61 (November 1987) 482–92. Reused as Chapter 3 of #A34.

(156) Digested lecture on "Meeting the Challenge of Biblical Fundamentalism," *St. Mary's Seminary and University Alumni Bulletin* 18 (Winter 1987) 1–3.

1988

(157) "The Burial of Jesus (Mark 15:42-47)," *CBQ* 50 (1988) 233–45.

(158) "The Annunciation to Mary, the Visitation, and the Magnificat (Luke 1:26-56)," *Worship* 62 (May 1988) 249–59. Reused as Chapter 6 of #A34.

(159) "The Annunciation to Zechariah, the Birth of the Baptist, and the Benedictus (Luke 1:5-25, 57-80)," *Worship* 62 (November 1988) 482–96. Reused as Chapters 4–5 of #A34.

1989

(160) "The Johannine World for Preachers," *Int* 43 (1989) 58–65.

(161) "Understanding the Bible," *Christopher News Notes* 313 (March 1989).

(162) "Johannine Writings," *New Catholic Encyclopedia*, Vol. 18, Supplement 1978–1988 (Washington: Catholic University of America, 1989) 219–21. See ##B56, 57.

(163) "A Personal Word," in Joel Marcus and Marion L. Soards, eds., *Apocalyptic and the New Testament Essays in Honor of J. Louis Martyn*. JSNTSup 24 (Sheffield: Sheffield University Press, 1989) 9–12.

(164) "The Contribution of Historical Biblical Criticism to Ecumenical Church Discussion," in Richard John Neuhaus, ed., *Biblical Interpretation in Crisis: The Ratzinger Conference on Bible and Church.* Encounter Series 9 (Grand Rapids: Eerdmans, 1989) 24–49. *Translations:* German (drastically abbreviated) in Joseph Ratzinger, ed., *Schriftauslegung im Widerstreit.* QD 117 (Freiburg: Herder, 1989) 81–97.

(165) "Apocrypha; Dead Sea Scrolls; Other Jewish Literature," *NJBC* article 67: §§1-56, 62-63, 72, 78-123.

(166) "Aspects of New Testament Thought," *NJBC* article 81: §§1-24, 118-57 (Christology, Resurrection, the Twelve).

(167) "Aspects of Old Testament Thought," *NJBC* article 77: §§152-63 (Messiah).

(168) "Biblical Geography," *NJBC* article 73: §§1-4, 32-115.

(169) "Canonicity," *NJBC* article 66: §§1-4, 20-43, 48-85, 87-101.

(170) "Church Pronouncements," *NJBC* article 72: §§3-9, 13-16, [25-35], 36-41.

(171) "Early Church," *NJBC* article 80: §§1-2, 5-33.

(172) "Hermeneutics," *NJBC* article 71: §§1-54, 71-92.

(173) "Texts and Versions," *NJBC* article 68: §§1, 3-4, 156-216.

(174) "Introduction to the New Testament," in Bernard W. Anderson, ed., *The Books of the Bible.* 2 vols. (New York: Scribner's, 1989) 2:117–24.

(175) "Reminiscence of David Noel Freedman," in *Twenty-fifth Anniversary of the Anchor Bible* (New York: Doubleday, 1989) 1–4. Privately printed for the November 19, 1989 meeting of the SBL at Anaheim, CA.

1990

(176) "The Resurrection in Matthew (27:62–28:20)," *Worship* 64 (March 1990) 157–70. Reused as Chapter 2 of #A37.

(177) "Infancy Narratives," in R. J. Coggins and J. L. Houlden, eds., *A Dictionary of Biblical Interpretation* (London: S.C.M., 1990) 311–12.

(178) "The Fundamentalist Challenge: Suggestions for a Catholic Response," *Catholic Update* (May 1990). See #B180. Reused in #A43. *Translations:* Spanish: "El Desafío Fundamentalista" (*Catholic Update* [April 2002]).

(179) "The Resurrection in John 20—A Series of Diverse Reactions," *Worship* 64 (May 1990) 194–206. Reused as Chapter 4 of #A37.

(180) "Biblical Fundamentalism: How Should Catholics Respond?" *St. Anthony Messenger* 98 (June 1990) 11–15. See #B178.

(181) "The Resurrection in John: Missionary and Pastoral Directives for the Church," *Worship* 64 (September 1990) 433–45. Reused as Chapter 5 of #A37.

(182) "Further Reflections on the Origins of the Church of Rome," in Robert T. Fortna and Beverly Roberts Gaventa, eds., *The Conversation Continues: Studies in Paul and John in Honor of J. Louis Martyn* (Nashville: Abingdon, 1990) 98–115.

1991

(183) "Catholic Faith and Fundamentalism," *Priests and People* 5 (1991) 134–36. Reprinted from pp. 137–42 of #A36.

1992

(184) "Communicating the Divine and Human in Scripture," *Origins* 22 (May 14, 1992) 1–9. NCEA Keynote Address, St. Louis, April 20, 1992.

(185) "Infancy Narratives in the Gospels," in David Noel Freedman, ed., *Anchor Bible Dictionary.* 6 vols. (New York: Doubleday, 1992) 3:410–15.

(186) "The Lucan Authorship of Luke 22:43-44," *SBL Seminar Papers* 31 (Atlanta: Scholars Press, 1992) 154–64.

(187) "The New Jerome Biblical Handbook: An Explanation," with Joseph A. Fitzmyer and Roland E. Murphy, *CBQ* 54 (1992) 735.

1994

(188) "Eschatological Events Accompanying the Death of Jesus, Especially the Raising of the Holy Ones from Their Tombs (Matt 27:51-53)," in John P. Galvin, ed., *Faith and the Future: Studies in Christian Eschatology* (New York: Paulist, 1994) 43–73.

(189) "How to Read the Resurrection Narratives," *Catholic Update* (March 1994) and *St. Anthony Messenger* 101 (April 1994) 10–16. Reused in #A43. Reprinted in *The Leaven* [newspaper of the Archdiocese of Kansas City, KS] 17 (April 5, 1996) 7–9. Australian ed.: "The Resurrection: Stories Tell It Best," *INFORM: Current Thinking on Catholic Issues* 42 (February 1995). *Translations:* Japanese in *Seinan Journal of Cultures* 10 (1996) 141–52.

(190) "The Christmas Stories: Exploring the Gospel Infancy Narratives," *Scripture from Scratch* (December 1994). See #B151.

1995

(191) "The Narratives of Jesus' Passion and Anti-Judaism," *America* 172 (April 1, 1995) 8–12. Reused in #A43. Reprinted in *Explorations* 10 (1996) 6–8, and in *Catholic Update* (March 1997). *Translations:* French: "Les récits de la Passion de Jésus et l'antijudaïsme: qui sont 'les juifs' mentionnés dans les récits de la Passion?" *Istina* 42 (1997) 130–31.

(192) "Scriptural Studies and the Church Today," *The St. Augustine Catholic* 6 (November/December 1995 [125th Anniversary of the Diocese Issue]) 12–13, 34–35. Reused in ##A43, B194. Reprinted in *Whence* (Sulpician Archive Bulletin, Spring 1996) 9–11.

1996

(193) "Lenten Stories from John's Gospel: Baptismal Dramas of Water, Light and Life," *Catholic Update* (March 1996); also as "Three Gospel Stories That Should Change Your Life," *St. Anthony Messenger* 103 (March 1996) 28–34. Reused in #A43 and, with adaptation, as Day Three (41–51) in #A45.

(194) "The Church and the Bible: A New Understanding," *St. Anthony Messenger* 104 (November 1996) 22–26. Reprints the first chapter of #A43, which was drawn from #B193.

(195) "How to Read the Passion Narratives," *INFORM: Current Thinking on Catholic Issues* 47 (February 1996). Considerably revised version of #B137.

1997

(196) "The Babylonian Talmud on the Execution of Jesus," *NTS* 43 (1997) 158–59. A response to Lou H. Silberman, "Once Again: The Use of Rabbinic Material," *NTS* 42 (1996) 153–55.

(197) "First and Most Perfect Disciple: Mary in the New Testament," *Scripture from Scratch* (May 1997); also as "Mary, The First Disciple," *St. Anthony Messenger* 104 (May 1997) 10–13. Reprinted in the Diocese of Springfield-Cape Girardeau *Mirror* 33 (November 28, 1997) 8–9; also in *The San Francisco Charismatics* 5 (January 1998) 1, 6, 8. Australian ed., with slight adaptation: *INFORM: Current Thinking on Catholic Issues* 58 (April 1998).

1998

(198) "The Gospel according to John—An Overview," *Chicago Studies* 37 (1998) 5–15.

(199) "The Holy Spirit as Paraclete: The Gift of John's Gospel," *Scripture from Scratch* (May 1998); also as "The Holy Spirit as Paraclete," *St. Anthony Messenger* 105 (May 1998) 12–15. Used as Day Seven (89–96) in #A45.

2000

(200) "John, Gospel and Letters of," in Lawrence H. Schiffman and James C. VanderKam, eds., *Encyclopedia of the Dead Sea Scrolls*. 2 vols. (Oxford and New York: Oxford University Press, 2000) 1:414–17.

C. Selected Reviews

1955

(1) Review of Jacques Dupont, *Les béatitudes: Le problème littéraire, le message doctrinale* (Saint-André and& Louvain: Nauwelaerts, 1954). *CBQ* 17 (1955) 522–25.

1956

(2) Review of Joseph Bonsirven, *Épîtres de Saint Jean*. VS 9 (2d ed. Paris: Beauchesne, 1954). *CBQ* 18 (1956) 114–15.

(3) Review of Willem Karel Maria Grossouw, *Revelation and Redemption: A Sketch of the Theology of St. John* (Westminster: Newman, 1955). *CBQ* 18 (1956) 208–10.

1960

(4) Review of Heinz Eduard Tödt, *Der Menschensohn in der synoptischen Überlieferung* (Gütersloh: Mohn, 1959). *CBQ* 22 (1960) 455–57.

(5) Review of Aileen Guilding, *The Fourth Gospel and Jewish Worship: A Study of the Relation of St. John's Gospel to the Ancient Jewish Lectionary System* (New York: Oxford University Press, 1960). *CBQ* 22 (1960) 459–61.

(6) Review of Maurice F. Wiles, *The Spiritual Gospel: The Interpretation of the Fourth Gospel in the Early Church* (New York: Cambridge University Press, 1959). *TS* 21 (1960) 142–44.

(7) Review of Bertil Gärtner, *John 6 and the Jewish Passover.* ConBNT 17 (Lund: Gleerup, 1959). *TS* 21 (1960) 144–45.

(8) Review of Wilhelm Thüsing, *Die Erhöhung und Verherrlichung Jesu im Johannesevangelium.* NTAbh 21,1-2 (Münster: Aschendorf, 1960). *TS* 21 (1960) 637–39.

1962

(9) Review of Karl August Eckhardt, *Der Tod des Johannes als Schlüssel zum Verständnis der johanneischen Schriften.* Studien zur Rechts- und Religionsgeschichte 3 (Berlin: De Gruyter, 1981). *CBQ* 24 (1962) 218–19.

(10) Review of Ceslaus Spicq, *Dieu et l'homme selon le Nouveau Testament.* LD 29 (Paris: Cerf, 1961). *TS* 23 (1962) 115–16.

(11) Review of Rudolph Schnackenburg, *Die Kirche im Neuen Testament: Ihre Wirklichkeit und theologische Deutung, ihr Wesen und Geheimnis.* QD 14 (Freiburg: Herder, 1961). *TS* 23 (1962) 465–67.

1963

(12) Review of Joseph Blinzler, Otto Kuss, Franz Mussner, eds., *Neutestamentliche Aufsätze: Festschrift für Prof. Josef Schmid zum 70. Geburtstag* (Regensburg: Pustet, 1963). *JBL* 82 (1963) 456.

(13) Review of Franz Zehrer, *Synoptischer Kommentar, 1: Kindheitgeschichte und Anfang des öffentlichen Wirkens Jesu* (Klosterneuburg: Klosterneuburger Buch- und Kunstverlag, 1962). *TS* 24 (1963) 293–94.

1964

(14) Review of Maurice Baillet, Josef T. Milik, and Roland de Vaux, *Les "Petites Grottes" de Qumran: Exploration de la falaise, les grottes 2Q, 3Q, 5Q, 7Q à 10Q, le rouleau de cuivre.* 2 vols. DJD 3 (Oxford: Clarendon Press, 1962). *CBQ* 26 (1964) 250–54.

(15) Review of Rudolph Schnackenburg, *God's Rule and Kingdom* (New York: Herder & Herder, 1963). *TS* 25 (1964) 257–60.

282 A Bibliography of the Publications of Raymond E. Brown, s.s.

1965

(16) Review of Dwight Moody Smith, Jr., *The Composition and Order of the Fourth Gospel: Bultmann's Literary Theory* (New Haven: Yale University Press, 1965). *TS* 26 (1965) 438–40.

1966

(17) Review of Ernest Best, *The Temptation and the Passion: The Markan Soteriology.* SNTSMS 2 (Cambridge: Cambridge University Press, 1965). *CBQ* 28 (1966) 338–40.

(18) Review of Heinz Eduard Tödt, *The Son of Man in the Synoptic Tradition* (Philadelphia: Westminster, 1965). *JBL* 85 (1966) 246–48.

(19) Review of David M. Stanley, *The Apostolic Church in the New Testament* (Westminster: Newman, 1965). *TS* 27 (1966) 99–101.

(20) Review of Ignace de la Potterie and Stanislaus Lyonnet, *La vie selon l'Esprit: Condition du chrétien.* Unam Sanctam 55 (Paris: Cerf, 1965). *TS* 27 (1966) 678–80.

1967

(21) Review of Charles W. Kegley, ed., *The Theology of Rudolph Bultmann* (New York: Harper & Row, 1966). *CBQ* 29 (1967) 151–53.

(22) Review of John H. Elliott, *The Elect and the Holy: An Exegetical Examination of 1 Peter 2:4-10 and the Phrase* βασίλειον ἱεράτευμα. NovTSup 12 (Leiden: Brill, 1966). *CBQ* 29 (1967) 255–57.

(23) Review of Otto Böcher, *Der johanneische Dualismus im Zusammenhang des nachbiblischen Judentums* (Gütersloh: Mohn, 1965). *JTS* 18 (1967) 469–71.

1968

(24) Review of J. Louis Martyn, *History and Theology in the Fourth Gospel* (New York: Harper & Row, 1968). *UQSR* 23 (1968) 392–94.

1969

(25) Review of A. J. Simonis, *Die Hirtenrede im Johannes-Evangelium: Versuch einer Analyse von Johannes 10,1-18 nach Entstehung, Hintergrund, und Inhalt.* AnBib 29 (Rome: Pontifical Biblical Institute, 1967). *Bib* 50 (1969) 121–23.

(26) Review of Odo Kiefer, *Die Hirtenrede: Analyse und Deutung von Joh 10,1-18.* SBS 23 (Stuttgart: Katholisches Bibelwerk, 1967), and of A. J. Simonis, *Die Hirtenrede im Johannes-Evangelium: Versuch einer Analyse von Johannes 10,1-18 nach Entstehung, Hintergrund, und Inhalt.* AnBib 29 (Rome: Pontifical Biblical Institute, 1967). *CBQ* 31 (1969) 98–100.

(27) Review of René Kieffer, *Au delà des recensions? L'évolution de la tradition textuelle dans Jean VI, 52-71.* ConBNT 3 (Lund: Gleerup, 1968). *CBQ* 31 (1969) 262–64.

(28) Review of Georg Richter, *Die Fußwaschung im Johannesevangelium: Geschichte ihrer Deutung.* Biblische Untersuchungen 1 (Regensburg: Pustet, 1967). *TS* 30 (1969) 120–22.

(29) Review of Walter Wink, *John the Baptist in the Gospel Tradition.* SNTMS 7 (Cambridge: Cambridge University Press, 1968). *TS* 30 (1969) 329–31.

(30) Review of Joseph Newbould Sanders, *The Gospel According to St. John.* BNTC (New York: Harper & Row, 1968). *TS* 30 (1969) 697–98.

1970

(31) Review of Herbert Leroy, *Rätsel und Mißverständnis: Ein Beitrag zur Formgeschichte des Johannesevangeliums.* BBB 30; (Bonn: Peter Hanstein, 1968). *Bib* 51 (1970) 152–54.

(32) Review of Jean Carmignac, *Recherches sur le "Notre Père"* (Paris: Letouzey & Ané, 1969). *CBQ* 32 (1970) 264–66.

(33) Review of Pierre Benoit, *The Passion and Resurrection of Jesus Christ* (New York: Herder, 1969). *TS* 31 (1970) 324–25.

1971

(34) Review of Rudolph Bultmann, *The Gospel of John: A Commentary* (Philadelphia: Westminster, 1971). *ThTo* 28 (1971–1972) 517–19.

(35) Review of Pierre Le Forte, *Les structures de l'Église militante selon Saint Jean.* Nouvelle série théologique 25 (Geneva: Labor et Fides, 1970). *Bib* 52 (1971) 454–56.

(36) Review of George Johnston, *The Spirit-Paraclete in the Gospel of John.* SNTSMS 12 (New York: Cambridge University Press, 1970). *CBQ* 33 (1971) 268–70.

(37) Review of Jacques Winandy, *Autour de la naissance de Jésus: Accomplissement et prophetie.* Lire la Bible 26 (Paris: Cerf, 1970). *CBQ* 33 (1971) 469–71.

(38) Review of Alfred Läpple, *Apocalypse de Jean: Livre de vie pour les chrétiens.* Lire la Bible 24 (Paris: Cerf, 1970). *CBQ* 33 (1971) 591–93.

(39) Review of David W. Wead, *The Literary Devices in John's Gospel.* Theologische Dissertationen 4 (Basel: Freidrich Reinhardt, 1970). *CBQ* 33 (1971) 617–18.

(40) Review of Samuel Sandmel, *The First Christian Century in Judaism and Christianity: Certainties and Uncertainties* (New York: Oxford University Press, 1969). *JAAR* 39 (1971) 234–36.

(41) Review of Harald Riesenfeld, *The Gospel Tradition* (Philadelphia: Fortress, 1970). *TS* 32 (1971) 301–303.

1972

(42) Review of Elio Peretto, *Ricerche su Mt. 1–2.* Scripta Facultatis Theologicae "Marianum" 25 (Rome: Edizioni Marianum, 1970). *CBQ* 34 (1972) 239.

(43) Review of André Lemaire, *Les Ministères aux origines de l'Église: Naissance de la triple hiérarchie—évéques, presbytres, diacres.* LD 68 (Paris: Cerf, 1971). *CBQ* 34 (1972) 371–72.

(44) Review of Leon Morris, *The Gospel According to John: The English Text with Introduction, Exposition, and Notes* (Grand Rapids: Eerdmans, 1971). *TS* 33 (1972) 138–39.

(45) Review of Willi Marxsen, *The New Testament as the Church's Book* (Philadelphia: Fortress, 1972). *TS* 33 (1972) 597.

1973

(46) Review of Anton Dauer, *Die Passionsgeschichte im Johannesevangelium: Eine traditionsgeschichtliche und theologische Untersuchung zu Joh. 18,1-19,30.* SANT 30 (Munich: Kösel, 1972). *JBL* 92 (1973) 608–10.

(47) Review of Siegfried Schulz, *Das Evangelium nach Johannes.* NTD. Neues Göttinger Bibelwerk 4 (Göttingen: Vandenhoeck & Ruprecht, 1972). *Bib* 55 (1974) 289–91.

(48) Review of Gerhard Delling, *Der Kreuzestod Jesu in der urchristlichen Verkündigung* (Berlin: Evangelischer Verlag, 1971/Göttingen: Vandenhoeck & Ruprecht, 1972). *CBQ* 35 (1973) 524–25.

1974

(49) Review of Günter Reim, *Studien zum alttestamentlichen Hintergrund des Johannesevangeliums.* SNTSMS 22 (Cambridge: Cambridge University Press, 1974). *TS* 35 (1974) 558–61.

(50) Review of Salvatore Alberto Panimolle, *Il dono della legge e la grazia della verità (Gv 1,17)* (Rome: Veritas, 1973). *TS* 35 (1974) 739–41.

1975

(51) Review of Martin Hengel, *Judaism and Hellenism: Studies in Their Encounter in Palestine during the Early Hellenistic Period.* 2 vols. (Philadelphia: Fortress, 1974). *TS* 36 (1975) 785–87.

(52) Review of Giuseppe Ferraro, *L' "ora" di Cristo nel Quarto Vangelo.* Aloysiana: Scritti pubblicati sotto la direzione della Pontificia Facoltà Teologica dell' Italia Meridionale, Sezione "S. Luigi" (Rome: Herder, 1974). *Bib* 56 (1975) 565–67.

1976

(53) Review of Donald P. Senior, *The Passion Narrative According to Matthew: A Redactional Study.* BETL 39 (Louvain: Leuven University Press, 1975). *CBQ* 38 (1976) 259–60.

(54) Review of Paul D. Hanson, *The Dawn of Apocalyptic* (Philadelphia: Fortress, 1975). *CBQ* 38 (1976) 389–90.

(55) Review of Michael Lattke, *Einheit im Wort: Die spezifische Bedeutung von "Agape," "Agapan," und "Filein" im Johannesevangelium.* SANT 41 (Munich: Kösel, 1975). *TS* 37 (1976) 483–84.

(56) Review of Martin Dibelius, *Commentary on the Epistle of James.* Hermeneia (Philadelphia: Fortress, 1976). *TS* 37 (1976) 487–88.

(57) Review of Felix Porsch, *Pneuma und Wort: Ein exegetischer Beitrag zur Pneumatologie des Johannesevangeliums.* Frankfurter Theologische Studien 16 (Frankfort: Knecht, 1974). *TS* 37 (1976) 684–85.

(58) Review of Eduard Schweizer, *The Good News According to Matthew* (Atlanta: John Knox, 1975). *USQR* 31 (1976) 296–97.

(59) Review of Michael D. Goulder, *Midrash and Lection in Matthew* (London: S.P.C.K., 1974). *USQR* 31 (1976) 297–99.

(60) Review of Jack Dean Kingsbury, *Matthew: Structure, Christology, Kingdom* (Philadelphia: Fortress, 1975). *USQR* 31 (1976) 299–300.

1977

(61) Review of Werner H. Kelber, ed., *The Passion in Mark: Studies on Mark 14–16* (Philadelphia: Fortress, 1976). *CBQ* 39 (1977) 283–85.

(62) Review of Robert Kysar, *The Fourth Evangelist and His Gospel: An Examination of Contemporary Scholarship* (Minneapolis: Augsburg, 1975). *JBL* 96 (1977) 146–47.

(63) Review of George M. Soares Prabhu, *The Formula Quotations in the Infancy Narrative of Matthew: An Enquiry into the Tradition-History of Mt 1–2* (Rome: Biblical Institute Press, 1976). *JBL* 96 (1977) 601–603.

(64) Review of Oscar Cullmann, *The Johannine Circle* (Philadelphia: Westminster, 1976). *TS* 38 (1977) 157–59.

(65) Review of Severino Pancaro, *The Law in the Fourth Gospel: The Torah and the Gospel, Moses and Jesus, Judaism and Christianity according to John.* NovTSup 42 (Leiden: Brill, 1975). *CBQ* 39 (1977) 287–89.

1978

(66) Review of Donald H. Juel, *Messiah and Temple: The Trial of Jesus in the Gospel of Mark.* SBLDS 31 (Missoula: Scholars Press, 1977). *BA* 41 (1978) 125.

(67) Review of James D. G. Dunn, *Unity and Diversity in the New Testament: An Enquiry into the Character of Earliest Christianity* (London: SCM, 1977). *CBQ* 40 (1978) 629–31.

(68) Review of Bruce M. Metzger, *The Early Versions of the New Testament: Their Origin, Transmission, and Limitations* (Oxford: Clarendon Press, 1977). *ThTo* 35 (1978–1979) 210–11.

1980

(69) Review of I. Howard Marshall, *The Epistles of John.* NICNT (Grand Rapids: Eerdmans, 1978). *CBQ* 42 (1980) 412–14.

(70) Review of Charles Kingsley Barrett, *The Gospel According to St. John: An Introduction with Commentary and Notes on the Greek Text* (2d ed. Philadelphia: Westminster, 1978). *TS* 41 (1980) 398–99.

(71) Review of Celestin Charlier, *Jean l'Évangeliste: Structure dramatique du quatrième évangile: Meditation liturgique du prologue* (Paris: Lethielleux, 1979). *TS* 41 (1980) 440.

1981

(72) Review of Joseph A. Fitzmyer, *To Advance the Gospel: New Testament Studies* (New York: Crossroad, 1981). *America* 145 (1981) 205–206.

1982

(73) Review of Bruno de Solages, *Jean et les Synoptiques* (Leiden: Brill, 1979). *CBQ* 44 (1982) 164–65.

(74) Review of Jan Lambrecht, *L'Apocalypse johannique et l'apocalypse dans le Nouveau Testament*. BETL 53 (Gembloux: Duculot, 1980). *TS* 43 (1982) 138–40.

(75) Review of Juan Mateos and Juan Barreto, *El evangelio de Juan: Análisis linguístico y comentario exegético* (Madrid: Cristiandad, 1979). *Bib* 63 (1982) 290–94.

1983

(76) Review of Christopher Rowland, *The Open Heaven: A Study of Apocalyptic in Judaism and Early Christianity* (New York: Crossroad, 1982). *TS* 44 (1983) 312–13.

(77) Review of Charles Kingsley Barrett, *Essays on John* (Philadelphia: Westminster, 1982). *TS* 44 (1983) 349.

(78) Review of Helmut Koester, *Introduction to the New Testament*. 2 vols. (Philadelphia: Fortress/Berlin: De Gruyter, 1982). *TS* 44 (1983) 693–95.

(79) Review of Leonhard Goppelt, *Theology of the New Testament* (Grand Rapids: Eerdmans, 1981–1982). *America* 148 (1983) 343–44.

1984

(80) Review of Godfrey C. Nicholson, *Death as Departure: The Johannine Descent-Ascent Schema*. SBLDS 63 (Chico: Scholars Press, 1983). *CBQ* 46 (1984) 586–87.

(81) Review of R. Alan Culpepper, *Anatomy of the Fourth Gospel: A Study in Literary Design* (Philadelphia: Fortress, 1983). *RevExp* 81 (1984) 487–88.

1985

(82) Review of Ernst Haenchen, *A Commentary on the Gospel of John*. 2 vols. Hermeneia (Philadelphia: Fortress, 1984). *TS* 46 (1985) 346–48.

(83) Review of Pheme Perkins, *Resurrection: New Testament Witness and Contemporary Reflection* (Garden City, NY: Doubleday, 1984). *Hor* 12 (1985) 365–67.

(84) Review of Eric Junod and Jean D. Kaestli, eds., *Acta Johannis*. Corpus Christianorum, Series Apocryphorum 1–2 (Brepols: Turnhout, 1983). *TS* 46 (1985) 132–33.

1986

(85) Review of Rosel Baum-Bodenbender, *Hoheit in Niedrigkeit: Johanneische Christologie im Prozess Jesu vor Pilatus (Joh 18, 28–19, 16a)*. FzB 49 (Würzburg: Echter Verlag, 1984). *CBQ* 48 (1986) 325–27.

(86) Review of Anthony Casurella, *The Johannine Paraclete in the Church Fathers: A Study in the History of Exegesis*. BGBE 25 (Tübingen: Mohr, 1983). *CBQ* 48 (1986) 738–39.

1987

(87) Review of Hans Dieter Betz, *2 Corinthians 8 and 9: A Commentary on Two Administrative Letters of the Apostle Paul*. Hermeneia (Philadelphia: Fortress, 1985). *TS* 48 (1987) 164–65.

(88) Review of Gary R. Habermas and Anthony G. N. Flew, *Did Jesus Rise from the Dead? The Resurrection Debate* (San Francisco: Harper & Row, 1987). *International Philosophical Quarterly* 27 (1987) 450–52.

(89) Review of Peter Hofrichter, *Im Anfang war der "Johannesprolog": Das urchristliche Logosbekenntnis—die Basis neutestamentlicher und gnostischer Theologie*. Biblische Untersuchungen 17 (Regensburg: Pustet, 1986). *CBQ* 49 (1987) 668–69.

(90) Review of Carsten Peter Thiede, *Simon Peter: From Galilee to Rome* (Exeter: Paternoster, 1986). *Bib* 68 (1987) 583–84.

1988

(91) Review of Hans Conzelmann, *Acts of the Apostles: A Commentary*. Hermeneia (Philadelphia: Fortress, 1987). *TS* 49 (1988) 530–31.

(92) Review of Peter Lampe, *Die stadrömischen Christen in den ersten beiden Jahrhunderten: Untersuchugen zur Sozialgeschichte*. WUNT 18 (Tübingen: Mohr, 1989). *HeyJ* 29 (1988) 359–60.

1989

(93) Review of Judith Lieu, *The Second and Third Epistles of John: History and Background* (Edinburgh: T & T Clark, 1986). *HeyJ* 30 (1989) 191–93.

(94) Review of Wolfgang J. Bittner, *Jesu Zeichen im Johannesevangelium: Die Messias-Erkenntnis im Johannesevangelium vor ihrem jüdischen Hintergrund*. WUNT 2nd ser. 26 (Tübingen: Mohr, 1987). *CBQ* 51 (1989) 147–48.

1991

(95) Review of Marie-Émile Boismard, *Moïse ou Jésus: Essai de christologie johannique*. BETL 84 (Louvain: Leuven University Press/Peeters, 1988). *CBQ* 53 (1991) 693–95.

(96) Review of Michael E. Stone, *Fourth Ezra: A Commentary on the Book of Fourth Ezra*. Hermeneia (Minneapolis: Fortress, 1990). *TS* 52 (1991) 546–48.

1992

(97) Review of John Ashton, *Understanding the Fourth Gospel* (Oxford: Clarendon Press/New York: Oxford University Press, 1991). *TS* 53 (1992) 744–46.

(98) Review of Reginald H. Fuller, *He That Cometh: The Birth of Jesus in the New Testament* (Harrisburg, PA: Morehouse, 1990). *AThR* 74 (1992) 101–104.

(99) Review of Kenneth Grayston, *Dying We Live: A New Inquiry into the Death of Christ in the New Testament* (New York: Oxford University Press, 1990). *Hor* 19 (1992) 131–32.

1993

(100) Review of Ernest Best, *The Temptation and the Passion: The Markan Soteriology*. SNTSMS 2 (2d ed. Cambridge: Cambridge University Press, 1990). *HeyJ* 34 (1993) 73–74.

(101) Review of Salvador Muñoz Iglesias, *Los Evangelios de la Infancia. I: Los Cánticos del Evangelio de la Infancia según San Lucas*. BAC (2d ed. Madrid: Editorial Católica, 1990); *Los Evangelios de la Infancia. IV: Nacimiento e infancia de Jesús en San Mateo* (Madrid: Editorial Católica, 1990). *JBL* 112 (1993) 341–43.

1994

(102) Review of Bruce M. Metzger, *Breaking the Code: Understanding the Book of Revelation* (Nashville: Abingdon, 1993). *PSB* 15 (1994) 289–90.

1995

(103) Review of Mark Coleridge, *The Birth of the Lucan Narrative: Narrative as Christology in Luke 1–2*. JSNTSup 88 (Sheffield: JSOT Press, 1993). *JBL* 114 (1995) 524–26.

1996

(104) Review of Jesús María Muñoz Nieto, *Tiempo de anuncio: Estudio de Lc 1,5–2,52* (Taipei: Facultas Theologica S. Roberti Bellarmino, 1994). *JBL* 115 (1996) 544–45.

(105) Review of Jesús María Muñoz Nieto, *El Mesías y la Hija de Sión: Teología de la redención en Lc 2,29-35* (Madrid: Editorial Ciudád Nueva, 1994). *JBL* 115 (1996) 545–46.

1997

(106) Review of Georg Strecker, *The Johannine Letters: A Commentary on 1, 2, and 3 John*. Hermeneia (Minneapolis: Fortress, 1996). *TS* 58 (1997) 352–54.

(107) Review of Rudolph Schnackenberg, *Jesus in the Gospels: A Biblical Christology* (Louisville: Westminster John Knox, 1995). *Int* 51 (1997) 431–32.

1998

(108) Review of William Klassen, *Judas: Betrayer or Friend of Jesus?* (Minneapolis: Fortress, 1996). *JBL* 117 (1998) 134–36.

See also the following review articles above: ##B80, 104, 117, 121.

D. Commercially produced audio/video tapes

(1) *The Gospel of John* (Cincinnati: St. Anthony Messenger Press, 1984; Deeside, Wales: Welcome Recordings, 2000) 12 audio cassettes.

(2) *New Testament Scholarship as We End One Century and Open Another* (Cincinnati: St. Anthony Messenger Press, 1997; Deeside, Wales: Welcome Recordings, 2001) 4 audio cassettes.

(3) *The Beginnings of the Church* (Cincinnati: St. Anthony Messenger Press, 1998; Deeside, Wales: Welcome Recordings, 2000) 6 audio cassettes.

(4) *The Paraclete: Spirit's Gift to the Church* (Cincinnati: St. Anthony Messenger Press, 1998; Deeside, Wales: Welcome Recordings, 2001) 4 audio cassettes.

(5) *A Retreat with John the Evangelist: That You May Have Life* (Cincinnati: St. Anthony Messenger Press, 2001) 3 audio cassettes.

(6) *The Infancy Narratives of the Gospels* (Cincinnati: St. Anthony Messenger Press 2002; Deeside, Wales: Welcome Recordings, 2002) 5 audio cassettes.

(7) *The Marys in the New Testament* (Cincinnati: St. Anthony Messenger Press 2002; Deeside, Wales: Welcome Recordings, 2002) 3 audio cassettes.

(8) *The Passion Narratives of the Gospels* (Cincinnati: St. Anthony Messenger Press 2002; Deeside, Wales: Welcome Recordings, 2001) 12 audio cassettes.

(9) *The Churches Paul Left Behind; The Challenge of Biblical Fundamentalism; Vatican II: 25 Years on and Into the Future* (Cincinnati: St. Anthony Messenger Press 2003; Deeside, Wales: Welcome Recordings, 2003) 4 audio cassettes.

(10) *Critical Questions and the Bible* (Cincinnati: St. Anthony Messenger Press 2003; Deeside, Wales: Welcome Recordings, 2003) 2 DVD's or 2 video tapes. More tapes may be released in the future by Welcome Recordings.

Prepared by Michael L. Barré, s.s., based on the compilation by Ronald D. Witherup, s.s.

Appendix Two

In Tribute to Raymond E. Brown, s.s.

Phyllis Trible,
"A Striving After Wind," Sermon at the Interreligious Prayer Service

John R. Donahue, s.j.,
"A Whisper from the Grave," Homily at the Closing Liturgy

"A Striving After Wind"

St. Mary's Seminary and University

October 17, 2003

Professor Phyllis Trible

Baldwin Professor of Sacred Literature, Emerita,
Union Theological Seminary

Scripture Readings: Ecclesiastes 3:10-15; John 16:20-24

Let us begin where many of us live: not with the joy of Jesus but with the enigma of Ecclesiastes.

"For everything there is a season and a time for every matter under heaven." These familiar words from Qoheleth, sage in ancient Israel, travel across cultures and centuries to sanction the rhythms, rituals, and regulations of life. The words proclaim order and appropriateness; they guard and guide the structures of existence.

> — This is the season of fall, a time to work and study.
> — This is the season of Simhat Torah, a time to rejoice in Scripture.
> — This is the season of Terror, a time to mourn and comfort.
> — This is the season of ordinary time, a time to reflect on how the mystery of Christ affects the lives of believers.

"For everything there is a season and a time for every matter under heaven."
But Qoheleth has more to say than the word of the seasonal and appropriate. That more startles, even offends us, for it seems to undermine all that we affirm as good and right and fit. The more that the sage speaks is the word of the wind.

The Word of the Wind

Consider an old man from the upper class in post-exilic Jerusalem. He lives in a world of cultural and religious upheaval where trusted formulas of faith have lost their vitality and new theological treasures have yet to appear. This man teaches in the Jerusalem academy. He is the author of many learned treatises who receives daily the esteem and affection of colleagues and students. He is also a businessman who has amassed considerable wealth and a philosopher who muses upon an acquisitive society that asserts the work ethic as noble, honorable, and profitable—a medium for greed.

This old man speaks out of his many experiences, which, on the basis of the evidence, have been rich and full and rewarding, and he testifies, "All is vapor and a striving after wind" (Eccl 1:2). All is insubstantial, futile, vain; all is nothing; all is emptiness; all is but striving after wind. Or we may translate and interpret the phrase, as some have done, "All is vapor and a vexation of the spirit." A striving after wind is, then, a vexation of the spirit.

This word of the wind disturbs us. It jars. We do not like it, for it seems to undercut what we affirm about life. Why, we claim values, not vapor. We seek meaning and purpose, even rewards, and so we do not want to hear that "all is vapor," futile and insubstantial, but a "striving after wind." Indeed, we do not believe it.

Yet who among us can escape this metaphor? who can pass it by? If Qoheleth came to us from an alien tradition, from a world with which we have nothing in common, then we might ignore or repudiate his words and go the way of our own faith. But that is not the case. The sage speaks as a child of Israel. He speaks to us, both Jews and Christians, in and through the Scriptures that have nourished, shaped, challenged, and disturbed our lives for millennia. Truly, the word of the wind is spoken from faith to faith.

From Futility to Joy

"I too have had a strong theological education," Qoheleth says, "and I perceive that this also is but a striving after wind. I know about biblical criticism, the names of the popes, the teaching of the rabbis, the strategies of pastoral care, the rituals for the Eucharist, and the debates about hermeneutics. Why, I pursued education to the highest levels of the doctorate in order to secure my standing in academe. Then I obtained an appointment to the faculty, published numerous articles and books, read papers at learned conferences, and did not perish at tenure review. Later I branched out into business and acquired a modest portfolio—some would say a substantial one.

"Meanwhile, in the midst of all of this acquiring of titles, esteem, and goods, I advocated the right causes: ecological sanity, prison reform, world peace, gay and lesbian rights, ethnic identities, the war on poverty, feminism, human rights, and nuclear disarmament. I supported the institutions of society, giving generously to charitable organizations, voting my conscience, and attending synagogue and church with regularity. Surely I affirmed the issues and values that you cherish. Moreover, throughout life I applied my mind to know wisdom and to perceive madness and folly. Now, as I come to the close of a blessed life, I perceive that all these things are but a striving after wind.

"For I know that whatever human beings do or think, they move toward death. Death is the end of all. It comes to professors and students, adults and children, men and women. The dust returns to the earth as it was and the wind (or the spirit) returns to the God who gave it. Vapor of vapors; all is vapor" (Eccl 12:1a, 7-8).

Thus the ancient teacher strips us of our claims to values, power, glory, and prestige. Yet his sobering words are not, I think, judgment and condemnation. They do not come with the authority of a prophet announcing divine judgment for sin. Instead, they come as words of invitation and challenge: to understand life as the wind of frailty and futility and to interpret this experience in the warp and woof of faith. And then what? Where does this understanding lead next? For some it may lead to nihilism, but not for the ancient teacher. After all, he is a child of Israel. For him, in a most unpredictable and inscrutable way, it led to affirmations of joy. Having stripped life to an awareness of its elusiveness and ephemerality, having faced futility and death, having relinquished claims to wisdom and power, this old man discovered joy as the gift of God. Thereby life became for him not a claim to self-importance, not self-centered gratification, but rather the recognition that God keeps us "occupied with joy in our hearts in the world that God has created" (Eccl 5:20). The enigma of Ecclesiastes, always present, makes room for the joy that God gives.

The understanding of life as joy in the world given by God highlights another use of the metaphor of wind in the book of Ecclesiastes. It is quite a different use from wind as frailty and futility. It is wind as divine mystery and divine creativity; wind as God's gift of life. This gift begins in the womb of woman. Once more there is the possibility of a play on the words "wind" and "spirit." We read, "As you do not know the way of the wind or how the bones grow in the womb;" *or* we read, "As you do not know how the spirit comes to the bones in the womb of a pregnant woman, so you do not know the work of God who makes everything" (Eccl 11:5). In its mystery and elusiveness, wind testifies to the presence of God the Creator in the womb of life.

The Wind of Creativity

Now these leaves from the notebook of a skeptical believer travel across the centuries of Israel's pilgrimage to be heard, understood, and appropriated by other sages in Jerusalem, one above all:

> There was a man of the Pharisees, named Nicodemus, a ruler of the Jews. This man came to Jesus by night and said to him, "Rabbi, we know that you are a teacher come from God; for no one can do these signs that you do, unless God is with that individual."

Jesus answered, "Truly, truly, I say to you, unless an individual is born anew, that one cannot see the rule of God." Nicodemus said, "How can one be born when already old? Can one enter a second time into a mother's womb and be born? Jesus answered, "Truly, truly I say to you, unless an individual is born of water and spirit, one cannot enter the realm of God. That which is born of the flesh is flesh, and that which is born of the spirit is spirit. Do not marvel that I say to you, 'You must be born anew.' The wind—the wind blows where it wills and you hear the sound of it, but you do not know where it comes or where it goes; so it is with everyone who is born of the spirit" (John 3:1-8).

Later in the gospel Jesus, speaking to the disciples, returns to birth imagery. This time, rather than contrasting a woman's womb to the spirit's womb, he uses birth imagery as a metaphor for the joy that life in God will bring. "When a woman is in labor, she has pain, because her hour has come. But when her child is born, she no longer remembers the anguish because of the joy of having brought a human being into the world. So you have pain now; but I will see you again, and your hearts will rejoice, and no one will take your joy from you" (John 16:22). Out of the anguish identified with birth emerged the joy of Jesus.

Wind, spirit, womb, and joy. With variations, abundant life in the Gospel of John resonates with imagery and messages in the book of Ecclesiastes. These resonances instruct us in the rich conversation that scripture carries on with Scripture. They show us myriad ways that faith seeks to understand itself, and so they encourage us to find places where these conversations intersect with our own lives as well as with the faith stands we take in an increasingly volatile and hostile world.

The Sovereignty of God

Lest you think that I am offering some idiosyncratic exegesis for the sake of a homily, let me tell you a story. Many years ago at Harvard Divinity School a visiting scholar concluded a lecture on biblical views of time with an exposition on Ecclesiastes. The gentleman had hardly completed the lecture before the hand of an impatient Harvard professor began waving in the air. "You should not have ended your lecture with Qoheleth," admonished the Harvard professor, "because Qoheleth has nowhere to go. It is a dead-end." Now that word was supposed to settle the matter. All who were present, Jews and Christians, were told in effect to forget Qoheleth, to leave it behind because "Qoheleth has nowhere to go." Was it by chance or the grace of God that about that time I heard the wind stirring in that stuffy lecture hall, moving from Qoheleth to John to begin a dialogue that enriches the faith of each? "You do not know the way of the wind," teaches Qohelet. "The wind blows where it wills," teaches Jesus.

Some years later I reported this incident to Raymond Brown. He enjoyed it—with a smile and a shake of his head. By nightfall my telephone was ringing, and the authentic voice said, "Here are a few articles you might want to read." Soon thereafter I asked Ray, "What is it you find most compelling in Ecclesiastes?" Immediately he answered, "The sovereignty of God."

As the twentieth century embodiment of John stood before me in the person of Raymond Brown, I heard yet again messages moving between Qoheleth and John, and in that movement my faith grew in understanding both the futility and the fullness of life. To affirm the sovereignty of God the Creator frees us from the burdens of labor to rejoice in our work, frees us to return with a difference to education, business, the daily routine of life, and the great causes and formidable threats of our time. That difference is the letting go of all strivings after wind.

Only the sovereign God gives life. Listen to Qoheleth: "I know that whatever God does endures forever; nothing can be added to it, nor anything taken from it." Now listen to the Evangelist: ". . . the Word was God. All things were made through the Word and without the Word was not anything made that was made."

Only the sovereign God gives life. Listen again to Qoheleth: Even with death approaching, we "scarcely brood over the days of our lives because God keeps [us] occupied with joy in [our] hearts" in the world that God has created (Eccl 5:20). Now listen to Jesus: This pain you know now, in my coming death, will not endure. Instead it will turn into joy as my presence continues among you. "And no one will take your joy from you." It is the gift of God (John 16:22-24).

The sovereignty of God, proclaimed by Qoheleth and Jesus, both of whom come to us as sages in the vast and diverse family of ancient Israel, provides the anchor for a faith that persists through all the circling years, through all the times and seasons of our lives, through all the differences, doubts, and delights of interreligious dialogue. This faith knows both an ill wind and a newborn spirit. It does not remove the enigma of life, but it does open itself to the joy that God sends. Living, as we do, in a mad, greedy, and terrifying world, we lay claim to the testimonies of these biblical sages even when our own faith falters. "All things were made through the Word and without the Word was not anything made that was made." "Whatever God does endures forever." Therein lies abundant life.

"A Whisper from the Grave"

Homily at the Final Liturgy of the
Raymond Brown Conference

Twenty-Ninth Sunday in Ordinary Time, October 18, 2003

John R. Donahue, S.J.

Scripture Readings: Isa 53:10-11; Psalm 33; Heb 4:14-16; Mark 10:35-45

Today's readings resound with exclamations of the saving love of God. Isaiah heralds the servant who through his suffering will justify many, which the church applies to Jesus. The Letter to the Hebrews speaks of a high priest who is able to sympathize with us in our weakness because he has been tested in every way, though sinless, and so we can "confidently" hope for God's mercy. The psalm sings beautifully that "of the kindness of the Lord the earth is full." Hebrews tells us that, because Jesus was a compassionate high priest who was tested like us, we can approach the throne of grace. The gospel reading concludes the Markan journey to Jerusalem, during which Jesus repeatedly spoke of his imminent suffering, only to be misunderstood by his disciples. This rhythm culminates in the desire of James and John for positions of power and the jealousy of the Twelve, which is countered by Jesus' own adoption of the role of Isaiah's servant as the Son of Man, who gives his life as a ransom for many. Liberating self-giving for others is to characterize the followers of Jesus.

Jesus makes the startling demands that those who would be great among his followers must be servants and only slaves need apply for first place. In almost forty years as a priest I have come to see again and again how this liberating service plays out in the myriad forms of service by "the priestly people of God." Last Thursday St. Mary's honored Bishop Walter Sullivan of Richmond, a classmate of Raymond Brown who was ordained with him fifty years ago. Bishop Sullivan was a compassionate priest who opposed war and violence in all forms, having served a number of years as President of Pax Christi. He stood in the rain outside the death house of a prison while a fellow human was being executed. In his homily Bishop Sullivan talked not about himself but about those classmates who have spent a lifetime in faithful service to others. Such self-giving for others shines forth also in parents at the bed of a sick child, in a spouse caring for another with Alzheimer's disease, in people giving their lives to protest injustice, in multiple institutions committed to enhancing the human dignity of downtrodden people. Here in Baltimore I think of Caroline House, Our Daily Bread, the House of Ruth, Mother Seton Academy, Marian House, and St. Ignatius Academy, along with priests, religious, and lay people working in pastoral teams serving local churches. As the poet Gerard Manley Hopkins said, "For Christ plays in ten thousand places, Lovely in limbs, and lovely in eyes not his."

Yet as we reflect on the gospel today a cloud overshadows the radiance of liberating service. The narrative begins with chosen disciples turning away from Jesus' prediction of suffering and asking instead for positions of authority in the coming kingdom. When their request is countered by Jesus the remaining ten become angry, not at their insensitivity or lack of sympathy for Jesus' suffering, but because they have been cut out of the power game. Jesus gives them a lesson on what true greatness means in his community: Gentile rulers lord it over their subjects, and their great ones make their authority felt (throw their weight around). "But it shall not be so among you," responds Jesus—a sentence that should be emblazoned on every letter of appointment to a position of authority in the church. Greatness in Jesus' community is a greatness of service. Gentile, that is, Roman, power was exercised primarily through force, intimidation, and an elaborate network of patronage that tried to assure absolute loyalty to the emperor. The way power is maintained in the secular world of rulers and ruled is anathema to true followers of Jesus.

Scripture is both a beautiful tapestry of God's loving deeds and a mirror that enables us to gaze at our own lives. Today's gospel summons us to reflect on the shadows that fall over church life today. Along with decades of service, the church especially in the United States has been devastated by the misuse of power. When forty years ago liberation theologians of all stripes called us to listen to the voice of victims and oppressed people they were marginalized as dissenters, and often still remain so. The horrible scandal that racked our community was rooted in an inability to hear the voice of victims as institutions of power were jealously guarded. Power continues to be maintained by patronage, fear, and networks of unquestioned loyalty. If self-giving service is a light in the dark corners of our society, misuse of power is an ecclesiastical SARS virus that threatens to smother the living spirit of the church. It shall not be so among you!

Today we also conclude a celebration in tribute to a Christian, a priest and scholar, Raymond E. Brown, s.s., whose life was spent in the liberating service of others. This was not the kind of direct service I talked about a few moments ago, but an equally demanding service of the quest for knowledge and of speaking truth to power. Through four decades he poured himself out in the daily labor of meticulous scholarship while traversing the world opening the treasures of God's word for all who had ears to hear—from parish study groups to curial cardinals. Though a person of great intellectual and personal power and a person deeply committed to the church, Raymond Brown never had much time for arguments about power and office.

Yesterday Burt Visotzky cited Rabbi Yohanan, who said that when we quote the teaching of a scholar who has died, that departed scholar's lips whisper from the grave. Let us listen in to Ray's whispers. In a notable address given at this seminary on October 1, 1979, Raymond Brown spoke of "Rethinking the Biblical Priesthood for All." When reflecting on the "priesthood of all believers," he wrote:

> Until we face the fact that hearing the word of God and living it out is the real source of sanctity in the Church, constituting true rank and privilege and honor, and until we appropriate this in our hearts we will not understand what the NT teaches us about priesthood. That is the challenge the Church will have to face in these next years as believing men and women who have heard their dignity in the service of Christ. [Reprinted in *The Critical Meaning of the Bible,* 102]

These next years that Father Brown talked about in 1979 have been our history over the last 25 years. Was this sage a prophet? Has this challenge really been met?

In preparing these reflections I searched somewhat in vain Raymond Brown's writings to see if he ever commented at length on today's gospel from Mark. Finally I came to see that he did, not in dialogue with Mark's gospel but in reflecting on a memorable section of John, which I see as the Johannine equivalent of today's gospel. I am speaking of the footwashing in John 13, which is a virtual Johannine mediation on today's gospel. All the same elements are there. The imminent death of Jesus overshadows the whole incident; disciples misunderstand the actions and teaching of Jesus; Jesus assumes the role of a slave by washing the disciples' feet; and this liberating service of self-giving is to be a model for his disciples.

In the final book published before his death, *A Retreat with John the Evangelist: That You May Have Life,* written in a very imaginative, almost playful manner, Father Brown assumes the role of "Translator" in dialogue with the "Evangelist." At one point, reflecting on the nature of the church, the Evangelist speaks to those making the retreat about what the Translator told him about disputes over power and office in the church. From his heavenly vantage point the Evangelist says:

> That is why, exactly at the supper where other followers of Jesus recounted the action of Jesus over bread and wine, I recounted the story of the washing of the feet. You may think me fanciful, but I imagined that in this action Jesus had left us a commentary on the outlook we must share in receiving the Eucharist. . . If most followers of Jesus had chosen to imitate the washing of the feet instead of

the breaking of the bread, I wonder if they would have overlooked the spirit of self-giving to the extent to which they have in disputes over the Eucharist.

The Evangelist continues, somewhat laconically,

> Although I think by the way your Translator raises his eyebrows he thinks I want you to agree with my outlook. I would be more modest, even if your Translator would never associate modesty with me. I do not offer a model to be imitated in our Johannine attitudes. Simply incorporate our attitudes into your larger picture and let them leaven the way you think and live. Your Translator tells me that from reading my Gospel Message he judged that I marched to a different drummer—an interesting metaphor. Yes perhaps we [Johannine Christians] did, but I humbly submit that you should incorporate our melody into the way you march. [*A Retreat with John the Evangelist*, 66]

Well, Raymond, scholar, teacher, friend, and inspiration for a generation, we are sad that your voice is but a whisper from the grave, but you have shown us how to march to a different drummer, and may we constantly hum that melody of the gospel you unfolded to us and the gospel you embodied for us—as we plod on toward that life in abundance that is your lasting inheritance.

Index of Ancient Sources

The indexes cover only the essays in the volume, not the Bibliography of the Writings of Raymond E. Brown, S.S.

Old Testament

Genesis

2:7	192n., 197n.
2:8-15	183
3:2-5	121
3:8-10	183
3:14-15	121
9:4	171
28:10-17	163
32:11	132n.
47:29	132n

Exodus

4:22	98
12	145
12:46	156n.
17:6	178, 194n.
19:16–20:17	184
34:27-35	183
34:33-35	196n.

Leviticus

19:18	132n.

Numbers

9:12	156n.
11:1-22	99
15:22-31	101
17:25	122

Deuteronomy

13:13-14	89n.
18:15	126
30:15-20	174
34	209

Joshua

24	197n.

Judges

18:2	122

1 Samuel

2:3	120

1 Kings

17:21	197n.

2 Kings

2:16	122

Job 174

1:6-12	121

Psalms

1:1	193n.
1:6	193n.
6:6	171
33	297
34:21	156n.
46:5-6	178
51:13	132n.
56:5	171
65:5	171
73	174
78	194n.
78:14-16	178
105	194n.
105:41	178
112:4	122
145:21	171

Proverbs

2:12-15	193n.
4:18-19	122
5:8	103
5:16	99
7:26	103
30:4	98

Ecclesiastes (Qoheleth)

1:2	293
2:13-14	131n.
3:10-15	292
5:20	294, 296
11:5	294
12:1a	294
12:7-8	294

Songs of Songs (Canticles)

3:1-4	183
3:4	198n.

Isaiah

2:5	131n.
5:20	122
6:9-10	37n.
12:37-43	37n.
26:10	132n.
40:3	126
42:1-4	174
45:7	122
49:1-6	174
50:4-9	174
50:10	131n.

Index of Authors (and Select Documents)

Strack, Hermann J., 105n., 107
Stump, Eleanore, 14n.
Suelzer, Alexa, 14n.
Suggit, John N., 197n., 198n.
Sullivan, Walter, 297–98
Sullivan, Francis, 251n.
Sungenis, Robert, 251n.
Sweet, John, 62n.
Swetnam, James, 195n., 197n.

Talbert, Charles, 51n, 89n.
Taylor, Michael J., 129n.
Teeple, H. M., 119, 131n.
Teixidor, Javier, 33n.
Temporini, Hildegard, 78n.
Thatcher, Tom, 191n.
Thomas, J. C., 107
Thompson, John, 80n.
Thompson, Marianne Meye, 155n., 157n.
Thompson, Trevor W., 90n.
Thyen, Hartwig, 155n.
Tolbert, Mary Ann, 81n.
Tombs, David, 190n.
Tovey, Derek, 105n.
Trapp, Michael, 83, 88n.
Trible, Phyllis, 292–96
Tuckett, Christopher M., 36n.

van Belle, Gilbert, 36n., 38n.
van der Horst, Pieter W., 80n., 104n., 105n.
van Heusden, Barend P., 39n.
van Unnik, W. C., 130n.

Vandecasteele-Vanneuvill, Fréderique, 115n.
VanderKam, James C., 33n., 129n.
Vanhoye, Albert, 235
Vatican Council II, 212, 240, 242, 244, 246, 251–52n.
Vawter, Bruce, 34n.
Veldheer, Kristine, 193n.
Verheyden, Jozef, 36n.
Vidler, Alexander, 14n.
Visotzky, Burton, 105–107, 299
von Wahlde, Urban C., 38n., 79n.
Vorgrimler, Herbert, 14n., 35n.

Wainwright, Arthur, 80n.
Ward, Graham, 192n., 198n.
Warford, Malcolm L., 250n.
Wengst, Klaus, 78n., 82, 88n.
Wigren, Tore, 89n.
Wilkens, Wilhelm, 167n.
Williamson, P. S., 39n.
Wink, Walter, 34n., 80n.
Witherington, III, Ben, 51n.
Witherup, Ronald D., 14, 250n., 252n.
Wolff, Hans Walter, 191n.
Worden, T., 198n.
Wrede, William, 88n.
Wright, N. T., 199
Wuerl, D. W., 257

Yuval, Israel Jacob, 115n.

Zumstein, Jean, 155n., 191n., 195n., 197n.